Clare of Assisi
and the
Thirteenth-Century Church

Religious Women, Rules, and Resistance

Catherine M. Mooney

PENN

UNIVERSITY OF PENNSYLVANIA PRESS

PHILADELPHIA

THE MIDDLE AGES SERIES

Ruth Mazo Karras, Series Editor
Edward Peters, Founding Editor

A complete list of books in the series
is available from the publisher.

Published by
University of Pennsylvania Press
Philadelphia, Pennsylvania 19104-4112
www.upenn.edu/pennpress

1 3 5 7 9 10 8 6 4 2

Library of Congress Cataloging-in-Publication Data
ISBN 978-0-8122-4817-3

Frontispiece. *Saint Clare Protects Her Sisters*, by Francesco
Tartaglia. San Giorgio Chapel, Protomonastery of Santa
Chiara, Assisi. Courtesy of Elvio Lunghi.

Clare of Assisi
and the
Thirteenth-Century Church

For
Caroline Walker Bynum
and
M. Brinton Lykes

Contents

Some Notes on Usage

I have anglicized many names of persons and places but sometimes retained Latin or Italian forms when these seem more apt.

Throughout this book, I have drawn on Latin editions of medieval texts, as indicated in the notes and bibliography. To make this book accessible to a wider public, however, I have, where possible, referred in notes to English translations of these Latin sources. Translations from the sources are mine unless otherwise noted.

The cover of this book depicts a fresco of Clare of Assisi and her religious sisters located in the San Giorgio Chapel of the Protomonastery of Saint Clare in Assisi. The artist, Francesco Tartaglia, has modeled Clare after Mary, the *Madonna della Misericordia*. The Mother of Mercy could always be identified by her one emblematic gesture—sheltering people under her mantle. Mirroring Mary, Clare in this fresco protects her own people, a crowd of kneeling Clarisse nuns. Indeed, her principal claim to fame by the early sixteenth century, when the fresco was painted, was as founder of a women's religious order, tellingly renamed the Order of Saint Clare shortly after her death. The papacy, in fact, had founded that order, and various popes in the course of Clare's lifetime had studiously rewritten the women's own origin story. In Clare and her sisters' minds, their community was founded by Francis of Assisi and they belonged to the same family as his Order of Lesser Brothers. Like Francis, these women saw themselves following in the footsteps of Christ. In this book, I recount the story of how Clare, in her own lifetime, came to be thought of as the founder—in deed and inspiration—of what became known shortly after her death as the Order of Saint Clare, and the story of how she and her monastery of San Damiano came to play an analogous "founding role" in the papally initiated order. Tartaglia's fresco captures Clare's dramatic transformation. By the end of her life, Clare, the self-described follower of Francis, was increasingly depicted instead as the female inspiration and cornerstone of a separate religious order; and Clare, the self-described imitator of Christ, was increasingly depicted instead as "another Mary."

Clare of Assisi
and the
Thirteenth-Century Church

Religious Women in the Thirteenth-Century Church

Clara claris praeclara meritis. So begins the bull for Clare of Assisi's canonization: "Clare outstandingly clear with clear merits."[1] It is one of myriad plays on her name, *Clara* in Latin and *Chiara* in Italian, both meaning "clear," "bright," "shining," or "brilliant." The puns proved irresistible for Clare's earliest hagiographers and have continued to appear in works about her ever since. Not in this book, however; not because I do not enjoy puns, but simply because the truth about Clare is not so clear to me. As I have explored her own writings, the hagiography, and scholarship about her, I have had to acknowledge that there is much about her life that remains opaque. There is, to be sure, much to be gleaned, but it is far from a full harvest when one relies principally on the sources closest to Clare's own life. My goal in this book has been to hew as closely as I could to those sources to see what might reasonably be established—and sometimes merely conjectured—about Clare and the religious Order of San Damiano. Understanding these women sheds important light on many other female religious like them in the thirteenth-century Church.

Such women and many thousands of men as well, were part of the vast *vita apostolica* movement. This religious renaissance had been in full swing for at least a century by the time Clare was born in 1193. Laity, religious, and clerics alike had been pioneering new paths in their pursuit of devout living. Full devotion to God was still sought, as it had been for centuries, by monks and nuns who lived withdrawn within monasteries, guided by one of the Church's canonically established rules, such as the Rule of Benedict. But in the twelfth and thirteenth centuries, new expressions of religious life were being articulated by a host of other spiritual seekers, including many who chose to live inserted within society, in the towns and cities that were reemerging across western Europe. Embracing the *vita apostolica*, the "apostolic life," meant many things, but it usually emphasized a life of material poverty, penance, and service to others, both through charitable works and by preaching the gospel.[2] Most famously, perhaps, this movement gave rise to the great mendicant orders, the Order of Lesser Brothers and the Order of Preachers, known colloquially today as the Franciscans and Dominicans. Francis of Assisi, born a century after the *vita apostolica* movement commenced, arguably represents its culmination. His charismatic exhortations to people of all walks of life echoed the movement's origins. His unplanned foundation of the Order of Lesser Brothers launched its future (cynics would say "demise") as an institution strictly regulated by the papacy.

No census records the number of people in this movement, but an array of genres that survive from this era—including sermons, saints' lives, chronicles, and testamentary bequests—attest to its overwhelming significance. Laypeople could adopt a *vita apostolica* lifestyle even as they remained in their family homes and engaged in their day-to-day employments. Largely unorganized at first, confraternities, guild associations, or groups allied with one of the mendicant orders eventually emerged to offer laymen and women a modicum of institutional structure for their devotional activities.[3]

The very newness of these religious lifestyles is reflected in the diverse names used to identify the men and women adopting them, names such as "brothers," "lesser brothers," "sisters," "lesser sisters," "poor men," *pinzochere*, and "beguines." What to call these groups has proved a challenge for historians. "New orders" works well for communities such as the Cistercians, who adopted a canonically approved rule and approximate our contemporary idea of a religious "order," a network of religious communities with a common juridical structure. But many groups emerging from the *vita apostolica* movement did not adopt an approved rule, belong to a network of communities, or share a defined juridical structure. While "quasi-religious" captures the similarity between many of these groups and traditional religious communities following an approved rule, it inaccurately suggests that they were not quite "true" religious, a suggestion contradicted by medieval descriptions of them as new "religions" (*religiones*), a term indicating their status as "religious." "Extraregular" works well as a description for the many groups that did not follow a canonically approved rule (*regula*), but it overlooks other groups that either adopted an approved rule or devised a new one. I will use the above phrases sparingly. In their place, I will often use the term "penitent" because "doing penance" was a meaningful catchphrase among those in search of the *vita apostolica*. Notably, Clare of Assisi and her sisters used it to describe their religious life. To a contemporary reader "penitent" might conjure pictures of flagellants harshly beating themselves and wailing aloud, but in the Middle Ages the term more broadly signified someone fully converted to religious living.[4] Such a life usually entailed various degrees of physical asceticism and material poverty, but it also represented a nexus of spiritual virtues including poverty, humility, and service to one's neighbor.

An especially sharp dividing line stood between the men and women who formed these new religious communities. By the early thirteenth century, men drawn to a communal expression of the *vita apostolica* might join one of the mendicant ("begging") orders to live poorly, penitently, and itinerantly, taking their good works and the gospel from place to place. Communities of similar female penitents also sprang up. Although somewhat less likely than their male counterparts to engage in itinerant good works and preaching because of social and religious constraints, they nonetheless came and went from their dwelling places, performed works of charity for their neighbors, and led lives marked by poverty, humility, and penance. Mendicant orders like the Franciscans and Dominicans united many men within single institutional structures bound by canonically approved rules. Their novelty lay particularly in two facts: (1) they were international orders directly answerable to the papacy, and (2) in contrast to monks who lived withdrawn in monasteries, mendicants, like the apostles, lived principally inserted in society.

In the early thirteenth century, female penitential communities lived independently from one another, even if some communities emulated the practices of another. In each house the women established their own self-styled form of religious life, some adopting an established rule, others devising their own. These communities were juridically answerable to their respective bishops, who expressed various degrees of interest in the women. The early thirteenth-century popes looked unfavorably upon this variegated and decentralized situation and set out to unite and regulate these disparate communities. Around 1218, beginning with Pope Honorius III (d. 1227), but shepherded especially by Cardinal Hugo dei Conti di Segni (later "Hugolino"; d. 1241),[5] the papacy founded its own religious order of women, the first of its kind. Like the male mendicants, the women's order would be under direct papal control. Unlike the male mendicants, however, the women were to be strictly cloistered. And since they would be cut off from society, unable to beg alms for their support, the popes planned also to provide the women's houses with lands, rents, and other income sources, refashioning them into a single monastic order of enclosed nuns.

In this book, I discuss the trajectory of the women's communities who coalesced into that papally founded order, focusing particularly on Clare of Assisi, her community of San Damiano in Assisi, and a few other houses that emulated San Damiano's religious lifestyle. Clare of Assisi began her religious life as a simple penitent. Inspired by Francis and devoted to poverty and penance, she soon attracted other women to join her. The women of San Damiano, as their house just outside Assisi was called, might have lived out the rest of their days as an independent house of penitents, closely allied with the Lesser Brothers, following their own rule based on Francis's precepts, earning some of their keep from the labor of their own hands and, for the rest, relying on alms they or the Lesser Brothers gathered. But Clare's growing renown, to say nothing of her and her community's special ties to Francis of Assisi, made San Damiano a lightning rod attracting the papacy's attention. The first papal strike arrived around 1219, when Hugo began to organize women's religious houses into a papal order and soon drew in San Damiano as well. But as long as Francis, San Damiano's protector, lived, Clare and her sisters safely escaped papal efforts to make Clare's community conform to the new order. That changed dramatically with Francis's death in 1226 and Hugo's elevation to the papacy as Gregory IX in 1227.

This book chronicles the journey through which Clare of Assisi's community of San Damiano was transformed into the flagship of the papal Order of San Damiano with Clare as its putative mother. The story of the San Damiano sisters illuminates the fortunes of other houses of penitent women wishing to emulate San Damiano who also became part of the new order. They constitute only a small group within the Order of San Damiano. Many other houses were more akin to traditional monasteries regulated by the Rule of Benedict; some of these houses had no relationship at all with Clare or San Damiano. I focus on Clare, San Damiano, and their kindred sisters in order to elucidate the fortunes of an expression of the female *vita apostolica* uniquely tied to the Franciscan movement. But their story also sheds light more broadly on other women outside the Order of San Damiano who had to contend with the same sorts of ecclesiastical pressures that confronted Clare and her sisters. I also devote particular attention to some of the better-known (and documented) women in the small circle surrounding Clare. This includes the Bohemian princess, Agnes of Prague, who battled alongside Clare to counter papal coercion that the women abide by certain rules. Since both Clare and the popes—but not always in the same ways—wanted Francis of Assisi's Order of Lesser Brothers to be linked to the women's religious life, the Lesser Brothers too play a prominent role in this book. In a nutshell, Clare of Assisi and the Order of San Damiano offer a micro-study of the trajectory of thirteenth-century religious women contending with a Church determined to regulate them.

Besides Clare's own writings and the hagiographic documents about her, this book explores numerous papal letters—many overlooked in most scholarship—and a series of competing rules issued to govern the women. Written variously by Francis, Pope Gregory IX, Agnes of Prague, Pope Innocent IV and, finally, Clare of Assisi and her allies, the very number of rules and authors reflects the extremely contested nature of regulating penitent women in the thirteenth century.

Clare of Assisi and the Order of San Damiano: Between History and Hagiography

It is fair to say that Clare of Assisi and the Order of San Damiano are located somewhere between "history" and "hagiography." Clare's canonization in 1255 and the first major *vitae* ("lives") that quickly followed both enlarged her image and froze it in time. This becomes especially apparent when these *vitae* and the eyewitness testimonies recorded for the process of her canonization are considered together with numerous earlier documents written by and about Clare and the women in her order. "History" and "hagiography" do not, of course, denote entirely discrete genres or spheres of knowledge. While "history" might evoke for some people a past that "really happened," most historians have always realized that the stories of the past that they tell are based on partial evidence and that the evidence itself reflects the particular perspectives of its creators. But there is a past that "happened" and, to varying degrees, one can reasonably confirm some of its features, for example, that a particular individual lived and exercised influence within a given society or that a certain event took place at a specific time. Putting these fragments together into a coherent narrative always involves interpretation, for the fragmentary evidence is not only the product of individuals with particular points of view, but also the very story a historian builds around that evidence is the result of her selection and reassemblage of those fragments. Every historical narrative entails a significant amount of "filling in the blanks" as bridges are built from one piece of evidence to another, allowing readers to imaginatively retrace the trajectories of historic figures such as Clare of Assisi and institutions such as the Order of San Damiano.[6]

Clare of Assisi and the women in the Order of San Damiano are between history and hagiography in several ways. First, the sources I use include both historical works—such as letters, religious rules, papal documents, and biographies—and hagiographic works, such as canonization testimonies and saints' *vitae* whose narratives seek principally to prove or publicize someone's sanctity. The "Clare of history" cannot be known apart from information conveyed in hagiographic documents about "Saint Clare." But neither can the significance of Saint Clare be appreciated apart from the events of Clare's life as we glean them from documentary sources. Throughout this book I draw liberally from all types of sources, trying to use them judiciously, sensitive to their varying purposes.

Second, and perhaps surprisingly, even my very chronological survey of Clare and her religious order necessarily locates them between history and hagiography. Beginning ostensibly with the Clare of history, who lived and died between 1193 and 1253, I proceed as systematically as I can from her birth, childhood, and youth through the series of events and controversies that marked her adult years and inventively transformed her into a religious founder. But even this historical Clare is between history and hagiography since her life story is inextricably tied to the story of her sanctity. Indeed, most of the details of her early life are recounted in testimonies taken down by churchmen directing the process for her canonization. Clare officially became Saint Clare only after her death, but that she had already become "Saint Clare" (and religious founder) during her life is amply proved by the lengths to which churchmen went in shaping her life story to fit their ends.

The history of hagiography is another way the spaces occupied by history and hagiography overlap, because Clare's story and that of her order are, in part and like most stories, very managed affairs. Even though I draw only from the earliest hagiographic accounts that date to the first years after Clare's death, one can discern Clare's sanctity subtly shifting its shape from one hagiographic text to the next. Certain stories recounted by the canonization witnesses just months after Clare died tellingly do not appear in the early hagiographic legends that drew on those testimonies. Others become embellished or altered to suit the hagiographer's and his papal patron's purposes.

Finally, I often have reason to focus on the ways recent historians have written about Clare and the Order of San Damiano. Clare was not always, for example, thought to be the author of a religious rule for San Damiano, but in recent years this has arguably become her greatest claim to fame. Historians have changed the Clare we know every bit as much as hagiographers have. Gentle, obedient, and hidden in an earlier period of historical scholarship, Clare more recently has been praised for her strength, subversive tactics, and eye-catching leadership. Some contemporary historical depictions of Clare as "valiant woman" are so over the top that they have become a sort of hagiography in their own right. *(nb, to Wendy Murray BK?)*

Methodological Assumptions

Key to my methodology is the conviction that chronology matters. It is a principle obvious to historians yet easy to overlook. Clare's four letters to Agnes of Prague, for example, are usually discussed together, not only because the sender and recipient of the letters are the same, but also because similar themes appear across them. Accordingly, I discuss all four letters in Chapter 5. But because other insights emerge when each letter is situated alongside documents and events from its same immediate historical period, I return to Clare's last letter, written long after the first three, in Chapter 9. Similarly, juxtaposing Thomas of Celano's 1228–1229 and 1246–1247 remarks about Clare and religious women with documents and events of the same periods highlights how markedly Thomas changed his story.

A second point related to chronology is that this book does not pretend to be a biography of Clare of Assisi. That would require a more fulsome treatment of Clare's life than I here present. I privilege sources written during her life or even shortly after it when these illuminate her life. For example, the *Acts* for the process of Clare's canonization, composed just months after Clare died, furnishes details regarding her early life that appear in no other sources.[7] But I am sparing in my use of the *Acts* because it pertains more properly to a discussion of Clare's afterlife as Saint Clare than her life per se—for the text's very purpose was to establish her as a saint. I have particularly left aside stories about Clare recounted in texts composed only many years after her death. For example, two fourteenth-century texts recount a meal that Clare and Francis shared together outside the little church of the Porziuncula.[8] The story is replete with fascinating details, including Francis's initial reluctance to eat with Clare, his companions' arguments persuading him to relent, what he said during the meal, and a glowing mystical rapture. Many scholars have challenged the historicity of this story because it places Clare outside her monastic enclosure. Other scholars liberally incorporate such episodes to construct fuller biographical portraits. They sensibly arrange such stories in some credible order, not according to the chronology of the texts that recount them, but as the episodes would have transpired in the course of Clare's chronological life. This "harmonized Clare"—harmonized insofar as chronologically disparate sources are plumbed for data the biographer unifies into a coherent biography—is an understandable endeavor, but not one that I attempt.[9] Rather than painting a full, fleshed-out portrait, I draw a more bare-bones profile. But getting that skeletal structure right is foundational because it is the bones, after all, that must bear the weight of the body.

I forgo the account of Clare's shared meal with Francis and various stories recounted in the *Acts* not because I challenge their historicity (although I sometimes do), but because I think it matters *when* a story is told. Stories, be they fictitious, real, or somewhere in between, are recalled when they most mean something. Their recollection tells us about the individuals doing the remembering and recounting and about their particular historical moments. In this book, I try to hear the voices that spoke *during* Clare's life. This puts me at the mercy of the documents that have survived, for surely many texts contemporary with Clare have been lost. Documents are fragile; some survive, some do not. The "survival of the fittest" documents is not necessarily the best guide to which accounts were most valued at the time. By so limiting myself, I know I lose those later stories; there are not many "charming Clare" stories in this book, but so be it. I prefer to consider the Clare that has happened to survive in documents contemporaneous with her life. One of the central Franciscan themes is *vestigia sequi Christi*, "following Christ's footsteps," the vestiges and traces he left behind. Playing on that same metaphor, I try to reconstitute aspects of Clare's journey by following her documentary vestiges. I chronologically follow the trail of texts like markers thrown on a path to help later travelers find their way. I have tried to learn, specifically, how Clare, the religious penitent, along with her allies, negotiated the religious identity of their communities vis-à-vis the Lesser Brothers, the thirteenth-century Church, and the Order of San Damiano. In this regard, Clare's portrait is a micro-painting of a larger landscape.

Third, and more positively, this more minimalist approach saves me from a well-known pitfall in Franciscan studies, one that transparently affects studies of Francis, for whom the medieval literature is vast, but also Clare. We creatively fill in the gaps in our knowledge by projecting into them our unconscious assumptions about who these figures were. Certain stories about Clare, for example, appear in narratives that scholars believe were initially composed while Clare was still alive. The only versions that have come down to us, however, have been reworked by later writers who took some of that early material verbatim, adapted other parts of it, and added to it passages composed only after Clare's death. What criteria does one use to adjudicate which stories originated in the mid-thirteenth century and which were embellished or written only later? How does one distinguish episodes that closely reflected Clare's actual experience or the situation of her order from those that conveyed the wishful thinking of a later writer? Too often such puzzles lead one into a kind of unconscious circular reasoning; the stories we judge to be authentically reflective of an earlier reality are those that happen to match our own projections. The episodes we thus deem more credible in turn serve to reinforce the images of Clare we already had. In short, it is very easy to keep creating a multiplicity of our own "Clares."

Fourth, while I am a minimalist in my approach to sources, I am not a reductionist; a skeptic by nature, I am not a deconstructionist out to destroy. To put it periphrastically in the words of two prominent medieval thinkers, I align myself less with Anselm's "I believe so that I can understand" than with Abelard's "I doubt and question so that I can understand." I know there is more than meets my eye and I will tentatively propose what that might be. But I prefer to build a sturdy raft that can float in the rough waters of hard questions than a showier ship easily capsized by that same sea. To that end, when I speculate about someone's intentions, actions, and other matters, I try to distinguish between what we can reasonably know and what we can only plausibly conjecture. Other matters I leave with a question mark, suspended until some new cache of documents or insightful analysis opens a fresh path of inquiry.

Fortunately, many matters which, on my own, I would have to leave unresolved, have been and are being addressed by many excellent scholars. Beginning just over a century ago, anniversaries commemorating events in Clare's life began to generate significant critical studies. In the 1890s, around the 700th anniversary of Clare's birth, Giuseppe Cozza-Luzi penned an influential study proposing Clare as the author of a religious rule that, until then, had been attributed to other authors.[10] The seventh centenary of Clare's entrance into religious life also saw the publication of studies still worth reading today. These include Livarius Oliger's and Ernest Gilliat-Smith's studies of the rules assigned to the women of San Damiano and Paschal Robinson's publications surveying Clare's life and writings.[11] More critical studies marked the 700th anniversary of Clare's death, the most enduring being Engelbert Grau's 1952 German translation of her writings, followed in 1953 by an English translation largely based on his work.[12] The first Latin edition of all the texts attributed to Clare appeared only in 1985.[13] Although I will take issue with some of these scholars, their contributions have long stood as exemplary islands in a sea of pious publications, some of which marry scholarship to devotion with decidedly mixed results. The decisive turning point in critical studies about Clare and the religious women related to her was 1993–1994, the eighth centenary of her birth. Since then, a steady stream of fine scholarship has appeared, exemplified by many edited volumes, often the results of Italian scholarly congresses.[14] Poor Clare Sisters in Umbria and Sardinia have also contributed to this renaissance, most notably producing a new critical edition of the rule attributed to Clare which corrects previous misreadings and systematically highlights the rule's multiple sources.[15] One of my goals in writing this book has been to make available to an English-language readership the fruits of these studies, until now largely overlooked this side of the Atlantic. As the pages that follow will show, my debt to these scholars is enormous. Often they have furnished just the stepping stones I needed to open new paths of analysis. I hope these paths, in turn, will furnish firm stepping stones for others.

Overview of Chapters

In Chapter 1, I explore the three principal sources of information regarding Clare's youth, family, early contacts with Francis of Assisi, and dramatic choice to flee her family home to be received as a penitent by Francis and his companions. Along with harvesting information about Clare's early life, I confront the dilemma that all three sources are hagiographic texts. Written only after Clare had died, these texts demand that I consider the extent to which their saint-making purpose has colored the portrait they paint of Clare's early life. The somewhat static and simple young "Saint" Clare who emerges in these texts will contrast in many respects with the more dynamic and complex Clare of later years, whose image is conveyed largely via texts composed contemporaneously with the events they chronicle.

Chapter 2 focuses on Clare's first years, from about 1211 to 1216, in the religious community of San Damiano. Francis gave Clare and her sisters a "form of life" (*forma vitae*), a term sometimes used to describe a plan of living that was less than a full-fledged religious rule and sometimes used, almost interchangeably, to connote a religious rule itself. The early evidence for such a document is crucial in Clare's case because throughout her life, she and her sisters in San Damiano would be assigned a variety of *formae vitae*, and these were at variance with or even contradicted some of the central religious values and practices prescribed by Francis. Clare and her sisters were determined to defend at least two features of their life explicitly articulated by Francis in his *forma vitae*—their intrinsic link with Francis and his brothers and a commitment to a life of radical material poverty. In this chapter I also consider one of the great debates about Clare and her sisters: did they initially live unenclosed like Francis and his companions, out and about in the world preaching and tending to the needs of others, or did they live a semi-cloistered or even cloistered life within the confines of San Damiano? I examine the most important proof text for this debate, a letter Bishop Jacques de Vitry wrote in 1216. Finally, I explore the sisters' life in San Damiano during their first years there.

In Chapter 3, I discuss recent scholarship that has radically revised our picture of Clare, penitent women, and the Order of San Damiano. Long thought to have been the founder of that order, it is now clear that Clare and her sisters were cajoled—some would even say forced—into joining an order of women founded by a papacy determined to regiment and enclose female penitents. I explain how the papal order was founded around 1219 and focus on the leading role played by Cardinal Hugo, one of the pope's advisers, a future pope himself, and a man who, for many years, would have a sometimes contested relationship with Clare. Papal letters and other texts suggest that other houses of religious women near Florence and in Siena, Perugia, and Lucca formed part of the new papal order before San Damiano even became associated with it. Explicit evidence indicates that the papacy considered Clare's community to be part of the new order at least by 1221, if not earlier. Hugo had a *forma vitae* drawn up—a document he would later call a "rule"— and assigned it to all the religious houses in the papal order, including San Damiano.[16] I first raise in this chapter and then elaborate further in later chapters evidence that the community of San Damiano showed more loyalty to Francis's *forma vitae* than to Hugo's newly imposed one.

In Chapter 4, I continue to explore San Damiano's role vis-à-vis the papal order by focusing on the pivotal years 1226 to 1230. Three key events precipitated a change in San Damiano's status within the papal order: in 1226 Francis of Assisi died, leaving Clare and her sisters bereft of a protector; in 1227 Hugo became Pope Gregory IX; and in 1228 Gregory canonized Francis. A succession of texts that appeared in the years 1228 to 1230 reveals how Gregory quickly used his new position to solidify San Damiano's place within the papal order. Clare's association with the now-sainted Francis and her own upwardly mobile reputation brought increasing cachet to the order, which churchmen soon artfully renamed the Order of San Damiano. As a trade-off, Clare was able to negotiate her community's singular status, winning from Gregory a Privilege of Poverty that allowed San Damiano to refuse the very sorts of property the pope was urging upon other monasteries in the order. I examine also an emerging clash between many Lesser Brothers and the papacy as they debated the nature of the Lesser Brothers' pastoral responsibilities toward religious women, a debate that elicited a pointed intervention by Clare.

I turn my attention in Chapter 5 to the earliest documents that Clare herself authored: four remarkable letters she sent to Agnes of Prague. A woman with prominent royal connections, Agnes had founded a monastery of the Order of San Damiano in Prague. After first discussing Clare's Latin literacy and the possibility that the letters were collaboratively composed, I show how Clare used these letters to instruct Agnes regarding religious themes and practices particular to Clare's and Francis's vision of religious life. In the course of the correspondence it becomes transparent that Clare had won a powerful ally to the cause of preserving a particular (and minority) style of religious life within the Order of San Damiano. Embedded within each letter, moreover, is evidence of some very this-worldly controversies involving Agnes and the papacy.

Chapter 6 details a series of controversies from the late 1230s to the mid-1240s about which *formae vitae* and rules should govern women in the Order of San Damiano. I discuss a unique and unsuccessful bid by Agnes of Prague to persuade Gregory IX to allow her monastery to follow a new *forma vitae* that she had devised, drawing on the pope's *forma*, on the one hand, and Francis's *forma*, on the other. I present evidence showing that at San Damiano, the sisters continued to adhere to the prescriptions Francis had given them even when these conflicted with Gregory's *forma vitae*. Finally, I discuss evidence that some women in the Order of San Damiano were organizing across monasteries to contest certain papal prescriptions. The monastery of Monteluce, probably trying to emulate the poverty of Clare's San Damiano, defied Gregory IX's wishes that they own property. In a coordinated campaign, with Agnes of Prague exercising important leadership, many monasteries in the order attempted to influence Pope Innocent IV to significantly alter his predecessor Gregory IX's *forma vitae* by dropping its stipulation that the women adhere to the Rule of Benedict. The clear subtext of their efforts was that they hoped to align themselves more with Francis of Assisi's *forma vitae*, but Innocent refused to release them from Gregory's *forma vitae*.

In Chapter 7, I discuss Pope Innocent IV's dramatic turnabout: he finally addresses the women's complaints regarding the Rule of Benedict by issuing a new *forma vitae* that bound the women instead to a rule that Francis had composed and the papacy in 1223 had approved for the Order of Lesser Brothers. This change, however, turned out to be merely cosmetic since both Benedict's and Francis's rules, in Innocent's mind, had no effective binding force beyond holding the women to the observance of poverty, chastity, and obedience. More substantively, Innocent's *forma vitae* laid out in detail his expectations for the Lesser Brothers. They were obligated to lend pastoral assistance to women in the Order of San Damiano and, momentously, to exercise juridic authority over them as well. The Lesser Brothers, women in the Order of San Damiano, and Rainaldo of Jenne, the cardinal protector of both orders, all reacted to these and other provisions in Innocent's game-changing legislation. Exploring all their views, I offer a new argument regarding why Innocent's *forma vitae* never succeeded. The near universal theory until now has been that Clare, above all, in tandem with (the minority of) women in other monasteries who shared Clare's views on poverty, defeated Innocent's legislation because it allowed communal property. I show how partial the evidence supporting that theory is and present new evidence that women in the order were probably more concerned that the Lesser Brothers were gaining too much juridic authority over them. Drawing then on two long overlooked letters, I present explicit evidence showing how Rainaldo of Jenne, in particular, engineered the failure of Innocent's *forma vitae*.

Chapter 8 focuses on yet another *forma vitae*, approved in 1253, for observance by the monastery of San Damiano, still struggling to establish a religious life independent from papal designs for the Order of San Damiano. I scrutinize the sometimes confusing evidence regarding the relationship between the Privilege of Poverty that Clare won in 1228 and this *forma vitae*, approved shortly before her death. After analyzing the *1253 forma vitae*'s remarkable contents, I turn to another knotty historical problem, the question of the text's authorship. Surveying evidence from the *forma vitae*'s appearance in the mid-thirteenth century through the present, I show how Clare emerged as the putative author of this text only in the late nineteenth century. While Clare's contribution to its composition was crucial, it is also likely that she was not the text's sole or even principal architect. Others too, whom I also discuss, undoubtedly had a hand in its composition. Even so, the *1253 forma vitae* strongly indicates that Clare was so determined to preserving her community's commitment to Francis of Assisi's original ideals that she was disposed to categorically withdraw her monastery from the papal Order of San Damiano. There is evidence within the *forma vitae* that she was doing just that.

In Chapter 9, I examine three brief texts, Clare's fourth and last letter to Agnes of Prague, composed probably in 1253, and a *Testament* and a *Blessing* attributed to Clare.[17] Her fourth letter is a poignant farewell to Agnes who, by the end of Clare's life, had become her intimate friend and influential ally. Even though Clare at this point was looking beyond her death to the divine life she expected to share, she showed her continuing engagement with this life. Citing the prophet Isaiah, she urged Agnes, who would survive her, to "run and not grow weary" and she embedded within the letter another biblical citation that appears to be a coded message regarding the Privilege of Poverty. As for the *Testament* and *Blessing*, I analyze the complex and lively arguments still going on regarding Clare's possible authorship of these texts. Focusing above all on the longer and more revealing *Testament*, I discuss the multiple ways the text accords well with themes we know characterized Clare's life. Even if she was the *Testament*'s intellectual author—a still open question—I point further to evidence suggesting that someone else, besides Clare, had a hand in composing both it and the *Blessing*. Finally, I conclude the book with my own assessment of the significance of Clare of Assisi, her allies, and the Order of San Damiano—and of how their journey illuminates the wider world of thirteenth-century women's religious communities negotiating the currents of ecclesial regulation. A "great woman" approach has often surrounded scholarship on Clare of Assisi. While this book shows that Clare was, indeed, an outstanding figure, it further establishes that her significance is best grasped when she is situated in a larger landscape populated by many other key actors, including popes, friars, sisters, allies who shared her views, and adversaries who did not. Clare's story, it turns out, is a single illuminating chapter in a larger narrative of women and men vying to define their religious identities within a Church more committed to unity and conformity than to diversity and difference.

Chapter 1

Clare's Childhood and Conversion to Religious Life, 1193 to 1211

"Saint" Clare casts a long shadow over the events of Clare's early life because most of the narrative details about this period derive from hagiographic sources composed only after Clare's death. Although there is a particular irony to beginning a chronologically ordered discussion of Clare's life with such late reports, it would be foolhardy to launch into an exploration of her writings and other texts contemporary with her life, as I do in later chapters, without considering her portrayal during the decades preceding their composition. The story built around Clare's family, childhood, and momentous contact with Francis of Assisi and his companions further sets the stage for understanding the evolution of the Order of San Damiano, the institution that would redefine Clare and her sisters as enclosed monastic nuns.

Sources for Clare's Early Life

Three hagiographic texts constitute the fundamental sources for Clare's early life. First and foremost is the *Acts* for the process of Clare's canonization, a text compiled in late 1253, just a few months after Clare's death.[1] The text, a fifteenth-century Italian translation of a no longer extant Latin original, survives in a single codex. It is especially prized for its eyewitness testimonies from twenty-one people who knew Clare personally. Many scholars refer to it as the primary and most fundamental historical source regarding Clare.[2] But it is also, by definition, a hagiographic work: its very purpose was to make Clare into a saint.

Two Latin legends, one prose, another verse, were composed shortly after
the *Acts*. The text usually referred to simply as the *Legend* is the prose account
of Clare's life composed sometime during Alexander IV's papacy (December
1254 to May 1261). Thomas of Celano, Francis of Assisi's first official hagiographer, has frequently been proposed—and quite recently reproposed—as its
author.[3] But the text, which survives in numerous manuscripts, requires a
critical edition before Thomas's authorship can be definitively established.[4]
The author used the *Acts* as a source, and many of the episodes he recounts
depend upon the witnesses' testimony. He claims also to have consulted Francis's companions and Clare's community.[5] The *Versified Legend*, closely related
to the *Legend*, survives in a single codex.[6] Its unknown author wrote also
during the papacy of Alexander IV, to whom he dedicated his work. Because
the *Versified Legend* lacks an account of Clare's canonization in 1255, some
scholars have theorized it was composed before the prose *Legend*, whose published versions do recount the canonization. This hypothesis fails to consider,
however, that many manuscript versions of the prose *Legend* similarly lack the
account of Clare's canonization. Scholars who have carefully examined and
compared the prose and verse versions of the "Legends" (the term I will use to
refer to both legends together) are inclined to think that the *Versified Legend*
followed the prose *Legend*[7]—indeed, the verse version might well refer to the
prose version[8]—but this chronology remains tentative until a critical edition
of the prose *Legend* appears.

Each of these three texts was composed only after Clare died in 1253. We
thus learn about Clare's life before she became a well-known saint only within
texts designed to make her into a well-known saint. By 1253, moreover, Clare's
identity was integrally tied to her redefinition as the founder of a monastic
order that had, in fact, been founded by the papacy. Sensitivity to the ways in
which hagiographic texts depict Clare's early life is thus a *sine qua non* for
understanding its meaning. "Saint Clare," monastic founder, is the lodestar
guiding the presentation of all the people and events of this period. They, in
turn, point to a Clare whose virtues and behavior aligned uncommonly well
with mid-thirteenth-century papal ideals of female sanctity.

Clare's Temporal, Social, and Geographic Location

Two of the most fundamental dates in Clare's life are disputed. She was born
in either 1193 or 1194 and left her family home to take up life as a penitent in

San Damiano in either 1211 or 1212.[9] While choosing one set of dates over the other only negligibly affects our understanding of Clare and the religious movement associated with her, it highlights a trend within the historiography of Clare studies. Scholars who favor the later dates depend upon Thomas of Celano's *First Life* of Francis, composed in 1228–1229. Scholars who favor the earlier dates rely instead on the *Acts* for Clare's canonization. Although it is true that this text post-dates Thomas's *First Life* by almost twenty-five years, it includes testimony from nine witnesses intimately familiar with Clare whose testimony collectively points to Clare having taken up residence in San Damiano in 1211.[10] Bona, a girlhood companion who lived with Clare (whether as a relative or handmaid is not clear),[11] and three other witnesses further note that Clare was about eighteen when she took up religious life, thus putting her birth at 1193.[12] The fact that most scholars until recently depended upon Thomas of Celano's dates rather than those of the multiple witnesses close to Clare subtly indicates how Clare studies have been unduly determined by the narrative of Francis and the friars. This narrative, while not a monolith, tended to exalt Clare (when it bothered to mention her at all), but always as an ancillary figure in the great male Franciscan drama.[13] One symbol of that era's end is the growing acceptance of Clare's sisters' testimony regarding her birth in 1193 and her conversion in 1211.[14]

Although characterizing saints' families as "noble" is boilerplate in much hagiography, Clare's family was, in fact, noble, if not quite at the pinnacle of Assisian society. Pietro di Damiano, a neighbor and witness for Clare's canonization, said that he "knew her father, Lord Favarone, who was noble, great, and powerful in the city. . . . Lady Clare was noble, of a noble family, and of an upright manner of life. There were seven knights of her household, all of whom were noble and powerful."[15] Giovanni di Ventura, household servant and also a witness, classified Clare's household as belonging to the *maiores* of the city, a term indicating the city's aristocratic families, rather than the size of the household as is sometimes claimed.[16] Clare's *Legend* describes her home as "rich and abundantly supplied." Part of it, standing on the northeast side of the piazza in front of the cathedral of San Rufino, survives even today.[17] This piazza was situated in the center of the "upper" section of Assisi, home to the city's other well-to-do and powerful families. San Rufino, which began to share the seat of episcopal authority with Santa Maria Maggiore in the mid-eleventh century, gradually took precedence and by the mid-twelfth century, the cathedral served as both a religious and political center of power in Assisi. Clare probably attended numerous liturgical events in the cathedral, whose grand expansion was just nearing completion in 1211, when she left her home for religious life.[18]

Clare's neighborhood was populated by supporters, including Clare's family, of the pro-imperial party known as the Ghibellines. In 1202 the *minores*—the upwardly mobile middle class—in Assisi rose up and proclaimed themselves an independent commune. The conflict that erupted between them and the more powerful *maiores* forced many of the aristocratic families into a sort of exile in Perugia, where they found allies. Arnaldo Fortini has proposed, albeit without explicit evidence, that Clare and her family, like many of the *maiores*, spent a few years, around 1202 to 1205, in nearby Perugia. It was perhaps there that she met and befriended two of the women who would later join her at San Damiano, Benvenuta da Perugia and Cecilia di Gualtieri.[19] This would explain Benvenuta's otherwise puzzling remark that she and Clare had lived in the same house before either had taken up religious life.[20]

Bona, Clare's childhood companion, testified for the canonization that Clare always stayed inside her home, hidden from public view.[21] Bona's single testimony, uncorroborated by other witnesses, well served the purposes of hagiography. A sheltered home life jibed well with Clare's later monastic enclosure, vaunted by a papacy avid to control and enclose the burgeoning women's movement. Indeed, heavy-handed plays on the theme of Clare's hidden and enclosed life pepper the early and later legends.

Some scholars claim that Clare first encountered Francis of Assisi when she heard him preach in the cathedral of San Rufino or in its piazza,[22] but no evidence establishes this. The few reports that Francis preached in that piazza are probably true, but they also had a life of their own within the hagiography. For example, in 1228–1229 Thomas of Celano reported that on one occasion Francis, remorseful for having eaten some chicken while ill, repented by publicly accusing himself while being dragged through Assisi with a rope tied around his neck.[23] The *Assisi Compilation*, which appears in an early fourteenth-century manuscript, elaborates by locating Francis's public humiliation in the San Rufino piazza, where Francis had just finished preaching.[24] Since the *Assisi Compilation* contains within it stories probably first reported by Francis's early companions around 1246, it is impossible to know what embellishment, if any, the story has sustained as new layers of text were added to the companions' account. In any case, Bonaventure's *Major Legend* about Francis, composed in the early 1260s, escalates the account further by moving Francis *inside* the cathedral and saying he *frequently* preached there.[25]

Bonaventure (d. 1274), the minister general of the Order of Lesser Brothers when he was writing his *Legend*, liked to stress that there had always been respectful ties between the church prelates and the Lesser Brothers. What better way to do that than to portray their founder as a welcome preacher inside the bishop's cathedral?[26] Bonaventure is the first to make such a claim, whereas other sources situate Francis's preaching in piazzas.[27] It is certainly plausible that Francis would have chosen the important piazza of San Rufino to preach penance and that Clare might have first encountered him there. But no medieval source says this and others, as I discuss below, suggest otherwise.

Clare's Peripatetic Journey from Penitence at Home to San Damiano

While still at home, Clare had already taken up the penitential life, according to the canonization witnesses.[28] They stress her exemplary youth—her holiness, upright life, and good deeds, including donations of food and alms to the poor. At some point Clare became personally acquainted with Francis of Assisi, the charismatic layman who preached penitence everywhere he went. "Doing penance" (*facere poenitentiam*) was central to Francis's identity; he exhorted his friars and laypeople alike to embark on this life.[29] Clare's blood sister Beatrice testified that it was Francis, having heard of Clare, who repeatedly sought her out to preach to her; Beatrice does not say where. Clare's *Legend*, which used the canonization testimony, carefully reframed these meetings to underline that it was Clare who sought out Francis.[30] Since Clare's companion, Bona, testified that Clare would meet Francis secretly to avoid being seen by her relatives, it seems likely they never met in her home or,[31] if they did, then at some point he became a *persona non grata* as her relatives caught on to their plans, leading the two to meet elsewhere.

Eventually Clare resolved to dedicate herself fully to a life of penance by "leaving the world" and entering *religio*, the term used to denote religious life. Just exactly what Clare envisioned for her religious life is not spelled out. Although *religio* could at this time mean a canonically approved religious institution bound by a rule, it was commonly used more expansively for an array of lifestyles adopted by men and women who sought religious perfection following a rule of their own devising or even no particular rule at all. These included individuals and married couples residing in their own homes and also groups of individuals sharing a common life. In the first years after Clare took up *religio*, it appears she continued to think of herself as a penitent, rather than as someone striving for canonical approval as a monastic nun, governed by an approved rule.

The first peripatetic weeks of Clare's conversion to religious life are shrouded in mystery, but one revealing constant is her association with Francis and his companions. She entered the path of *religio* at Francis's behest on the night of 27–28 March 1211, Palm Sunday and Monday of Holy Week, significantly, the last week of the Lenten penitential season.[32] Francis remained intimately involved in every step of her journey toward San Damiano, suggesting that the *religio* Clare adopted was the *religio* he extolled. Clare surreptitiously fled her family home and first made her way to Santa Maria della Porziuncola, Saint Mary of the Little Portion, a small rural church, some six kilometers from Clare's house, where Francis and his companions often resided. The bishop of Assisi had perhaps been in on the plan. In a conspicuous display during a liturgical service earlier that day, he had personally given Clare a palm.[33] Several canonization witnesses report that when Clare arrived at the Porzioncula, Francis tonsured her hair,[34] a ritual act that symbolized a rite of initiation, a sign of penance, and flight from the world.[35] The *Legend* author rewrote the witnesses' testimony to underscore that not only Francis but also his brothers received Clare into their "new army of the poor" (*nova militia pauperum*).[36]

The next day Francis sent Clare to San Paolo delle Abbadesse,[37] a monastery alongside the Chiascio river in Bastia, some four kilometers from the Porziuncola. The nuns there followed the sixth-century Rule of Benedict, arguably the most venerable monastic rule. Clare's blood sister Beatrice, Lord Ranieri, and Giovanni di Ventura all testify that when Clare's relatives wanted to wrest her from the church of San Paolo and bring her back to Assisi, she showed them her tonsured head. It was this, claims Ranieri, that convinced them to give up.[38] The *Legend* elaborated the episode, attributing their change of heart to Clare's brave spirit and love more than the sight of her tonsure:

> After the news reached her relatives, they condemned with a broken heart the deed and proposal of the virgin and, banding together as one, they ran to the place, attempting to obtain what they could not. They employed violent force, poisonous advice, and flattering promises, persuading her to give up such a worthless deed that was unbecoming to her class and without precedent in her family. But, taking hold of the altar cloths, she bared her tonsured head,

maintaining that she would in no way be torn away from the service
of Christ. With the increasing violence of her relatives, her spirit
grew and her love—provoked by injuries—provided strength. So,
for many days, even though she endured an obstacle in the way of
the Lord and her own [relatives] opposed her proposal of holiness,
her spirit did not crumble and her fervor did not diminish. Instead,
amid words and deeds of hatred, she molded her spirit anew in
hope until her relatives, turning back were quiet.[39]

These hagiographic texts suggest that Clare had resolutely decided to "do penance" for the rest of her life. The radicality of a young woman of her social
status fleeing her home late at night and then "hurrying" six kilometers to
meet an unusual group of poor penitent men points to her resolve.[40] Her relatives—how many or who the texts do not state—were understandably cha-
grined and did their utmost to persuade Clare from a proposition they found
beneath their class standing. Clare probably exchanged words with them, but,
significantly, the witnesses for her canonization highlight her performative
defiance, when, clinging to the altar cloths, she showed them her shorn hair.
    Why Francis led Clare to the monastery of San Paolo has been a matter of
much speculation. Few scholars believe he thought it a fitting religious home
for his protégé, given his own vision of religious life. The nuns of San Paolo
lived primarily enclosed and, while they practiced personal poverty, they also
benefited corporately from lands and other common property. At the time,
five chapels with benefices belonged to San Paolo.[41] The fact that Clare remained there perhaps some eight days raises the possibility that her stay was
always a temporary expedient.[42] The *Versified Legend* suggests that Francis
placed her there only until God would reveal her final destination.[43] Perhaps
neither he nor Clare had fully thought out where she might reside.[44] Mean-
while, the monastery offered certain short-term advantages. Besides being
close to the Porziuncola, it was, importantly, under the bishop of Assisi's jurisdiction and thus constituted a juridically fitting residence for an Assisian
woman who had just committed herself to religious life.[45] Furthermore, in
1198 Innocent III had issued a bull prohibiting under pain of excommunication anyone not acting on behalf of the bishop from using violence there.[46]
The monastery therefore served, theoretically, as a safe haven. Clare performa-
tively invoked her right to sanctuary when she grabbed hold of the church
altar cloths. This qualifies the pictures offered in the Legends. Both Legends,
after accusing Clare's relatives of behaving violently toward her, state that they

abandoned their quest to bring her home only because of her own "unconquerable perseverence" (*invicta constantia*).[47] Neither Legend mentions any
papal prohibition against the use of violence within the monastery, but perhaps this, together with her tonsure's proof of a ritualized commitment, are
what made her constancy "unconquerable."

Why did Clare leave San Paolo? No source unambiguously answers the
question. Beatrice testifies, without further explanation, that Francis and two
of his companions, Philip and Bernard, led Clare to another place.[48] Fortini
suggests that the nuns themselves might have sent Clare away, fearing retribu-
tion from her family, who had perhaps been emboldened by recent imperial
victories undermining the bishop's authority in Assisi.[49]

Fortini further conjectures that the nuns would not have been justified in
keeping "a girl not inclined to accepting the Rule of Saint Benedict and living
in community." But there is no evidence anywhere that Clare ever objected to
living in community or to accepting the Rule of Benedict, which, importantly, could be flexibly adapted. The Rule was definitely assigned to the San
Damiano community by 1221, if not earlier, and it would remain so for most
of Clare's life. As I discuss in later chapters, we do not know Clare's attitude
toward this rule: neither she nor most of her contemporaries say that she willingly observed it, only reluctantly observed it, or even observed it at all. There
is, on the other hand, explicit evidence that she wanted to follow written
guidelines Francis gave her and her sisters. Regarding the Rule of Benedict, in
1238 Pope Gregory IX would assert that Clare and her sisters had "since the
time of their profession" observed a "rule" (of his devising) assigned to them.
His rule happened to enjoin also upon the sisters the observance of the Rule
of Benedict.[50] In 1243, while Clare was still alive, Pope Innocent IV repeated
Gregory's claim almost verbatim, but he notably added that the Rule of Benedict had been binding on the sisters even during Gregory's pontificate regarding *only* "obedience, the renunciation of property, and perpetual chastity"
or, in other words, what became the three traditional religious vows.[51] If this
is true (and in Chapter 6 I discuss ulterior reasons that may have prompted
his claim), then the lengthy Rule of Benedict would have meant nothing in
particular to Clare since the three vows were observed generally by communities of penitents and all monastics regardless of other guidelines or rules they
might follow. In sum, arguments about the Rule of Benedict's positive, negative, or negligible meaning in Clare's life are conjectural.

Many scholars, with more persuasive force, point to discrepancies between the religious rule approved in the year Clare died, 1253, and the Rule of

Benedict as observed by the nuns of San Paolo to suggest that Clare objected to the latter. Although it is certain that Clare herself contributed important passages to the 1253 rule, it is less certain that what Clare had come to think by 1253 accurately reflected what she thought as a young woman just beginning her religious life in 1211. However, one conviction well attested in both the 1253 rule and her earliest writings (mid-1230s) regards her commitment to a life of poverty in line with Francis's vision. Like him, she intimately linked poverty with humility and considered them to be the foundation of religious life. Her blood sister Beatrice testified that Clare sold her entire inheritance and gave the proceeds to the poor.[52] The sequence of Beatrice's testimony, supported by that of another witness, suggests that this was one of Clare's first acts following her conversion. One might surmise that such an act would have been unwelcome by the nuns of San Paolo who were accustomed to receiving dowries and corporate possessions, but Marco Bartoli suggests that Clare offered to join the servants at the monastery. Even so, he surmises that Clare abandoned San Paolo because she was unable to practice personal poverty to her satisfaction.[53] But no sources ever call Clare a servant or explain why she moved on. It makes just as much sense to think everyone agreed from the start that her stay would be temporary because, in her mind, she had already committed fully to Francis's religious movement.

Indeed, only days after she arrived at San Paolo, Francis and Philip led her to the church of San Angelo di Panzo, three kilometers east of Assisi's town center. Formerly described by scholars as a group of Benedictine nuns, we know now that the women residing there were recluses, a community of noninstitutionalized penitents who followed no approved religious rule.[54] Those, like Fortini, who argue that the Rule of Benedict was not to Clare's liking contend that San Angelo appealed to Clare precisely because it was not a monastery; there she could lead the freer, less regulated life of a penitent. Some scholars conjecture, based on San Angelo's location, that Clare went there for greater seclusion.[55] Its location may be significant for another reason: it lay just a half kilometer beneath the Eremo delle Carceri, a hermitage where Francis and his companions sometimes withdrew. Clare was thus closer, sharing the same western slope of Mount Subasio.

A single but highly revealing episode is reported about Clare's stay in San Angelo. The prose *Legend*, the sole early source for this incident, dedicates an entire chapter to the story of Clare's younger blood sister, Agnes, joining Clare at San Angelo.[56] Closely united in their family home, Clare had prayed that they might continue together in the service of God. The *Legend* author highlights Clare's virginal purity, a leitmotiv throughout his work: Agnes had perhaps been contemplating "carnal marriage" rather than virginal marriage to Christ.[57] Clare's prayers were answered and Agnes arrived at San Angelo some sixteen days after Clare's conversion.[58] The author readily depicts the young Clare in the role of religious leader: Clare, "who perceived more about the Lord," began to teach her younger sister and "novice."[59] This is certainly a case of hagiography, with the benefit of hindsight, retrojecting onto the two sisters the later event of Clare being named head of her community and "founder" of a religious order initiated by the papacy.

Agnes's conversion story offers numerous parallels with Clare's: she fled the family home and was subsequently pursued by relatives. "Twelve men, burning with anger and hiding outwardly their evil intent, ran to the place [and] pretended [to make] a peaceful entrance." Led by Agnes's and Clare's paternal Uncle Monaldo, the men had already given up on retrieving Clare. When Agnes refused to go with them, they seized her. The *Legend* graphically describes the men's violence against the young girl. They were perhaps emboldened because San Angelo lacked the papal protections granted to San Paolo. "One of the knights in a fierce mood ran toward [Agnes] and, without sparing blows and kicks, tried to drag her away by her hair, while the others pushed her and lifted her in their arms." This is probably one of the seven knights who the witness Pietro had said resided in Clare's home. Agnes screamed to Clare for help. "While the violent robbers were dragging the young girl along the slope of the mountain, ripping her clothes and strewing the path with the hair [they had] torn out, Clare prostrated herself in prayer with tears." Then God miraculously intervened: Agnes became too heavy to carry. Other men ran from nearby fields to help the group absconding with Agnes, but her body could not be budged. This elicited further violence: Agnes's enraged uncle raised his hand to strike her dead, but was stymied when his hand was itself struck with an excruciating incapacitating pain. Predictably, an unqualified victory concludes the story. When Clare approached and asked her relatives to desist, they bitterly abandoned the near-dead sister, and she arose, rejoicing that she could devote the rest of her life to God. Notably, Francis, too, makes an appearance in the story: he tonsures Agnes and, with Clare, teaches her about the Lord's path.[60] Like Clare, Agnes was received into religious life by Francis himself. The story has many of the earmarks one expects to find in a narrative about a holy girl dedicating her life to God: family opposition, brave resistance, and miraculous triumph. As I will discuss, however, the family's resistance to the girls' choice of religious life was probably more than mere hagiographic embellishment.

Clare soon left San Angelo, with Agnes, one presumes.[61] Clare's blood sister Beatrice testified, without explaining why, that Clare stayed there only a few days.[62] The *Legend* notes cryptically: "She went to the church of San Angelo in Panzo, but *since* her spirit was not completely at peace, upon Francis's counsel, she moved to the church of San Damiano" (emphasis mine).[63] The *Legend*'s backward glance over forty years later reveals nothing more. So why did Clare move to San Damiano? The small church was under the jurisdiction of the bishop of Assisi, making it a fitting residence for a new penitent. The place was also connected to Francis, being the first church he repaired, and, like the Porziuncola, the brothers stayed there. Marina Righetti Tosti-Croce's architectural and archaeological investigations suggest it served as a hospice for the poor and sick,[64] a ministry we know Francis and his companions engaged in. Lying less than a kilometer from the southeastern gate of Assisi's town walls, San Damiano (named for a physician saint) was ideally situated for such work.[65] That the sisters resided in the "church" (*ecclesia*) of San Damiano may be telling, since this was a term for religious communities given to charitable work, including in hospices.[66] The *Acts* note that Clare healed sick persons brought there.[67] Marino Bigaroni's architectural study suggests that a key reason for Clare's sojourns at San Paolo and San Angelo before moving to San Damiano was that the structure required further work before it could accommodate Clare and other women.[68] Significantly, thereafter, it seems that a few brothers continued to reside alongside the women. All this suggests a plausible scenario in which Francis and Clare had indeed had a plan, perhaps from the very beginning, for her and other women to join Francis's brothers and engage in a similar ministry at one of their sites.

Clare's Family Dynamics

The figures in Clare's family take shape in the Legends largely in light of the roles they played vis-à-vis Clare's religious life. Her mother, Ortulana, receives special attention in the *Acts* and Legends. She eventually joined Clare in San Damiano, although when is not known.[69] In 1238 a list of the monastery's residents fails to list Ortulana so she was probably dead by then.[70] But years later, the sisters frequently recall Ortulana in their canonization testimonies. Since the clerics interviewing them probably elicited this testimony, it is worth pondering at what point narrative history elides into managed hagiography replete with pious embellishment. No clear line demarcates these genres; narrative history is itself "managed," that is, told by someone with a point of view and goal. Pious depictions of Ortulana and Agnes's dramatic flight to become Clare's "novice" illustrate how elusive it is to ascertain seven and a half centuries after the events the extent to which hagiographers have inventively adapted stories to propagate particular images of Clare's family which, in turn, help shape a particular saintly image of Clare.

The witnesses testify to Ortulana's pious life both before and after she joined San Damiano. Before entering, she was known for her prayer, piety, attention to the poor, and pilgrimages to shrines in the Holy Land, Rome, and Sant'Angelo, a shrine in southeastern Italy.[71] Living together in San Damiano, Clare and Ortulana once modestly attributed each to the other the cure of a young boy.[72] A portent Ortulana received while pregnant with Clare is particularly highlighted, a stock feature of medieval hagiography. Standing before a cross, a voice told Ortulana that "she would give birth to a great light which would greatly illumine the world."[73] The Legends claim that Ortulana chose the name "Clare" because of this prophecy.[74] Word plays with "Clare" (*Chiara*), which means "clear," and terms like "light" (*lume*) and "illuminate" (*illustrare*) abound in texts about her. Especially heavy-handed is the opening line of the bull for her canonization, *Clara claris praeclara meritis*, "Clare outstandingly clear with clear merits." And who could miss the coincidence that Clare, who became known as the "little plant" (*plantula*) of Francis, had a mother whose Italian name, Ortulana, meant "gardener," a wordplay featured in the *Bull of Canonization* and Legends: "Ortulana, . . . the excellent gardener who brought forth such a plant in the garden of the Lord"?[75]

In contrast to Ortulana, a cloud of suspicion hovers over Clare's father, Favarone, son of Offreduccio, son of Bernardino.[76] Favarone was a knight who implicitly plays the role of the absent father.[77] The witness Pacifica, a distant relative of Clare who had lived just across the piazza from her, remarked cryptically that she had never seen Clare's father.[78] Favarone was not entirely absent because the witness Pietro said he knew Favarone and was aware that he and Clare's other relatives were interested in having her marry.[79] However, in stark contrast to Ortulana, Clare's father is left entirely out of the *Bull of Canonization* (1255). He is also not named among the group of twelve male relatives, led by Clare's Uncle Monaldo, who had tried to seize Agnes when she joined Clare. Maybe Monaldo was named because he was the oldest son of Favarone's father and therefore the *paterfamilias* of the clan,[80] but even so, the near total silence regarding Clare's father has struck scholars as odd.[81]

The story of pious young girls like Clare and Agnes confronting family opposition with brave resistance is common in medieval hagiography, but in their case, it is also probably quite true. In fact, Clare's siblings might offer some clues about their possibly absent father and family tensions. She had just two blood sisters, both younger. The youngest, Beatrice, joined Clare and Agnes at San Damiano in 1229. Since Ortulana probably died before 1238, and Agnes died just after Clare in 1253 and before the canonization inquest began, that left Beatrice as the only family member able to testify. In surprisingly brief testimony, she alluded to Clare's holiness as a child and offered a few details about Clare's interactions with Francis and her conversion. As to Clare's life in San Damiano, Beatrice supplied a clipped laundry list of virtues bereft of any illustrative details. Probably by the time the canonization commissioners interviewed her, the twelfth witness, they no longer sought or needed to record more details substantiating Clare's "virginity, humility, patience, and kindness," and so forth.[82] They valued Beatrice's testimony principally for details about Clare's life prior to entering San Damiano.

Clare had no brothers, a significant fact because it greatly enhanced the three sisters' possibilities for inheritance. Women's opportunities to inherit and control property had been steadily improving. Clare and her sisters offer a striking case study of significant female economic freedom and autonomy.[83] The marriages of well-born girls were integral to an extended family's social and economic well-being. Clare and her sisters would disappoint their family's hopes by forgoing marriage to become religious. The blow this dealt to their family is borne out by the canonization testimonies. Pietro di Damiano testified that Clare's "father and mother and her relatives wanted her to splendidly marry a great and powerful man in keeping with her nobility. But the young woman, who was at that time about seventeen years [old] or so, could in no way be persuaded because she wanted to remain a virgin and live in poverty, as she then showed when thereupon she sold her entire inheritance and gave it to the poor."[84] Just what is meant by "inheritance" (heredità) here is not entirely clear. Benedetto Vetere thinks a passage in the prose Legend suggests it referred to a specific share of the family's property allotted to Clare independently, rather than simply wealth set aside for a dowry.[85] But in any case, dowries had become a sort of pre-mortem inheritance. They had grown sizably in patrician families like Clare's eager to elevate their status; their transfers underlined the interdependence of fathers and daughters.[86]

Clare apparently had free and unambiguous control over how she would dispose of her property. Her family, avid not to lose it, apparently had no legal recourse—or at least none they were willing to invoke—to regain it. The only road open to them, it seemed, was to buy Clare out, but she refused. One sister testified that Clare's "relatives wanted to give her a better price [for her inheritance] than any of the others [buyers], but she did not want to sell it to them; instead she sold it to others so that the poor would not be defrauded."[87] Just what trickery Clare's family might have deployed to defraud the poor is not spelled out. What is clear is that Clare deeply mistrusted, overtly opposed, and pointedly defied her relatives.

Clare's forceful personality was probably a factor in her successful resistance to her family's overtures to sell her inheritance to them. Notably, Beatrice, who joined Clare some eighteen years later, also maintained control over her property or, at least, a portion of it. The youngest, Beatrice was the least conspicuous of the three sisters. Unlike Clare and Agnes, she never governed a monastery. Her canonization testimony gives no hint that she held any special stature within the San Damiano community. None of the other witnesses ever mention her.[88] Beatrice said that Clare "sold her *entire* inheritance and *part* of the inheritance of the witness [Beatrice] and gave it to the poor" (emphasis mine).[89] It is reasonable to suspect that Agnes, who joined Clare in 1211, also controlled property that was then sold to benefit the poor.[90] Perhaps some sort of deal had been struck based on the family's experience of losing Clare's (and possibly Agnes's) share of the inheritance in 1211 that explains why, around 1229, just a "part" of Beatrice's inheritance had been sold. Beatrice was, after all, Favarone's and Ortulana's last child to inherit. Without knowing the extent of the property given to the three daughters, we cannot judge how much its loss impacted the family, although the fact that they tried to buy back Clare's property indicates that it was not inconsiderable. Favarone probably deplored this loss of property. If so, it would constitute one more reason for the authors of the *Bull of Canonization* and the Legends to forgo assigning him any lofty place in their accounts. The loss of property also adds essential context to the violent behavior of Uncle Monaldo and the other relatives who tried to bring Clare and Agnes back to the family fold. They were losing not only family members but also—and this may have rankled more—property.

Three more interrelated points based on Clare's sale of her family inheritance can be adduced. First, the common hagiographic trope—the young woman who refuses her family's wish that she marry—becomes in Clare's case something more. It is a clash about property. Clare does not simply leave wealth to become poor. She takes wealth with her to fund the poor. Second, Clare's action seems eminently "Franciscan."[91] She could have followed a more traditional path and used her property as a sort of dowry to join a monastery that allowed corporate property, such as the monastery of San Paolo, where she first stayed. Or she could have relinquished the property to the family she left behind. Clare's relatives would understandably have worried about her ties to a fledgling, ragtag group of religious men who, in 1211, had as yet no written approved rule. Moreover, the men's life, and apparently Clare's as well, was predicated in part on their commitment to forgo all wealth. This became part of the written record for the friars in 1221, when Francis quoted Matthew's gospel at the outset of his *Earlier Rule* telling the brothers that they should "go, sell everything you have and give it to the poor."[92] Although the papally approved *Later Rule* (1223) did not demand this, it still advised it.[93] Third, Clare's adamant insistence that she dispose of her family property suggests that she could be inflexible, efficaciously inflexible one might add: Clare got her way. Although one might wish that the early sources revealed fuller details about Clare's personality, this particular characteristic will be abundantly corroborated not only in her own writings, such as her letters and her contributions to the 1253 rule, but also in the *Acts* for her canonization, the *Bull of Canonization*, and the early Legends. All these documents will show that Clare could be uncompromising and tirelessly resolute about the poverty she thought she and her sisters should observe. She would be just as insistent that her community of San Damiano be intrinsically tied to Francis of Assisi and his religious brothers.

Chapter 2

The Early San Damiano: A House of Penitents, 1211 to ca. 1216

Shortly before she died in 1253, Clare of Assisi firmly asserted that her San Damiano sisters' commitment to a life of poverty and their inextricable ties to Francis of Assisi and his brothers dated to her community's very beginnings. Her lucidity on these points contrasts sharply, however, with the opacity of those early years. In this chapter, I examine the three texts scholars have most associated with this period. The first is Francis of Assisi's *forma vivendi*, his guide or rule for Clare's religious life, a text that purportedly dates to her earliest years in San Damiano but survives only in a text composed toward the end of her life. I then turn to a letter written in 1216 by Bishop Jacques de Vitry, who describes his first encounter with the Lesser Brothers, as Francis of Assisi and his friars were known, and the Lesser Sisters, women many scholars think include Clare and her first companions. Jacques's famous passage is, in fact, the first textual witness to the existence of Lesser Brothers and Lesser Sisters. Because it is so frequently invoked as proof that Clare and her sisters originally engaged in apostolic ministries outside San Damiano alongside the Lesser Brothers, I explore in detail the various ways the passage might be interpreted. Finally, I draw on information provided by the *Acts* for Clare's canonization to probe what life might have been like for the San Damiano women during their earliest years.

Francis's *Forma Vivendi*, or Proposed Way of Life

Not long before she died, Clare pithily commented on what she believed was the heart of her community's life in San Damiano. While her description of San Damiano showed it to be remarkably like other houses of simple penitent women, she notably highlighted the community's singularity by tying it securely to Francis of Assisi and the Lesser Brothers. Her remarks are found within a text known as the *forma vitae*, literally "form of life." The text, perhaps redacted only in the late 1240s or early 1250s, is a religious rule articulated primarily in the canonically correct and impersonal language required by the thirteenth-century papacy. Sometimes identified as "Clare's rule" or "Clare's *forma vitae*," it is clear that the text contained not only Clare's significant contributions, but those of others as well. To distinguish it from other similarly entitled legislative texts I discuss in this book, I will refer to it as the *1253 forma vitae* since that is the year the papacy approved it. The most compelling passages within it are two unusual and highly personalized passages placed at the very center of the text (divided, in later extant versions, into twelve chapters). In each passage, Clare speaks in her own first-person voice and then includes verbatim quotations from Francis as well. In the first passage, Clare leads with her vocation "to do penance" and then lays out the mutual ties binding her and her sisters to Francis and his brothers:

> After the Most High Heavenly Father saw fit by His grace to enlighten my heart to do penance according to the example and teaching of our most blessed father Saint Francis, shortly after his own conversion, I, together with my sisters, willingly promised him obedience. When the Blessed Father saw we had no fear of poverty, hard work, trial, shame, or contempt of the world, but, instead, we held them as great delights, moved by piety he wrote a form of life [*forma vivendi*] for us as follows: "Because by divine inspiration you have made yourselves daughters and handmaids of the most High, most Exalted King, the heavenly Father, and have taken the Holy Spirit as your spouse, choosing to live according to the perfection of the holy Gospel, I resolve and promise for myself and for my brothers always to have the same loving care and special solicitude for you as for them." As long as he lived he diligently fulfilled this and wished that it always be fulfilled by the brothers.[1]

Clare has effectively inserted one "form of life," Francis's, within the larger *1253 forma vitae*, thus anchoring it in the words of Francis himself.[2] One might be tempted to squeeze some meaning out of the differing valences between the terms *forma vitae*, literally "form of life," and the more dynamic *forma vivendi* (form for living), but thirteenth-century usage does not bear the weight of such hair-splitting. Differing variations of these terms were often used interchangeably. All "forms of life" regarded the "form," "way of life," or "manner of living" that a religious community would follow, and many were detailed enough to be described as "rules." Francis's *forma vivendi*, as quoted by Clare, is exceptional for its brevity, evoking the women's life in grand terms.

It should be kept in mind that there is no independent manuscript tradition for Francis's *forma vivendi*, its sole source being the *1253 forma vitae* written a full forty years or so after Francis would have composed his *forma vivendi*. Most scholars date the latter to around 1212 or 1213, some few to 1215 or even later, but all these dates are speculative.[3] Anthologies of Clare's and Francis's writings often naively present Francis's quoted words as a stand-alone text,[4] but its meaning cannot be fully grasped apart from the significance that Clare poured into it when she placed it in the very center of the rule she wanted the Church to approve for her and her sisters' life in San Damiano just before her death.

The language of the *forma vivendi* certainly rings true to Francis's exhortative style. He was inclined toward simple, pithy, grand—even grandiose—summary statements. And the "gospel" mentioned in this *forma vivendi* for Clare's community was central to his vision of religious life. Comparing the two rules he authored for his brothers bears this out and also sheds light on his rhetorical style. His *Earlier Rule* (1221) began thus: "The rule and life of these brothers is this, namely: to live in obedience, in chastity, and without anything of his own, and to follow the teaching and footprints of our Lord Jesus Christ, Who says . . ." At this point, to spell out his deepest convictions about religious life, Francis simply inserted a number of gospel verses that quoted Jesus himself. These included (but in longer form than I here present) "go, sell everything and give it to the poor," "come follow me," "if anyone wishes to come after me . . . , let him deny himself and take up his cross and follow me," and so forth.[5] Most scholars agree that Francis had a large hand in the composition of the *Earlier Rule*, written gradually over time. Avid to incorporate Scripture, he called on the friar and biblical scholar Caesar of Speyer to help him embellish his own more plain-spoken style.[6] The lengthy 1221 text has a highly exhortative and meandering quality. Poetic and inspirational, it lacks the juridic specificity that the canonically savvy popes and curia of the thirteenth century expected. Not surprisingly, this rule never received papal approbation. Francis was pressed to write another one that could pass papal muster.[7] With divisions and problems growing among the friars, Francis began around this time to withdraw as their administrative leader and to withdraw physically from them as well, albeit still exercising charismatic authority.[8]

His very reworked *Later Rule*, which Pope Honorius III approved in 1223, is a much tighter text. Gone are many of the scriptural quotations and lyrically poetic passages about prayer, thanksgiving, and other inspirational themes. In their stead, one finds terse, precise regulations regarding key administrative matters, some entirely overlooked in the earlier rule, such as how the minister general was to be elected. Francis had significant help writing this rule. The *Assisi Compilation* states that Francis's early companion and secretary, Brother Leo, and also one Brother Bonizo from Bologna, an expert in canon law, assisted him.[9] More significantly, just a few years after the rule was approved, Pope Gregory IX, recalling the period when he served as the prelate responsible for the Lesser Brothers, claimed his own influence over the *Later Rule*. He wrote: "while we held a lesser rank [as Cardinal Hugo], we stood by [Francis] both as he composed the aforesaid Rule and obtained its confirmation from the Apostolic See."[10] While Francis is considered the intellectual author of the *Later Rule*, it is clear that the *Earlier Rule* better captured his unique rhetorical style. For this reason, it is quite believable that Clare's quotation of Francis's exhortative *forma vivendi* is an authentic expression of Francis's voice.

Clare's recollection provides two pivotal insights about her conception of religious life. First, late in life she recalled that her sisters' early life was integrally tied to Francis's inspiration. The overriding importance of this conviction is signaled by the highly unusual format of her presentation: she interrupts a legislative text, the *1253 forma vitae*, with her highly personalized first-person voice, then encloses within that the first-person voice of Francis himself. Furthermore, after Francis describes the women's manner of life "according to the perfection of the gospel"—his shorthand phrase for the central virtues of poverty and humility[11]—he concludes with a promise that he and his brothers will "care" for the women, which means attend to them spiritually and probably assist them materially as well. This promise is no mere trifle meant to adorn the legislative text; rather, Clare is asserting that her community's relationship with Francis and the friars is absolutely intrinsic to the "form of life" Francis prescribed for them.

Second, the term Clare uses for Francis's advice, *forma vivendi*, connoted a canonical status below a "regularized" monastery, that is, a group of women living according to one of the Church's approved religious rules (*regulae*). In the twelfth century the term *regula* usually referred to one of the well-established rules such as the Rule of Benedict or the Rule of Augustine. Joseph Conwell notes that professing a *vita* (life) differed from professing a *regula* (rule). *Forma vitae* and its variations might well be used in the early days of a penitential community; the religious association of the Humiliati is a case in point.[12] Many groups would intentionally couple the terms *vita* and *regula* as they evolved toward a more juridically recognized entity. Perhaps this explains Thomas of Celano's nomenclature: writing in 1228–1229, he called the very brief text Francis first brought the pope around 1209 or 1210 both a "form of life" and a "rule."[13] By 1245–1247, with the friars fully established as an "order" (*ordo*), Thomas called it simply a "rule for his [Francis's] life."[14] Similarly, while the *Earlier Rule* and *Later Rule* each described their contents as a "rule and life,"[15] the pope, approving only the *Later Rule*, used only the juridically key term "rule."[16]

San Damiano in its earliest years was a charismatic community of religious women called "to do penance," as Clare noted. Embracing a life of "poverty, hard, work, trial, shame" and "contempt of the world," the women were as yet unregulated by any juridically sanctioned rule. Francis's *forma vivendi* was probably quite consciously so termed in light of San Damiano's noncanonical, unregulated status.

If San Damiano, like so many other religious houses, began its life without an approved rule, then we might ask who, if anyone, had authority there? In the *1253 forma vitae*, Clare observed that "I, together with my sisters, willingly promised *him* [Francis] obedience" (emphasis mine). Her statement, included within a papally sanctioned rule, transparently asserts that the women belonged to Francis's *fraternitas* (for lack of a more inclusive term).[17] Was it Francis, then, who "ruled and governed" the sisters during those first years? The women's promise of obedience and Francis's distinguished stature certainly meant he exercised effective authority, but it was the bishop of Assisi, Guido II, who wielded official authority over San Damiano and, it is worth noting, over Francis and his brothers too. Luciano Canonici believes that the bishop even authorized Francis's and Clare's Palm Sunday night escape plan. Pacifica testified for the canonization that during Clare's first years in San

Damiano, "saint Francis, together with the bishop of Assisi, commanded" Clare to eat at least half a roll of bread on the days of the week—Monday, Wednesday, and Friday—that she had been eating nothing at all. That Bishop Guido accompanied Francis strongly suggests—Francis's personal authority aside—that it was the bishop who officially presided.[18] This paralleled the situation of most houses of penitent women in north-central Italy. But notably, Benvenuta and Amata referred to the same incident and spoke of Francis's command, not even mentioning the bishop. Benvenuta, an eyewitness, would have seen him.[19] Did she attribute greater authority to Francis? Or did the canonization commissioners, assisted by the friars Leo, Angelo, and Marco, prefer to accentuate Francis's authority over Clare because it better conformed to the picture they wished to present in 1253 when they were questioning the sisters?

It is often assumed that the women of San Damiano would have been forced to adopt one of the Church's approved religious rules in order to conform to the Fourth Lateran Council's decree *Ne nimia*, issued in 1215.[20] This may be so, but the decree's stipulation that any new expression of "religious life" (*religionum*)—often misleadingly translated as "order"—needed to adopt an approved rule would not have immediately affected San Damiano. Lateran IV's legislation aimed to stem the multiplication of diverse *forms* of religious life cropping up in independent or interrelated communities. As an independent house of penitent women authorized by the bishop of Assisi, however, San Damiano was already duly incorporated into the ecclesiastical structure and was thus not subject to the council's decree.[21] Moreover, there was a natural lag time, sometimes lengthy, between the promulgation of conciliar decrees and their enforcement. This, in part, explains why prelates at the Second Council of Lyon (1274) issued another decree, *Religionum diversitatem*, which essentially repeated *Ne nimia*, aiming to suppress the proliferation of new types of religious life (*religionum diversitatem*) and also any religious "orders" (*diversorum ordinum*) that had arisen without papal approbation since 1215.[22] For years after Lateran IV, as I discuss in Chapter 3, houses of extra-regular women were still being gradually regularized in accordance with *Ne nimia*.

While Bishop Guido exercised juridic authority over San Damiano, Francis's word also weighed heavily. Perhaps because his responsibilities toward his friars so often kept him away from San Damiano, he set down in writing specific guidelines that Clare and her sisters carefully observed. As I will discuss, these written prescriptions eventually sparked controversy between the papacy and religious women aligned with Clare.

Jacques de Vitry's 1216 Letter

The Fratres Minores et Sorores Minores

A key proof text for some scholars who argue that Clare's original intention in 1211 was to lead a life essentially like that of the mendicant friars appears in a letter written by Jacques de Vitry in 1216, just five years after Clare's conversion.[23] Appearing around four decades before the *1253 forma vitae*, the *Acts*, and both Legends, many scholars believe the text to be the earliest witness to the manner of life led by Clare and her followers during their initial years.[24] Jacques's letter has been used to argue further that the San Damiano women were explicitly grouped together with the Lesser Brothers, were known by the parallel title of Lesser Sisters, and had the freedom to come and go as they wished during their early years in San Damiano.[25]

Since claims about the likeness of the women's manner of life to the friars' mendicant way of life are often made as brief assertions resting on Jacques's letter, I think it important to consider in a more detailed fashion the provocative passage thought to support them. Closer scrutiny of Jacques's text shows that while such claims about the women cannot be ruled out, importantly, none are proved by his letter. I agree essentially with scholars such as Lilly Zarncke, Ernest McDonnell, Maria Pia Alberzoni, Jacques Dalarun, and Lezlie Knox, who consider the letter's language too general to know if it refers specifically to Clare and her sisters.[26] I suggest further that the letter even less likely refers to Clare and her sisters if it is interpreted to mean that the women in question carried on an active apostolate *outside* San Damiano.

Jacques de Vitry was one of the most astute and forward-thinking observers of his time in terms of recognizing the importance of new religious groups. A Parisian master, canon regular, and bishop, Jacques had the opportunity to live in a variety of settings, including his native France, the Low Countries, Italy, and the Holy Land.[27] In 1216 he traveled from Liège in the Low Countries to Perugia to be consecrated bishop by Honorius III, who himself had just been elevated to the papacy.[28] Along with observations about other matters, Jacques shared a revealing comment about religious men and women in a letter that he sent almost certainly to a group of his friends back in Liège.[29] The letter is prized not only for its reference to the Lesser Sisters but also as the very first written testimony regarding the Franciscan movement. The great nineteenth-century historian Paul Sabatier thought it provided a more vivid and precise description of Francis's ministry than any single passage contained in his early biographies.[30] The passage, which represents less than 7 percent of the entire letter, is rendered thus in a widely available English translation:

> I found one consolation in those parts, nevertheless: many men and women [*multi enim utriusque sexus*], rich and worldly, after renouncing everything for Christ, fled the world. They are called Lesser Brothers and Lesser Sisters [*fratres minores et sorores minores*]. They are held in great esteem by the Lord Pope and the cardinals. They do not occupy themselves with temporal affairs, but work each day with great desire and enthusiastic zeal to capture those souls that were perishing from the vanities of the world and to bring them along with them. They have already borne much fruit through the grace of God, and have converted many, so that whoever hears them says "Come" [Rev 22:17; Jn 1:46] and one circle of hearers draws another.
>
> They live according to the form [*formam*] of the primitive Church of which it is written: "The multitude of believers was of one heart and one soul" [Acts 3:32]. They go into the cities and villages during the day, so that they convert others, giving themselves to active work; but they return to their hermitages or solitary places at night, employing themselves in contemplation.
>
> The women live near the cities in various hospices. They accept nothing, but live from the work of their hands. In fact, they are very much offended and disturbed because they are honored by the clergy and laity more than they deserve.
>
> The men of this Order [*religionis*], with much profit, come together once a year in a determined place to rejoice together in the Lord and to eat together. They draw up and promulgate their holy statutes with the advice of good men and have them confirmed by the Lord Pope. After this they disperse for an entire year throughout Lombardy, Tuscany, Apulia, and Sicily.[31]

The Lesser Sisters Disappear

Because this passage has been used for such varied interpretations, it is worth discussing in detail the identity of these "lesser brothers and lesser sisters." The phrase has a fascinating history of its own among scholars who first studied and wrote about this text. The most stunning revelation was the discovery by R. B.

C. Huygens that "lesser sisters" had been entirely omitted from all but one of the previously published Latin editions and quotations of the letter.[32] Jules de Saint-Genois, who had discovered the manuscript of the letter, first published it in its entirety in 1849.[33] Although his edition was unreliable in important respects, it correctly included Jacques's reference to the "lesser brothers and lesser sisters."[34] But Saint-Genois's edition, published in a relatively inaccessible journal, was little known[35] and was superseded by Reinhold Röhricht's late nineteenth-century edition.[36] Huygens noted that influential scholars—including Paul Sabatier, Heinrich Boehmer, Leonhard Lemmens, and Girolamo Golubovich—contented themselves with reprinting Röhricht's edition rather than consulting the manuscript themselves.[37] Huygens found Röhricht's edition riddled with errors and found it almost beyond belief that no scholar thought to double-check the original manuscript on reading that Jacques's reference to "many men and women" was represented later in the letter as "lesser brothers" alone.[38] His judgment is perhaps too harsh given that women's identities had for so long been routinely swallowed up within masculine pronouns and substantives under the guise of putatively neutral inclusive language.

What truly stuns, however, is Röhricht's omission. In the caption to the following manuscript reproduction, I have divided the Latin lines to correspond to the same lines in the manuscript. Note that while *fratres* is abbreviated, each and every letter of *et sorores minores* appears.

One can only wonder at Röhricht's reasons for silently omitting the phrase. Perhaps he found the mention of female and symmetrical counterparts of the brothers to be so dissonant with the received wisdom at the time he was writing that he decided to "correct" what he judged to be Jacques's wrong-headed perception. Alternatively, Röhricht may have bowdlerized the text simply because he found the possible existence of *sorores minores* in early Franciscan history to be potentially too explosive. Perhaps the very history of the letter's textual editions proves an excellent example of how porous the boundaries joining so-called objective history and hagiography can be.

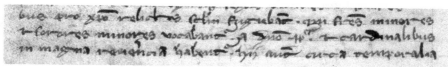

Figure 1. . . . *bus pro Christo relictis seculum fugiebant, qui fratres minores et sorores minores vocabantur. A domno papa et cardinalibus in magna reverentia habentur. Hii autem circa temporalia.* . . .
University Library, Ghent, Ms. 554, f. 2.

Interpreting Jacques's Meaning

Jacques's reading of the situation is his own and needs to be considered on its own terms. He was renowned for his promotion of some of the emerging expressions of religious life; his association with the beguines of the Low Countries is legendary. He promoted his own devotion to the beguine Marie of Oignies by writing her biography, a copy of which he later gave as a spiritual aid to Cardinal Hugo,[39] the very man who would exercise so much influence over Francis and his brothers and Clare and her sisters. Among the topics Jacques raises in his newsy 1216 letter are religious women in the Low Countries, for whom he won Pope Honorius III's permission that they be able to live together communally and exhort each other, apparently without being subject to an approved rule. These "religious women" (*religiosis mulieribus*) offer one case among many of a new expression of religious life (*religio*) that fell outside the reach of the Fourth Lateran Council's decree imposing the adoption of an approved rule. Jacques's letter commented also on the Humiliati in Milan, a combined group of canons, regulars, and laypeople at the forefront of the *vita apostolica* in Italy.[40] It was entirely in keeping with Jacques's interests that as he moved south through Italy, he would be alert to new religious movements there also, movements that departed from more traditional and easily identifiable expressions of religious life such as monks, nuns, hermits, and canons.

His intriguing remarks about the lesser brothers and lesser sisters have admitted a variety of interpretations. These begin at the most basic level with decisions about how to render Jacques's passage using modern orthography. Modern editors and translators have to carefully decide a host of issues when they publish medieval manuscripts since these often lack paragraphs, punctuation, and capitalization. The late thirteenth-century manuscript containing Jacques's Letter 1, which employs a cursive minuscule, does not capitalize *fratres minores et sorores minores*.[41] It makes an altogether different impression when one renders this phrase as "Lesser Brothers and Lesser Sisters," as one sees in the translation above, instead of as "lesser brothers and lesser sisters," as I have been doing in most of this chapter. When Jacques wrote his letter in 1216, Francis's lesser brothers were still seven years from receiving a written rule approved by the papacy. Hagiographic sources relate that Francis and some of his brothers had received oral confirmation from Pope Innocent III in 1209 or 1210 for a very brief written "form of life and a rule." Thomas of Celano says it consisted primarily of "words from the holy gospel," supplemented by "a few other things necessary for the practice of a holy way of life."[42] It was sufficient to win Innocent's oral approval, but hardly constituted a canonically approved rule. In this light, "lesser brothers" might seem an apt description of the new group. On the other hand, at some point in the evolution of the brothers from a small charismatic band orally authorized by the papacy into a large organized institution regulated by the papacy, the proper name Lesser Brothers best captures their reality.

In any event, considering the matter in 1216 from the perspective of Jacques de Vitry, a man being introduced to these men and women for the first time, one must consider the possibility that Jacques took the names lesser brothers and lesser sisters to be an informal designation, much as other devout people of the time might be called a brother or sister of penance without necessarily pertaining to one of the groups formally recognized as the Brothers and Sisters of Penance, who would eventually be given their own canonically approved rule. Many identifiable and recognized religious groups evolved and took their official titles initially from informal movements. And many informal movements never coalesced into clearly identifiable and recognized religious groups. Huygens had to make an interpretive judgment call when he inserted capitalization into his published version of the manuscript of Letter 1. But the difference between "lesser brothers and lesser sisters" and "Lesser Brothers and Lesser Sisters" could be as significant as the difference between "poor men" and the group known as the Poor Men of Lyon.

It might have been especially meaningful to the recipients of Jacques's letter to know that there were in Italy not only men but also women involved in the *vita apostolica*. Huygens argues persuasively that Jacques's 1216 letter, which lacks a greeting, was addressed to his friends back in the region of Liège. Internal evidence within the letter confirms this.[43] It is likely that any such group of friends included women and, perhaps, only women.[44] His mention of "lesser sisters" participating in the *vita apostolica* in Italy might have been not only a newsy report but also a conscious message of support to religious women in Liège.

The very ambiguity surrounding Jacques's description of the lesser brothers and lesser sisters is revelatory of the Umbrian scene surrounding Assisi. He perceptively realized that he was encountering something altogether new, paralleling in excitement what he had witnessed in the north. Ironically, the phrase "lesser sisters"—until recently expunged from so many editions—riveted the attention of thirteenth-century churchmen much as it rivets the attention of historians today. Just a year or so after Jacques penned his letter,

Cardinal Hugo, the future Pope Gregory IX, would encounter an array of women's groups as he traveled through north-central Italy. They no doubt included women like those Jacques described and perhaps other "lesser sisters" as well, who were known to exist in Italy at that time, some without any concrete ties to Francis and his followers. For example, a community of women founded in Verona around 1210 were identified in 1224 as *sorores minores*, and Italy abounded with examples of penitent "brothers and sisters" sharing religious life and serving lepers or other needy groups.[45]

Identifying the Lesser Sisters

But should we so easily identify the *sorores minores* whom Jacques mentions with Clare and her growing community of sisters, or do they refer to other women? There are several matters to consider. First, while Lesser Brothers became a title formally applied to Francis's early followers, there is no evidence of an equivalent parallel formal, or even informal title, ever being applied to Clare and the women of San Damiano. The men and women Jacques encountered could have included Francis's friars, already approved orally by Innocent III, and any nonsanctioned, independent, and informally organized female penitents who, as Jacques said, renounced the world to lead lives of poverty and humility. It is worth noting that Jacques's comments embrace more than one community of women because he employs the plural when he refers to their "hospices" outside the "cities." The women he calls "lesser sisters" were thus a phenomenon throughout the region.

Second, if Jacques did recognize these men and women as followers of Francis, it is curious that he never mentions Francis, or Clare herself for that matter. This was, of course, Jacques's first exposure to the Franciscan movement, and it is unlikely he had met either Francis, who was already becoming well known, or Clare, who was probably not well known.

A third point, indirectly related to identifying the women in the passage, regards decoding just what Jacques is saying about the women per se. He emphatically noted that both men and women belonged to this movement, and he pointed out certain traits that distinguished them. Did he also point out shared characteristics? Key to correctly interpreting Jacques's meaning is determining at just what point after his initial mention of "lesser brothers and lesser sisters" he diverges to discuss the men and women separately. This is not self-evident, in part because after mentioning "both sexes" Jacques proceeds to make a number of statements about "them"; that is, he uses gender-neutral pronouns such as "they" and gender-neutral verbs such as "they go into" without noting whether "they" includes both men and women or only one of these groups. The most obvious and grammatically transparent reading would be to assume that Jacques continues to be speaking of both groups until he indicates clearly, by using gender-specific terms such as "men," "women," or "these women" (*hae*), that he is speaking of just one of the groups. But undermining this assumption is the fact that Jacques narrows his focus to men alone while still employing gender-neutral language.

The question then arises, at just what point in his discussion of this gender-neutral "them" does he cease speaking of both groups and begin speaking of one alone? The manuscript version of the letter, which does not divide the passage into paragraphs, offers little help on this point. The English translation cited above has paragraphs; this in itself suggests an interpretation the Latin may not have originally borne. According to this paragraphing, the first paragraph seems to be about both men and women, the second paragraph about men, the third paragraph about women, and the fourth paragraph, again, about men.[46]

To reexamine this question, I present below my more literal translation of the passage, followed by the Latin text as edited by Huygens. I have divided the passage into five pericopes, capitalizing words or phrases that I highlight in my discussion. Note that I begin the second pericope with "These ones, moreover" (*hii autem*) and the third pericope with "These same ones, moreover" (*Ipsi autem*). Although it may seem a small matter, this makes sense because the two phrases appear to be syntactically related. Moreover, the Latin text has at just these very places a *punctus*, that is, a punctuation mark that indicates there should be some sort of pause or stopping point before *hii* and *ipsi*.[47] I indicate in the Latin text the places of all the *puncti* that appear in the manuscript. I here simply summarize what I have elaborated at greater length elsewhere.[48]

Pericope 1
I found one consolation in those parts, nevertheless: indeed, many people of BOTH SEXES rich and worldly, have been fleeing the world, renouncing everything for Christ; they [*qui*] are called lesser brothers and lesser sisters. They are held [*habentur*] in great esteem by the lord pope and the cardinals.

Pericope 2
THESE [ONES], MOREOVER, do not occupy themselves in any way with temporal affairs, but work every day with ardent desire

and eager zeal to draw back from worldly vanities souls who are being lost and to lead them along with them. And through the grace of God they have already borne great fruit and many have been saved, such that whoever hears [them] says, "Come," and [thus] one circle [of hearers] draws another circle.

Pericope 3
THESE SAME [ONES], MOREOVER, live after the manner of the primitive church, of whom it was written, "the multitude of believers was of one heart and one soul." By day they go into the cities and towns to benefit others through active work; but at night they return to their hermitage or solitary places where they are free to devote themselves to contemplation.

Pericope 4
THE WOMEN, HOWEVER [or "indeed"], abide together in various hospices near the cities; they accept nothing, living instead from the work of [their own] hands; moreover they suffer and are troubled because they are honored more than they wish by clergy and laity.

Pericope 5
THE MEN, HOWEVER [or "moreover"], in this religious life [*religionis*] come together with manifold profit once per year in a determined place so that together they might rejoice in the Lord and feast, and they draw up and promulgate their holy directives, with the counsel of good men, and [their directives are] confirmed by the pope; after this, indeed, for the entire year, they disperse throughout Lombardy, Tuscany, Apulia, and Sicily.

In the Latin text, a forward slash (/) indicates places in the text where the copyist has placed a *punctus* to indicate a pause. Italicization calls attention to the letter's gender-neutral terms and verb endings.

Pericope 1
Vnum tamen in partibus illis inveni solatium, / multi enim UTRI-USQUE SEXUS divites et seculares omnibus pro Christo relictis seculum fugiebant, / *qui* Fratres Minores et Sorores Minores vocab*antur*. / A domno papa[49] et cardinalibus in magna reverentia habe*ntur*,

Pericope 2
/ HII AUTEM circa temporalia nullatenus occupa*ntur*, / sed fer-
venti desiderio et vehementi studio singulis diebus labora*nt* / ut ani-
mas que pereunt a seculi vanitatibus retraha*nt* et eas *secum* duca*nt*. /
Et iam per gratiam dei magnum fructum feceru*nt* et multos lucrati
/[50] sunt, ut qui audit dicat: / veni, / et cortina cortinam trahat.

Pericope 3
/ IPSI AUTEM[51] secundum formam primitive ecclesie vivu*nt*, de
quibus scriptum est: / multitudinis credentium erat cor unum et
anima una. / De die intra*nt* civitates et villas, ut aliquos lucrifacia*nt*
operam da*ntes* actione; / nocte vero revertu*ntur* ad heremum vel
loca solitaria vaca*ntes* contemplationi.

Pericope 4
/ MULIERES VERO iuxta civitates in diversis hospitiis simul com-
morantur; / nichil accipiunt, sed de labore manuum <suarum> vi-
vunt, valde autem dolent et turbantur, quia a clericis et laicis plus
quam vellent honorantur.

Pericope 5
/ HOMINES AUTEM illius religionis semel in anno cum multi-
plici lucro ad locum determinatum conveniunt, / ut simul in domino gaudeant et epulentur, / et consilio bonorum virorum suas
faciunt et promulgant institutiones sanctas et a domno / papa con-
firmatas, / post hoc vero per totum annum disperguntur per Lum-
bardiam et Thusciam / et Apuliam / et Siciliam./[52]

As noted, Jacques's subjects of discussion in pericopes 1 (men and
women), 4 (women), and 5 (men) seem clear. But about whom is Jacques
speaking in pericopes 2 and 3? Logically, one should assume he is still speaking
about the brothers and sisters whom he introduced in pericope 1. They would
be the antecedent for these ones" (*Hii*) in pericope 2 and for "These same
ones" or "They" (*Ipsi*) in pericope 3. But there is a strong case to be made that
Jacques has, by the third pericope, narrowed his discussion to the brothers
alone even though he continues to speak using gender-neutral pronouns and
verbs for an unspecified "them." This opens the door to the possibility that his
discussion of the brothers began yet earlier in pericope 2.

My purpose in the following discussion is not to argue strongly for a single interpretation, but rather to show that, ultimately, the passage admits several possible interpretations. Too often scholars have argued in favor of one interpretation alone, one that reflects the scholar's assumptions (and sometimes wishful thinking) regarding the respective roles of early religious women and men associated with Francis of Assisi. My goal is to show how broad the valid spectrum of interpretation is for this passage.

First, what is the evidence that pericope 3 concerns the brothers alone? We know from evidence external to Jacques's letter that the behavior he describes in that pericope corresponds to the practice of the early friars: "By day they go into the cities and towns to benefit others through active work; but at night they return to their hermitage or solitary places where they are free to devote themselves to contemplation." The fourth pericope shows a very conscious shift to "women," indicating he intended to contrast the women who live near the cities in hospices with the people he has just been discussing: those who go in and out of the towns and reside in hermitages or solitary places, that is, the men.

If it is the case that Jacques has shifted his focus to men in pericope 3 even while continuing to speak of a gender-neutral "they," then we should ask further if he had shifted his focus yet earlier in the passage. This interpretation too is possible. In that case, Jacques's comment about working ardently every day to save souls from worldly vanities would regard, specifically, the lesser brothers' well-known evangelizing activity. As I noted before, the most obvious and compelling reading of pericope 2, at first sight, is that Jacques is still speaking of both the men and the women. Grammatically, they should be the antecedent for *hii*, "these ones." But what if the *hii autem* of pericope 2 is paired with the *Ipsi autem* of pericope 3? *Ipsi* can be rendered simply as "they" or as "these same ones." Jacques uses the term *ipsi* liberally in his writings, and he uses it in both senses, sometimes as the simple pronoun "they," and at other times as an intensive pronoun to signal to his readers that he is speaking still of the *very same* people about whom he has been speaking. If *Ipsi* here means "these same ones," then his subject in pericope 2 would also be the brothers.[53] It is relevant to note, moreover, that elsewhere in Jacques's writing, without apprising the reader, he similarly shifts from a discussion of both men and women to a discussion of men alone.[54] The ambiguity marking the second pericope, however, remains. Jacques appears somewhat more likely to be discussing both the brothers and sisters, but the reader cannot know for certain at what point in the passage his subject becomes the men alone.

Do the Lesser Sisters Include Clare and Her Sisters?

How broadly or narrowly one understands Jacques's remarks to apply to the sisters as well as the brothers affects how likely it is that they include the women of San Damiano. For example, if one presumes the sisters and the brothers went into the cities and towns to work, one must consider whether Clare and her sisters also shared this active apostolate with the brothers. Virtually no explicit evidence, and perhaps no explicit evidence at all, exists to shore up such a claim. None of Clare's surviving writings, which admittedly are few, ever even slightly suggests that the non-serving sisters like Clare had ever gone outside San Damiano. The sisters who testified for Clare's canonization speak often about her early religious life. At least five of them had joined Clare before 1216, the year Jacques wrote his letter.[55] None alludes to an active life outside San Damiano (to be sure, as their statements were recorded by the canonization commissioners). A jar of oil that Sister Pacifica said had been miraculously replenished in the summer of 1212, soon after Clare began living in San Damiano, had been placed on a "wall" (*murello*) by Clare for a friar questor for refilling.[56] A friar questor was a man who begged to help sustain the women materially. Why would Clare have called for his assistance if the sisters themselves could regularly come and go? The Legends, sermons, papal privileges, and other documents regarding Clare and the women of San Damiano are also silent about any movements on the part of the sisters beyond San Damiano, the sole exception being the "serving sisters."[57] We do not know at precisely what point in San Damiano's history such sisters were incorporated into community life. By October 1221, at the latest, it is probable that serving sisters resided at San Damiano since they are mentioned in a new *forma vitae* assigned by that date, or somewhat earlier, to San Damiano and eight other women's houses by Cardinal Hugo (later Gregory IX).[58] In 1253 Sister Angeluccia testified that Clare would send them outside, but Angeluccia provides no other particulars about them.[59] More to the point, her testimony implies that going outside was the province of the serving sisters alone. The one piece of potential counter evidence is a brief act documenting a sale of land to Sisters Maresebelia, Angeluccia, and Clare in September 1217 on which would eventually be built the San Damiano-allied monastery of Foligno. It is not certain, however, if the "Clare" in question is Clare of Assisi. If it was, it indicates she could and did leave San Damiano for important business.[60] In any case, the preponderance of evidence regarding the first years of life at San Damiano reveals nothing about Clare and her sisters leaving San

Damiano. Thus, if Jacques's remark about urban activity is taken to include the lesser sisters, then it is less likely that he was referring also to the women of San Damiano.

It is significant too that Jacques devoted an entire chapter of his *Historia occidentalis* to the friars and their order. He had encountered Francis of Assisi in person in 1219. Jacques, as bishop of Acre, had traveled to Damietta, Egypt, to accompany a crusading expedition. Francis, whom it seems Jacques had not seen before this time, had also traveled there in order to preach to the Sultan of Egypt. Jacques entitled his chapter on the friars "On the Order and Preaching of the Lesser Brothers." He presents a rather global image of the order which, by then, in the 1220s, he had come to know much better.[61] He comments on the friars' founder, their religious ideals, manner of living, rule, structure, meetings, recruiting, membership requirements, and so forth. Yet Jacques says nothing about any lesser sisters or other women who may have been associated with the brothers.[62] Is it possible that by 1220 Jacques omitted the women in order to align his *Historia* with the recently launched papal initiative to cloister such women apart from the friars?

In sum, although it is not impossible to think that Clare and her sisters were the lesser sisters cited by Jacques in his letter of 1216, there are reasons to doubt this, especially if Jacques's passage is interpreted in a way that includes the sisters alongside the brothers undertaking an active urban apostolate. A broad interpretation of Jacques's passage leads one to think that his lesser sisters in 1216 were probably other women inspired by Francis or at least by the same values that motivated the lesser brothers. Roger of Wendover (d. 1236) preserves an account of a woman from Burgundy who, in 1225, approached some friars and insisted on adopting their rigorous way of life. Barefoot, wearing a sack garment and haircloth, she "took up the office of holy preaching." Known for her holiness, she traveled from one place to another for many years, preaching especially to women.[63] During and after Clare's life, such women would be increasingly denounced by the papacy.

Jacques might be more narrowly interpreted, of course. If only pericopes 1 and 4 regard the women, then Jacques's claims about the lesser sisters are simpler: they renounced the world for Christ; were esteemed by prelates, clergy and laity; and lived poorly from the work of their own hands in hospices near the cities. This narrower reading could describe the life of Clare and her sisters in 1216. Still, it is worth bearing in mind that they are never identified as lesser sisters in any documents. Perhaps evidence of this early title simply has not survived or, more sinisterly, was intentionally suppressed as the

papacy prodded Clare and her sisters to become cloistered nuns while simultaneously ostracizing the lesser sisters and other women emulating the lifestyle
of the Lesser Brothers.[64] The fact that such questions about the lesser sisters
are so difficult to answer reminds us that the traces of most of these women,
whether penitents residing primarily within their hospices or others serving
their neighbors in towns, are mostly lost to us. Never having received the civic
and ecclesiastical approbation and institutional support that helped male
groups like the Lesser Brothers and the Order of Preachers flourish, such
women left far fewer records for us to plumb.

Although it is unlikely that the San Damiano women led an urban apostolic life in 1216—indeed, the jar of oil incident probably pushes this date
back to 1212—it is conceivable that during their very earliest days they had
enjoyed some freedom to come and go from San Damiano and engage with
others. But such freedom of movement—if indeed it ever existed—would be
quashed once a religious rule was assigned to (and also enforced) at San Damiano. Their early days by then might have constituted just the sort of dangerous memory that becomes suppressed, leaving for posterity only arguments
ex silentio about Clare and her sisters' earliest practices.

The Internal Life of San Damiano: Evidence Gleaned from the *Acts* (1253)

What transpired within San Damiano and how Clare and her sisters first organized themselves is virtually impossible to reconstruct. The *Acts* provide
some bare-bones information regarding the first women who joined Clare.
Witnesses' comments about themselves or other sisters suggests there was a
steady flow of women into the monastery during those early years. By 1212, at
least five women had entered and there could well have been others; the canonization commissioners never asked the women to tally their numbers for
any given period, information that was perhaps general knowledge and taken
for granted.

Many sisters were related by blood or closely connected, even for this
small town of some two to four thousand inhabitants.[65] Clare's blood sister
Agnes joined her in 1211.[66] The first witness, Pacifica, a neighbor and distant
relative who also lived on the piazza San Rufino, says she joined San Damiano
at or about the same time as Clare, thus probably also in 1211.[67] The second
witness, Benvenuta da Perugia, who entered in September 1211, says that she

had lived with Clare (possibly in Perugia when Assisians sought exile there).[68] The third witness, Filippa, knew Clare since childhood and began her life in San Damiano in 1215.[69] Clare's "niece" Balvina di Martino (actually, the daughter of Clare's cousin) arrived sometime before 1217.[70] Cristiana di Bernardo da Suppo, entered in 1219 and knew Clare in Assisi. She must have known Clare fairly well because she was in Clare's house the night Clare fled her family home and could supply details about what happened.[71] Other women close to Clare whose names are unknown to us may also have entered in these years. Later, more relatives and acquaintances would enter, including another "niece," Amata (1228), Clare's blood sister Beatrice (1229), and, at some unknown date, her mother Ortulana.[72] San Damiano, in short, was in many ways a family affair.

The story about the jar of oil being mysteriously filled in 1212, told to suggest an early divine presence at San Damiano, inadvertently revealed also the presence of friar questors.[73] Comments about friars elsewhere in the *Acts*, although often bereft of specific dates, suggest friars were closely allied with the women and commonly present. Indeed, the *1253 forma vitae* would later declare that friars, perhaps four—a chaplain, a clerical companion, and two lay brothers—had "always" assisted the women in their poverty.[74] When a heavy door fell on Clare in 1246, three friars were sufficiently close to help lift it off.[75] The *Acts* frequently mention friars occupying the posts of questor, preacher, chaplain, and, eventually, "visitator" on behalf of the papacy.[76] It is very likely that a few friars regularly resided in a structure close by or even attached to San Damiano.[77]

We know little about how the women first organized themselves. The texts referring to this period—the *Acts*, the two Legends, Clare's brief references in the *1253 forma vitae*—were all written decades later and have little to say about the early community's structure, day-to-day routines, and work and division of labor. Common sense suggests there was little formal hierarchy. The women were probably few and frequently closely related or well known to each another. In fact, six of the eight women known to have joined San Damiano prior to 1220 (there may have been others) were related to Clare, lived with her, or had been long-time and often close friends.[78] The first clear sign of organizational development in San Damiano appears three years after Clare's conversion, when Francis asked her to take over the "rule and governance" (*regimento et governo*) of the sisters around 1214.[79] It is likely none of the sisters had been formally in charge until then. Perhaps the community had grown to twelve or thirteen, highly symbolic numbers recalling the apostles, or the apostles with their leader, Christ. This was the moment some groups sought formal organization or approval—one thinks of Francis and his eleven companions who traveled to Rome in 1209 or 1210 to seek Innocent III's approval.[80]

Most of the women whose backgrounds we know seem to have come from the upper echelons of society. Giovanna Casagrande's survey of the twenty-four sisters who gave testimony or are named in the *Acts* indicates that seven women belonged to Clare's family circle and six others hailed from well-off families (two of whom were notably aristocratic). The backgrounds of eleven sisters are unknown. That the early sisters came from a socially restricted circle hardly surprises. They knew each other and, further, well-off women figured prominently in the poverty movement: having wealth to renounce, they were more likely to value voluntary poverty as a religious ideal. An irony of the poverty movement is that its prestige derived in part from the halo effect of the rich and powerful.[81]

The serving sisters constituted a more muted and even enigmatic group in San Damiano. As noted, they are mentioned in a *forma vitae* Cardinal Hugo assigned to San Damiano and other women's houses.[82] The document can be dated between his second and third journeys as papal legate (May 1218–October 1221), the most probable date being between spring 1220 and 1221.[83] I will therefore refer to it as the 1220–1221 *forma vitae*. We do not know at what point before this *forma vitae* that serving sisters joined any of these communities, how many there were, and how much their work and prayer differed from those of the other sisters. One wonders if serving sisters undertook most of the manual tasks, leaving the other sisters freer for contemplation or reading, as was the case in some monastic communities. The serving sisters are mentioned in passing in the *Acts* when Clare exhorted them to praise God on the occasions when she sent them outside where they would see people, creatures, beautiful trees, flowers, and bushes.[84] The serving sisters were clearly enshrined in the 1253 rule, described as those "serving outside the monastery" (*servientibus extra monasterium*) and thus distinguished from sisters bound by the rule's law of enclosure.[85] Contrary to a romanticized notion of San Damiano, but wholly in keeping with thirteenth-century religious life, the very existence of serving sisters reveals that a two-tiered society existed within the community, however much affection and mutual respect might have bound the women. Boccali wonders if Lucia of Rome, who had been brought to San Damiano as a little girl, was perhaps poor or orphaned.[86] Often such girls became serving sisters in the monasteries of the well born. Residing in San

Damiano, where humility was especially prized, probably softened any class distinctions they might otherwise have experienced. Even after Clare took charge of governing San Damiano, she would wash the sisters' feet. Once, having done so for a serving sister, Clare bent to kiss the sister's foot. When the sister abruptly pulled it away, she accidently struck Clare in the mouth.[87] The episode encapsulates a wonderful religious reversal, the saintly mother serving the probably less saintly sister and, lurking beneath this spiritual reversal also a class reversal, the refined lady Clare, leader of San Damiano, bowing before the simple and significantly unnamed servant.

The early sisters' daily routine is also unknown. Cardinal Hugo's *forma vitae*, assigned by 1221 at the latest, prescribed the Divine Office. Sisters who testified for the canonization sometimes indicated the time of day by referring to parts of the Office, such as Matins or Terce. Most of these references cannot be dated, but among those that can, the earliest refers to 1225.[88] One wonders how many years before that the sisters had been praying the Office—as early as 1211? Or were they in that period too engaged with charitably tending to others in their hospice? Did they begin to pray the Office only later when they were urged to adopt more conventionally monastic practices?

The same silence surrounds the early sisters' work and other activities. The witnesses frequently mention Clare's work spinning corporals and altar linens.[89] Cloth-work was common in women's religious houses; perhaps the other San Damiano sisters did this too. When Jacques de Vitry claimed that the "lesser sisters" who resided in hospices "lived by the work of their own hands," he could have meant this. Such labor might generate "alms" of some sort as a token of gratitude. So too might work tending the poor, sick, or travelers who stopped at hospices outside towns, an apt description of San Damiano perhaps. In any case, our view of the early San Damiano community should not be determined by descriptions of the community in later years or by idealized assertions regarding San Damiano's "absolute poverty." Francis himself approved a just return for honest labor.[90]

The canonization witnesses report some specific information about Clare during these early years, besides her very reluctant assent to govern San Damiano. Several sisters note that, sometime before 1217, Francis and Bishop Guido forcibly restrained her extreme fasting. The canonization commissioners no doubt relished such stories. Clare's total fasts on some days and partial fasts on others, they record, harmed her health. The sisters, in fact, were astonished that she could even survive. During Lent and the weeks before Christmas, Clare fasted on bread and water six days a week, easing up only slightly on Sundays when, if available, she would drink a small amount of wine.[91]

Other witnesses described Clare's harsh sleeping arrangements in those first years. She slept on a bed of branches or twigs (*sarmenti*) before Balvina di Martino entered by 1217 and, after that, at some point, on a coarse board. Agnes di Oportolo, who entered in 1220, says that for most of the years they lived together, Clare slept on a mat. Francis had ordered her to sleep on a sack of straw after "she fell ill," which might refer to the chronic illness that befell Clare in 1224.[92]

Clare's food and sleeping practices are among the few that can be dated and, in both cases, Francis obliged her to temper them. This suggests a severely austere "early" Clare, albeit the "later" Clare was still an ascetic. Alas, the witnesses say nothing about how Clare reacted to Francis's mitigations besides the fact that she obeyed, a virtue duly noted by the canonization commissioners.[93] By around 1238, when Clare wrote about fasting to her collaborator Agnes of Prague, she appears to have softened her attitude. After outlining Francis's recommendations on fasting—which, while more lenient that Clare's early practices, were still quite demanding—Clare glossed Scripture and implored Agnes: "because neither is our flesh the flesh of bronze, nor our strength the strength of stone, but instead we are frail and prone to every bodily weakness, I am asking and begging in the Lord that you be restrained wisely, dearest one, and discreetly from the indiscreet and impossibly severe fasting that I know you have imposed on yourself, so that living, you might profess the Lord, and might return to the Lord your reasonable worship and your sacrifice always seasoned with salt."[94] Perhaps she preached moderation without practicing it herself. Benvenuta noted that Clare used "rough haircloths and shirts for herself, but was very merciful to the sisters who could not endure such harshness and willingly gave them consolation."[95] She had worn a sort of coarse wool or hemp beneath her garments while still at home.[96] She then escalated her asceticism in San Damiano, wearing the bristled side of an animal hide or a garment of knotted horsetail hair against her skin.[97] The sisters confiscated such garments after Clare fell ill.[98] Her customary routine included other ascetic disciplines as well, but these are usually impossible to date with precision. Even allowing for the sort of embellishment a canonization inquiry might encourage, Clare appears to have been almost frighteningly harsh with her own body. Were it not for the many counterbalancing comments about her gentleness and joy, she would cut a fearsome figure.

One final event can be placed during Clare's first years in San Damiano, a refreshingly telling episode. Cecilia, commenting on Clare's spirit of prophecy, reported that when "Saint Francis had sent five women to be received in the monastery, Saint Clare lifted herself up and [said she] would receive four of them. But she said that she did not want to receive the fifth because she would not persevere in the monastery, even if she stayed there for three years. After she did receive her because of great pressure [*molta importunità*], the woman stayed hardly a half year. Asked who this woman was, Cecilia replied, Lady Gasdia, daughter of Taccolo."[99] The story is telling for three reasons. First, while some sisters acknowledged Clare's role in their decisions to join San Damiano,[100] here we see Francis proactively expanding the women's numbers. If he sent five women at once in this instance, he probably sent others also to the community he helped found. The episode signals his personal involvement with and high regard for San Damiano and probably also his conviction that the sisters shared the same gospel vision as he and his brothers. Second, Clare's dissent from Francis's opinion—striking in itself—reveals, in this instance anyway, that she was a better judge of character. Finally, despite Clare's protest, Francis still insisted—and Clare complied—that she accept the novice.

It should be borne in mind that Cecilia reported this extraordinary disagreement in 1253, decades after Francis had been raised to the status of Saint. Her report was just the sort of threatening memory that the thirteenth-century hagiographers who had access to the *Acts* suppressed, thus consigning the story to oblivion until the sixteenth century, when Sister Battista Alfani portrayed a more assertive Clare.[101]

We can only wonder at what Clare might have said to Francis when the novice Lady Gasdia gave up after only six months. Clare had predicted she would depart even if she managed to stay "three years," probably the length of the probationary period a new entrant's vocation would be tested before definitive acceptance. At some point, a set of rules developed to govern such decisions. Just how those rules evolved, as the next chapter shows, is a matter of considerable debate.

Chapter 3

The House of Penitents Becomes
a Monastery, ca. 1211 to 1228

For centuries, scholars have debated how and when the penitent women of
San Damiano evolved into a monastery, bound formally by one of the
Church's approved religious rules and governed specifically by a set of constitutions articulating the details of their life. In many respects, the San Damiano women would follow the same trajectory as other thirteenth-century
religious women. Cistercian and Dominican women too, for example, often
began as houses of penitents who were then compelled to accept increasing
church regulation and enclosure.[1] There has been lively division too about
how the very "Order" of San Damiano began, what role Clare did or did not
play in its foundation, and what specific rule her community might actually
have observed.[2] To launch my discussion of the San Damiano community's
evolution, I offer one traditional perspective and then a revised portrait that is
rapidly gaining ground.

A Traditional Portrait

One long-popular view of Clare and her sisters generally adheres to these
points. First, Francis (or sometimes Francis with Clare) founded the community of San Damiano. More specifically, they founded the very *religio*, the
particular expression of religious life, at San Damiano. However historians
might tip the balance between Francis and Clare, both figured as the principal
inspirations for religious life there.

Second, the radically poor life practiced at San Damiano quickly inspired both already existing and entirely new women's religious houses to pattern themselves after San Damiano. Medieval and modern historians colloquially identified this ensemble of houses as the "Second Order" because it presumably succeeded, they thought, Francis's "First Order" of friars. A variety of names were early attached to this women's order, including the "order of poor ladies," "order of poor nuns," and "order of poor enclosed ladies," titles often not capitalized in medieval documents. Whether or not this was owing simply to the medieval propensity not to capitalize proper names or to the fact that the identity of this network of women was still inchoate is not always clear. But scholars often identified the early women of San Damiano as *the* Poor Ladies. They were also considered the institutional foundation stone of the Order of San Damiano, renamed, not long after Clare's death, as the Order of Saint Clare.

Third, the early "regularization" of San Damiano was understood in light of the Fourth Lateran Council's decree, *Ne nimia*, issued in 1215. To limit the ever-growing proliferation of new expressions of religious life—a diversification that had been flourishing since the eleventh century—the decree required all new religious houses to accept one of the Church's already approved religious rules.[3] Thus, perhaps as early as 1216 but certainly by 1218/1219, Clare's community agreed to follow the Rule of Benedict to conform to the Lateran decree.[4]

Fourth, around 1218, Cardinal Hugo dei Conti di Segni, an enthusiastic supporter of the friars who was also keen to organize the many female penitent communities he encountered as papal legate, composed a legislative text—a *forma vitae*—to unite these communities.[5] Monastic houses often had such legislative texts to adapt and lend specificity to official rules such as the Rule of Augustine or the Rule of Benedict.[6] When Hugo [aka Hugolino] assigned his *forma vitae* to a community, he coupled it with the Rule of Benedict, probably to satisfy the demands of *Ne nimia*. The term *forma vitae*—which Francis used for both the brief text he presented to Innocent III in 1209–1210 and the text Clare said Francis gave her community shortly thereafter—indicated a canonical status below a "rule" (*regula*) which formerly "regularized" a religious group. Hugo's longer and more formal *forma vitae* set forth the customs or constitutions that were to accompany the Rule of Benedict and even "overrule" it when the two texts conflicted. His text is sometimes called his "constitutions," to distinguish it from the great rules, and also a "rule" because it reads like a rule (and, indeed, he would eventually call it a rule himself).[7] Certainly by 1219, Clare and San Damiano had accepted both the Rule of Benedict and Hugo's *forma vitae*, although the extent to which either was actually followed continued to be a matter of debate. San Damiano would, in fact, cycle through three *formae vitae* or rules between 1211 and 1252. Then, just before Clare's death, yet a fourth *forma vitae*—the one incorporating first-person quotations from Clare and Francis—would become San Damiano's official rule, a triumph for Clare since it contained provisions she had fought for her entire life.[8]

A Revised Portrait

In recent years, a revised portrait has been modifying the foregoing account. As long ago as the 1930s, Lilly Zarncke explored long-overlooked ecclesiastical documents and proposed that neither Clare nor Francis founded the Order of San Damiano.[9] A few years later Herbert Grundmann similarly recognized that the order, launched in fact by Cardinal Hugo, had at first existed independently of both Clare and Francis.[10] Although neither Zarncke's nor Grundmann's arguments had much effect upon Franciscan historiography of the time, they gradually gained momentum with scholarship by Roberto Rusconi, Werner Maleczek, Luigi Pellegrini, and, especially, Maria Pia Alberzoni.[11] The main contours of this newer portrait include the following.

First, Francis and Clare founded the individual community of San Damiano. Conceived originally as a house of penitents (perhaps even *sorores minores*), San Damiano was part of the vast movement of women's penitential houses, most of which, like San Damiano, existed independently of each other.

Second, gradually some houses sought to emulate some of San Damiano's practices, but without becoming together with San Damiano an institutional entity with a single overarching governing structure or even formal ties. These houses included, for example, communities in Spello, Foligno, and Monteluce (Perugia) in Umbria and houses in Arezzo and Monticelli (near Florence) in Tuscany.[12]

Third, in late 1218, Cardinal Hugo, on his second of three journeys through north-central Italy as papal legate of Tuscany and Lombardy, began organizing the disparate and autonomous houses of pious women he encountered. Emblematic of many female penitents of the time, these women—many well-to-do—were known especially for their pronounced practice of material poverty.[13] Hugo wanted both to offer some institutional protection to these houses and, in the spirit of *Ne nimia*, to impose a degree of uniformity among them, which, for Hugo, included strict enclosure, a feature he thought essential for monastic women. To that end, he requested and received power from Pope Honorius III to exempt the houses from episcopal control and place their lands and any churches they included directly under the authority of the Holy See.[14] In essence, the pope sundered these houses from their respective bishops and authorized the creation of the first women's religious order directly under papal control. Honorius here followed the regularizing footsteps of his predecessor, Innocent III, who had tried (unsuccessfully) to gather diverse women's communities in Rome into a single, enclosed convent.[15] Many of these women, and perhaps some of their benefactors who set lands aside for them, would have welcomed exemption from episcopal control. Some of the women, for their part, would similarly have welcomed independence from benefactors who still controlled aspects of the women's lives.[16] The communities in Hugo's new order went by various titles during its early years, one oft-use title being the "order of poor ladies of the valley of Spoleto or Tuscany" (*religionis pauperum dominarum de Valle Spoleti sive Tuscia*). A key point to note is that this order existed entirely apart from San Damiano.

Fourth, Hugo sent letters in July 1219 to three of the women's communities being incorporated into his new order. He decreed that the communities—Santa Maria di Gattaiola in the diocese of Lucca, Santa Maria outside Porta Camollia in Siena, and Santa Maria di Monteluce in Perugia—follow the Rule of Benedict along with his own *forma vitae*.[17] The *forma vitae* was probably composed around 1218–1219 after Honorius III had empowered Hugo to place the communities under papal control. With an eye to promoting the new order, the register for Hugo's third legation in 1221 included a written form to facilitate the transfer of communities from bishops to the papacy. A bishop had only to fill in a few blanks, specifying, for example, his own name, city, and the name of the women's religious house. It would then receive the same privileges the papacy had conferred upon the monasteries of "Perugia, Siena, and Lucca." Besides attesting to Hugo's ambitions for his order's expansion, the transfer form specified also that the women would live in conformity with his *forma vitae* and the "order [*religionis*] of the poor ladies of the Valley of Spoleto or Tuscany."[18] Years later, in 1228, just after Hugo had become Pope Gregory IX, he reflected back on the origins of his order, recalling that when he was "still in a lesser office, while on legation in the regions of Tuscany and Lombardy," he gave a "form and way of living" to all the "Poor enclosed nuns,"[19] the title that was gradually superseding the "order of poor

ladies" named in the transfer form. Indeed, Hugo had already made perpetual
enclosure a requirement in his letter to the monastery of Monteluce in Perugia in 1219.[20]

Fifth—and this is key—although Hugo seems always to have wished and
considered San Damiano to be part of his order, the process of effectively incorporating it was contested and far more gradual. The earliest known version
of his *forma vitae* (ca. 1220–1221) indeed names San Damiano. It prominently
lists San Damiano as the lead monastery of nine named monasteries. Making
Clare's community (now a monastery in Hugo's view) the flagship of the order
won it the cachet not only of Clare but also of Francis. Yet, notably, Hugo's
1221 form for bishops to transfer communities to his order names three communities, Perugia, Siena, and Lucca, the communities he wrote letters of incorporation to in July 1219, but not Assisi, which it seems should have been
named had it then been part of Hugo's order. As I will elaborate, although
Hugo certainly founded the order, he would eventually propagate the incor-
rect notion that Francis founded it, with Clare playing an exalted role, a claim
belied by other medieval evidence. For example, Hugo's contemporary biographer, writing after Hugo had become Pope Gregory IX, notes that when the
pope, a "planter and cultivator of Order[s] [*Religionis*]," was still Cardinal
Hugo, he "established [*instituit*] and brought to completion the new orders
[*Ordines*] of the Brothers of Penance," "the Enclosed Ladies," and "the Order
of Minors," an unambiguous reference to the three orders that early Franciscan hagiography would later claim Francis had founded.[21] Around 1228–1229,
Thomas of Celano also acknowledged Hugo's role establishing the Order of
Poor Ladies, a title that would begin to be displaced by Order of San Damiano only in the late 1220s.[22] In 1250 Rainaldo of Jenne, the order's then cardinal protector, also identified Gregory as the founder.[23]

The First Monasteries in Hugo's Order

A central question raised by this new research is this: how and when did
Clare's San Damiano become part of Hugo's order? Before examining this
issue, it is important to reconsider the evidence in favor of the traditional
portrayal of Clare as founder of an order. A key text is a letter Hugo sent 27
July 1219 to the monastery of Santa Maria in Monticelli near Florence. He
wrote it a few days before the letters he sent to the monasteries of Siena, Perugia, and Lucca. It resembles those letters insofar as it incorporates Monticelli

into his order, but it also differs in some slight but significant ways. First, the letter to Monticelli similarly decrees that the women accept the Rule of Benedict but makes no mention at all of Hugo's *forma vitae*. Second, and related, it makes this important provision: "besides the general Rule of Blessed Benedict, you have voluntarily imposed upon yourselves the regular observances [*observantias regulares*] of the Ladies of Saint Mary of San Damiano at Assisi."[24] Some scholars have assumed that San Damiano was the model, indeed, the motherhouse so to speak, not only of the Monticelli monastery but also of the other monasteries to whom Hugo was sending letters of incorporation even though these did not name San Damiano.[25] San Damiano thus figured as the founding inspiration for all the women's houses being regularized and united in a similar style of religious life. Note too that Hugo, following Cistercian practice, conspicuously adds "Saint Mary," the name he regularly used for monasteries in his order, to the title of the already named San Damiano.

In the *1253 forma vitae* Clare pointedly referred to following Francis's *formula vivendi* when San Damiano began. Never in her (admittedly brief) writings does she ever mention Hugo's *forma vitae*. Clare had been living in San Damiano for some eight years when Hugo wrote his 1219 letter to the monastery of Monticelli acknowledging their adherence to San Damiano's "regular observances." It is worth noting, first, that these seem surely tied to Francis's *formula vivendi*. By 1219 the San Damiano women would have added to it other practices based on new contributions from Francis, both oral and written, attested to in the late 1230s and again in the early 1250s.[26] The women's own experience surely shaped their way of life as well, especially since Francis was mostly absent, occupied with cares related to the rapidly expanding friars. Second, these "*regular* observances" are lexically tied to a *regula*, some written document or rule, the term being used perhaps more loosely in "regular observances" than when it denotes one of great religious rules such as the Rule of Benedict.[27] Third, even later than 1219, there is evidence of San Damiano's specific practices influencing other monasteries. For example, in February 1223, the nuns of San Apollinare in Milan were adopting the "order and rule of Blessed Damiano in the Valley of Spoleto near the city of Assisi" for observance, a phrase that might well connote San Damiano's "regular observances." Only later, in November 1224, does the bishop of these "poor sisters," at the request of Hugo, officially consign their community over to Hugo.[28] Fourth, Hugo's stipulation, on the one hand, that the monasteries of Siena, Perugia, and Lucca were to be bound by the Rule of Benedict together with his *forma vitae*, and his stipulation, on the other hand, that the monastery of Monticelli was to be bound by the Rule of Benedict together with the "regular obser-vances" of San Damiano, suggests a parallelism between his *forma vitae* and San Damiano's "regular observances." Thus, although Hugo was avid to estab-lish San Damiano as first among his order's monasteries, it appears that Clare and the women of San Damiano, adhering to practices rooted in Francis's *formula vivendi*, had another idea. This crucial point would be repeatedly con-firmed in documents leading up to Clare's death.

Hugo's *Forma Vitae*

The earliest version of Hugo's *forma vitae* probably appeared shortly after Honorius III had given Hugo permission in 1218 to organize houses of reli-gious women under the papal see. Hugo likely relied on curial officials to re-dact the *forma vitae*, but he surely oversaw its composition and approved its every detail. The salutation of the 1220–1221 version of Hugo's *forma vitae* names nine monasteries. Significantly, San Damiano is named first before the others. Also named were the monasteries of Perugia, Siena, and Lucca, which had received Hugo's letters of incorporation in 1219. The women in all the monasteries are referred to collectively as abbesses and sisters, thus confirming that in Hugo's eyes, Clare was an abbess and the first among others in the new order.

The text offers an excellent entrée into Hugo's vision for women's reli-gious life. About one-sixth the length of the Rule of Benedict, the 1220–1221 *forma vitae* comprises some 2,400 Latin words. Hugo, a canon lawyer, self-presents as a stern legislator in his opening lines:

> Every true religion [*vera religio*] and approved institute of life en-dures by certain rules and requirements, and by certain disciplinary laws. Whoever wishes to lead a religious life will deviate from righ-teousness to the degree that she does not observe the guidelines of righteousness, unless she has diligently striven to observe a certain correct rule and discipline for living. She runs the risk of falling at the point where, in virtue of her free choice, she neglected to set for herself a sure and stable foundation of making progress.[29]

His *forma vitae* aims to make clear to each sister "what she should do and what she should avoid, lest, excusing herself perhaps because of ignorance, she dangerously presume what is not allowed and prohibited, or lest, little by little through laxity and detestable sloth, she more dangerously neglect and condemn it." Full compliance is expected: "In virtue of obedience we strictly enjoin each and every one of you, and we command that you humbly and devotedly accept this form of life . . . and that you and those who follow you strive to observe it inviolably for all time." In contrast to Francis's and Clare's repeated association of humility with poverty, especially in following or imitating Christ, poor and humble, Hugo has associated humility with obedience, stating also that the sisters' life should be "in imitation of those who have served the Lord without complaint." He enjoins the women to observe the Rule of Benedict—also known for its emphasis on obedience and humility—"in all things which are in no way contrary" to his own *forma vitae*.[30]

The most prominent feature in Hugo's *forma vitae* is its insistence upon enclosure. A truly religious woman, for him, was a strictly enclosed woman. He demanded perpetual enclosure when he incorporated the monasteries of Monticelli (near Florence) and Monteluce (Perugia) in July 1219.[31] His *forma vitae* discusses enclosure explicitly and reinforces it implicitly via other world-renouncing regulations. Circumscribing and limiting the women's physical sensations was part and parcel of the proposed *fuga mundi*, their world renunciation: they were to be cut off from the world tangibly by way of walls, orally and aurally by way of silence, visually by way of curtains and veils, and even gustatorially by way of fasts. Only the sense of smell escapes Hugo's strictures.

Material enclosure and separation from the world are the first themes to appear in the *forma vitae* and they also recur later. For example, since the women had "abandoned and despised the vanity of the world," it was fitting that they "remain enclosed the whole time of their life."[32] Enclosure in many medieval monasteries might better be termed semi-enclosure, because a monk or nun could leave the enclosure for many reasons.[33] For Hugo, such reasons were virtually nonexistent: "After they have entered the enclosure of this religion and have assumed the religious habit, they should never be granted any permission or faculty to leave, unless perhaps some are transferred to another place to plant or build up this same religion."[34] Letters to various monasteries show that accepting perpetual enclosure was Hugo's sine qua non for the women to win the coveted prize of exemption from episcopal authority. A particularly clear example is the letter he later sent as pope in 1227 to the nuns of Spoleto. Noting that when he was still a cardinal they had won episcopal exemption, Gregory therefore decided in their favor in a dispute with their bishop.[35] His *forma vitae* aimed to keep not only the nuns in, but also everyone else out. While special personages such as a cardinal, bishop, or chaplain, might enter the sisters' enclosure on exceptional occasions, even they had to be accompanied by others as a sort of insurance against impropriety.[36] Rigorous silence was enforced both among the sisters and between them and outsiders.[37] When outsiders were allowed entrance, Hugo's *forma vitae* required "the ladies [to] most zealously guard against being seen by seculars or persons from the outside."[38]

Hugo laid down strict rules policing the physical borders of the women's enclosure. Structural barriers stood at the center of a sister's most intimate exchanges with outsiders: she communicated with her confessor through a *locutorium*, a sort of screen, grille, or other separator. A grille also stood between her and the priest giving her communion. A cloth covered the grille between the cloister and the church so that no sister could see anything happening in the chapel, including the centrally important sacrifice of the Mass.[39] The monastery door was to be guarded by a mature, diligent, and discreet sister. Although portresses were common in large medieval monasteries, Hugo's insistence is striking: the portress should "so diligently take care of and guard the key to the door, that the door could never be opened without her or without her knowledge." Just two lines later, the *forma vitae* reiterated that the portress and her substitute should "zealously take care and beware that the door never remains open, except when it can be fittingly done for a very short time." And immediately again: "Let the entrance be very well secured with door panels, strong beams, and iron bars. Let it never be left without a guard, except perhaps for a moment, unless it is firmly locked with a key."[40] Rigorous and repetitious, Hugo's preoccupation in the *forma vitae* led Chiara Augusta Lainati to call it "a hymn to strict enclosure."[41] Her romanticized characterization is matched by Hugo's wishful confidence that uniform observance of the *forma vitae* across all the monasteries in the order would "unite and join in a bond of love those sisters who are separated by the distance between places."[42] Separating themselves physically from this world and its inhabitants would achieve, Hugo believed, an invisible unity more powerful than physical distances.

The *forma vitae*'s prescriptions regarding fasting and abstaining from food were similarly harsh. The women were to fast every day, which meant they were to eat but one meal.[43] Outside of Lent, on Wednesdays and Fridays—both traditional days of penitence—they were to abstain also from wine, potage, and cooked foods (*pulmentum*), unless it happened to be a saint's feast day.[44] In that case, they could eat fruit and raw vegetables if available. Fasting customs suggest they usually abstained from dairy foods and eggs. Moreover, they were to fast on bread and water on four days of the week during Lent, on three days during Advent, and, if they wished, on the vigils of solemn feast days. Compared to other rules, such as the Rule of Benedict or either of Francis of Assisi's two rules (1221 and 1223), Hugo's food-related requirements were unstintingly severe, although he did allow the abbess to excuse adolescents, the elderly, and any sisters who were physically or mentally infirm.[45]

Hugo's *forma vitae* called for an ecclesiastical visitor or a cleric he designated to pay regular visits to the women's monasteries to "zealously seek the truth . . . about the observance of their religious life [*religio*]." The visitor was authorized to "reform and correct" whatever was not in compliance with the rule and *forma vitae*.[46] A great admirer of Cistercians, whom he often chose as his own confessors, Hugo appointed a Cistercian, Ambrose, to be the women's official visitor.[47] Hugo also mimicked a Cistercian practice by naming all the houses in his new order after the Blessed Virgin Mary.

He concluded his *forma vitae* decreeing that it "be diligently and everywhere observed in a uniform way by every sister." To the above absolute injunction, however, he immediately attached a key escape clause: "But if the far-seeing discretion of the Roman Church, by reason of the nature of the place or concern for individuals, decides that some sisters should receive a dispensation in some necessity, other sisters who do not need a similar dispensation should firmly guard and live up to their manner of life."[48] Hugo seems already to know that he would liberally deploy such dispensations. He was, after all, incrementally building the order from a hodgepodge of religious foundations throughout north-central Italy. Enclosure, strict fasting, and other demanding rules surely introduced dramatic changes into the day-to-day lives of many of these women. His *forma vitae* thus revealed rather rigid ideals for religious women along with an acknowledgment that the diverse existential realities of their communities would sometimes warrant flexibility. In subsequent years, even from his enhanced position as Pope Gregory IX, he would still be confronting the variety of monastic practices within the order, many existing through dispensations, others through negligence, disregard, or even disobedience.

For now, Hugo became "Father and Lord" of these women's monasteries, a role later more familiarly identified as "cardinal protector." Hugo's Order of Enclosed Ladies and Francis of Assisi's Order of Lesser Brothers were, in fact, the first religious orders to be linked to the papacy via cardinals. The prelates' mediating and authoritative role attested to the papacy's new ascendancy over increasingly centralized religious orders.

San Damiano's Relationship with Hugo's Order and the Order of Lesser Brothers

At what point, however, did San Damiano effectively enter the ambit of Hugo's monastic order? His transfer form, available since 1221, notably cited as models the monasteries of Siena, Monteluce, and Lucca, but not San Damiano in Assisi. One would think it would be named had it then belonged to—indeed, held primacy of place within—Hugo's order. This might help narrow the date of the *forma vitae* that names San Damiano from 1220–1221 to after the appearance of the 1221 transfer form. Tellingly, Monticelli, which had adopted San Damiano's regular observances was also left out.[49] Alternatively or in addition, both omissions might indicate that Hugo preferred not to present the Franciscan-identified Assisi and Monticelli as models for his monastic order. In any case, this is one of many indicators that despite Hugo's presentation of San Damiano as the flagship monastery within his order, it remained something of an outlier, exceptional in its style of religious life.

Clare and her sisters decidedly thought of themselves as simple "penitents."[50] Sister Filippa testified just after Clare's death that she joined Clare in 1215 so that they could together "do penance" and that when Francis had exhorted Clare to adopt religious life, he spoke of Christ's passion and death.[51] Abundant testimony from Clare's sisters and acquaintances who were questioned for her canonization shows that she identified herself as a follower of Francis—and Francis was himself first and foremost a lay penitent. While some houses of penitent women desired speedy regularization for the legitimization and fund-raising cachet it yielded, others did not.[52] There is no evidence the women of San Damiano themselves sought to change their status.

At some point, Clare and Hugo met. The *Legend* (ca. 1256–1260) about Clare reports that Hugo, both as Bishop of Ostia and later as Pope Gregory IX, frequently wrote to Clare seeking her help.[53] At most, however, two letters of this stated abundant correspondence survive. Hugo wrote the first letter while still a bishop, therefore prior to his elevation to the papacy in 1227. The letter's earliest attestation is the late fourteenth-century *Chronica XXIV Generalium*.[54] Kajetan Esser's conjectured date of 1220 for this letter has, over time, been transformed into a relatively secure, or even "certain," date in much scholarship.[55] The letter is revelatory because Hugo addresses it to "lady Clare," the "mother of his salvation" and the "handmaid of Christ." He clearly esteems Clare, asking for her prayers and admiringly referring to the "rigor of life" he observed at San Damiano. Some scholars have suggested that he visited the community precisely to learn more about the way of life houses like Monticelli said they wanted to emulate.[56] But notably, Hugo fails to address Clare as "abbess" as one would suppose if San Damiano had adopted his *forma vitae* with its mandated requirement to observe the Rule of Benedict. He also fails to name any order in the letter's salutation or otherwise link San Damiano to any other communities. These omissions might fortify Esser's conjectured 1220 date, since the ca. 1220–1221 *forma vitae* was addressed to San Damiano and other "monasteries." Moreover, it included Clare among the "abbesses," Hugo's term for the superiors in each of the four letters sent to monasteries of women he was organizing in 1219. It seems possible that Clare and the women of San Damiano were not fully incorporated into Hugo's order until he sent the 1220–1221 (or perhaps more likely 1221) *forma vitae* to them.

What about the San Damiano women's relationship with Francis? Despite Francis's towering importance to Clare and her sisters, he, remarkably, never once mentions them in any of his writings. Accounts of his relationship with Clare and her community occur only in texts (and a modest number of images) composed after his death.[57] There, the tenor of their relationship oscillates, often reflecting events that transpired long after he had died. Thus, in periods when the Lesser Brothers wanted less to do with the Order of San Damiano, Francis is portrayed putting greater distance between himself and Clare.

In his lifetime, however, Francis himself did have something to say about women. Two texts from the early 1220s are particularly relevant and will provide a touchstone for later controversies dividing the friars, the papacy, and the Order of San Damiano regarding the friars' pastoral obligations toward the order. Francis's *Earlier Rule* (1221), the long, meandering, and exhortatory text laced with Scripture and reflective of his personal style, categorically states: "*Absolutely no woman may be received to obedience* by any brother, but after spiritual advice has been given to her, let her do penance wherever she wants" (emphasis mine).[58]

Although Francis says nothing about Clare and San Damiano, virtually all later sources—not just Clare herself—agree that Clare and her community posed the one significant exception to this rule. Clare stated in the *1253 forma vitae* that she and her sisters "willingly promised [Francis] obedience."[59] New brothers were, notably, "received into obedience" when they joined the Lesser Brothers.[60] It is not surprising that San Damiano would have been an exception: Francis founded it, felt special affection for it, and proactively expanded the community by sending it new members. His own friars begged bread for the sisters and resided alongside them.

But in 1221 Francis prohibited the friars from receiving into obedience (and thus becoming responsible for) any other female penitents. He probably had no desire for multiple San Damianos. When the papacy refused to approve Francis's *Earlier Rule*, he, assisted by canonists and Hugo himself, composed another. This *Later Rule* was approved in November 1223 by Honorius III, the very pope who had encouraged Hugo to convert independent houses of penitents into a network of regulated nuns' monasteries. So it comes as no surprise that this later papally approved rule entirely replaces Francis's earlier prohibition regarding penitent women. The drift of papal policy was to transform houses of penitents into monasteries of nuns and to provide the nuns, some newly enclosed, with appropriate pastoral care. Fittingly then, Francis's *Later Rule* comments instead on the friars' relationship with "nuns' monasteries" (*monasteria monacharum*): the friars may enter them as long as they have the pope's permission.[61] Francis would have welcomed this clear stricture limiting his friars' responsibilities for the pastoral care of nuns, a ministry he never envisioned.

The status of San Damiano at this time would appear then to be in transition: a house of penitent women committed to the ideals and practices Francis had taught were being invited, cajoled, or perhaps even forced to join a papally initiated religious order of enclosed monastic women. Simultaneously, the Order of Lesser Brothers, officially ratified in 1223, was itself changing, its rule delineating firm boundaries between them and monastic women. Would San Damiano continue to be an exceptional case? While documents from this period reveal little, evidence from the years just following Francis's death in 1226 will show that the critical shift in San Damiano's situation took place in those very years.

Chapter 4

Turning Point: Negotiating San Damiano's Singularity, ca. 1226 to 1230

Multiple documents point to a clear change in San Damiano's status by about 1228. The precipitating conditions for this turning point included Francis of Assisi's death in October 1226, Hugo's election as Pope Gregory IX in March 1227, and Gregory's canonization of Francis in July 1228.

Francis's death cleared the way for Gregory to make the Lesser Brothers responsible for the pastoral care of his order of "poor enclosed nuns." Given that Francis had never planned to found his own male Order of Lesser Brothers, it is even less likely he planned to found an associated female branch.[1] Francis had laid down clear strictures limiting the brothers' associations with religious women. His 1221 rule prohibited various associations with women, including female penitents, and his 1223 rule barred the brothers from entering nuns' monasteries without express papal permission.[2] Francis's death, however, freed Gregory to expand the brothers' responsibilities without any worry about how the saintly founder might react. In December 1227 Gregory sent Minister General Giovanni Parenti a letter, *Quoties cordis*, commanding him and subsequent ministers general to accept the pastoral care of all the monasteries of poor enclosed nuns.[3] But the Lesser Brothers, like other mendicant orders, were reluctant to assume the *cura monialium*, the pastoral care of nuns. It entailed a stability at odds with their itinerant lifestyle and absorbed attention they preferred to devote to other constituencies.

Many scholars suppose that when Gregory went to Assisi in July 1228 to canonize Francis that he visited Clare at San Damiano. Although there is no documentary proof, it is a reasonable supposition since the San Damiano women treasured their ties with their "father" and founder, Francis. Moreover, a visit would allow Gregory to speak to the women about conforming their lives more closely to his notion of a monastic community. As later documents show, Clare and her sisters hewed as closely to Francis's *forma vitae* as possible. Busy though he was, Francis had always accorded Clare and San Damiano an exceptional status by, for example, having friars assist them,[4] instructing them orally and in writing,[5] and, according to various sources, even residing at San Damiano when ill.[6] Francis's fame within his own lifetime would have made it difficult for any prelate, including Hugo, to contravene Francis's will for San Damiano. As Thomas of Celano himself noted in his *First Life* of Francis, written at the behest of Hugo-Gregory IX, Francis's life was marked by so many signs of sanctity that "no one dared to speak against him."[7] Gregory would know that the halo effect shining on San Damiano after Francis's canonization would shine as well on the papal order, including San Damiano. Indeed, he would soon rebrand it as the Order of San Damiano. Importantly, since Francis had pledged that he and his friars would always "have the same loving care and special solicitude" for San Damiano as he had for his friars,[8] Gregory could feel justified—now that he had cast San Damiano as the symbolic motherhouse of his order—in charging the Lesser Brothers with the *cura monialium* for all the order's monasteries.[9] Whether or not Gregory actually visited Clare after the canonization little matters. *That* something took place then is all but certain.

This is the best explanation for a rapid succession of texts that seem to address San Damiano's new circumstances. Tellingly, all five texts are explicitly tied to Gregory IX. They include (1) a letter Gregory sent Clare and her sisters, probably before 16 July 1228; (2) Rainaldo of Jenne's August 1228 letter announcing that Gregory had put him in authority over the women's monasteries; (3) a privilege Gregory granted to San Damiano in September 1228; (4) Thomas of Celano's observations about Clare and the Poor Ladies included in his 1228–1229 *First Life* of Francis, commissioned by Gregory; and (5) Gregory's September 1230 decree, *Quo elongati*, settling various points of concern brought to him by the Lesser Brothers. Together, the first four texts suggest that Gregory was intensifying his control over San Damiano. Furthermore, the third and fifth texts indicate that Clare negotiated hard to protect her vision of religious life while the papacy sought to assert more authority over San Damiano.

Gregory's 1228 Letter to Clare

The first text is thought to be Gregory's second surviving letter to Clare, usually dated shortly before Francis's canonization on 16 July 1228.[10] The Irish Franciscan Luke Wadding (d. 1657) found the letter in the mid-thirteenth-century formulary of Marino di Eboli (d. 1286), vice chancellor for Innocent IV. It was Marino, apparently, who identified the sender as Gregory and the recipient as Clare. Wadding accepted the identification without explaining why. He placed the letter under this rubric: "To the beloved Daughter Clare, Abbess, and to the community of enclosed Nuns of San Damiano in Assisi,"[11] but the letter is usually transcribed and translated with this rubric transferred to the letter itself, as if it were Gregory's actual greeting to the women. Thus, before analyzing this letter it is worth noting what is now left out of most introductions to it: lacking a salutation in its earliest manuscript version, we must put our faith in Marino di Eboli's attribution. Esser thought the letter might instead have been a general letter circulated to all the monasteries in the order, and a few contemporary scholars such as Alberzoni have been persuaded by his view.[12]

However, since no similar letter to another community has been located since Esser first made his suggestion in 1953, it is worth considering what the letter might mean if it were sent to Clare and her sisters alone, as other scholars still suppose.[13] If Gregory was indeed writing to Clare and her sisters shortly after he had drawn them further into his order's ambit, then several comments take on special meaning. At once striking and poignant, Gregory writes to a community that is suffering and in turmoil. He opens his letter by calling the women's attention to the necessary relationship between their espousal to Jesus Christ and enclosure, which allows them to direct their affections solely to God: "Therefore, since above all things you are bound to love your Spouse, Who loves those who love Him and makes them co-heirs, you should delight with all your affections in Him alone, so that nothing may ever separate you from His love. For divinely inspired to this end you have chosen to place yourselves in an enclosure, so that you may profitably renounce the world and all that is in it and, while embracing your Spouse with an untainted love, run after the odor of His ointments, until He introduces you into the chamber of His mother to be refreshed forever by the sweetness of His love."[14] Enclosure was, of course, the most powerful *leitmotiv* in his *forma vitae*. Gregory's strict expectations represented a departure from what was likely a more moderate form of enclosure practiced at San Damiano.

Clearly unambiguous in this short letter is that some difficult event had recently befallen the women. Gregory hopes that "those things which now seem bitter will become wholesome and sweet for you, what is hard will become soft and what is rough will become smooth, so that you will exult, if you merit to suffer these things for Christ Who endured for us the passion of an infamous death."[15] Gregory refers to his own trials and asks the women for their prayers.[16] He "commands" them then, as he says he has done before "to walk and live in the Spirit, forgetting the past and straining toward what lies ahead, as the Apostle says, by striving for better gifts." This, says Gregory, will make them virtuous and glorify God. It will also bring joy to Gregory, who loves them as his "special daughters."[17]

The letter obviously regards a recent change affecting the women, one known to both them and Gregory. At first sight, forgetting the past could allude, obliquely, to the loss of their beloved Francis, but he had died over twenty months earlier and, in any case, Gregory would never recommend or expect Francis to be forgotten. Indeed, the women's present struggles with things (plural) that are bitter (*amara*), hard (*dura*), and rough (*aspera*), certainly extend beyond the single, momentous loss of Francis. They would more likely refer to being called to greater conformity with the harsher provisions of Hugo's *forma vitae*. Addressing Clare as "abbess"—a monastic title she seems intentionally to have eschewed in her writings—Hugo appears to have wanted to impose upon San Damiano not only strict permanent enclosure behind grilles, but also a host of other regulations meant to bring their life into conformity with other monasteries in his order. His *forma vitae* was quite austere in terms of the silence, fasting, sleeping conditions, and so forth, but notably said nothing at all about forgoing possessions. The omission contrasted sharply with the *forma vitae* Francis had given San Damiano. The past Gregory calls Clare and her sisters to forget—if, indeed, they are the letter's recipients—very plausibly refers to Francis's *forma vivendi* which Gregory now wished to replace with his own *forma vitae*.

Rainaldo of Jenne's 1228 Letter

After Hugo became Pope Gregory IX in March 1227, he handed over the duties of his role as "Father and Lord" of the monasteries to Bishop Rainaldo of Jenne.[18] Rainaldo announced his new post 18 August 1228 in a letter, an original of which still exists, dispatched to various monasteries, including San Damiano.[19] Addressed to "the abbesses and communities of poor monasteries" (or perhaps "Poor Monasteries"), the letter suggests the still-evolving state of an order that would soon begin to be identified as the Order of San Damiano. Rainaldo indicates San Damiano's preeminence by placing it first in the list of addressees. How one translates this salutation bears on one's understanding of San Damiano's new-found position and the order's institutional physiognomy. Rainaldo begins his letter:

> To the mothers, sisters and daughters, to the very dear handmaids
> of the Spouse Christ, the Son of God, to the abbesses and commu-
> nities of poor monasteries of San Damiano of Assisi, of Santa Maria
> of Vallegloria, of Perugia, of Foligno, of Florence.

> [Matribus, sororibus et filiabus, carissimis ancillis Christi Sponsi,
> Filii Dei, abbatissis ac conventibus pauperum monasteriorum sancti
> Damiani de Assisi, Beatae Mariae Vallisgloriae, de Perusio, de Fulgi-
> neo, de Florentia.][20]

In my translation above, San Damiano appears as the first in a list of twenty-four monasteries. The following twenty-three monasteries each bore the name Santa Maria, a practice the Cistercian-friendly Hugo had promoted. In contrast to the 1220–1221 *forma vitae*, the Virgin's name has been dropped from San Damiano's title, an omission possibly reflective of Clare and San Damiano's resistance to a more Cistercian-like identity.[21]

Some other translators, however, suggest that this group of twenty-four monasteries is already a single order named after the San Damiano house. Omaechevarría's widely used Spanish translation misleadingly adapts Rainaldo's greeting to the abbesses and communities of "the poor monasteries" (*pauperum monasteriorum*) to "the Poor (Ladies) of the monasteries" (*[Damas] Pobres de los monasterios*) followed by the list of twenty-four monasteries. This implies an institutional identity absent within the letter itself.[22] Armstrong's widely used English translation offers yet another reading:

> To my dear mothers, sisters, and daughters, the servants of Christ
> the Spouse, the Son of God; to the abbesses and communities *of the
> poor monasteries of Saint Damian of Assisi*: Santa Maria de ValleGlo-
> ria, Perugia, Foligno, Florence. (emphasis mine)[23]

Inserting a colon after "Saint Damian of Assisi" and following this title with the twenty-three remaining houses imposes a clear organizational structure on this group. It turns the community of San Damiano at the head of the list into the order to which the other twenty-three communities belong: they become the monasteries "of San Damiano." Alberzoni rejects such a reading, believing that the less specific "communities of poor monasteries"—as my own rendering above also suggests—is the all-encompassing rubric for all twenty-four houses listed, including San Damiano. The title reflects the fact that Gregory's order was still evolving, incorporating diverse houses collectively designated simply as "poor monasteries." The text is correctly rendered either as I and Alberzoni have done or as Armstrong has done. The latter possibly retrojects back into 1228 a slightly later institutional reality. The monasteries were probably just on the cusp of being designated the *Order* of San Damiano (emphasis mine). Boccali was apparently aware of the ambiguity in Rainaldo's address when, following Oliger, he described Rainaldo's letter as referring "to 23/24 monasteries."[24] Gregory was notably still employing in this period other names to identify this collection of monasteries. For example, in October 1228, he refers to the "order of the poor enclosed nuns" (*Ordinem pauperum Monialium reclusarum*) in a letter he sent to one of the twenty-four monasteries, Santa Maria in Todi.[25] The title "Order of San Damiano" begins to appear sporadically in the sources in 1229, with other titles still in use.[26] For example, in 1234, Gregory referred to the *religio* "of the poor enclosed nuns" (*Religione pauperum Monialium inclusarum*) in a letter to Agnes of Prague.[27]

Rainaldo's letter announced to the women that the pope wanted him to be responsible for their care (*cura*). His first act, announced in the letter, was to appoint one "brother Philip" as their visitator (*visitatorem*). Rainaldo summed up the visitator's oversight role, detailed more fully in Hugo's *forma vitae*, as including full powers to advise, command, and even punish the women.[28] The brother is Philip Longo (the Tall), one of Francis's earliest and close companions. He had a troubled trajectory in Franciscan history and hagiography. In early and more reliable documents about him, he appeared as an admired companion of Francis who also assisted the community of San Damiano. The chronicler Jordan of Giano, writing about 1262, recast Philip as having zealously solicited letters from the papacy to defend the Poor Ladies against people disturbing them. He did so, according to Jordan, against Francis's wishes and while the saint was away in the East in 1219–1220.[29] Rusconi has shown how this demonization of Philip is essentially unreliable, better reflecting a rift in the early 1260s between the friars and the (by then renamed) Order of Saint Clare.[30] Jordan wrote that when Francis returned, he got Cardinal Hugo to rescind the letters granted to Philip. Alberzoni intriguingly theorizes that the "letters" rescinded included the *forma vitae* Hugo sent to San Damiano in this same convenient period of Francis's absence. Francis would be, in effect, using his status to protect San Damiano from being hijacked into Hugo's network of monasteries.[31] Although this remains speculative, the force of Francis's clout is not: it explains why so much evidence about a critical change in San Damiano's status comes only after his death.

Whatever happened in 1219–1220, Philip's appointment as visitator in August 1228 constituted a turning point for many of Hugo's monasteries. First, either a certain Pacifico or Philip Longo is the first known Lesser Brother to be appointed to this role. Brother Pacifico, whose Franciscan identity is still debated, had been appointed visitator by Hugo by April 1226.[32] Soon claiming the office to be too great a burden, Pacifico resigned, precipitating Rainaldo's decision to appoint Brother Philip. Both appointments had occurred in the critical period surrounding Francis's death (3 October 1226). Previously, when Gregory was still Cardinal Hugo, he had appointed a Cistercian, Ambrose, to this position. Either Pacifico or Philip as the first Lesser Brother to hold the post would have represented a striking shift not only for the women, but also for the friars. Rainaldo's letter suggests that Philip, "zealous" for the nuns' welfare, had perhaps lobbied on their behalf and at some considerable cost to himself. As an early companion of Francis, Philip knew the community of San Damiano quite well and was further aware of Francis's regard for them.

Philip's appointment would have been personally meaningful to the women of San Damiano. Clare knew him even before she moved to San Damiano. Philip, along with Francis, had urged her to take up religious life.[33] He was one of the friars with Francis who led Clare from the monastery of San Paolo to San Angelo di Panzo.[34] With Francis and Clare, Philip successfully inspired Cecilia di Spello to join San Damiano in 1213–1214.[35] It seems likely that Gregory and Rainaldo were quite consciously shifting the order into the Franciscan ambit in part to enhance its appeal to Clare and her sisters, who would probably have been delighted with Philip's appointment. Such a move boldly affirmed the women's Franciscan provenance and identity, assuaging some of their fears as Gregory enhanced his control over them.

Gregory's 1228 Privilege of Poverty

The third document indicating the change in San Damiano's status is one of the most important documents in the community's history, the Privilege of

Poverty granted by Gregory to San Damiano. This Privilege of Poverty—
which I capitalize given its historic importance—was conceded to San Damiano in September 1228, just one month after Rainaldo's and Philip's
appointments. A papal privilege was a formal acknowledgment of some special favor or exception being conceded. The Privilege of Poverty was granted
specifically to San Damiano and not to other religious houses. In some 180
words, including the formal salutation and closing, it allows the women to
reject possessions. Sounding several Franciscan themes, Gregory wrote:

> As is evident, you have renounced the desire for all temporal things,
> desiring to dedicate yourselves to the Lord alone. Because of this,
> since you have sold all things and given them to the poor, you pro-
> pose not to have any possessions whatsoever, clinging in all things
> to the footprints of Him, the Way, the Truth, and the Life Who, for
> our sake, was made poor.[36]

Gregory's Privilege of Poverty then elaborates the women's proposal to live
"most high poverty" by interweaving biblical language from the gospels and
the Song of Songs.[37] Rather than representing any sort of change in the life of
the women of San Damiano, the privilege seems to grant them the right to
continue living as they already had been. The *Versified Legend* noted that Clare
petitioned "that her new Order created in poverty might *continue* [in poverty]
with the Holy See's protection" (emphasis mine).[38]

    If Clare and her sisters had been practicing strict poverty since their earli-
est days, why would Gregory in 1228 bother granting them a special privilege
to continue doing so? Probably because while his *forma vitae* is silent on the
subject of owning property, the Rule of Benedict—which accompanied his
forma vitae—permitted, indeed presumed, corporate monastic possessions.
Income by way of lands and other immovable possessions ensured a cloistered
religious community's survival. When he was still a cardinal, Gregory had realized that the "poor enclosed nuns" required such steady income, however
modest, if they were to have the wherewithal to devote themselves principally
to the sort of religious life he envisioned for them. He wanted to thus secure
San Damiano, but Clare had to have recognized that San Damiano's poor
mendicant life would cease if it agreed to adopt the practices prevalent among
other monasteries forming part of Gregory's order.

    Clare summarized her uncompromising views about poverty in the rule
composed shortly before her death. There she shrewdly validated her

community's poor life by once again quoting Francis himself, a passage some-times referred to as his *Last Will* for Clare and her sisters. She writes:

> In order that we as well as those who were to come after us would
> never turn aside from the holy poverty we had embraced, shortly
> before his death he repeated in writing his last wish for us. He said:
> "I, little brother Francis, wish to follow the life and poverty of our
> most high Lord Jesus Christ and of His most holy Mother and to
> persevere in this until the end; and I ask you, my ladies, and I give
> you my advice that you live always in this most holy life and pov-
> erty. And keep careful watch that you never depart from this by rea-
> son of the teaching or advice of anyone."[39]

Unconventional for many women, Clare and her sisters followed the mendi-cant practice of living by alms, perhaps supplemented by the work of their own hands and whatever food they might cultivate in San Damiano's garden. The friar questors who lived alongside San Damiano went out and begged on the women's behalf.

After Francis's death, Gregory had, in fact, tried to alter Clare's convic-tions about poverty. Explicit evidence appears in the *Acts* for Clare's canoniza-tion, the bull announcing her canonization, and also the early Legends. Three witnesses for Clare's canonization testify that Gregory tried to coax Clare into accepting possessions. Benvenuta da Perugia said Clare "especially had a great love of poverty. Neither Pope Gregory nor the Bishop of Ostia [Rainaldo] could ever make her consent to receive any possessions. Moreover, blessed Clare sold her inheritance and gave it to the poor. Asked how she knew these things, [Benvenuta] replied she was present and heard the Lord Pope tell [Clare] that he wanted her to receive possessions. This Pope personally came to the monastery of San Damiano."[40] The witness Filippa explicitly linked the dispute with the Privilege of Poverty. Filippa said that Clare "was such a lover of poverty that when the begging [brothers] of the monastery brought back whole loaves of bread as alms, she reproachingly asked: 'Who has given you these loaves of bread?' She said this because she preferred to receive broken loaves of bread as alms rather than whole ones. She could never be persuaded by the Pope or the Bishop of Ostia [Rainaldo] to receive any possessions. The *Privilege of Poverty* granted to her was honored with great reverence and kept well and with great diligence since she feared she might lose it."[41] The witness Pacifica gave a similar report, albeit without mentioning Rainaldo.[42] These testimonies were gleaned serially from the very first three of the twenty-one witnesses testifying. The three were among the sisters who had been with Clare the longest and thus knew her original intentions and so might logically object more strenuously to the pope's attempt to reshape their self-identity. No doubt, the canonization commissioners, for their part, were aware of the overriding significance of this issue. They thus made sure to cover it at the outset of their inquiry. The presence of Francis's early companions Leo and Angelo, together with the friar chaplain Marco, probably reinforced this point. No other witnesses commented on the dispute; the commissioners would not have needed further testimony, especially since two of the first sisters could claim eyewitness status.

Only the third witness, Filippa, mentioned the Privilege of Poverty (dated 17 September 1228). The order of topics presented in her testimony above obliquely suggests that it was granted only after Clare had refused to comply with Gregory's wishes. This could lend credence to the supposition that Gregory's visit took place not long before Francis's canonization 16 July 1228.[43] But since Filippa and Benvenuta noted that Rainaldo too was involved in trying to change Clare's mind, the dispute might have taken place after he had been appointed caretaker of the order, that is, after 18 August 1228. Whatever the case, Gregory's clash with Clare took place in the critical few years following Francis's death.

Both Legends, however, are explicit in placing the dispute only *after* Clare had received the Privilege, which suggests that the pope had had second thoughts about the women's poverty. This sequence of events is also plausible. As the order grew, so did Gregory's conviction that cloistered monasteries required possessions for their support. This would provide context for Filippa's remark that the Privilege was reverently honored and carefully guarded since Clare "feared she might lose it."[44] Understanding Gregory's sentiments, Clare realistically calculated that he might reverse his position. The *Versified Legend* depicted Clare's controversy with Gregory this way: "A new thing! Because of poverty's honor, the Virgin petitions that her new Order created in poverty might continue with the Holy See's protection. Although it is something unusual that the poor Clare asked, nevertheless it is granted, and a papal letter confirms the title of blessed poverty upon them. Afterwards, because of the cruel violence of a corrupt time, although the Pope wanted to grant her some land and promised to release her from her vow, she resisted. She was heard saying to the Pope: 'I do not want to be absolved from following Christ completely.'"[45] Although the author does not name the pope, the context of the passage, coupled with testimony from the *Acts*, makes clear that it is Gregory IX. He had been donating land to many women's monasteries as part of his campaign to ensure strict enclosure,[46] and Gregory's contemporary biographer recounts that Gregory went to great expense to meet the material needs of the monasteries.[47] The prose *Legend*'s chronology of events is similar: first the pope granted the Privilege, then Clare categorically refused Gregory's gift of possessions.[48]

One significant difference, however, has generated a long scholarly debate that, while still alive, is losing some vigor: the prose *Legend* claims that the pope who granted the Privilege was Innocent III (r. 1198–1216) and that he himself drew up the "first draft" of the text.[49] Doubts about the authenticity of this earlier Privilege date as far back as 1759, when Sbaraglia, an editor of Franciscan documents, noted that he thought the text attributed to Innocent III was a forgery.[50] In 1995 Werner Maleczek published a magisterial essay that convinced most scholars that Innocent never issued such a privilege. Among Maleczek's arguments are these: the alleged Privilege is conveyed in manuscripts many scholars date to the fifteenth and sixteenth centuries; it pretends to be a solemn papal privilege yet treats a matter far less weighty than Innocent's similar privileges; its address does not conform to Innocent's style; it refers to the *regularis vita* of San Damiano before the house even had a religious rule (*regula*); San Damiano had no need for a privilege of poverty in 1216 since it was in good standing with the diocesan bishop who approved of the women's poverty (but it did need one in 1228 when Gregory pressed Clare to accept possessions); the Privilege attributed to Innocent III contains a clause allowing individuals to transfer out of San Damiano and into less rigorous forms of religious life, a possibility sharply opposed by canon law and by Innocent, himself a canon lawyer; and the *Legend* author who attributed the Privilege to Innocent proved himself to be unreliable when reporting papal documents elsewhere and had motives for wanting to draw Innocent into his hagiographic portrayal of Clare. In a final coup de grâce, Maleczek offered multiple reasons to explain why the very text of a privilege attributed to Innocent III would have been fabricated in the fifteenth century by sisters involved in the Franciscan Observant reform and who were zealous to prove the ancient lineage of their order's allegiance to radical material poverty.[51]

Based on the little-read *Versified Legend*, I would add one more argument to Maleczek's against the authenticity of Innocent III's alleged Privilege. In the passage that I quoted above, the *Versified Legend* emphatically corroborates that the Privilege should be attributed only to Gregory and not to either

Innocent alone or to Innocent first, followed by another Privilege from Gregory. The passage recounts, in order, two related incidents: first, the granting of the Privilege and, second, Clare's dispute with the pope. The pope in both episodes in the *Versified Legend* is clearly Gregory IX. Here is yet one more reminder of the importance of establishing a critical edition of the prose *Legend*. If it preceded the *Versified Legend*, then defenders of the authenticity of Innocent III's Privilege will have one more argument in their favor. Even so, this would still do little to allay doubts raised by the testimony in the *Acts*, the absence of reliable documentary evidence for a privilege before 1228, and, indeed, various arguments adduced by Maleczek.

However one dates the Privilege, Clare proved a formidable opponent, rejecting compromise when it came to San Damiano's practice of poverty. After recalling Clare's and her sisters' desire to renounce all material goods and live without possessions, Gregory continues in his Privilege:

> Therefore, we confirm with our apostolic authority, as you requested, your proposal of most high poverty, granting you by the authority of the present [document] that no one can compel you to receive possessions.[52]

But Gregory's concession falls short of an enthusiastic endorsement of the sisters' request to live without possessions. As Joan Mueller and Pacelli Millane note, rather than positively affirming their radical renunciation, Gregory merely states negatively that "no one can compel you to receive possessions."[53] The prose *Legend* spells out his concern in language even stronger than the *Versified Legend*: "Pope Gregory . . . loved this holy woman intensely with a fatherly affection. When he was [attempting to] persuade her that, because of the events of the times and the dangers of the world, she should consent to have some possessions which he himself willingly offered, she resisted with a very strong spirit and would in no way acquiesce. To this the Pope replied: 'If you fear for your vow, We absolve you from it.' 'Holy Father,' she said, 'I will never in any way wish to be absolved from the following of Christ.'"[54] Gregory concluded the Privilege with a customary anathema, threatening with God's wrath anyone who might violate or oppose the Privilege.

Despite Gregory's bold assurance, however, Clare had good reason to doubt his commitment to preserving San Damiano's singular status within his order. Filippa confirmed this when she concluded her report of the dispute between Clare and the pope by noting that Clare "feared" she could lose the

Privilege.[55] Until her death, Clare would tenaciously hold the papacy to the Privilege she won when she struck her bargain with Gregory and agreed to fuller incorporation into his order. Her sisters were apparently just as staunch: although few documents survive from San Damiano's early history, the sisters still preserve today an original manuscript of the Privilege of Poverty.[56]

Only a very few other monasteries in San Damiano's sphere of influence managed to obtain a similar privilege regarding their poverty. The struggle this entailed and the short-lived nature of these other privileges points to the papacy's reluctance to allow any women's monasteries to live without regular income.[57]

Thomas of Celano's *First Life* of Francis (1228–1229)

A brief but powerful witness to Gregory IX's authority over San Damiano comes in Thomas of Celano's *First Life* of Francis. Thomas, who received his commission from Gregory himself, began writing sometime after Francis's canonization on 16 July 1228, probably finishing the work in early 1229. The *First Life*, therefore, like the three documents just discussed, dates to the critical period following Francis's death and Gregory's ascent to the papacy. Gregory, both as cardinal and pope, had taken an avid interest in Francis and the friars. In keeping with his organizational bent, he actively promoted their institutionalization, achieved in 1223 when Honorius III formally approved their religious rule. Gregory, who commissioned Thomas's text, not surprisingly emerges as a star in the *First Life* for the role he played in Francis's and the friars' lives.

Thomas's description of Clare and the women associated with her seamlessly accords with Gregory's monastic plan for religious women. The few pages Thomas devotes to Clare and her sisters are a panegyric, both poetic and ethereal.[58] Even the most concrete subjects in his passage point heavenward. Thomas transforms Francis's rebuilding of the church of San Damiano, his post-conversion act of piety, into an expansive building metaphor: Francis was rebuilding the universal Church, founded by Christ and in need of renewal. Of Clare we learn not the details of her life in Assisi or even about her conversion. She is, instead, "the most precious and strongest stone of the whole structure, standing as the foundation for all the other stones." Thomas thereby positions Clare as the foundation not just of San Damiano, but of all the communities in the "excellent Order of Poor Ladies and holy virgins" (*excellentissimus ordo pauperum Dominarum*), the "noble structure of precious pearls [that] arose above [Clare]."[59] The qualities he exalts in them echo Gregory's ideals of women's monastic life: charity, humility, virginity and chastity, highest poverty, abstinence and silence, patience, and contemplation, although it is notable that none of these virtues relate explicitly to enclosure. Thomas presents not an idealized portrait of San Damiano but one of multiple communities in the entire order. Thomas makes Clare the order's heroine and foundation, placing her and her sisters in a direct line of descent from Francis, the builder. This means, of course, that the rest of the communities also descend from Francis. Thomas's lofty encomium has to be bereft of most narrative details for to recount the actual chronology of events would undermine the narrative Gregory wished to propagate. Even so, Thomas's cryptic conclusion to his 1228–1229 description of the Order of Poor Ladies points to a rich backstory that begs to be told: "For the moment let this suffice concerning these virgins dedicated to God and most devout servants of Christ. Their wondrous life and their renowned practices [*institutio gloriosa*] received from the lord Pope Gregory, at that time Bishop of Ostia, would require another book and the leisure to write it."[60] Thomas, of course, never wrote that book. The women's *institutio*, the same term Lateran IV's *Ne nimia* used to refer to legislative texts, here rendered as "practices," is in fact an unmistakable reference to Hugo's *forma vitae*. Thomas thus enigmatically acknowledged the pope's formative role in founding this Order of Poor Ladies, an order that now, in Thomas's recounting, sparkled with Clare as its illustrious leader and "Saint" Francis as its inspiration.

Did Thomas also claim Francis as the founder of three orders? An oft-cited proof-text appears in Thomas's *First Life*. The Church, he writes, was "being renewed in both sexes according to [Francis's] form, rule and teaching [*formam, regulam et doctrinam*], and there is victory for the triple army of those being saved."[61] Just what Thomas meant by "triple army," however, is not immediately clear to modern readers. With hindsight, some scholars want to identify it with the three religious orders associated with Francis, the first order of Lesser Brothers, second order of Poor Ladies, and third order of laity.[62] But its context belies this. In the preceding passage, Thomas had recounted how Francis went from town to town inspiring all types of people to convert: "Men ran, women also ran, clerics hurried, and religious rushed to see and hear the holy one of God, who seemed to everyone a person of another age. People of all ages and both sexes hurried to behold the wonders which the Lord worked anew in the world through his servant."[63] After elaborating Francis's power to affect all kinds of listeners, Thomas concluded with his famous remark about the "triple army" being saved. Certainly, Thomas was referring to the three types of people he had just described, namely, laity of both sexes, clerics, and religious. The larger historical context confirms this. Augustine of Hippo first made famous this tripartite division of society and thereafter the typology recurred frequently in medieval texts,[64] including Bonaventure's *Hexaemeron*.[65] It was the Franciscan hagiographer Julian of Speyer who, around 1232–1235, creatively reinterpreted Thomas's comment to be an allusion to the by then established three orders, a transposition sometimes accepted at face value by modern scholars unfamiliar with the medieval typology and persuaded by the institutionalized portrait of Francis as founder.[66]

Gregory IX's *Quo elongati* (1230)

Francis's death, especially in light of his charismatic leadership, posed a formidable challenge to his followers: would they be able to remain faithful to the radical program he had set before them? For some Lesser Brothers, their founder's vision of religious life seemed too extreme to maintain once they had grown from a small charismatic band to a sprawling institution. In fact, Francis's uncompromising views regarding the brothers' poverty, education, and obligation to work had caused controversies among the brothers even while he was alive. Shortly before Francis died, realizing how susceptible his vision was to diverse interpretations, he attempted to end the matter with his brief, but powerfully worded *Testament*, which aimed to clarify the papally approved 1223 rule. He recalls the pivotal features of his conversion and religious vision and also lays out strict instruction regarding some controversial issues dividing the brothers. He concludes with a categorical statement about the binding character of his *Testament*:

> And let the general minister and all the other ministers and custodians be bound through obedience not *to add to* or *to take away* from these words. And let them always have this writing with them together with the Rule. And in all the chapters which they hold, when they read the Rule, let them also read these words. And I strictly command all my cleric and lay brothers, through obedience, not to place any gloss upon the Rule or upon these words saying, "They

should be understood this way." But as the Lord has given me to
speak and write the Rule and these words simply and purely, may
you understand them simply and without gloss and observe them
with a holy activity until the end.[67]

Yet who is the faithful interpreter and who the unfaithful glosser is in the eye
of the beholder. As the Lesser Brothers strived to interpret and uphold the
1223 rule, they found themselves divided on a number of issues, including the
rule's provision regarding the friars' relationship with nuns' monasteries: "I
strictly command all the brothers not to have any suspicious dealings or conversations with women, and they may not enter the monasteries of nuns, excepting those brothers to whom special permission has been granted by the
Apostolic See."[68]

By 1230, evolving circumstances left Francis's stricture increasingly open
to diverse interpretations. These had momentous ramifications for the friars'
access to three related categories of nuns: those in all monasteries in general,
those in monasteries belonging specifically to Gregory's "order of poor enclosed nuns," and, within that order, the women in the monastery of San
Damiano (whose members Clare herself tellingly referred to as sisters and ladies but never as nuns).[69]

Francis's earliest companions knew San Damiano and respected Francis's
special commitment that he and his friars would always be tied to the women
and attend to their needs. The friars' entrance into San Damiano, a simple
house of penitents, was probably quite easy. After Hugo sent the women his
forma vitae by or before 1220–1221, there are no indications that entrance was
any more difficult. Circumstances suggest that Francis may have approached
Hugo to insist on San Damiano's Franciscan identity, but the sources are
mostly silent. Even after Francis's death in 1226, when Gregory began to assert
greater control over San Damiano, Clare was able to argue for San Damiano's
singularity, as the Privilege of Poverty attests. Gregory's effort to cajole Clare
into his order perhaps played a part in both his 1227 mandate to the friars,
Quoties cordis, charging the friars with the *cura monialium* of his order, and
also his appointment around that time of a friar as visitator. Both actions may
have assuaged Clare.

But over time, many Lesser Brothers grew wary of their growing responsibilities toward nuns in Hugo's order and, indeed, toward other nuns. This
was one of many matters regarding the 1223 rule and Francis's *Testament* that
came to a head at the Lesser Brothers' May 1230 chapter meeting in Assisi.

They wondered just what Francis intended when he said in his rule that friars needed special papal permission to enter women's monasteries. Did he mean only the poor enclosed nuns—as an oral tradition among them had long circulated?[70]—or did he mean all women's monasteries? The question seems to have arisen in part because increasing numbers of friars, including their leadership, wanted it to mean all monasteries, to help stem their growing pastoral responsibilities toward nuns.

Unable to come to any resolution, the Lesser Brothers dispatched a delegation to meet in person with the pope. Among the seven friars in the delegation, at least two, Anthony of Padua and Leo of Perego, were known to be friendly to the papacy's desire to regularize, enclose, and monitor women's religious houses.[71] The other brothers in the delegation, led by the minister general, Giovanni Parenti (whom Gregory had charged with the *cura monialium* of his order), included Haymo of Faversham, Gerard Rusinol, Gerard of Modena, and Peter of Brescia.[72] In contrast to Francis's early companions from Umbria, this group was notably more international, educated, and allied with the papacy. Only Gerardo of Modena seems to have known Francis; Salimbene says he was close to him, albeit not one of the original twelve companions.[73] A generation distant from Francis, these friars were largely unfamiliar with the primitive *fraternitas* of the simple Umbrian friars.[74] They had no personal ties to San Damiano and likely wanted to reduce their burden of caring for the spiritual needs of religious women.

Gregory answered the friars on this and other questions in *Quo elongati* (September 1230), a document of enormous import for the Lesser Brothers. He first had to articulate his position on the status of the 1223 *Later Rule* and Francis's *Testament*. In language reminiscent of his canonization bull for Francis,[75] the pope revealingly reminded the friars that he was intimately familiar with Francis. He asserted that he knew—in a way that the friars apparently did not—the saint's true "intention" (*intentionem*). Francis's language in the *Testament* had been unequivocal: he bound the brothers to full observance of all he commanded in both the *Later Rule* and the *Testament* and charged that his words were never to be glossed. Gregory did not so much gloss Francis's words as reject them outright. The rule's command that the brothers observe the holy gospel was simply too difficult if it meant obeying all its precepts, rather than simply those points articulated in the rule. Gregory, the canon lawyer, further stated that the *Testament* was not binding: Francis could not oblige the brothers, especially the ministers, to something about which he had not consulted them. And he had no right to bind his successors.[76]

Regarding the specific matter of the friars' contacts with nuns, Gregory declared:

> Finally, it is written in the Rule that "the brothers should not enter
> the monasteries of nuns, except those [brothers] to whom special
> permission has been granted by the Apostolic See." Up to now the
> brothers have interpreted this passage as referring to the monasteries
> of the Poor Cloistered Nuns for whom the Apostolic See exercises a
> special concern. This interpretation is believed to have been handed
> down by the provincial ministers in general chapter through a stat-
> ute at the time when the Rule was approved and blessed Francis was
> still alive. Nevertheless, you have asked for a clarification. Does this
> mean all the monasteries without exception, since the Rule excepts
> none, or does it refer only to the monasteries of the aforesaid [Poor
> Cloistered] Nuns? We respond: the prohibition affects the commu-
> nities of nuns of every description. And by the term monastery we
> mean the cloister, the living quarters, and the inner shops. Those
> brothers to whom the superiors have granted permission by virtue
> of their maturity and suitability may go into the other areas to
> which lay people also have access in order to preach or beg alms,
> with the exception always of the monasteries of the aforesaid Clois-
> tered Nuns. No one has any access to them without the express per-
> mission of the Apostolic See.[77]

Gregory's clarification, alas, could have been clearer, but in essence he issues three directives regarding entrance into monastic enclosures. First, the
pope clarifies specifically which women's monasteries are affected according to
his reading of the *Later Rule*. Gregory corrects the friars' oral tradition by stating that they needed special papal permission to enter *all* women's monasteries, not just those of the poor enclosed nuns.

Second, Gregory specifies which areas of a monastery were off limits
without special permission. When the *Later Rule* prohibits entrance without
special permission to a monastery, it meant, specifically, the inner, more cloistered domain, which included the nuns' living quarters, shops, and perhaps
also spaces such as an inner courtyard and garden. Entrance into this inner
section of *any* monastery required special papal permission.

Third, Gregory deals with access to the more exterior section of a monastery. This might include, for example, an outer courtyard adjacent to the

monastic walls where goods were dropped off or a parlor where visitors could meet with a nun face-to-face or through a grille. Gregory here makes an extraordinary distinction (and one wonders if the delegation suggested it). Brothers could enter the outer areas of monasteries *not* belonging to the poor enclosed nuns as long as they had permission of a religious superior; they did not need papal permission. However, to enter even the outer enclosure of a monastery belonging to the poor enclosed nuns, papal permission was required. Friars seeking to lighten their pastoral burden must have been delighted with the pope's pronouncement.

Clare's famous reaction to Gregory's interpretation was immediate and vehement, but why she reacted this way is not fully transparent. Gregory's 1230 ruling in *Quo elongati* introduced something new into San Damiano's situation, but what? It must have regarded one or more of three matters: (1) the friars' access to the inner domain of San Damiano, (2) their access to its outer domain, and/or (3) the papacy's control over one or both of these. Prior to Francis's 1223 *Later Rule*, it is unclear what access the friars had to San Damiano's inner and outer domains. It might have been relatively easy and free. This might have continued to be the situation even after the 1223 *Later Rule*, with its strictures about entering nuns' monasteries, until the death of Francis in 1226 since it is plausible that Francis might have used his influence with Cardinal Hugo to protect San Damiano's special status. But certainly after Francis's death, if not before, the friars' interpretation of their rule was that they needed special papal permission to enter, minimally, the inner domain of San Damiano. It bears recalling that in 1227, Gregory had put the pastoral care of the poor enclosed nuns in the hands of the Lesser Brothers' minister general, relegating to him the power to grant the special permission needed to enter San Damiano (and other monasteries of the poor enclosed nuns).

Clare, for her part, would certainly have wished to preserve the friars' ease of access to her community. Now, in 1230, Gregory unceremoniously slammed the door shut. He took back the power he had granted the minister general to allow access to San Damiano and other monasteries of the poor enclosed nuns. And worse, his distinctions between the outer and inner domains of monasteries, on the one hand, and between the poor enclosed nuns and all nuns, on the other hand, now made even the outer domain of San Damiano off-limits to friars lacking special permission. Whether Clare was most angered by the enhanced regulation of the friars' access to the inner domain, outer domain, or both little matters. Ultimately, she was objecting to the heightened papal gatekeeping and whatever bureaucratic red tape for permission it would entail. The new stipulations would surely slow and even threatened to halt altogether visits from beloved friars such as Leo, Angelo, Philip Longo, Elias of Assisi, and others.

Both early Legends report Clare's reaction. On receiving word of Gregory's new ruling, she promptly ordered that the friars who begged food for San Damiano be sent away. The *Versified Legend* says she exclaimed: "From now on, we do not want questors for our bodily food, since by his decree the pope removed the disciples of the Word."[78] Clare's decision could be construed as a reaction of despair: losing our preachers, we have lost our appetites as well. But the prose *Legend* is less ambiguous. Clare implicates Gregory as the culprit responsible for both losses. Clare proclaims: "Let him [Gregory] now take away from us all the brothers since he has taken away those who provide us with the food that is vital."[79]

Clare's move was consciously strategic. She knew that Gregory worried about the women's material sustenance. For that very reason, he had earlier tried to press property upon them. Because they were cloistered, sending the questors away, if not tantamount to self-starvation—after all, they might still have received alms or harvested produce from their own garden—would surely intensify the precarity of their material situation. Clare's "hunger strike," as this episode has popularly been described, has lent sheen to her modern persona. She becomes the courageous woman valiantly challenging the highest male authority in the Church. The episode indeed strikes that chord, but also sounds another note. Most hunger strikes, including this one, are tactics strategically deployed to provoke either feelings of guilt or public embarrassment or both in order to achieve a specific goal. Clare's decision was a calculated gambit, one that she won straightaway according to the Legends. The episode is usually portrayed as a conflict between Clare and Gregory, but it also places the friars center-stage. They are the third party to the conflict. If the pope gives them permission, they are his emissaries, liaising the monastery of San Damiano with Gregory. If the pope does not give them permission, their absence functions as a direct blow to Clare and her community who had felt one with them and relied upon them since their earliest days. When Clare dispatched the friar-questors, she was probably delivering a double rebuke, one to Gregory and another to those Lesser Brothers who wanted to minimize their pastoral obligations to the women. Bartoli believes Clare's gesture declared her belief that she controlled who could and could not enter San Damiano.[80] To the friars' leadership, she was saying, "If you do not wish to be here pastorally, you need not be here at all."

Both Legends narrate that as soon as Gregory heard that Clare had banished the brothers—which she surely broadcast specifically in his direction—he rescinded his decree. Safely washing his hands of the controversy, Gregory gave up his role as papal gatekeeper and ceded control (again) to the friars' minister general, Giovanni Parenti.[81] The pope's famous reversal was perhaps not the full retreat that the Legends suggest. After all, his 1227 *Quoties cordis* showed he wanted the friars to assume more responsibility vis-à-vis the nuns in his order. Reversing *Quo elongati* merely continued the status quo. Importantly, the reversal may have affected San Damiano alone; we do not know if it pertained to all the monasteries of the poor enclosed nuns. It was a compromise that apparently satisfied Clare. She and the San Damiano-friendly friars may well have reminded Giovanni Parenti of Francis's early promise to her community: "I resolve and promise for myself and for my brothers always to have the same loving care and special solicitude for you as for them."[82]

San Damiano's Growing Influence

By late 1220s, Clare and the monastery of San Damiano had attained a certain acclaim, a trace of which survives in the *Acts*. Around the time of Francis's death in 1226, Sister Cecilia says she heard Clare's mother Ortulana recount a prophetic experience she had around the time of Clare's birth. A voice told Ortulana that she would give birth to "a great light who would greatly illumine the world,"[83] thus explaining the origins of Clare's name, *Chiara*, "clear," "shining," "bright." The story suggests that others had begun to see Clare as someone who would leave her stamp on the world, the very sort of insight that prompts saintly mothers to look back and recall prophetic signs. Thomas of Celano's relatively brief remarks about San Damiano in his *First Life* (1228–1229) could hardly have been more effusive. He announced to the world beyond Assisi Clare's and San Damiano's special relationship to Francis. The point would surely please his patron, Gregory IX, who wanted to establish a direct line of descent from Francis to his order of enclosed nuns. Thus Thomas, in his section on Clare and her sisters, connects the dots between Francis's rebuilding of San Damiano (and the Church universal), Francis's conversion of Clare, Clare's foundational role in the order of poor ladies, and the example Clare presented for others. Thomas's poetic description of Clare and her sisters as the ideal religious women,[84] would not have been lost on his audience, which certainly included female penitents emulating the religious life of

Francis's itinerant and apostolic friars. Thomas's message to them was Gregory's: to follow Francis, follow Clare, the "foundation stone" of the enclosed papal order.

Clare's and San Damiano's growing fame also increased Clare's clout at the bargaining table. Her ability to win the Privilege of Poverty from Gregory in 1228 and maneuver him into reversing *Quo elongati's* provisions regarding the friars' access to San Damiano display her pluck and power. Gregory struck a bargain with Clare because he needed her in his order to strengthen its attraction to other religious women.

San Damiano had grown not only in prestige but also in size. Having begun as a small, humble community of penitents outside Assisi, it soon commanded the attention of the city itself. In 1233 the Assisi commune made a gift to the *operi sancti Damiani*, an apparent building project. Notably, the gift appeared just third in the commune's list, following gifts made to building projects at the cathedral of San Rufino and the grand church of Saint Francis.[85] By 1238, a legal document indicates that fifty-one sisters resided at San Damiano.[86]

At some unknown point in the monastery's history, the sisters began going out to other women's religious houses to share their knowledge and style of religious life. The *Acts* refer to one Sister Balvina, apparently one of Clare's early companions, who left probably between 1215 and 1230 for the monastery of Vallegloria, where she remained and became abbess.[87] Clare sent Pacifica for one year also to Vallegloria to "inform the sisters" there.[88] Late sources state that Clare's blood sister Agnes spent many years at Monticelli, the monastery that in 1219 had petitioned to follow the *observantias regulares* of San Damiano.[89] Clare sent her relative, Balvina di Martino, for a period of seventeen months to the "monastery of Arezzo along with a lady who had been sent there."[90] These women were among Clare's first companions. It made sense that Clare would send them out as pioneers to proselytize and inform other female penitents desirous of emulating San Damiano's religious lifestyle. San Damiano would next extend its reach beyond Tuscany and Umbria, when the politically powerful Princess Agnes of Prague joined the order and became one Clare's most significant allies.

Chapter 5

Clare's Letters to Agnes of Prague, ca. 1234 to 1238

Clare's words, deeds, and style of religious life during the first forty years of her life reach us only indirectly, gleaned through the scrim of a few letters sent to her, two rules that purported to regulate life at San Damiano, the Privilege of Poverty she won from the pope, Thomas of Celano's brief description of her in the *First Life*, a few other church documents, and hagiographic texts penned years after this period. It is only in about 1234 that we hear, for the first time, Clare's own voice in a letter she sent to Agnes of Prague. Clare was just over forty years old and in the next few years she would write two other letters to Agnes. Then, shortly before Clare died in 1253, she sent a fourth and final letter to her friend. These four Latin letters, all that survive of Clare's correspondence, disclose key aspects of her spirituality and personal convictions absent in other works ascribed to her.

It was thought that another letter, to one Ermentrude of Bruges, also survived. The seventeenth-century Franciscan chronicler Luke Wadding (d. 1657) is the sole source for the letter.[1] Somewhat darker in mood than Clare's letters to Agnes, it shares some themes but diverges stylistically. More problematic, however, is Antonio Melissano de Macro's (fl. 1700) claim that Wadding's text is a mere summary of two letters that Clare sent to Ermentrude.[2] This, together with the letter's lack of an early attestation, has led most scholars to doubt the letter's authenticity,[3] although it is included, with caveats, in many editions of Clare's writings.[4] Clare must have carried on a correspondence with many people, including other religious women and some friars, but such letters have never been located.

Clare's four letters to Agnes are widely held to be authentic. The *Legend of*

Blessed Agnes of Bohemia (ca. 1283 to 1322), which, to be sure, aimed to portray a strong relationship between Agnes and the (by then) "Saint" Clare, claimed that Clare "comforted [Agnes] maternally, reverently, and affectionately by her *frequent* and gracious letters" (emphasis mine).[5] That these four letters to Agnes survive at all suggests their particular significance.[6]

Clare's Latin Literacy

The lyrically elegant Latin in these letters reflects a knowledge of the *ars dict-aminis*, the medieval rhetorical art of letter writing. Clare's theology, if not highly complex—these are brief letters, not treatises—nonetheless conveys theological nuance and profound sentiment. The letters also strike a dissonant note with how Clare's contemporaries described her education. The witness Agnes di Oportulo, noting that Clare enjoyed listening to learned sermons, told the canonization commissioners that Clare herself "had not studied letters" (*epsa non havesse studiato in lectere*).[7] The Legends concur. The *Versified Legend* says, for example, that Clare enjoyed listening to learned men even though she herself did not understand "writing" (*scripture nescia*).[8] The particular turns of phrase in these passages are unambiguous. Not having studied "letters" meant, specifically, that she had not studied Latin. Not understanding "writing" meant that she was unable to read Latin. If Clare could not read Latin, then, a fortiori, one would suppose that she could not write Latin.

And yet most contemporary discussions of the letters rarely address this point. In their lengthy commentary on the letters, Edith Van den Goorbergh and Theodore Zweerman note simply that Clare's "writings show that she had mastered Latin very well."[9] This appears to be the unspoken assumption of most scholars commenting on the letters.[10] Perhaps the question is passed over in silence because it recalls so many unfounded scholarly suspicions regarding the authenticity of other works by women. Joan Mueller, attuned to such suspicions, argues strongly that Clare herself wrote the letters, perhaps assisted by one or more of her sisters. She adduces points against any friar's intervention and for a more likely female authorship, but without addressing the assertions regarding Clare's lack of literacy.[11]

Occasionally, the question of Clare's literacy is broached obliquely, without reference to her contemporaries' claims that she was unlearned in Latin. Thaddée Matura, for example, rightly notes that whether Clare "herself wrote or dictated these texts in Latin, or received help from one or more secretaries" is unresolvable since "contemporary witnesses are lacking." On the basis of Clare's social class alone, he concludes that she would have known how to read and write Latin, better than Francis in any case, a plausible but not certain conclusion. Matura points to the "unity of inspiration and also of style" characterizing the letters and two other texts often attributed to her, the *1253 forma vitae* and *Testament*. The import of his remarks seems aimed at strengthening Clare's authorship.[12]

A few scholars have acknowledged the problematic medieval evidence against Clare's literacy. Fidel Aizpurúa concludes that "the most sensible thing to say is that, although Clare had the formation that an aristocratic girl would receive . . . , she was, in terms of her literary skill, incapable of writing and structuring a single one of the works attributed to her." Aizpurúa continues: "Therefore, she had to avail herself of secretaries, people well-versed in the art of writing. Nevertheless, we can say that even though it is not an easy task to distinguish the ideas and sentiments of Clare from the literary thicket that was in style at that time, it is possible to locate the fundamental components of her thought. And that is what is most interesting."[13]

How do we unravel the dilemma of Clare's supposed lack of Latin alongside the existence of four elegant Latin letters? One solution is simply to discard the possibility of Clare as their author. But while Clare's putative lack of Latin literacy poses a dilemma, several points tip the balance significantly in favor of her literacy and, especially, her authorship of the letters. First, Clare's social status does suggest that she might have learned some Latin prayers at home, and perhaps more. Italy was known for its relatively strong tradition of lay literacy. Early thirteenth-century Tuscany and Umbria, which boasted more secular primary schools than most areas of western Europe, were making education at all levels more accessible to a larger swath of society.[14] Clare's cultural milieu, in short, suggests that an aristocratic young girl might well learn how to read and even write some Latin at home, albeit this would not qualify as having "studied Latin," a phrase implying formal study in a school.

Second, the unlearned woman who was, in spite of her ignorance, wise and adept at understanding the intricacies of theology was a favorite trope among thirteenth- and fourteenth-century Italian hagiographers.[15] Agnes di Oportulo or the scribe who recorded her testimony might have been playing off this trope.

Third, Clare could have acquired a modicum of Latin literacy through repeated exposure to the Latin liturgy, especially the lengthy Divine Office. The witnesses for Clare's canonization allude several times to the Latin prayers or scripture verses the sisters recited. For example, the last words the dying Clare spoke to Agnes di Oportulo were from Psalm 115, *Pretiosa in conspectu Domini mors sanctorum eius* (Precious in the sight of the Lord is the death of his saints).[16] Angeluccia noted how Clare would turn over in her mind the hymn *Vidi aquam egredientem de templo a latere dextro* (I saw water coming forth from the temple on the right side).[17] The ease with which the sisters interlace vernacular remarks and Latin citations reminds us that women's monastic communities were steeped in Latin. Boccali even assumes that since the sermons Clare loved to listen to were learned, they must have been in the learned language of Latin.[18] But by the thirteenth century Italian preachers were usually preaching in the vernacular, especially before women's monastic and lay audiences. Bonaventure, for example, made it a point to preach in French before a group of Parisian nuns even though his French was so deficient he felt compelled to apologize. But even vernacular sermons could be a vehicle for learning Latin, for preachers sometimes cited texts in Latin before glossing them in the vernacular.[19]

More problematic is the *Versified Legend*'s explicit claim that Clare could not read Latin. But this is exactly the sort of flesh that hagiographers liberally added to the bare bones of canonization testimonies and other fragments of information in order to present a full-bodied and colorful saint's story. Clare had already resided in San Damiano some thirteen years when she wrote her first letter to Agnes. For many if not all of those years she had been hearing and reciting Latin. Knowing liturgical Latin, however, still falls short of the literacy required to *compose* letters like those addressed to Agnes.

However, a fourth point, the existence of the Latin letters in an early manuscript of Czech provenance—the region where the original letters were most likely preserved—strengthens arguments for the letters' authenticity, at least insofar as it suggests that Latin letters were actually dispatched to Agnes of Prague. Similarly, their early translation into German places them close to their recipient Agnes; one of the languages common in Prague at that time was German.[20]

Fifth, all the manuscripts and early published versions, without cavil, ascribe the letters to Clare. Medieval editors believed Clare to be their author. This, in fact, is the principal criterion for attributing many texts to medieval authors, male or female, and it should not be rejected lightly in the case of these letters.

Sixth, the contents of the letters accord well with what we know about Agnes and Clare from papal and other documents. It is true that some of the issues dealt with remain rather cryptic; they make sense only in light of these other documents. But this in itself points to the letters' authenticity, for if they were ascribed to Clare without being by her, it is unlikely that the forger would have left the reader in the dark regarding "Clare's" meaning, for that would undermine the forger's very message.

Since Latin was the only viable language for these letters, given that Agnes would have had little exposure to Umbrian Italian, we should more specifically ask whether Clare is the "sole" author of these letters. I do not mean here to point to the various written sources, such as the martyrdom of Agnes of Rome (ca. 291–ca. 304), that are incorporated into the letters.[21] Medieval writers often drew extensively on other sources while creating very original works—one thinks immediately of writers such as Benedict of Nursia. Rather, I suggest it would hardly be surprising to learn that Clare had an amanuensis. Scribal assistance was quite common, even for writers who knew Latin and were skilled in the *ars dictaminis*. Alfonso Marini and Timothy Johnson discuss three verses in Clare's fourth letter that include the revealing terms *inquit* or *hoc inquit* for "she says." These phrases—often omitted from translations—were probably included to persuade the reader that the words taken down were faithful to what had been dictated—and they are incontrovertible evidence that the fourth letter was dictated.[22] But what if Clare dictated her letters in the vernacular? Thirteenth-century scribes were adept translators. Even though sermons to the laity and nuns were commonly preached in the vernacular, when they were written down—often in the form of notes taken on the spot—they were usually recorded in Latin, thought to be a more proper and precise vehicle. Until the fourteenth century, "literary bilingualism," the ability to take down in Latin what was spoken in the vernacular, lay at the heart of Latin sermon composition.[23] The same process might have applied to Clare's letters, which happen to share many features of a medieval sermon. Emore Paoli, recognizing the stylistic unity of the letters, thinks a single secretary might have assisted her in writing all four letters,[24] and Attilio Bartoli Langeli suggests Francis's close early companion Brother Leo as the possible scribe. We know Leo worked as a scribe and made creative contributions to other literary projects. He was close to Clare and her sisters: he was present when Clare died, participated in her canonization process, and entrusted Francis's very breviary to Clare's successor, Sister Benedetta, when the community relocated from San Damiano to the monastery of Santa Chiara in Assisi.[25] A scribe might not only have added Latin polish to Clare's expression, but also embellished her ideas with felicitous phrasing or well-chosen scriptural quotations. In this case, he or she would more accurately be termed a "redactor."

In sum, one can marshal arguments pointing to the plausibility that Clare was significantly literate in Latin. But there remains an undeniably discordant note between Agnes di Oportulo's and the hagiographers' claims that Clare was not proficient in Latin and the striking Latin eloquence of the letters to Agnes of Prague. Of course, medieval notions of authorship were far more embracing than modern notions, which expect a "true" author to conceive and arrange every word of a text. Medieval authors often drew extensively and verbatim from other texts and also relied on helpful collaborators to create "their own" texts. Clare may well have relied on assistants who not only translated her vernacular words into Latin, but also embellished them to better convey her thought. In modern parlance, she is indisputably the "intellectual author" of these letters; in medieval parlance, she is quite simply the *auctor*.[26]

The Letters

Agnes of Prague (ca. 1211–1282) was one of nine children and the last daughter of King Přemysl Otakar I and his second wife, Queen Constance of Hungary.[27] Raised and educated in Poland, Bohemia, and Austria, Agnes's peripatetic childhood was owing, in part, to her father's attempts to cement political alliances by betrothing her to various royal suitors, including a son of Henry the Bearded, duke of Silesia; Henry, son of Emperor Frederick II; Henry III, king of England; and, eventually, Emperor Frederick II himself. Death, in one case, and politics in others undid negotiations with the first three candidates. Agnes, perhaps about seventeen when Emperor Frederick sought her hand in the first of two attempts, also played a role. Her *Legend* (ca. 1283–1322) states that she preferred marriage to Christ over marriage to "any mortal being no matter what his status or prominence," a claim supported by Clare's first letter to Agnes.[28] Evading marriage to an emperor required astute diplomacy, and Agnes showed hers when she wrote to Gregory IX to enlist his aid. Ostensibly, the pope supported her resolve to remain a virgin for pious reasons, but surely too because an alliance between Frederick II, his arch enemy, and the Přemysl house was not to Gregory's advantage.[29]

Agnes asked the Franciscan friars who had settled in Prague in 1233 to instruct her concerning what her *Legend* anachronistically called the rule of

St. Clare.[30] She began to divest herself of riches and founded two institutions. Following the example of her cousin, Elizabeth of Hungary, she built and endowed with income and property the hospital of Saint Francis for the poor and sick, placed under the care of a recently founded military order, the Crusaders of the Red Cross and Star. The *Legend* reports she also built, at her own expense, the monastery of Saint Francis. It housed both the Lesser Brothers and, elsewhere in the monastic complex, sisters who were anachronistically identified as of the Order of St. Clare.[31] At Agnes's request, Gregory IX sent five sisters from Trent to be the first members of this community. Seven highborn Bohemian virgins soon joined them in November 1233, followed on Pentecost, 11 June 1234, by Agnes herself—named abbess—and seven more noblewomen.[32] It is important to note both that Agnes contacted Pope Gregory first, not Clare, and that the sisters he sent from Trent followed his *forma vitae*. Thus, Agnes's monastery began as fully part of Gregory's order. Both the correspondence she soon struck up with Clare and other signs suggest that, at this initial stage of Agnes's religious life, she was still finding her way about how best to be a follower of Francis. Indeed, it is possible that Clare herself and her allies initiated contact with Agnes in order to draw the influential princess toward their interpretation of religious life.[33] Mueller thinks that Agnes intended her monastic community to be separate from the endowed hospital, but the documents suggest the two foundations were, from the beginning, linked.[34] For example, in spring 1234, Agnes's brother, King Wenceslas, referred to the "cloister in Prague built in honor of Saint Francis and the hospital *belonging* [*pertinens*] to it" (emphasis mine).[35] Later that year, Pope Gregory referred to them together as "a monastery *with* [*cum*] a hospital" (emphasis mine),[36] a connection he would certainly favor given his preference that monasteries in his order have regular income streams. Perhaps in founding these institutions, Agnes had given little thought to how this linkage would affect her religious life both financially and spiritually. A few months after joining the monastery, she had asked her brother Přemysl to donate an estate he had previously given her to the hospital to support its poor.[37] Nevertheless, six months later a connection between her monastery and the hospital is apparent in a letter that her mother, Queen Constance, wrote donating other estates "to the Hospital *of* the Cloister [*Claustri*] of Saint Francis." The gift was to the hospital, but it is not transparent that the queen had no thought of any benefit to the monastery. Constance put herself in charge of the estates' profits so that she could do with them as she thought God would want.[38] Perhaps she envisioned some support for her daughter's monastery. In any case, this apparent linkage between the hospital and monastery would, by the time Clare wrote her second letter to Agnes, become a source of contention.

Dating the Letters

Clare's letters to Agnes can be dated with reasonable precision by relating the contents of the letters with other datable documents, such as papal letters, or known events, such as Agnes's entrance into monastic life. Table 1 notes various scholarly opinions regarding the precise date of each letter and concludes with my own opinion, to which I return in my discussion of the letters.

The Letters' Spiritual Teaching in Historical Context

The contents and character of these four letters, despite the many years that separate them, are remarkably homogenous. They attest to Agnes's close alignment with Clare's vision of religious life, even when that put Agnes at loggerheads with the papacy. Each letter includes both Clare's spiritual teaching and some information, however allusive, regarding specific historical events. Two of the letters appear to include Clare's responses to specific questions posed by Agnes. Since none of Agnes's letters to Clare survives, what Agnes might have written must be gleaned in *grosso modo* from Clare's responses. I will supplement this information by considering numerous papal letters to Agnes's monastery and other women's monasteries engaged in negotiating the issues that concerned Clare and Agnes.

Clare's spiritual teaching plays off the historical circumstances surrounding at least three, and perhaps all four, letters. Letter 1, written probably just after Agnes entered the monastery in June 1234, includes elaborate plays regarding Agnes's rejection of marriage to the emperor and choice of marriage to Christ. Clare notes, for example, how inviolate virginity surpasses earthly marriage, contempt of the world surpasses honors, and poverty (with its eternal riches) surpasses temporal wealth. Letter 2 was likely written when Agnes was trying to win papal guarantees allowing her monastic community to live without the material support provided by the hospital of Saint Francis that she helped establish. Clare spiritually foregrounds poverty, equates it with perfection, and pointedly deems it the "one thing necessary."[39] This is a striking transformation of the biblical phrase from the Martha-Mary story that deemed contemplation the one thing necessary. Clare's spiritual teaching in letter 3 is, *prima facie*, less obviously tied to the matters at hand. Agnes had

Table 1: Scholarly Opinions Regarding the Dates of Clare's Letters to Agnes

	Letter 1	Letter 2	Letter 3	Letter 4
Robinson (1910)	shortly before 30 August 1234	ca. 1235	ca. 1237–1238	period before Clare's death 11 August 1253
Vyskočil (1932)	1234	ca. 1236–1 May 1238	post-14 April 1237; probably post-5 May–pre-18 December 1238	shortly before 11 August 1253
Fassbinder (1936)	before 11 June 1234 (when Agnes entered the monastery)	1234–1239	early 1238	August 1253
Olgiati & Lainati (1977)	perhaps post-5 June 1235	1235–1238	before 1238	1253
Grau (1980), followed by Godet (1985)	before 11 June 1234	1234–1238	early 1238	shortly before 11 August 1253
Paoli (1995)	after 11 June 1234	1234–1238, probably post-spring 1237–winter 1238	spring 1238	February–early August 1253
Mueller (2001)	after 11 June 1234	spring 1235–winter 1238	July–October 1238	shortly before 9 August 1253
Boccali (2001)	1234	1237/1238	1237/1238	July 1253
Mooney	after 11 June 1234	ca. May 1235–1238, probably closer to 1238	ca. 11 May–18 December 1238	before 11 August 1253

Sources: Robinson, "Writings of St. Clare," *AFH* 3 (1910): 437, 439; Vyskočil, *Legend of Blessed Agnes*, 75, 79, 82, 84–85, 88; Fassbinder, "Untersuchungen über die Quellen zum Leben der hl. Klara," *FS* 23 (1936): 298–99; Olgiati and Lainati, "Scritti di Chiara d'Assisi," in *Fonti francescane* (1977), vol. 2, 2283 n. 2, 2287 n. 1, 2289 n. 1, 2293 n. 1; Grau, "Schriften der heiligen Klara," in *Movimento religioso femminile*, 202 and see table, 201; Godet, *Écrits*, 18; Paoli, in *FF* (1995), 2225–28; Mueller, *Letters* (2001), 27 for letter 1, 53 (cf. 215, 217) for letter 2; Mueller, *Companion to Clare*, 158–59 (cf. 149) for letter 3, and 164 for letter 4; Boccali, LegCl, 10.

written to Clare requesting clarification regarding rules of fasting, which Agnes was then negotiating with the papacy. She wanted her monastery, like San Damiano, to follow Francis's advice on fasting. One of Clare's spiritual themes in this letter regards the mystical body of Christ insofar as Agnes's poverty, humility, and faith join her to God and simultaneously support weaker members of God's body. Perhaps there is an analogy between this mystical union and the material (and spiritual) union that common fasting rules would forge between Agnes's and Clare's communities. Clare's comments regarding tasting God's "hidden sweetness" and seasoning one's sacrifice "with salt" might or might not be related to the letter's attention to fasting.[40] Letter 4, which Clare composed shortly before she died, is her farewell to Agnes. She seems to be contemplating the end of her own earthly life as she reflects spiritually on the end awaiting those who yearn for God.

Despite the varying historical circumstances of the letters, a striking number of spiritual themes emerge across them. References in one letter elucidate those in others such that the letters can be fruitfully discussed as a coherent unit. Four complexly linked spiritual themes—poverty, the imitation of Christ, contemplation, and divinization—crescendo across them.[41] Clare's development of these themes could appear entirely spiritual in the sense of sounding theological points that rise above day-to-day realities. However, as I will show in my discussion, the themes are inextricably bound with the particular circumstances impinging upon Clare, Agnes, their communities, and probably some other communities as well within the Order of San Damiano. In this chapter I will focus especially upon the first three letters, all composed in the mid- to late 1230s. In them, Clare diplomatically raises three topics regarding the women's religious practice—their poverty, their fasting, and the religious rule they were bound to observe. Close attention to these topics foregrounds stark tensions that existed between Agnes's monastery in Prague and the papacy in the 1230s. Clare seems surely implicated in these struggles and they, in turn, inform the articulation of her spiritual themes. Clare and Agnes appear as allies uncomfortable with a papacy bent on enforcing a particular style of monastic life upon all religious women, a style at odds with Clare's vision of religious life as she understood it from Francis. That vision placed particular emphasis on the complex overlapping themes of poverty, the imitation of Christ, contemplation, and divinization.

Letter 1

Poverty is the theme that comes across most powerfully in the letters. For Clare, as for Francis, it was a multivalent leitmotif. "Poverty" denotes not only material poverty, but also humility, this too suggesting that Clare shared Francis's own understanding of poverty, which always entailed humility. Related motifs in Clare's letters include contempt for the world, praise of virginity, and embrace of the cross. As Frederic Raurell and Joan Mueller have shown, Clare's first letter, especially, echoes language found in the legend of the early virgin-martyr Agnes of Rome (d. ca. 304).[42] It plays on the opposition between Agnes of Prague's rejection of worldly honors and wealth (by her refusal to marry the emperor) and her choice of Jesus Christ as spouse, a marriage requiring her to be both virgin and poor. Clare wrote the letter around Pentecost (11 June) 1234, the day Agnes entered the monastery of Saint Savior.

The Franciscan virtues of poverty and humility are inextricably and repeatedly linked in Clare's other three letters as well. In her third letter, Clare says that she, Agnes, and the other sisters follow "in the footsteps of the poor and humble Jesus Christ."[43] This enables Agnes, like the Virgin who held Christ in her womb, to contain him who holds her and all things within himself.[44] In her second letter, Clare approvingly acknowledges Agnes to be "someone zealous for the holiest poverty, in a spirit of great humility."[45] In her last letter, she exclaims to Agnes, "O marvelous humility! O astonishing poverty!"[46]

Poverty is more than a spiritual theme, however lofty, in Clare's letters. Agnes wanted her monastery to emulate, at least in part, the strict material poverty practiced at San Damiano.[47] Agnes is sometimes, like Clare, set up as a poor woman contesting at every turn Gregory IX's wish that her monastery be secured by a regular source of revenue. Notably, with *Cum relicta seculi* (May 1235), Gregory established that Agnes's monastery would be permanently linked to the hospital of Saint Francis and its possessions.[48] Both entities were under papal control, a fact Gregory pointed out to Agnes shortly after she became a nun.[49] Barbara Newman wryly notes: "Although [Gregory] had granted St Clare her 'privilege of poverty' in 1228 under intense pressure, he was most reluctant to give Agnes a similar dispensation, and instead showered St Savior with endowments and exemptions that would have made a Benedictine abbess green with envy."[50]

Gregory's largess aside, it is not clear that Agnes, at the moment she was just beginning her religious life, had fully charted the ways her monastery would be poor. Gregory's *Cum relicta seculi* states clearly that she and her community petitioned (*vestris supplicationibus*) that their monastery be *permanently* linked to the hospital. They knew, of course, that the hospital had been generously endowed with income-producing lands by Agnes, her brother Přemysl, and her mother, Queen Constance.[51] Moreover, the letter's Latin allows that Gregory's grant of the hospital's revenues to the monastery formed part of the women's petition, notwithstanding some translations that affirm that Gregory foisted the revenues on the women.[52] Perhaps influenced by later hagiographic accounts, such translations retroject back into Agnes's monastic beginnings a commitment to material poverty that was not yet fully formed. Art historian Jeffrey Hamburger notes tellingly that Agnes's private living quarters about the time she entered the monastery were "of a size befitting her royal status."[53] In July 1235 Gregory made further provisions securing the economic health of her monastery.[54]

Letter 2

At some point, probably between May 1235, when the hospital and monastery were formally linked, and spring 1238, Agnes apparently contacted Clare for advice about her religious life. Clare's second letter indicates that Agnes was receiving diverse counsels. Clare forcefully urges Agnes to live in utmost poverty and to listen to the "Minister General Elias." This is Elias of Assisi, also known as Elias of Cortona, who governed the Lesser Brothers from 1232 to 1239 during which time the letter must have been written. Most scholars further narrow this letter to the years 1234–35 to 1238, precisely the period when Agnes was negotiating with the papacy as to the customs of religious life to be practiced in her monastery.

Clare writes briefly but says she knows that Agnes would gladly welcome a longer letter for her "consolation."[55] Someone in authority over Agnes had apparently been trying to weaken her proposal to pursue the perfection of religious life. Clare's opening greeting sets the theme for her letter: "Clare, useless and unworthy handmaid of the Poor Ladies, sends her greetings and the prayer that Agnes may always live in utmost poverty [*summa paupertate*]."[56] For Clare, poverty is intrinsic to perfection. She writes to Agnes that God "has made you shine with the honors of so much perfection . . . so that once you have been made a diligent imitator of the Father who is perfect, you may deserve to be made perfect." Extending the notion of Agnes as imitator, Clare elaborates that Agnes, despising an earthly kingdom and imperial marriage, has been made an "imitator of holiest poverty" (*aemula sanctissimae paupertatis*), one who with humility and love has "clung to the footsteps of him with whom you have been worthy to be united in marriage."[57] Imitating poverty and imitating the Father who is perfect are, if not one and the same, intimately allied.

Clare communicates her own tough tenacity, admonishing Agnes to "be mindful, like a second Rachel, of your purpose [*propositi*], always seeing your beginning [*videns principium*]."[58] The term *propositum*, it is worth noting, often denoted, like *forma vitae*, norms for a way of life.[59] "Rachel" in the Middle Ages was often a figure for contemplation.[60] She was also the younger, or "lesser" sister of Leah.[61] Early Christian writers such as Jerome (d. 419) and Augustine (d. 430) thought Rachel's name derived from the Hebrew terms "to see" and "to begin."[62] Thus, Clare reminds Agnes to be mindful, to hold before herself in a contemplative fashion her commitment, "always seeing [her] beginning."[63] Agnes the "poor virgin" and, one might add, the "lesser sister" should "embrace the Poor Christ," "gaze upon, examine [and] contemplate" him, "look upon and follow" the spouse "who made himself contemptible" for her sake and for whom she has, in imitation, made herself contemptible.[64] Clare quite possibly echoes this second letter many years later in her last letter when she divides Christ's life into three phases and associates its beginning (*principium*) with poverty. Indeed, poverty, the poverty and humility of the poor Christ, seemed to be the beginning and foundation of Clare's religious life. In her first two letters to Agnes, both penned when Agnes herself was beginning religious life, Clare hammers home that the foundation of Agnes's religious life should similarly be poverty and humility.

Gregory IX's bull canonizing Francis of Assisi in 1228 compares and contrasts interestingly with Clare's letter. The pope contrasts Rachel, who represents contemplation that is beautiful albeit sterile, with Leah, who represents a more fleshly fecundity. Francis descended, wrote Gregory, from Rachel to Leah so that he could scatter his seed and bear fruit that he would bring back to eternity.[65] Gregory thus captures an important duality in the life of Francis, who alternated between contemplative withdrawal from and active insertion within society. Clare's and Agnes's religious life, more singly focused on enclosed contemplative withdrawal, could, by contrast, be more simply associated with Rachel alone.

Clare is cautiously cryptic in her second letter about the person— probably a powerful ecclesiastic—whom Clare considered a threat to Agnes's religious life. The likeliest and indeed about the only obvious candidate, most scholars agree, is Gregory IX. Clare's first warning is oblique:

Confident, joyful, and eager, may you proceed with caution along
the path of blessedness, believing nothing, agreeing to nothing that
might turn you from this purpose [*proposito*] or place a stumbling-
block in your way that keeps you from fulfilling your vows to the
Most High in that perfection to which the Spirit of the Lord has
called you.[66]

Invoking the authority of the "Most High" provided Agnes an unassailable
religious rationale for parting ways with even the pope. Years later, the Franciscan Angelo Clareno (d. 1337) would consider Clare a saint because, to remain true to her commitment to poverty, she forthrightly refused to obey the
pope. Angelo was probably recalling the hagiographic accounts of Gregory's
attempt to press possessions upon Clare, but Clare's own words in this letter
confirm how fearless she could be. Remarkably, Angelo reported that Gregory
excommunicated Clare for her disobedience, a fact not verified in any other
source. Even so, Angelo's mistaken belief or polemical invention evokes what
appears to be a genuine facet of her personality.[67] Clare's letter also reveals her
to be a political pragmatist, advising Agnes to avail herself of a strategic ally,
Elias, against the unnamed authority:

Now concerning this, so that you may walk more tranquilly along
the way of the Lord's commands, follow the advice of our venerable
father, our Brother Elias, minister general. Prefer his advice to the
advice of others and consider it more precious to you than any gift.
Indeed, if someone tells you something else or suggests anything to
you that may hinder your perfection and that seems contrary to
your divine vocation, even though you must respect him, still do
not follow his advice; instead, poor virgin, embrace the Poor
Christ.[68]

"Our venerable father, our Brother Elias" Clare calls him. Some scholars
have pointed to the possessive pronoun "our" as a sign that Clare thought the
friars and sisters belonged to a single order.[69] Salimbene, who refers many
times to the "Order of St. Clare" in his chronicle, notably refers to Clare herself as pertaining to the "Order of St. Francis," a term he occasionally uses for
the friars' order.[70] It is probably closer to the mark to say that Clare thought
they belonged to a single family. Clare, at this point in history, would have
appreciated not only the juridical distinction between the Order of Lesser

Brothers, officially constituted once the pope approved their rule in 1223, and her own religious community, but also the now quite distinct lifestyles that separated the itinerant friars from the enclosed sisters. Clare's conscious quotation from Francis's *forma vivendi* in the 1253 rule suggests that even in their earliest years the men and women were two groups, both distinct and allied, for Francis states: "I resolve and promise for myself and for my brothers always to have the same loving care and special solicitude for you as for them."[71] Clare's repetition of "our" more tellingly connotes, to my mind, that Clare saw Elias as an ally in a conflict between "us" (Clare, Agnes, Elias, and others committed to Francis's vision of religious poverty) and "them" (Gregory IX and, quite possibly, friars who judged Francis's initial vision unsuitable for the friars' changed circumstances).[72] Notably, Clare's blood sister Agnes of Assisi seems also to involve Elias with negotiating her community's position on poverty before the papacy.[73]

Elias, who until recently was often demonized in scholarship relying on later polemical treatises, had, in fact, enjoyed Francis of Assisi's complete confidence during Francis's lifetime. He was awarded the plum position of provincial in the Holy Land.[74] Just a short time after Francis renounced his leadership in 1220 of the rapidly expanding group of friars, Elias took over command of the Lesser Brothers.[75] Francis respectfully called Elias minister general during these years.[76] Only after Francis's death in 1226 would Elias's post be downgraded by Thomas of Celano (and subsequent hagiographers and chroniclers) to "vicar"—a linguistic sleight of hand that allowed them to accentuate Francis's unique preeminence throughout his lifetime.[77] But even Thomas noted that Elias was chosen specifically by Francis to be his "mother" and to be "father of the other brothers."[78] Nothing seems to have ruffled the two men's close cooperation despite the fact that Elias's first stint as minister general from 1221 to 1227 was fraught with challenges. He had, for example, to win papal approval for the friars' rule and to resolve an array of knotty governance issues that might easily have stumped (or even undone) the singularly unbureaucratic and charismatic Francis. In 1227, Elias was replaced as minister general, only to be elected again in 1232. Francis's high regard for Elias, coupled with the fact that sources contemporary to Elias's periods of governance almost universally praise him,[79] make it unsurprising that Clare looked to Elias to defend her and Agnes's allegiance to Francis's ideals. Elias had, furthermore, a long and trusted relationship with Gregory IX, whom he represented, for example, in negotiations with Gregory's enemy, Frederick II.[80] Elias and Gregory, it is true, were about to clash seriously at the time Clare was telling Agnes to follow Elias's advice. In May 1239, Elias would be deposed from his second term as minister general and then excommunicated, but this was a future unknown to Clare when she was writing her second letter to Agnes.[81]

It appears that once Agnes became firmly committed to separating her monastery from the hospital of Saint Francis, she astutely used her considerable influence to urge Gregory to reverse his commitment that the two entities be linked. Gregory's correspondence with other women's monasteries shows that he was becoming increasingly convinced that enclosed women required a regular income in order to survive. In 1235, for example, he offered an indulgence of forty days to "all the faithful" in exchange for their charity to the nuns of Monteluce in Perugia whom he described as weighed down by extreme poverty.[82] Two years later he gave them a church with all its belongings, and two months after that he exempted them from paying the tithe on the lands he had given them.[83] But Agnes of Prague was seeking to emulate the life of poverty recommended to her by Clare. She was in a singular position to do so since she could rely on the support of a powerful intercessor, her brother, who in 1230 had become King Wenceslas I of Bohemia (d. 1253). In 1237 he wrote to Gregory, who needed the king as an ally against Frederick II, asking him to accede to his sister's wishes.[84] Just what those "wishes" were was apparently understood between the two men but not laid out explicitly in the letter.[85] It seems, however, that they might well have included Agnes's objection to her monastery's association with the hospital of Saint Francis.

Some combination of the formidable team composed of Agnes, her brother (King Wenceslas), Clare, and Elias ultimately persuaded Gregory to reverse his earlier agreement that the hospital be permanently linked to the monastery. The separation was final in April 1237, when the pope wrote to the abbess and enclosed sisters in Prague acknowledging King Wenceslas's and the local bishop's donation of the monastery's lands to the Holy See, without even mentioning the hospital of Saint Francis. Gregory tellingly calls the women the "enclosed nuns of San Damiano."[86] On the very same day, Gregory accepted the hospital of Saint Francis under his own protection and entrusted it and its related lands to an order of canons,[87] the Crusaders of the Red Star mentioned in Agnes's *Legend*. After this, momentously, Gregory wrote to Agnes confirming her renunciation of the hospital and granting her monastery a privilege of poverty, importantly echoing some of the very same language found in the Privilege he had granted to Clare and San Damiano: "you cannot be compelled to accept possessions."[88] Perhaps Clare's second letter had prompted Agnes's renunciation of the hospital. In any case, given the ex-alted economic and social status of many of the nuns in Agnes's monastery and the largess they received from the Bohemian nobility, Gregory may have had little fear that the women would suffer genuine want.[89] Even so, his will-ingness to reverse course belies attempts to paint him as the unmitigated vil-lain vis-à-vis Clare's and Agnes's projects for a religious life of poverty. He was perhaps simply and, one might argue, reasonably averse to cloistered women living without regular means of support. Yet, when faced with the dogged opposition of Clare, Agnes, and others, he also evinced a capacity for compro-mise. Somewhat more cynically, one might suppose that Gregory reversed his position due only to the overwhelming pressure of the King of Bohemia, whose alliance he needed, and perhaps that of other formidable opponents, possibly including Clare.

The poverty of Christ that Clare called Agnes to contemplate and imitate forges, according to Clare, a relationship with Christ more intimate than mar-riage. Clare frequently employs nuptial imagery in her letters to Agnes, im-ages she occasionally expresses in erotically evocative language. Such imagery was perfectly suited to Clare's correspondent since it played upon the well-known fact that Agnes had forgone marriage to an emperor in order to be-come a religious. Clare writes to her in her first letter: "you are now held fast in the embraces of the one who has adorned your breast with precious stones."[90] Years later, in 1253, she will paraphrase the Song of Songs: she imag-ines Agnes sighing after her heavenly Spouse who draws her into his wine cellar, "happily [*feliciter*] embraces" her, and kisses her with "the most blissful [*felicissimo*] kiss of [his] mouth."[91] That this apparently traditional nuptial im-agery evokes also, for Clare, poverty is made clear by her insertion of the ad-verb "happily" (*feliciter*) into the Song verse since that term came directly from Gregory's paraphrase of the same Song verse in the Privilege of Poverty he conceded to San Damiano in 1228.[92]

Nuptial imagery alone was insufficient to evoke the richly multilayered union with God that Clare describes. In her first letter to Agnes, she had called Agnes not only spouse but also "spouse and mother and sister of my Lord Jesus Christ." The triplet seems to have been central to Clare's thinking, for she repeated it in slightly adapted form some fifteen years later when she wrote her final letter to Agnes.[93] Once again, Clare's language echoes that of Francis, who called faithful men and women penitents "spouses, brothers, and mothers" of Jesus Christ.[94] As Giovanna La Grasta points out, Clare's use of nuptial imagery is specifically Franciscan.[95] Rather than evoking only the traditional notion of the female saint as the virgin who renounces earthly men to become the spouse of Christ, Clare's nuptial imagery sounds the dynamic Franciscan notion of following the poor Christ. The early hagiographic legends about Clare will mostly ignore this larger notion, describing her conventionally as a cloistered, monastic, virginal spouse of Christ and linking her poverty particularly to contemplation. Clare's spousal imagery in her second letter is more multilayered: she exhorts Agnes to contemplate and be like the poor Jesus. The union to which she calls Agnes falls just short of what might be termed divinization:

> If you suffer with him, with him you will reign,
> grieving with him, with him you will rejoice,
> dying with him on the cross of tribulation,
> with him among the splendors of the saints,
> you will possess heavenly mansions.[96]

Clare's description of Agnes's union with Christ is lyrically evocative, but there is still a certain externality separating the two. This disappears in Clare's third and fourth letters.

Letter 3

In Clare's third letter, she responds to Agnes's request for clarification regarding the practice of fasting vis-à-vis the church calendar and feast days. On the heels of having won a privilege of poverty in April 1238, Agnes tried to persuade Gregory to allow her monastery to observe a new *forma vitae* that she had devised, drawing, in part, on Francis's *forma vivendi*. As I elaborate in Chapter 6, on 11 May 1238, Gregory denied Agnes's request and definitively confirmed that his *forma vitae* was to be followed.[97] It was in this period, probably after Gregory quashed Agnes's own *forma vitae*, that Agnes sought Clare's advice about fasting practices. She may have been seeking a fallback plan so that her monastery might align at least with the fasting customs Francis had given San Damiano. As I will show, Clare probably responded between 11 May 1238, when Gregory rejected Agnes's *forma*, and 18 December 1238, when Gregory responded to Agnes's and her sisters' request about fasting.

Clare's two-part letter begins with a soaring spiritual sermon. She rejoices at Agnes's happiness and growth, progress Clare associates with Agnes's "following in the footsteps of the poor and humble Jesus Christ."[98] Clare is probably celebrating the privilege of poverty that Agnes and her community had just won. Clare's exultant tone almost mutes her periodic allusions to the enemies that would, if they could, defeat Agnes. These enemies seem in some instances to be spiritual, such as the "stratagems of the cunning enemy, the pride that destroys human nature, and the vanity that beguiles human hearts."[99] But elsewhere in the letter it seems Clare may be including actual human enemies who themselves pose spiritual threats. She advises Agnes to ignore "all those who in this deceitful and turbulent world ensnare their blind lovers."[100] Clare proposes the path of poverty and humility against the enemy's main snare, pride.[101] While her comments certainly regard Agnes's inner spiritual life, they likely concern concrete circumstances as well. Clare had already shown her willingness to be confrontational when she resisted Gregory's and Rainaldo's attempt to press possessions on San Damiano and when, in her second letter to Agnes, she referred in barely veiled language to an authority figure trying to turn Agnes from radical poverty. Since Clare notes in this third letter that proud kings and queens fail to recognize poverty and humility as the path to possession of Christ,[102] perhaps she has in mind someone suggesting a style of poverty seemingly more in keeping with Agnes's aristocratic lineage. She may even have been alluding to Agnes's lovingly protective mother, Queen Constance, and her brother, King Wenceslas.

Whatever the case, Clare's joyful confidence that Agnes is defeating and will continue to defeat such worldly enemies sets the letter's dominant tone. The Franciscan leitmotiv of following the poor and humble Christ, sounded in her first two letters, subtly changes in this letter in that the "following" becomes so intimate that the division between the follower and Christ dissolves. Clare's language evokes what came to be termed the mystical body, the single spiritual body that unites Christians with each other and with Christ. Since Agnes was intent on adopting some of San Damiano's religious practices, Clare may have introduced this theme to underscore the women's unity in Christ. Sharing her joy at Agnes's progress, Clare writes "and I breathe again in the Lord with elation equal to my knowledge and belief that you are supplying in wonderful ways what is lacking both in me and in the other sisters who are following in the footsteps of the poor and humble Jesus Christ."[103] Elaborating on her joy, she continues shortly thereafter: "And, to use the very words of the Apostle himself, I judge you a co-worker (1 Cor 3.9; Rom 16.3) of God himself and one who holds up the members of his ineffable Body who are giving way."[104]

In contrast to many discussions of the mystical body, which accentuate the headship of Christ over the rest of the lesser (human) members of the mystical body, Clare here points to Agnes's active collaboration with God. The drooping members of God's body recall not only the human members of God's body, but God's own suffering limbs in his human incarnation. God's and humans' participation in one body means that they cannot be spoken of discretely: when Agnes upholds other members, she is also upholding God and participating in his life-giving sustenance of others. Clare may well be thinking of herself and her sisters, since she has just told Agnes: "you are supplying in wonderful ways what is lacking both in me and in the other sisters."[105] Identifying Christ's body with the Church, she might even have had in mind the ways in which a commitment to poverty was renewing and uplifting the institution.[106]

Note too a certain play in Clare's words. When she writes "to use the very words of the Apostle himself," Clare is certainly conscious that St. Paul's words, included in the New Testament, are themselves God's own Word. Making God's Word her words is another way that Clare is assimilated into God. Commenting on the connection between contemplation and transformation, Clare suggests a theology of divinization: "Place your mind in the mirror of eternity; place your soul in the splendor of glory; place your heart in the figure of the divine substance; and through contemplation, transform your entire being into the image of the Divine One himself, so that you, yourself, may also experience what his friends experience when they taste the hidden sweetness that God alone has kept from the beginning for those who love him."[107] Clare's third letter has moved through four elements central to Clare's spirituality: (1) the practice of poverty (and humility), which is the foundation of (2) the imitation of Christ, (3) contemplation, and (4) divinization. Each flows seamlessly into the next element, as the one living poorly in imitation of Christ is drawn up into the very life of God.

Clare's triple counsel to Agnes to place her mind in "the mirror of eternity," her soul in "the splendor of glory," and her heart in "the figure of the divine substance"—all references to Christ—indicates that Agnes, or anyone else so doing, is contained within God. Clare does not mean that one enters into God in the sense of being drawn above or outside of this world. Clare instead consciously reverses this movement to restore a sort of equilibrium between God and humans whom she wants to depict in a single unity. She embraces a paradox: God brought down into humanity and individual humans, themselves, containing God. Clare's model is the Virgin Mary who "gave birth to a Son Whom the heavens could not contain" and who yet carried him in "the tiny enclosure of her sacred womb."[108] The "soul of a faithful person" is like Mary, writes Clare, because it is "greater than heaven, since the heavens and the rest of creation together cannot contain their Creator and only the soul of a faithful person is his dwelling place and throne."[109] Clare then completes the circle by reiterating in a single sentence that we contain God and God contains us: "So, just as the glorious Virgin of virgins carried him physically, so, you too, following in his footsteps especially those of humility and poverty, can without any doubt, always carry him spiritually in your chaste and virginal body, containing him by whom both you and all things are contained."[110] In contrast to Clare's this-worldly incarnational focus, later hagiographic depictions of her will make her into a supremely otherworldly figure. The mystical body that Clare evokes in her letters has both an otherworldly and this-worldly dimension. Poverty for Clare—and Francis—was not in the mold of early medieval monastics aiming to strip themselves of this-worldly possessions in order to attain heaven. The poverty that Clare preached to Agnes was a vehicle for identification with God, who had become human and poor. Joining themselves to the poor Christ made God present on earth, within history, and among humans.[111]

The last part of Clare's third letter includes her clarification—based on Francis's counsels—regarding the rules for fasting and abstention throughout the liturgical year. The very detail of this discussion allows us to date the letter with reasonable confidence. In a brief letter to Agnes's monastery dated 9 April 1237, Gregory noted that the abbess, with the counsel of the monastic visitator, could relax the perpetual fast, the "fasting every day" prescribed in his *forma vitae*. "Perpetual fasting" meant that a single daily meal could be taken of so-called Lenten foods, which likely excluded meat, dairy, and eggs.[112] Gregory said he was relaxing these fasting and abstention norms owing to the Prague monastery's cold and intemperate climate.[113] His dispensation probably continued in effect even after he reconfirmed his *forma vitae* for observance at Agnes's monastery in March 1238,[114] as made clear in his letter of 5 May 1238, which lays out in greater detail the fasting and abstention rules he wanted the women of Prague to follow.[115] These too were dispensations insofar as they relaxed what he had legislated in his *forma vitae*. So, for example, instead of the *forma vitae*'s "fasting every day," the sisters could take two meals and also eat dairy products on Sundays and Thursdays. Furthermore, where his *forma vitae* called for the women to fast on bread and water on four days of the week during the Greater Lent and three days of the week during the Lent of Saint Martin (Advent), his May 1238 letter allowed them on those

Table 2: Chronologically Ordered Comparison of Documents on Fasting

HUGO-GREGORY'S FORMA VITAE (ASSIGNED TO THE PRAGUE MONASTERY 1234, RECONFIRMED AND RESENT 4 MAR 1238)	Gregory, Pia meditationes pensantes (5 May 1238), to Abbess & Enclosed Handmaids of the Prague monastery	CLARE'S 3RD LETTER TO AGNES (PROBABLY BETWEEN 11 MAY AND 18 DECEMBER 1238)	Gregory, Ex parte carissime (18 Dec 1238)
	Circumstances: Since the cold climate makes the women unable to observe the Rule's (i.e., Forma vitae's) rigor, Gregory wants to temper its austerity.	Circumstances: Agnes has asked Clare to clarify what were the feasts that Francis had urged them to celebrate in a special way with various kinds of food.	Circumstances: Agnes and her sisters proposed to Gregory certain observances regarding when and when not to fast. He repeats these in the letter and grants their request, acknowledging that it is an exception to the "rule" [his forma vitae]. He said Agnes and her sisters had proposed:
Fasting PERPETUAL (i.e., one meal per day)	Fasting The Rule [Forma vitae] says you should ALWAYS FAST ON LENTEN FOOD (i.e., one meal per day) but [now] you may eat two meals Sundays and Thursdays	Fasting THE HEALTHY EAT LENTEN FARE EVERY DAY, INCLUDING FERIAL AND FEAST DAYS, but two meals ought to be taken on Sundays AND ON CHRISTMAS	Fasting THE HEALTHY EAT LENTEN FAST EVERY DAY, INCLUDING FEAST DAYS, but not on Sundays OR ON CHRISTMAS
Abstention [no allowance mentioned]	Abstention[1] ON WEDNESDAYS AND FRIDAYS OUTSIDE OF LENT NO POTAGE OR WINE (UNLESS IT IS A SAINT'S FEAST); FRUIT AND FRESH VEGETABLES ARE ALLOWED	Abstention Gregory allows milk products on Sundays and Thursdays	Abstention [no allowance mentioned]

Table 2: Chronologically Ordered Comparison of Documents on Fasting

Feast days	Feast days	Feast days	Feast days
NO ABSTENTION ON SAINTS' FEAST DAYS [without specifying feast days]	*No obligatory fasting on:* •*Easter*	FRANCIS SAID *no obligatory fasting:* •DURING THE ENTIRE *Easter* WEEK	[Agnes and sisters proposed] *no obligatory fasting on:* •THE ENTIRE *Easter* WEEK
	And the solemnities of: •*the Blessed Virgin Mary* •*the Apostles* •*Christmas*	And the feasts of: •*Holy Mary* •*the holy Apostles* UNLESS THE FEASTS OCCUR ON A FRIDAY [i.e., then there is fasting].	And the solemnities of: •*the Blessed Virgin* •*the Apostles* UNLESS THE FEASTS OCCUR ON A FRIDAY [i.e., then there is fasting]
		ON THURSDAYS DURING ORDINARY TIME, FASTING IS A PERSONAL CHOICE; EVEN SO, THE HEALTHY AND STRONG ALWAYS EAT LENTEN FARE [i.e., fast, except on Sundays & Christmas].	ON THURSDAYS DURING ORDINARY TIME, FASTING IS A PERSONAL CHOICE
Lents DURING THE GREATER LENT: BREAD AND WATER FOUR DAYS PER WEEK ST. MARTIN'S LENT [ADVENT]: BREAD AND WATER THREE DAYS PER WEEK	Lents ON THOSE DAYS WHICH THE RULE [*FORMA VITAE*] HOLDS YOU TO FAST ON BREAD AND WATER DURING THE GREATER LENT AND LESSER LENT [ADVENT], *you may have a repast, just as you do on all the other "lenten" days* [i.e., the "perpetual fast" of every day]	Lents [not mentioned]	Lents [not mentioned]

1. Gregory IX, *Licet velut ignis* (9 February 1237), in *BF* I, pp. 209-10, enjoined the abbesses and sisters of the Order of San Damiano, and any brothers dwelling with them (perhaps as questors or serving brothers) to the Cistercian practice of abstaining from meat.

days to have a repast similar to their practice on the other days when they did not have to abstain from all food except bread.[116]

By comparing Clare's third letter, written explicitly to respond to Agnes's request for clarification regarding fasting, with Gregory's *forma vitae* and his two dated letters, one can surmise that Agnes had asked for Clare's counsel only after the Prague monastery had received Gregory's fasting guidelines of 5 May 1238. One can unequivocally deduce, moreover, that Agnes then conveyed Clare's guidelines on fasting to Gregory and asked him to allow her monastery to adopt them. Table 2 facilitates this comparison by placing the documents in a proposed chronological order.[117] This points to the ways in which one document possibly (although not necessarily) influenced practices or language regarding practices found in the later documents.

Comparing a few points in Clare's third letter to Gregory's three documents suffices to show how Agnes used Clare's guidelines to try to influence Gregory's provisions for the Prague monastery. Clare noted (in agreement with Hugo-Gregory's *forma vitae*) that healthy sisters were to fast daily. In his May 1238 letter, Gregory named some exceptional days when the fast was suspended and the sisters could eat two meals. These included Easter week and the feasts of Christmas, the Blessed Virgin Mary, and the Apostles. Clare, who told Agnes that Francis wanted to suspend fasting on special days, named the same days as Gregory, but qualified that if the feasts of Mary or the Apostles fell on a Friday, then healthy sisters were obliged to fast. Here too Clare perhaps follows Francis, who in his rules singled out Friday as a special day of fast and whose "writing" she had just cited to Agnes.[118] Clare's advice seems clearly to have prompted Agnes's and her sisters' request to Gregory that he allow them to follow the same observances counseled by Clare. Thus in his December 1238 letter responding to Agnes and her sisters, Gregory repeats the details of their request before granting it. As Table 2 illustrates, the conformity between Clare's advice to Agnes and those details strongly suggests that Agnes wrote to Gregory only after she had received Clare's letter.[119] Notably, Gregory's letter does not mention Clare (or Francis or San Damiano). It would be interesting to know if Agnes and her sisters consciously chose either to mention to Gregory Clare's advocacy in favor of certain fasting practices or to omit it as the most politic approach to winning his concession. As his letters of April 1237 and May 1238 show, he was amenable to allowing monasteries to modify their observance of his *forma vitae* for reasons of climate or other particular circumstances. Now, in December 1238, he allowed Agnes's monastery to follow fasting practices in place at San Damiano.

Clare's third letter to Agnes allusively raises another practical (and controversial) question: what rule should the women be observing? Clare explicitly stated that the fasting rules she was laying out were drawn from Saint Francis's teaching. So even in the late 1230s, when Clare wrote this letter—years after Clare had agreed to accept Gregory IX's *forma vitae*—she was still looking to Francis as the ultimate arbiter regarding their religious practice. This is minimally true regarding fasting, as her letter indicates, but it is probably also true regarding other issues. In a passing phrase Clare reveals that she is drawing this teaching from a *written* document—what "blessed Francis's written text says" (*ut scriptum beati Francisci dicit*).[120] Despite having Gregory's *forma vitae*, Clare still had recourse to a text composed by Francis—by then dead some twelve years—when she advised Agnes about practices that Clare transparently conveys were still in place at San Damiano. This text is, unfortunately, no longer extant, but its ancestor was probably Francis's pithy *forma vivendi*, quoted within the *1253 forma vitae*, that set forth in broad, muscular language the central purpose of Clare's community. The more detailed text from which Clare now drew probably set forth a set of practices that had developed over time within San Damiano in conjunction with Francis's occasional guidance.[121] The prologue to the *1253 forma vitae* includes two related remarks: Bishop Rainaldo, the then protector of the Order of San Damiano, refers to what Francis had passed on to Clare and her sisters "in writing" (*scripto*); and the pope at that time, Innocent IV, similarly acknowledges that Francis had given the women a *formula*.[122] As Chapter 6 elaborates, Agnes was eager to have her monastery incorporate Francis's written guidelines into their daily life.

Before leaving Clare's third letter, it is worth noting that although the fasting regulations she advocated were exceptionally strict, she pointedly concluded her letter to Agnes counseling moderation, "because neither is our flesh the flesh of bronze nor our strength the strength of stone. . . . I am asking and begging in the Lord that you be restrained wisely, dearest one, and discreetly from the indiscreet and impossibly severe fasting that I know you have imposed upon yourself."[123] This moderating note will again be sounded in the *1253 forma vitae*.

Letter 4

One other letter from Clare to Agnes survives; it was written shortly before Clare's death in 1253, after a long hiatus in Clare's correspondence. I discuss

Letter 4 here to highlight the remarkably consistent contours of Clare's spiritual teaching over so many years but will return to it again in my discussion of the close of Clare's life.

Rather than any sort of qualitative change, a subtle shift in Clare's vision of religious life marks the letter. While in her first two letters she devoted more comment to the virtues of poverty and humility, together with the imitation of Christ, in her last two letters of ca. 1237–1238 and 1253, she tipped the balance toward contemplation and divinization. This shift makes sense in light of the letters' historical circumstances. Clare's first two letters were written when Agnes was beginning religious life, striving to establish particular religious customs and grasp their spiritual underpinnings. By the third letter, with Agnes fully invested in aligning her monastery with the customs of San Damiano, Clare explicitly acknowledged Agnes's advances and broached in greater depth the topics of contemplation and mystical union with God.

Her greeting in Letter 4 again evokes the notion of the mystical body: she calls Agnes "the other half" of her soul. Imitation of Christ in this letter is patterned less on the human Christ, whose life one was to copy, than the divine Christ. Imitating or following the human Christ, however closely, suggests a certain distance: one places one's feet in the footsteps left behind by the other, the one who is always just ahead. But the divine Christ Clare invokes in her last letter is enjoyed now; there is sensual contact, even penetration, as porous boundaries are continually crossed: one shares in a "sacred banquet," takes in a "glorious vision," and, drawn into the "wine cellar," is kissed with the "kiss of [His] mouth."[124] Of course, this was only a foretaste of a fuller future enjoyment. Clare's letter is eschatological, pointing to that future beyond, all the while insisting that it can be tasted even now through contemplation.

Significantly, Clare returns to a metaphor she briefly introduced in her third letter when she advised Agnes to "place your mind in the mirror of eternity."[125] Clare now elaborates, interweaving the themes of imitation, contemplation, and divinization. The vision of Christ, she announces, is the "mirror without tarnish": "Look into this mirror every day, O queen, spouse of Jesus Christ, and continually examine your face in it, so that in this way you may adorn yourself completely." The spouse, Agnes, is to wear "flowers and garments made of all the virtues," a phrase that recalls Clare's first letter when she explained how the spouse, Christ, would adorn Agnes with metaphorical gems.[126]

Clare seems acutely aware of her own approaching death which, for her, represented a passage to full life with God. She retrospectively traces the trajectory of the spiritual life through three stages, correlating them, respectively, with the virtues of poverty, humility, and love. Those first virtues of poverty and humility flourish into love, the fruit of contemplation and the earthly beginning of divinization. She joins poverty and humility to love in two ways. First, she shows how poverty and humility, together with love, all reside within the mirror one contemplates: "Moreover, in this mirror shine blessed poverty, holy humility, and love [*caritas*] beyond words, as you will be able, with God's grace to contemplate throughout the entire mirror."[127] The mirror metaphor plays off the ancient Christian belief that humans are made "in the image and likeness" of God. Although the image was subsequently tarnished by sin, all are called to recover their resemblance to Christ, God's perfect Image.[128] Clare exhorts Agnes to contemplate this untarnished mirror, Christ, because it will reflect back to Agnes her true resemblance to him. She sees within that Christ-mirror the virtues she must imitate, namely, poverty, humility, and love.

Second, Clare looks both back to the foundational virtues of poverty and humility and forward to the future deified life of love. She does so by describing Christ, the mirror, in three distinct temporal periods—a beginning (*principium*), a middle, and an end.[129] His life begins in poverty: "Look closely, I say, to the beginning of the life of this admired one, indeed at the poverty of him who was wrapped in swaddling clothes and placed in a manger."[130] This beginning recalls Clare's admonition to Agnes regarding poverty in her second letter, when she told Agnes to be like a second Rachel, remembering her "purpose [*propositum*]" and "always seeing your beginning [*principium*]."[131] As then, Clare now also speaks of poverty and humility as distinct yet inextricably related virtues. She concludes her commentary on the first period of Christ's life: "O marvelous humility! O astonishing poverty! The King of the angels, the Lord of heaven and earth is laid to rest in a manger!"[132] Clare associates Christ's midlife with humility, then again, in the same breath, rejoins it to poverty: "Consider the midst of his life, his humility, or at least his blessed poverty, the countless hardships, and the punishments that he endured for the redemption of the human race." The end of Christ's life is characterized by love: "Indeed, ponder the final days of this mirrored one, contemplate the ineffable love [*caritatem*] with which he was willing to suffer on the tree of the cross and to die there a kind of death that is more shameful than any other."[133]

Like earlier letters, this one too is bound to its immediate historical circumstances. Beneath Clare's rhetorically charged language that seems to soar above the mundane world lies her awareness of her own imminent death, transformation, and union with God. Steeped in Scripture by her years of li-turgical prayer, she probably recalled as she wrote this letter what the evange-list John wrote in another letter: "we know that when he shall appear we shall be like him, for we shall see him as he is."[134] Perhaps too she recalled the apostle Paul, whose words she had made her own in her third letter: "We see now in a mirror darkly but then face to face."[135] Paul then recalls the virtues which will last: faith, hope, and love. Clare would certainly have agreed with Paul that love is the greatest virtue, but as her fourth letter shows, Clare's trip-let of virtues is Francis's rather than Paul's: for Clare, love is the culmination of a life of poverty and humility. Yet, however elevated the language of Clare's last epistle, it too was rooted in the deep soil of her this-worldly battles, as my discussion of the next fifteen years separating this last letter from her earlier letters will show. In fact, when I return to Clare's fourth letter again in Chap-ter 9, I will be able to show how Clare's apparently otherworldly focus in this last letter is only part of the story, for Clare has subtly imbedded within the letter another decidedly this-worldly message.

Chapter 6

Contested Rules, Late 1230s to ca. 1246

Clare's voice falls silent after her third letter to Agnes of Prague, around 1238, until shortly before her death in 1253. We learn narrative details about Clare's life in this time only in the saint-making *Acts* recorded for her canonization process in late 1253. Two miraculous cures attributed to Clare can be dated, respectively, to 1239 and 1241.[1] Another colorful incident took place in 1246 when a large monastery door fell on Clare. Some sisters feared Clare had been killed, but when three brothers ran and lifted the door, they found her unharmed.[2] The sisters' testimonies indicate that Clare's thaumaturgical power within San Damiano had continued since 1212, when a jar of oil had miraculously refilled. The canonization commissioners would certainly have welcomed such reports.

Although Clare remains a mostly opaque figure during these years, papal letters offer arresting details about religious women in the monasteries most closely allied with San Damiano. They suggest some of the very this-worldly issues that probably preoccupied Clare and her sisters. More particularly, several letters make pointed comments revolving around the papacy's ongoing attempts to effectively regulate the lives of the women in the Order of San Damiano.

Gregory Reconfirms His *Forma Vitae* (1238)

In the late 1230s, Gregory IX reconfirmed and reissued his *forma vitae* for all the monasteries in the Order of San Damiano. Significantly, the earliest known version was sent to Agnes of Prague's monastery on 4 March 1238.[3] He reissued it when an array of neuralgic points impinged upon the sisters' relationship with the papacy. Indeed, an air of contestation surrounded Gregory's—and after him, Innocent IV's—dealings with many of the order's monasteries. All the conflicts seem to revolve around the women's desires to align their communities more closely with Francis's and Clare's interpretation of religious life. This includes Agnes's failed attempt to receive papal permission to follow Clare's and Francis's advice on fasting practices, as discussed in Chapter 5. Further conflicts that I explore in this chapter include Agnes's bid to make Francis's *forma vitae* part of her monastery's rule, efforts by the sisters of Monteluce in Perugia to divest themselves of property that Gregory gave them, and numerous monasteries' petitions to jettison entirely their obligation to observe the Rule of Benedict.

Gregory showed himself willing to bend on some matters. He relaxed some fasting and clothing prescriptions for monasteries in cold climates, such as Prague.[4] He allowed Agnes of Prague (rather than her entire monastery) to view the solemnity of the Mass five times a year, something impossible according to his *forma vitae*, which required that a cloth cover the grille joining the sisters' quarters to the chapel.[5] Her petition to physically see the liturgy dovetails with her *vita*'s report that she loved the beauty of churches and "richly furnished" her convent with "precious ornaments pertaining to divine services."[6] Gregory's mitigations reflect, on the one hand, the women's desire for diversity in adhering to his *forma vitae* and, on the other hand, their acute consciousness that departures from the rule—even a commonsensical request regarding the need for warmer clothing in cold climates—required explicit papal approval. Gregory could accede to such requests precisely because "exceptionally" mitigating the rule was another way to reiterate its binding normativity.

But Gregory would brook no diversity on matters he thought central to the good ordering of religious life. Well-suited to his profession of canon law, he is aptly characterized as a man with a legal—some would say a "legalistic"—cast of mind. He appreciated the charismatic and poetic Francis, but also valued law, order, and uniformity. Gregory's guiding hand had touched nearly all the early Franciscan rules. He had been directly involved with the composition and papal approval of Francis's 1223 rule. He similarly oversaw the 1221 *Memoriale propositi*, the rule intended to regulate the lives of lay penitents.[7] His *forma vitae* for the monasteries in his order for women was simply one more instance of his project to regulate all the various religious lifestyles (*religiones*) he encountered. It echoed the policies of Innocent III and Honorius III before him and embraced not only Franciscans, but Dominicans and other orders as well.[8]

Perhaps Gregory thought this reconfirmation with its insistence upon full compliance would stem the sisters' petitions for certain freedoms from the *forma vitae*'s prescriptions. That would prove not to be the case.

Gregory Rejects Agnes of Prague's and Francis's *Formae Vitae* (1238)

Agnes of Prague provides the first and perhaps boldest example of resistance. Around the time of—but likely before—her attempt to persuade Gregory to allow her monastery to adopt Francis's rules on fasting, she tried to replace his *forma vitae* with her own. In this light, her gambit with Clare for adopting Francis's fasting rules was probably a fallback position that followed upon Gregory's refusal to ratify her version of a *forma vitae*. In his letter of 11 May 1238 to Agnes, he states she submitted a new *forma vitae* that combined passages from the "rule of the Order of San Damiano" (as Gregory was then identifying his *forma vitae*) with Francis's *formula vitae*, a text that had clearly evolved over time. As early as 1219 Gregory, then Cardinal Hugo, had permitted the nuns of Monticelli to adopt San Damiano's "regular observances" (*observantias regulares*), a phrase probably indicating a written document informed by Francis. Around 1238, when Clare advised Agnes on fasting, she noted she was drawing on what "blessed Francis's written text says" (*ut scriptum beati Francisci dicit*).[9] Now, Gregory's letter to Agnes similarly attests to a written document. He describes Francis's *formula vitae* as simple—indeed, "facile" is actually more on the mark. Gregory was likely quite intentional in using the diminutive *formula* to refer to Francis's *forma*. In a dense passage, Gregory recalls the time when he was still a cardinal:

> Saint Francis gave [Clare and her sisters] not solid food, but that which seemed suited to newborns, a milk drink, a *formula vitae*. Long ago, it was brought to us on a small leaf of paper by our beloved son, the Prior of the hospital of Saint Francis in Prague. A discreet and prudent man, he humbly entreated that We confirm by apostolic authority a *forma*, composed from the aforementioned *formula* and certain chapters contained in the rule of the Order of Blessed Damiano, presented to us by him under your seal.[10]

The dizzying number of rules named in this passage includes, first, Francis's *formula vitae*. Second is a *forma* (i.e., "form of life") that Agnes seems to have put together, quite possibly with the help of the prior of the hospital of Saint Francis. It drew on Francis's *formula vitae* and also passages from a third rule, the "rule" of the Order of San Damiano, Gregory's own *forma vitae*. Apparently Agnes was trying to alter it so that her monastery might more closely resemble the women's religious life prescribed by Francis. Quite likely, either Clare or the friars advising Agnes—or both—had been urging Agnes to follow this path. Francis's close companion Elias, whom Clare mentioned in her second letter to Agnes, figured importantly among Agnes's counselors. What a loss that her *forma vitae* neither survives nor is described in any detail by Gregory.

Gregory issued a resounding "No" to Agnes's entrepreneurial legislation, which he elaborated in three points. Gregory writes in his first point that Clare and her sisters "solemnly professed that *Rule* [Gregory's *forma vitae*] which was composed with careful zeal and accepted by St. Francis, and afterward confirmed by the same Pope Honorius."[11] The surprising claim that Francis "accepted" the prelate's *forma vitae* should be considered alongside other white lies in this passage. Gregory states that the *forma vitae* "was composed with careful zeal." In fact, it shows little significant order, repeats itself needlessly, duplicates what the Rule of Benedict had stated more clearly, and devotes inordinate attention to some topics while entirely disregarding others that would appear in any carefully executed religious legislation.[12] Another white lie regards Gregory's repeated and loose use of the term "rule" (*regula*). His conscious semantic choice to now call his *forma vitae* a rule conferred on it an official canonical status it did not have. It is true his *forma vitae* had been officially approved by Pope Honorius III, whereas Francis's "*formula*" and Agnes's proposed *forma vitae* had no official ecclesiastical standing whatsoever. But Gregory's *forma vitae* had been consistently given to monasteries along with the Rule of Benedict precisely because a rule, not just a *forma vitae*, had been mandated by the Fourth Lateran Council.[13] This was certainly one of the reasons he initially called his text a *forma vitae*. But by 1238 when he wrote to Agnes, his order was firmly established and he was the reigning pope. So much time had passed since Lateran IV and circumstances had so changed that he probably felt entitled to call his *forma vitae* a rule. So he now used the term "rule" to elide two texts, his *forma vitae* and the Rule of Benedict, effectively hiding the former under cover of the latter.

Gregory's inflated use of the term "rule" and his exaggerated claim that it had been carefully composed suggest one should be circumspect as well in evaluating his claim that Francis had accepted his rule. Gregory is writing revisionist history, creating a new story line to strengthen his position. There is no other reliable early evidence that Francis ever explicitly accepted Gregory's *forma vitae*—none during Francis's lifetime, none even in the thirteenth-century hagiographies of Francis that consistently vaunt the friendly relationship between the two men. In Gregory's early letters to women's monasteries joining his order, he referred to his *forma vitae*, yet he never connected it with Francis. Nor did his written form for transferring religious houses to his order mention Francis. Certainly the politically astute Gregory would have recognized that name-dropping "Francis" alongside his *forma vitae* would have given it just the stature it needed to attract houses of penitent women. It is incredible that he would have remained silent on this point. Years later, Gregory's successor Innocent IV wrote to Agnes, lifting points almost verbatim from Gregory's 1238 letter with its outsized claims. But after Innocent similarly stated that the *forma vitae* had been "composed with careful zeal," he tellingly omitted the grandiose claim that it had been "accepted" by Francis.[14]

The timing of Gregory's assertion that Francis accepted his *forma vitae* is also too convenient. He articulated and inserted it into a letter to Agnes of Prague, a woman bent on aligning her monastery with San Damiano and Francis's teachings. Perhaps most importantly, Francis, long dead, was unable to contest Gregory's claim. At the very moment the pope needed to shore up the Franciscan credentials of his order and rule, he knew he could safely invoke the saint's authority. It is also no coincidence that just two days before Gregory's 11 May letter to Agnes, certainly after he had received her proposed *forma vitae*, he had written to her with another startling claim: Francis had "instituted three Orders [*tribus Ordinibus*] throughout the world."[15] Gregory here shows transparently that he is not above stretching the truth. It was well known that Francis inspired numerous laypeople to undertake lives of poverty and penitence, but he neither instituted nor founded an institutional entity that could be qualified as a lay order in the sense of a discrete body with a rule and governance structure.[16] It was Gregory, the legislator, who redacted a rule in 1221 for these penitents, thereby founding such an order. He now similarly attributed his institution of an order of monastic nuns to Francis, helped, no doubt, by Julian of Speyer's earlier claim along these same lines.[17]

Making Francis the founder nicely set the stage for Gregory's claim two days later on 11 May: if Francis, the alleged founder of the women's order, himself accepted Gregory's *forma vitae*, then why should the pope even consider Agnes's request to follow a *forma vitae* that drew on Francis's earlier *formula*? Gregory's second point aims to strengthen his case: "Clare and her sisters put aside the *formula* [of Francis] and have been observing the same *Rule* [that is, Gregory's *forma vitae*; perhaps also the Rule of Benedict] in a laudable manner from the time of their profession [*Professionis*] until the present."[18] Regardless of when this "profession" took place, there are strong reasons to believe Clare had never put aside Francis's *forma*, albeit she may have been sensibly discreet about publicizing this fact. Robinson describes Gregory's claim that Clare and her sisters were laudably observing Gregory's rule as "an assertion in which the wish may well have been 'father of the thought.'"[19]

True to his own centralizing style, Gregory in his third and final point rejecting Agnes's *forma* declares that it had "been determined that this *Rule* [Gregory's] be uniformly observed everywhere by all who profess it" and that "grave and insupportable scandal" would arise from any deviations from his rule. "Other Sisters of this Order . . . seeing the integrity of the *Rule* violated, may with disturbed hearts waver in its observance. God forbid!" Why then, does Gregory conclude by noting that mitigations previously granted to Agnes's monastery allowing the women to adapt or ignore certain provisions of his rule would remain in effect? He would, moreover, gladly consider future requests to "temper the rigor of some aspects of the *Rule*."[20] So much for the "insupportable scandal" aroused by diversity. In fact, a quick perusal of the *Bullarium Franciscanum* and its hundreds of papal letters shows that Gregory (and other popes) showered women's monasteries with exceptions to the rule regarding clothes, fasts, property, and so forth.

Indeed, it was not diversity per se that proved so threatening as Francis's very *forma vitae*. Brought to Gregory on what he describes as "a small leaf of paper," it might have contained prescriptions explicitly at odds with Gregory's well-honed convictions regarding women's monastic life. The danger of Francis's milk-drink-parading-as-a-rule was probably its very failure to mold penitent women into regulated, enclosed monastic nuns, secured by income.

Revealingly, Gregory cryptically alluded to forces aligned against him. After ordering Agnes to obey, he added that she should disregard "whatever might be suggested to you by someone who maybe zealous, but has no knowledge."[21] Gregory is perhaps making a veiled reference to Clare or Elias, both advocates of Francis's *forma* for religious life. Had word reached him of Clare's earlier counsel to Agnes to prefer Elias's advice over that of "someone" (quite possibly Gregory) who deserved respect but did not understand Agnes's vocation?[22] In any case, Agnes, on the receiving end of both Clare's and Gregory's cautionary advice not to listen to an ill-advised "someone," could hardly have

avoided seeing Gregory's letter as a tit-for-tat against Clare's and Elias's pro-
posals. Gregory possibly had Elias and other friar-advisers in mind when he
wrote in another letter "to all the faithful" in 1236 reminding them to respect
his *forma vitae*'s strictures against freely entering the monasteries of the Order
of San Damiano.[23] The Franciscan chronicler Thomas of Eccleston, although
not always well informed, later tellingly linked Gregory's excommunication of
Elias with his association with the "poor ladies": Brother Elias "went without
permission and against the general prohibition of the minister general [Albert
of Pisa] to visit the houses of the Poor Ladies; for this reason he seems to have
incurred the sentence of excommunication decreed by the pope [Gregory
IX]."[24] Gregory respected Elias but would have rejected his meddling with the
Order of San Damiano.

Who Really Ruled San Damiano?

The disjuncture between religious life envisioned by Clare and defined by
Gregory has prompted numerous scholars to speculate about Clare's allegiance
to his *forma vitae*. At one extreme, Heribert Roggen and Paschal Robinson
have wondered if Clare and the sisters of San Damiano ever truly observed
Gregory's rule.[25] At another extreme, Chiara Augusta Lainati and Ignacio
Omaechevarría have said that there is no reason at all to mistrust Gregory's 1238
testimony (echoed, in part, by Innocent IV) that Clare had put aside Francis's
formula and observed Gregory's rule.[26] Papal pronouncements aside, a review of
four concrete topics—enclosure, poverty, the sisters' relationship with the friars,
and fasting—shows that, on balance, the women of San Damiano were adhering to Francis's rather than Gregory's prescriptions for religious life.

Enclosure, so strictly mandated in Gregory's *forma vitae*, has often been
suggested as a feature of his rule that would not have been to Clare's liking. Of
the four topics, it is the only one for which we have no explicit evidence of
Francis's wishes for Clare and her sisters. Perhaps that helps explain why no
stark opposition can be established between Gregory's wishes and the practice
(or wishes) of the sisters of San Damiano. As I showed in Chapter 2, Jacques
de Vitry's testimony about "lesser sisters" is insufficient to prove whether the
San Damiano community initially observed enclosure or not. Like penitent
women allied with other orders such as the Cistercians, it is plausible that the
San Damiano women managed a hospice and observed an informal semi-
enclosure or even none at all.[27] After Clare's death, her sisters recounted that

when she heard of five friars who had been martyred in Morocco in 1220, she too yearned for martyrdom,[28] but such a holy desire hardly establishes Clare's lack of allegiance to enclosure, as some suggest.[29] The *1253 forma vitae* that Clare helped compose shortly before her death somewhat relaxes enclosure compared to Gregory's rule, but it enforces it nonetheless. Lainati argues that if Clare had the mettle to resist Gregory when he wanted her to accept possessions for her monastery, then she could just as well have resisted him on enclosure too had she strongly opposed it.[30] Might Clare's acceptance of enclosure have constituted a sort of trade-off for winning the Privilege of Poverty? In sum, the evidence is simply too thin to establish Clare's attitude toward Gregory's imposition of enclosure.

While enclosure permeates Gregory's *forma vitae*, poverty—so central to Francis's vision of religious life—is conspicuous by its absence. Poverty had been a dominant trait of many of the religious houses Gregory first drew into his order. Perhaps for that reason he felt little compelled to say much about it, its practice being simply assumed and summed up in the order's early and oft-used title, the "poor enclosed nuns." Even so, it is striking that aside from a few comments regarding the women's ascetic life—their meager clothing, bedding, and so forth—the *forma vitae* does not treat poverty as a theme. This silence made the more detailed Rule of Benedict, by default, the text that regulated the women's poverty and possessions. Benedict stated that any man with possessions who joined the monastery had to give them all to the poor or to the monastery.[31] Insisting on the individual poverty of each monk, Benedict permitted corporate ownership of lands and other goods. Francis, in contrast, insisted on both individual and corporate poverty for his brothers. This seems to have been Clare's and her sisters' ideal as well, although as I show further below, their poverty did not entirely prohibit corporate property. Like Francis's 1221 and 1223 rules, the 1253 rule recommended that a woman entering the order "go and sell all that she has" and "distribute the proceeds to the poor" (with no allowance that anything be given to the monastery).[32] Clare wrote in that rule that Francis was "moved by piety" to write his *forma vivendi* for the sisters when he saw that they "held as great delights" "poverty, hard work, trial, shame, [and] contempt of the world."[33] It was owing to the sisters' choice to live "according to the perfection of the gospel," which for Francis always entailed radical poverty, that he promised that his friars would always "have the same loving care and special solicitude" for the women that he himself had. Gregory had to concede to Clare the Privilege of Poverty, giving the women license to refuse possessions, precisely because he accepted the traditional monastic view of poverty articulated in Benedict's rule. Regarding religious poverty, Clare and her community thus conformed to Francis's *forma vivendi* rather than Gregory's *forma vitae*. Clare's correspondence with Agnes points also to her wish that the Prague community similarly adopt Francis's vision of poverty and resist Gregory's material endowments. In her third letter, Clare appears to celebrate the Prague monastery's reception of its own privilege of poverty.

Clare similarly stands with Francis rather than Gregory on the topic of the sisters' relationship with the friars. Gregory's *forma vitae* does not even mention Francis, a glaring omission given Gregory's (later) claims that Francis "accepted" Gregory's rule and "founded" the women's order. His decree *Quo elongati* (1230) threatened to severely limit the friars' access to San Damiano. His categorical rejection of Agnes's 1238 petition to incorporate Francis's *forma* as part of the Prague monastery's observance showed that the pope had little sympathy for preserving what must have been a profound symbol for women committed to maintaining their ties with the saint. But Clare—and Agnes too, it appears—saw their communities as integrally tied to Francis's family. Clare had to react swiftly to reverse Gregory's *Quo elongati* and ensure that the friars could continue to minister to her sisters. She was probably evoking the shared lineage between sisters and friars when, in a letter to Agnes, she referred to the then minister general of the friars as "Our venerable father, our Brother Elias."[34] This is certainly why she included Francis's verbatim promise that the friars would always show "loving care and special solicitude" for her sisters in the rule she coauthored shortly before her death. The San Damiano women surely preferred Francis's promise of relationship with the friars over Gregory's rule, which simply ignored the topic.

The fourth and final topic of fasting presents incontrovertible evidence that San Damiano was not conforming to Gregory's guidelines. Clare's third letter to Agnes laid out the fasting practices that Clare had in writing from Francis. These differed markedly from Gregory's guidelines in the *forma vitae* and also from the exceptions he permitted at the Prague monastery. Clare's letter, as discussed in Chapter 5, shows that the San Damiano community was abiding by Francis's teachings.

Thus, Clare's stance on poverty, relationship with the friars, and fasting all lead to the conclusion that Clare and her sisters hewed to Francis's teachings. Therefore, to accept at face value Gregory's (and later Innocent's) claim that Clare laudably observed Gregory's *forma vitae* ignores evidence regarding the actual practices in place at San Damiano. It also underestimates Gregory's willingness to adapt the truth for what he believed was a good cause. Indeed, as Robinson surmised, Gregory's assertion was mere wishful thinking.[35] Whatever his *forma vitae*'s formal status at San Damiano, Clare's allegiance was to Francis's *forma vivendi*. The San Damiano community, like so many religious communities before them, felt free to adapt their rule as they saw fit.[36] In fact, as I discuss in Chapter 7, Innocent IV himself would soon state that the Rule of Benedict bound women in the Order of San Damiano to simply observe only the three vows in general, rather than the rule's many particular provisions.

Poverty and Possessions Contested: The Sisters of Monteluce

One wonders whether Clare would have objected to Gregory's *forma vitae* being observed by other monasteries of the Order of San Damiano. Before the revised historiography of the Order of San Damiano, when historians thought of Clare and Francis as its founders, it made sense to think that Clare would take an active interest in the rule assigned to all the monasteries in *her* order. Knowing now, however, that San Damiano was incorporated into an order already established and managed by the papacy throws Clare's investment in the order's many and diverse monasteries into question.

Monasteries in the towns of Spello, Foligno, Perugia (Monteluce), Arezzo, Monticelli (near Florence), and Prague would have interested Clare[37] because they wanted to emulate San Damiano's practices. Clare sent her sisters to some monasteries to teach San Damiano's way of life. Clare may have even been involved in the purchase of land for the Foligno monastery.[38] Clare and Elias were apparently quite interested in Agnes of Prague's and Agnes of Assisi's monasteries, especially regarding poverty, as correspondence with the two women shows.

Clare never mentions the monastery of Monteluce, but it may be where her own blood sister Agnes had moved, instead of to the more often cited Monticelli.[39] In any case, papal letters provide tantalizing evidence regarding the Monteluce sisters' dramatic struggle to divest themselves of corporate property. Indeed, they seem to have changed course several times in their practice—and perhaps also in their embrace—of material poverty. Pope Honorius classed them among those women desirous of fleeing worldly riches when Hugo accepted them into his new network of religious houses under the Holy See in 1218. They were expected to remain a poor community.[40] In

January 1228 Hugo, now Pope Gregory, granted them the right to receive some books, a small altar, and other possessions donated to them by a Brother Angelo. Under pain of excommunication, the pope prohibited them from selling, donating, or otherwise alienating these things.[41] In June 1229 he granted them a privilege of poverty. Using language almost identical to the Privilege he issued San Damiano, Gregory notes that the sisters themselves requested the privilege: "Desiring to be dedicated only to the Lord, you have given up your longing for temporal goods. Because of this, you sell all things, give to the poor, and propose to have no possessions, clinging in all things to His footprints who, for us, was made poor, the way, the truth and the life."[42] By July 1231, perhaps finding themselves in difficult economic straits, the nuns accepted (or had imposed upon them?) Gregory's own donation to them of a mill, fields, vineyards, olive groves, and gardens.[43] Over the course of the next few years, the pope continued to assist them with various concessions and favors. For example, describing the nuns as burdened by great poverty, he issued an indulgence to Christians who would give alms to the monastery and another to pilgrims who would visit the site.[44] Gregory was clearly determined to place their monastery on a firm economic footing.

But at some point, perhaps after exempting the nuns from a tithe they owed the papacy for a church he gave them in 1237,[45] it appears the women either had a change of heart and no longer wanted so many possessions or had, perhaps, never welcomed Gregory's largess and decided to reject it. In March 1239 Gregory shot off a letter forbidding them in the direst of language from selling, exchanging, or otherwise alienating any of their property without first receiving express permission from the Holy See. He had evidently got wind of or had reason to fear that the Monteluce women had plans to give up some property that he believed essential to the good ordering of their religious life. Gregory sent similar letters, about this time, to the monasteries of Spoleto and Spello, and quite possibly others as well.[46] It had been only about a year since Gregory had allowed Agnes of Prague's monastery to separate from the income-generating hospital of Saint Francis. Perhaps he worried that her success in renouncing property was giving other monasteries similar ideas.

Then, remarkably, at some point after Gregory's stern prohibition, the nuns of Monteluce (but not Spoleto or Spello) went ahead anyway and alienated property without obtaining the requisite papal permission.[47] We know this because Gregory's successor, Innocent IV, wrote to the bishop of Perugia in May 1244 telling him to recover the nuns' possessions and to tell them they should not do this again.[48] Whether the nuns had openly defied the papacy or just taken clever advantage of a vacancy in the Holy See from November 1241 until Innocent IV's election in June 1243 is not clear. The women's shifting economic fortunes do make clear, however, that poverty and possessions continued to be a neuralgic point between the papacy and certain monasteries of the Order of San Damiano.

Gregory's thinking on the subject of property had probably evolved since he was papal legate, from an early insistence that the monasteries remain poor to an acknowledgment that cloistered monasteries required more support.[49] At that earlier time, religious houses had been received into the new order and granted episcopal exemptions with the clear stipulation that they had to remain without property. But years of experience seem to have led Gregory to believe that property was a necessary condition for good religious observance.

Excursus: Absolute Poverty and San Damiano's Sale of Land

For Gregory, religious poverty was not an all or nothing issue; it was painted in shades of gray rather than black and white. His tempered approach is often contrasted with Clare of Assisi's more radical stance. But it is worth considering more closely the meaning of phrases often attached to Clare's vision of poverty, phrases such as "absolute poverty" and living without "any possessions whatsoever." Such language evokes an ostensibly black and white world that Gregory rejected and that Clare embraced. It is true, also, that the Privilege Gregory granted the women of San Damiano appeared semantically more radical than the almost identical privilege conceded to the nuns of Monteluce. Whereas Gregory freed the sisters of Monteluce from accepting "any possessions," he freed the San Damiano women from accepting "any possessions whatsoever" (*nullas omnino possessiones*).[50] Whether this is a distinction without a difference or something more, it is worth underlining a point seldom discussed: the women of San Damiano owned possessions, not only clothing, housing, and food, but also land. A legal document from 1238 is often cited for its revelation that the San Damiano community then numbered fifty-one, including Clare. The document's principal content, usually ignored, regards the transfer and sale (*venditio*) of an enclosure and the land alongside it to the chapter of the church of San Rufino.[51] Omaechevarría thinks the transaction is an example of the community violating its own principle against holding landed possessions,[52] but this only points up how misleading it is to speak of "absolute" poverty, as if poverty were not always relative. Gregory's Privilege allowed them to refuse possessions but sheds no light on what they did possess. Alas, no details survive indicating how Clare's community came to own the land or how they used the sale's proceeds. But the sale adds realism and perspective to the San Damiano women's poverty. Their differences with Gregory were a matter of degree, defined by where they positioned themselves within the gray zone of poverty, adjudicating how many possessions were compatible with it and how many exceeded its bounds.

Attempts to Jettison the Rule of Benedict

By the time Gregory IX died on 22 August 1241, Agnes of Prague had lost several key battles but had yet to give up her fight for greater autonomy from the pope's *forma vitae*. After the fifteen-day papacy of Celestine IV (d. 10 November 1241), the papacy remained vacant for some twenty months. When Innocent IV ascended the papal throne on 23 June 1243, Agnes probably thought she had a new opportunity to win some concessions. She wrote to him just a few months after he had become pope. No longer abbess, she could still command a pope's attention because of her powerful social status. Although her letter is not extant, its contents can be gleaned from Innocent's response to her on 13 November 1243.[53] She wrote regarding the provision in Gregory's *forma vitae* that stated: "We give you the *Rule of Saint Benedict* to be observed in all things which are in no way contrary to that same *Form of Life* that was given to you by us and by which you have especially chosen to live."[54] Agnes and her sisters complained to Innocent that they found it "impossible" to simultaneously follow "two rules" (*duae regulae*), namely, the Rule of Benedict and Gregory's *forma vitae*. Innocent's response intimates that the women were anxious, scrupulously quaking at the prospect that they might violate one or the other of these rules. Therefore, they asked Innocent to strike from Gregory's *forma vitae* two phrases, "by virtue of obedience" and "the Rule of Blessed Benedict."[55]

Innocent firmly declined and sought, ostensibly at least, to allay the women's anxieties. He tellingly explained his refusal by offering Agnes the same three points that Gregory IX had given her in 1238 when she asked him to approve the *forma vitae* that she had cobbled together from Francis's *forma vivendi* and parts of Gregory's *forma vitae*. First, Innocent noted that the abbesses and sisters in the monastery of San Damiano in Assisi and all the other sisters in the order had solemnly professed Gregory's "carefully composed" and papally approved *forma vitae*. Second, these sisters had "laudably observed it from the time of their profession until the present." Third, it had been "uniformly observed everywhere by all." If it were now not to be so observed, it might lead to "grave and insupportable scandal. . . . Other sisters of this Order," seeing the "full content of the rule [i.e., the *forma vitae* including its passage regarding the Rule of Benedict] thus violated or altered, might with disturbed hearts waver in their observance."[56] Innocent's reasons and even his very choice of words, especially his third point, so closely follow Gregory's 1238 refusal that it is clear that someone in Innocent's papal chancery had thoroughly reviewed and drawn on that prior correspondence between the papacy and Agnes.

Agnes was perhaps not being fully forthcoming with Innocent when she requested these two changes. Writing to Innocent in the very first months of his papacy, she hoped, it seems, that a change of pope might bring a different response than her earlier request to Gregory that the women be freed to follow a *forma vitae* more in line with Francis's. Innocent's response, mimicking Gregory's so closely, was at once barbed and humorous. He was saying, in effect, "asked and answered."

It strains credulity to think that Agnes and her sisters were truly suffering a crisis of conscience about observing two rules. Gregory's *forma vitae* made it crystal clear that it took precedence whenever it conflicted with the Rule of Benedict. The timing of the women's alleged moral quandary is also suspicious. As Gilliat-Smith noted, there seems to be more of "the wisdom of the serpent than the simplicity of the dove" in the women's plaints: "If their consciences had been in reality as grievously afflicted as they alleged, they would have hardly waited twenty years before making any attempt to rid themselves of a burden so intolerable."[57] The sisters' stated anxiety about the impossibility of following two rules seems instead to be just a pretext to win greater freedom to shape their own religious life. A closer consideration of the two phrases that Agnes wanted struck from Gregory's *forma vitae* shows this to be so. First, dropping any mention of the Rule of Benedict would leave the sisters with no explicit regulations regarding a host of issues—including corporate ownership of property. Whereas the Rule of Benedict explicitly allowed it, Francis's *forma vitae* would not have. Since Agnes had failed to win Gregory's approval of her *forma vitae* incorporating Francis's *forma*, she now tried instead to simply nullify Benedict's rule. Second, although deleting the other phrase "by virtue of obedience" might seem still to regard the unwanted Rule of Benedict, that is not the case. After all, if the women had succeeded in having the single phrase

"Rule of Benedict" removed, then only one rule would be left, Gregory's *forma vitae*. There would be no problem adhering to this one rule "by virtue of obedience." Notably, Gregory bound them "by virtue of obedience" specifically to his own *forma vitae*. Thus, if that phrase too were removed, Agnes and her sisters would not have been bound by obedience to observe even Gregory's *forma vitae*. Whether or not they intended such an extreme strategy is difficult to gauge. It was, in any case, fully consonant with their unambiguous goal: to gain the autonomy they needed to hew more closely to the *sui generis* religious life practiced at San Damiano.

My suggestion that Agnes might have been engaging in subtle but ultimately unsuccessful diplomacy clashes with her hagiographic depiction as a self-abnegating and obedient daughter of the Church. Her *vita* describes her as "bound . . . by the obligation of obedience, which abounds with many victims" and "intent on observing the rule, not overlooking a single jot or tittle."[58] But circumstantial evidence—even within her own written "saint's life"—suggests that Agnes wanted to change the direction of church control over her monastery. Just after praising Agnes's obedience, her *vita* discussed her refusal to accept possessions that Lord John Cajetan, cardinal of the Apostolic See, was pressing upon her "on account of the evils of the age and the threatening dangerous times" (*propter maliciam dierum et instancia temporum periculosa*).[59] The language echoes Gregory's when he tried to persuade Clare to accept possessions "on account of the events of the times and the dangers of the world" (*propter eventus temporum et pericula saeculorum*).[60] The parallel between Pope Gregory and Clare, on the one hand, and Cardinal John Cajetan and Agnes, on the other, could be a hagiographic device to strengthen Agnes's imitation of Clare, a leitmotif in the *vita*.[61] But it may also be an example of Agnes's struggle to limit her monastery's possessions.[62] She was certainly "like" Clare insofar as both women were adroit politicians pursuing their own religious agendas.[63]

Retaining the Rule of Benedict but Reducing Its Binding Force

Agnes was by no means alone in her complaints about two rules. In April 1244, just months after her exchange with Pope Innocent, Rainaldo, the order's protector, forwarded to the entire Order of San Damiano the letter *Cum universitati vestrae*, in which Innocent addressed the same concerns.[64] Other monasteries had also been voicing worries about being bound to observe both the Rule of Benedict and the *forma vitae*. Apparently, the women had been communicating among themselves and decided to launch a concerted effort to influence the papacy's regulation of their life. With Gregory gone, they were collectively seizing the moment to win a concession. That more protests about the same issues followed Agnes's and Innocent's correspondence suggests that she or she together with some collaborators (Clare? Elias?) were spearheading the effort. We do not know how the women communicated with each other, perhaps by letter, or perhaps assisted by friars or others traveling from one house to the next. Nor do we know how their concerns reached the papacy, whether by letters, emissaries, or delivered *viva voce* to Innocent by their papal liaison, Rainaldo. What is certain, however, is that mere coincidence cannot account for so many objections about two rules cropping up simultaneously in monasteries as distant as Bohemia, Italy, and Spain.

Subsequent papal correspondence suggests that the matter remained alive. Innocent's letter to the entire order, sent by Rainaldo in April 1244, was sent again to monasteries in August 1244. Was this because certain monasteries continued to complain? Or is it that the letters intended for the entire order were each sent to some monasteries at various times? In any event, the papacy continued to try to quell the women's protests. Tellingly, the *Bullarium Franciscanum*'s version of the August letter relies on an autograph located in the monastery of Santa Chiara in Assisi, the monastery to which the San Damiano sisters moved after Clare's death.[65] The fact that Clare and the San Damiano sisters saw fit to preserve the letter, addressed specifically to them, underlines its significance.[66] About one year later, Innocent would send almost identical letters to monasteries in Barcelona and Salamanca in Spain.[67] The sisters' dissatisfaction appeared widespread and difficult to silence. Future archival work will probably discover more letters in other monasteries.

In defending Gregory's *forma vitae* with its explicit insistence on the Rule of Benedict, Innocent articulated an astounding claim in his letters to Agnes, the entire order, and the monasteries in Barcelona and Salamanca: the women were bound by the Rule of Benedict regarding *only* the three vows. Innocent claims he was acting on precedent in thus solving the dilemma of two rules. Gregory IX had himself declared the same thing, explains Innocent: "And thus We also declare just as our predecessor of pious memory, Pope Gregory, declared in the presence and hearing of Our venerable Brother, the Bishop of Ostia [Rainaldo], that the aforesaid Rule of Saint Benedict does not bind you unto anything except obedience, the renunciation of property, and perpetual chastity, which things pertain to the essence of every type of religious life [or "order"] [*quae substantialia cujuslibet Religionis existunt*]."[68] Rainaldo himself was likely the pope's source for this information. This is an early and telling clue that Rainaldo had a vested interest in the rule or rules binding the order he oversaw, an interest that would profoundly influence the order's trajectory, as I show in Chapter 7.

Innocent surely had the Fourth Lateran Council's legislation in mind when he noted in his letter to Agnes that the Rule of Benedict was the most distinguished of all the Church's approved rules and that it rendered the women's religious life "authentic" (*authentica*), in other words, canonical.[69] But there is a decided irony in Innocent's position as he, on the one hand, exalts the Rule of Benedict as the "most distinguished" of all the religious rules, but on the other hand, reduces its binding force to the three religious vows. Although Innocent appeals to Gregory's own opinion (as alleged by Rainaldo) that the Rule of Benedict bound the women only in the matter of the three vows, this was certainly not Gregory's intention when he first prescribed his *forma vitae* together with the rule in 1219 on the heels of Lateran IV, for he stated explicitly that the Rule of Benedict was to be "observed in all things which are in no way contrary" to his *forma vitae*.[70] It would be absurd to make such a comment if the rule was not binding in anything beyond the vows. Now, however, Innocent asserts that the Rule of Benedict functioned merely as a symbolic and official stamp of approval, nothing more. Considered in this light, Innocent's letter is less an outright refusal of Agnes's and the other sisters' request to be freed from the rule than a sort of face-saving compromise. Invoking Gregory as his precedent, he nullified virtually every prescription in the rule, leaving only the vows. And certainly none of the women had been seeking release from the vows.

In November 1245 Innocent reissued Gregory's *forma vitae*, thus making known his intention to be a faithful continuator of Gregory's vision of women's religious life. Innocent's version made few, and mostly slight, changes to Gregory's *forma vitae*. One, however, should be noted: instead of stating that the *forma vitae* had been given to them by "our predecessor of holy memory, Gregory," as Innocent did in a version of Gregory's *forma vitae* that he sent out in July earlier that year, his new version more boldly asserted that the *forma vitae* was "given to you [sisters] by Us."[71] Innocent, using the papal royal "we" to refer to himself, here takes greater ownership of Gregory's *forma vitae* and emphasizes his own investment in its observation and enforcement. Vásquez believes that Innocent sent copies of the *forma vitae*, unsolicited, to all the women's monastic communities in the order.[72]

That Gregory IX had continued to grant dispensations throughout his fourteen-year-plus papacy regarding clothing, fasting, and possessions might have been a clue to him at some point that his *forma vitae* required updating, but perhaps being the *forma vitae*'s original redactor blinded him to its deficiencies. One might have thought Innocent IV freer to acknowledge this, but he too clung to the *forma vitae* even as he busily granted dispensation after dispensation to those seeking them. The very day that Innocent denied Agnes's request to have mention of the Rule of Benedict struck from Gregory's *forma vitae*, he sent her community another letter confirming and expanding their dispensations from its full observance.[73] Indeed, the number of papal mitigations included in the *Bullarium Franciscanum* indicates a papal chancery office ever occupied authorizing exceptions to the rule. But after repeated and confident declarations supporting Gregory's *forma vitae*, Innocent would finally see the light and reverse course in 1247, issuing an altogether new rule that would dramatically affect both the Order of San Damiano and the Lesser Brothers.

Chapter 7

Innocent IV's *Forma Vitae* and Its Aftermath, 1247 to 1250

After years defending the viability of Gregory's *forma vitae*, his successor, Innocent IV, finally came to the conclusion that it was time for a new *forma vitae*. Whatever his personal involvement in the text's redaction, its contents appear to reflect his own wishes regarding the Order of San Damiano. On 6 August 1247 he sent a copy of it to all the monasteries in the order.[1] He quickly followed with a letter on 23 August that sketched his two principal reasons for issuing the new legislation. First, he wanted to give peace of mind to wavering souls (*fluctuantibus animis*),[2] a phrase that recalled his earlier letters to Agnes of Prague and the women in the Order of San Damiano whose minds had wavered (e.g., *mentis tuae fluctibus*) over the difficulty of observing two rules.[3] Citing both their rule (the Rule of Benedict) and their *forma vitae* (Gregory IX's), Innocent again acknowledges the women's scruple of uncertainty (*ambiguitatis scrupulus*) and uneasy consciences. Although some think this passage uses two modes to name the women's one *forma vitae*,[4] this dual reference is instead a transparent allusion to Agnes's and the other sisters' earlier complaints about having to observe both the Rule of Benedict and Gregory's *forma vitae*. Innocent's new legislation aims to address these very complaints. He had been decidedly won over—or quite possibly worn down—by the women's relentless petitions. Second, Innocent no longer wanted to allow ever more exceptions to Gregory's *forma vitae*. He complained that so many and so great a variety of dispensations had been handed out that the women seemed to have "many rather than a single profession." In other words, the very diversity of the women's religious life from one monastery to the next was destroying the order's essential unity (a unity, to be sure, that had, in fact, never been realized). He therefore deemed it necessary to "correct their Rule and *forma vivendi*." Innocent concluded his letter stating categorically that all the sisters would now be obliged to follow the new rule and *forma vitae* sent to them in his recent bull of 6 August.[5]

Paradoxically, Innocent's *forma vitae*, or rule, as it is also commonly known, proved to be both a momentous change and a non-event. It was momentous insofar as it represented a thoughtful and concerted effort to address concerns voiced over the years by many monasteries in the still growing Order of San Damiano. It was a non-event in that it seems not to have been adopted by many monasteries, Innocent's categorical directive to them notwithstanding. Most recent scholarly treatments of Clare and the Order of San Damiano therefore readily dispatch Innocent's legislation. Some few take the trouble to highlight its most notable features,[6] while most dwell almost exclusively on the provisions that proved so objectionable to Clare of Assisi that, they say, she decided to take up her pen and write her own rule.[7] But Innocent's rule was much more than an insignificant stepping stone between Gregory's *forma vitae* and the *1253 forma vitae*. Both its contents and its ultimate failure elucidate pivotal struggles involving control over the Order of San Damiano. It also proffers tangential evidence for reassessing authorship of the *1253 forma vitae* commonly attributed to Clare of Assisi.

I begin this chapter probing Innocent's stated reasons for issuing a new *forma vitae*, including his desire to address the women's complaints about the Rule of Benedict constituting a second rule. Their complaint, of course, was a mere pretext to hew more closely to Francis of Assisi's prescriptions for religious life and to maintain ties with Francis's order. In the second part of this chapter, I turn my attention to the friars themselves. Responding to the women's petitions, Innocent's new rule assigned starring roles to both Francis and the Lesser Brothers. Understanding the friars' complex relationship with the papacy and the women in the Order of San Damiano is fundamental to assessing both the text and its reception. Finally, I reexamine the reasons why Innocent's *forma vitae* failed. Almost all scholars agree that it was not warmly received, and most contend, further, that the prime movers behind its failure were Clare of Assisi and other women in the order. Some scholars further cite resistance by the Lesser Brothers. Rarely mentioned, however, is the role played by Rainaldo of Jenne (the future Pope Alexander IV), the cardinal responsible for both the Order of San Damiano and the Order of Lesser Brothers. I will show that his role was critical in causing the demise of Innocent's rule. This lays the groundwork for Chapter 8, where I reassess Clare of Assisi's role in redacting the famous *1253 forma vitae*.

Innocent IV's Reasons for Issuing a New *Forma Vitae* (1247)

Correcting Gregory IX's Forma Vitae

Probably out of deference to his predecessor, Innocent initially described his legislation as a correction, or mere revision, of Gregory's *forma vitae*. But while Innocent unsurprisingly adopted many features of Gregory's rule, he also radically rewrote other aspects of it and altogether expanded it, so much so that it can only be considered Innocent's own *forma vitae*. Several years later he would acknowledge that others saw it as new: he referred to his work, alternately within a single letter, as a "new rule or *formula*" and then, more modestly, as an adaptation of Gregory's.[8] Nomenclature aside, the pope obviously intended to give a fresh start to the women's order by specifying many regulations about the women's religious life that had been either left undefined, imprecisely defined, or ill defined in Gregory's *forma vitae*. These additions make his text almost twice as long as Gregory's.

Innocent was being quite forthcoming when he told the women he was updating the *forma vitae* to eliminate dispensations and respond to their grumbling about two rules. Part of his strategy for making dispensations unnecessary, apparently, was to embrace the breadth of actual practices within the monasteries. This probably explains why he relaxed the fasting regulations, a frequent topic in papal dispensations. Fasting in Innocent's *forma vitae* was less strict than it had been in both Hugo's *forma vitae* and Clare's third letter to Agnes of Prague (see Table 2 in Chapter 5). Clare—albeit at the behest of Francis and Bishop Guido—had early forsaken her extreme fasting and, in 1238, had counseled Agnes away from excessive fasting. Even so, Clare was a martinet alongside Innocent, perhaps because as a poor, enclosed woman she used fasting to express the self-abnegation that someone privileged and unenclosed might have expressed by renouncing money, status, or other worldly riches.[9] Whereas Clare wanted the healthy sisters to fast (take just one meal) every day except Sundays and Christmas, Innocent advised a fast only between the Exaltation of the Cross (mid-September) and the Resurrection (late March or April). He also added several feast days on which the women were not to fast. Other times, except Fridays, they could have wine, fish, and potage, and, except during the two Lents, also eggs and dairy products. He granted other fasting relaxations to young girls and serving sisters.[10] Some other norms were only slightly relaxed. For example, he authorized certain types of people to enter the monastery, including doctors, blood-letters, and anyone who had to help in a crisis, such as a fire, an accident, a threat of some kind, or other danger.[11] Innocent was merely incorporating into the *forma vitae* a permission that both Gregory and he, quite possibly influenced by Agnes of Prague, had already explicitly granted to the women's order: friars who needed to enter the monasteries on account of some danger could freely do so.[12] Innocent's *forma vitae* now extended this permission to anyone, although as I show below, he expected Lesser Brothers to often be close by.

The most discussed feature of Innocent's *forma vitae*—indeed the one point often cited in discussions that otherwise summarily dispatch the text—regards its treatment of poverty or, more precisely, corporate ownership of goods. Although often treated as a relaxation, it is in fact just another instance of Innocent's attempt to bring his *forma vitae* into line with the actual practice of most monasteries. After noting that sisters who left the enclosure for some reason had, upon their return, to turn over to the abbess or another appointed sister anything they happened to receive while outside, the *forma vitae* then added this more general observation: "Regarding this, it is permissible for you to receive and hold in common rents and possessions and freely to retain them."[13] This language echoed a concession Innocent had made the previous year to fourteen monasteries.[14] Nor would many monasteries in the Order of San Damiano have thought that corporate possessions conflicted with their monastic vocation since this had been the traditional, commonly accepted practice.[15] Next, the *forma vitae* set forth rules regarding a procurator, a person outside of the monastery who might assist the sisters with property sales, exchanges, and so forth.[16] At this very time, Innocent was similarly approving the office of procurator for the friars.[17] His *forma vitae*'s comments about possessions would be banal and hardly worth mentioning were it not for the fact that this centuries-old practice of corporate monastic property was precisely what Clare of Assisi and her monastery of San Damiano, the symbolic flagship of the order, resisted when she sought and obtained the Privilege of Poverty.

Innocent's other relaxations were few and almost negligible: Gregory's *forma vitae* allowed the women to leave the enclosure if superiors sent them to found or establish another monastery; Innocent further authorized them to leave to reform, correct, or govern another monastery; to avoid a significant expense; or for some other religious (*pia*) or reasonable cause.[18] Innocent slightly eased the women's material life: he allowed them to have two "or even more" tunics instead of the two alone permitted by Gregory, and Innocent allowed the women's pillows to be filled with "wool or even feathers," instead of just the hay or straw allowed in Gregory's *forma vitae*.[19]

But numerous other details resist easy analysis: was he incorporating practices he knew already existed in some monasteries, for which he had perhaps granted dispensations, or was he outlining new regulations of his own making? His comments on the scapular, the design of the window through which the women received communion, and his injunction that sisters who had to leave the enclosure not eat, drink, or sleep outside the monastery without permission, fall into this puzzling category.[20]

Rich details regarding women's religious life can be gleaned from Innocent's *forma vitae*: set times were allotted for all the sisters to do useful and honest work, a topic not touched upon in Gregory's *forma vitae*. Like Cistercians, the women were to use sign language while maintaining the rule of silence. Innocent's *forma vitae* reveals that in a period when the chalice was beginning to be withheld from the faithful, the sisters still received communion in both species. Serving sisters who left the enclosure and even sisters who remained within were allowed to wear decent shoes.[21]

Especially striking are regulations that tighten control over the women and suggest a decided distrust. Gregory's *forma vitae* had strictly enjoined that they not be seen by others, but said nothing in particular about their headdress.[22] Innocent, on the other hand, prescribes it in compulsive detail: "They should uniformly and decently cover their heads with headbands or a garment that is entirely white, but not curious, in such a way that the forehead, cheeks, and neck are, as is fitting, covered; nor should they dare to appear before unknown people in any other way. They should also wear a black veil that extends over the head, so wide and long that it comes down both sides until the shoulders and behind it should extend a little beyond the hood of the tunic."[23] With their faces so covered, the women would hardly see much even of each other. A note of mistrust is similarly sounded in new regulations regarding the women's sleeping arrangements. All were to sleep in a common dormitory; each sister would "have her own bed separated from the others." The abbess's bed was to be positioned so she could see everyone, with a lamp kept burning the entire night.[24] Obviously, this arrangement made infractions against silence and especially sexual propriety less likely. Gregory's *forma vitae* had stipulated that the monastery door be vigilantly guarded, kept closed, locked with a key, and bolted with iron bars.[25] Innocent went further: "In each monastery there should be just one door for entering and leaving the enclosure. . . . This door should be positioned as high as reasonably possible, such that one reaches it from the outside by means of a ladder that can be raised up. This ladder, zealously secured by the sisters by an iron chain, should be raised up from the recitation of compline until prime the next day, and [also] during the period of daily rest and visitation, unless an obvious need or clear advantage sometimes requires otherwise."[26] Whereas Gregory's *forma vitae* required a single carefully guarded key for the monastery door, Innocent's *forma vitae* required two different keys: at night the door would be double-locked, with the portress guarding one key and the abbess the other.[27] Such additions belie facile descriptions of Innocent's rule as "basically a milder version of [Hugo's]."[28]

Responding to the Women's Complaints About Two Rules

As dramatic as some of Innocent's changes to the *forma vitae* appear, all pale alongside his strategy to end complaints about the impossibility of following two rules. These complaints, as I discussed in Chapter 6, had surely been a pretext to win a rule more conformed to Francis's *forma vivendi*. Although Innocent had categorically countered that move in 1243–1244, he now just as categorically capitulated, or so it seemed. He makes this bold concession in the very prologue to his *forma vitae*: "We, acceding to your pious prayers, grant to you and those who come after you the observance of the *Rule* of Saint Francis."[29] Here Innocent acknowledges that he had known all along that the sisters' desire to align themselves more closely with Francis of Assisi's vision of religious life lay behind their complaints regarding the Rule of Benedict being a second rule.

But the *Rule* of Francis that Innocent now assigned to the women was not Francis's brief *forma vivendi*, which Clare of Assisi would quote so definitively within the *1253 forma vitae*. Nor was it any longer a set of written prescriptions that may have grown out of it; for example, the document that Agnes of Prague drew on to fashion her own *forma vitae*, the one Innocent refused to approve.[30] The *Rule* of Francis Innocent commits the women to observe was rather the very rule the papacy had approved for the Order of Lesser Brothers in 1223. Telling the women they were to be bound by the same rule as the friars only appeared to be a grandiose concession. For just as he held the Rule of Benedict to bind them only in the matter of the three vows, so now would the *Rule* of Francis. In other words, both rules were mere window dressing: the regulations in force would be those detailed in Innocent's *forma vitae*. Leonhard Lemmens noted how ironic it was that the Order of San Damiano's first rule to mention Francis was also the first to state they could own property, a right so at odds with Francis's notion of religious poverty.[31]

The Lesser Brothers and Innocent IV

The Lesser Brothers and the Order of San Damiano Prior to Innocent's **Forma** Vitae

But Innocent's *forma vitae* did more than replace one symbolic rule with another. By showcasing Francis's *Rule* in the *forma vitae*'s opening lines he was announcing in so many words that the friars and the sisters in the Order of San Damiano shared a common descent from Francis and were both bound, in some sense, by a single rule. He was radically reconfiguring the Order of San Damiano by tying it juridically to the Lesser Brothers.

This was no impulsive move on Innocent's part. He had been moving the two orders in this direction for some time. Although it happened by fits and starts, Gregory IX himself had been pressing the Lesser Brothers to take on the *cura monialium* of the women's order that he first founded. While the friars' response cannot be summed up simply—indeed, close ties between various friars and women's monasteries had existed since the time of Francis—it is the case that the friars' leadership seemed generally to have been wary of such ties.[32]

Innocent's correspondence with the friars before he issued his *forma vitae* underlines, however, the futility of the friars' resistance. On 17 July 1245 Innocent addressed a letter to the Minister General Crescentius of Jesi and all the Lesser Brothers responding to their request to be freed from the pastoral care of women in the Order of San Damiano. Expressing his "paternal solicitude," he offered them a compromise for the sake of their "peace and tranquility." The friars would be bound to continue their pastoral care in all the monasteries committed to them since the papacy of Gregory IX, but absolved from accepting such care in monasteries not already in their charge. Even so, the pope slyly upped the ante: the women already in their care would be under the provincial ministers' "jurisdiction and correction" (*jurisdictioni, et correctioni*).[33] With a brief stroke of the pen the two orders were now, somehow, juridically bound, a path Innocent would continue to pursue.

In the ensuing months, Innocent dropped any pretense of a compromise. It seems certain that he had received complaints about it. In October 1245 he took back his earlier deal with a new letter to the minister general and all the provincials. Again expressing his "paternal solicitude," this time he acted for the sake of the "peace and welfare" of his "beloved daughters in Christ, the enclosed nuns of the Order of San Damiano." The minister general and provincials, he wrote, would take charge of the "visitation, correction, and reformation" of the enclosed nuns "in both head [i.e., abbess] and members," tasks that Gregory's *forma vitae* had assigned to the monastic visitator. Innocent's letter added a laundry list of attendant tasks. The friars were to see to the sisters' official customs, preach to them, hear their confessions, celebrate solemn Masses, consecrate monastic altars, preside at religious professions, and tend spiritually to the nuns during their illnesses, deaths, and burials.[34] A follow-up letter to all the abbesses and nuns in the Order of San Damiano confirmed that friars duly appointed by their provincial ministers could freely enter the monasteries under circumstances the pope spelled out. Innocent's letter shows, significantly, that the women or their allies had been contacting him and requesting this change. Their petitions mirror those of Dominican women, who were in this same period making similar requests vis-à-vis the Order of Preachers.[35]

Crescentius and other friars were perplexed by Innocent's moves to tie them juridically to the Order of San Damiano. So, in 1245, they asked him to clarify for them the meaning of their *papally approved* rule, which, ostensibly, forbade their entrance into nuns' monasteries. They singled out Francis's own words within their rule: "I strictly command all the brothers not to have any suspicious dealings or conversations with women, and they may not enter the monasteries of nuns, excepting those brothers to whom special permission has been granted by the Apostolic See."[36] Earlier, in 1230, Gregory—much to some friars' delight—had strictly interpreted this passage to apply to the inner cloister of all nuns' monasteries and to the inner *and* outer cloister of monasteries in Gregory's order of "enclosed nuns." Although Gregory insisted he knew Francis's true "intention" when he wrote his rule, Innocent apparently disagreed. In mid-November 1245, he responded to the Lesser Brothers' 1245 request with a new take on Francis's *Rule*: the friars could not enter the inner cloister of monasteries in the Order of San Damiano without papal permission; but Innocent said nothing about—and thus left open—their access to the outer cloister.[37]

Some friars, it appears, resisted their new responsibilities.[38] In early November 1245 Innocent sent the same letter he had sent in October to the minister general detailing the brothers new duties of visitation, correction, and reformation to the minister general and the provincial minister of the March of Ancona.[39] It is possible that this provincial required special prodding, especially since Innocent sent the letter to both men yet again in September 1246.[40] And other letters besides these sought to impress upon the Lesser Brothers of the March of Ancona that they were obliged to provide pastoral care for the women's monastery in Ascoli Piceno.[41] An order repeated suggests an order ignored.

Innocent continued to escalate the brothers' responsibilities, particularly by emphasizing their juridical duties. In June 1246 he wrote to fourteen women's monasteries in Italy, Spain, and France placing them—at their request, he says—under the minister general and provincials of the Lesser Brothers. The women's petition had to do with their enclosure, which required the presence of friars at their monasteries for spiritual and temporal assistance. Innocent's letter specifically placed the women under the minister general's and provincials' "supervision and teaching" (*magisterio et doctrina*). That *magisterio* should be rendered as "supervision," with its attendant meanings of direction and guidance, rather than simply as "teaching," seems clear not only because the second term, *doctrina*, itself captures the notion of teaching, but also because Innocent made the Lesser Brothers responsible for the "office of visitation" with its tasks of "correcting and reforming."[42] That same day, another letter to the same effect went to the minister general.[43] Some friars must have thought that the Order of San Damiano was being collapsed into the Order of Lesser Brothers, for the next month Innocent wrote an appeasing letter to Crescentius and the provincial ministers purporting to clarify and delimit the jurisdictional status of the two orders. Claiming he did not want to so multiply the friars' duties that their contemplation suffered, he nonetheless repeated that the women were under the friars' "supervision and teaching." But he added that the friars should show the women the friars' own "Constitutions" (Francis's 1223 rule). In a sense, the pope was trying to have it both ways. Giving the friars *magisterio* over the women, he was also giving a nod of assent to the Lesser Brothers' rule and its strictures regarding their dealings with women. Innocent concluded with the reassurance they certainly sought: "We are not proposing to incorporate [the women] into your Order."[44] But Innocent's correspondence binding the two orders together continued.[45] Indeed, it was consonant with a pattern of papal policy: Innocent was similarly entrusting women's religious houses to the Order of Preachers.[46]

In May 1247, Innocent announced in letters to Crescentius and the brothers that he wanted them to convene a general chapter in July in his presence.[47] Crescentius had not convoked a general chapter since his election as minister general in May 1244. In attendance at the chapter in Lyon was Rainaldo, the friars' protector, but not Crescentius. In principle, his presence was required, but he pled old age.[48] Other factors, such as his aversion to public appearances, possible antipathy toward Innocent IV, or fear of appearing in Lyon, where Frederick II might attack him, might also have been at play. Whatever the explanation, Crescentius was immediately removed as minister general. Innocent would also refuse to ratify Crescentius's election as bishop of Assisi in 1247.[49] Perhaps another chink in the two men's relationship was their failure to see eye to eye on the friars' obligations toward the Order of San Damiano.

The friar Thomas of Celano provides more direct testimony regarding things that concerned the friars in the years just before Innocent's *forma vitae* appeared. At the general chapter of Genoa in 1244, Crescentius had charged the brothers to "send him in writing whatever they reliably knew about the life, miracles, and prodigies" of Francis. He and the chapter wanted Thomas of Celano to redact a new *Life* of Francis, in part because so much had transpired since Thomas had completed his *First Life* in 1229. The deep divisions that rent the Order of Lesser Brothers included sharp disagreements about how to interpret Francis's *Rule*, so part of Thomas's brief was to set the record straight regarding Francis's true intentions.[50] Twice charged with compiling a *Life* of Francis, first by Gregory IX and now by the friars themselves, Thomas was as close to an official biographer as there was at the time.

Thomas's *Second Life* suggests a sea change in the friars' attitudes toward Clare, religious women, and the *cura monialium*. In his *First Life*, Elias played a lead role as one of Francis's most intimate companions. Thomas singled him out as one of the only companions, for example, privileged to see Francis's stigmata during his life, and as the only companion Francis chose to care for him in his illness as a "mother" and for the other brothers as a "father."[51] Thomas reports that it was Elias who cajoled Francis into speaking to a woman whom Francis had at first ignored because he had once expelled a demon from her.[52] Writing his *First Life* at the request of Gregory IX after the pope had drawn San Damiano into his order, Thomas called Clare "the strongest and most precious stone" in the foundation, and he called the order itself "a noble structure of the most precious pearls."[53] One of the most touching scenes in Thomas's *First Life* is when the crowd accompanying Francis's recently deceased body from the Porziuncola to Assisi pauses at San Damiano for Clare and her sisters to see their beloved father one last time. The women glimpsed him through the small window adjoining their cloister to the chapel and, overcome with grief, they kissed his hands. Thomas, poignantly depicting the women's struggle to keep command of themselves even as they cried out in anguish, captured their heart-rending lamentations in a series of direct quotations.[54]

Less than two decades later, Thomas of Celano, now writing at the behest of the friars, radically revised his depiction of these earlier stars, partly through delicate omission, but partly also through pointed, even acerbic, commentary. Between the two works, of course, the women's one-time ally Elias had been deposed as minister general, his fortunes fallen so low that David Burr dubbed him "The Name That Cannot Be Named."[55] If we can believe Thomas of Eccleston, writing in the mid-thirteenth century, Elias had been tarred in part for his very association with the "poor ladies."[56] Thomas of Celano's *Second Life* alludes to Elias, always unfavorably, but refuses to name him.[57] Elias, of course, had made enemies for many reasons, so his absence in the text might be owing to other factors.[58] More significant is the fact that Clare too joins the ranks of those "Who Cannot Be Named." She does, however, make a sneaky, pseudo-anonymous appearance. Thomas writes that when Francis "spoke with a woman, he would speak out in a loud voice so that all could hear. He once said to his companion: 'I'll tell you the truth, dear brother, I would not recognize any woman if I looked at her face, except for two. I know the face of this one and that one, but any other, I do not know.'"[59] Thomas knew no reader would believe that Francis would fail to recognize Clare or his friend Jacopa di Settesoli.[60] This is Clare's biggest role in the *Second Life*; she is one of the two faces in Francis's otherwise unabashedly anti-women comment. Equally anonymous and unnamed is the Order of San Damiano, which Thomas refers to just once as the "Order of holy virgins."[61] Thomas is judiciously trying to capture Francis's true intentions without cavalierly disrespecting the claims of diverse factions within the order.[62] Even so, the line he walks between Francis's commitment to Clare and her sisters, on the one hand, and the Lesser Brothers' fears about the *cura monialium*, on the other hand, leads him to portray Francis as an unmitigated misogynist.

Thomas of Celano is telling his readers much more about the situation surrounding him in the 1240s than he is about Francis during the saint's life. From Francis's own writings and Thomas's *First Life* to Thomas's *Second Life*, Francis beats a straight path away from women. Francis himself was reluctant to have the friars become involved in the supervision of penitent women, and he wanted to avoid even the appearance of impropriety. He wrote in his *Earlier Rule*: "Wherever they may be or may go, let all the brothers avoid the evil regard and frequent company of women. No one may counsel them, travel alone with them or eat out of the same dish with them. When giving penance or some spiritual advice, let priests speak with them in a becoming way. Absolutely no woman may be received unto obedience by any brother, but after spiritual advice has been given to her, let her do penance wherever she wants."[63] There might be a note of misogyny in his allusion to the "evil regard" (*malo visu*) of women, but he might just as well have been referring specifically to women who would lasciviously regard the friars rather than to all women in general. Francis's next advice in the *Earlier Rule* suggests as much, for, rather than blaming women as temptresses for the sexual indiscretions of any friars, Francis blames the friars themselves. This sets Francis apart from many of his contemporaries, who were quick to shunt blame away from religious men and onto women, who are caricatured as carnally weak and morally compromised.[64] Making his own the words of Scripture, Francis writes:

> Let us all keep close watch over ourselves and keep all our members clean, for the Lord says: Whoever looks at a woman with lust has already committed adultery with her in his heart (Mt 5:28); and the Apostle: Do you not know that your members are a temple of the Holy Spirit? (1 Cor 6:9) Therefore, whoever violates God's temple, God will destroy (1 Cor 3:17).
>
> If, at the instigation of the devil, any brother commits fornication, let him be deprived of the habit he has lost by his wickedness, put it aside completely, and be altogether expelled from our Order.[65]

The more canonically succinct text of Francis's *Later Rule*, which simply forbids the brothers from having "suspicious contacts or conversations with women," also fails to fault women for men's sexual indiscretions.[66] An oftquoted line attributed to Francis comes to us via one Brother Stephen: "Remarking one day that women who lived together in monasteries were called 'sisters,' [Francis] was extremely troubled by this and is reported to have said: 'The Lord has dispensed us from having spouses, now the devil has procured sisters for us!'"[67] Francis's caustic comment is transparently related to the women being condemned as "lesser sisters," "minoresses," and so forth in papal letters beginning in the early 1240s. Dalarun notes that this "brutal expression of the saint's will" could derive from legends such as Thomas of Celano's *Second Life*. Notably, the quotation was passed on not by Stephen of Narni himself, but only indirectly. A fourteenth-century manuscript attributes it to Thomas of Pavia, who, if the text is indeed his, would have been writing in the wake of more troubles in the 1260s, when the Lesser Brothers were again resisting papal overtures for them to assume the *cura monialium*.[68]

Thomas's *First Life* provides some positive evidence regarding Francis's relationships with women beyond what we know of his association with Clare and her community. Thomas writes that Francis renewed the Church "in both sexes"; crowds of women and men flocked to hear him preach; Francis provided a pattern of teaching and an example of holy deeds for both sexes.[69] About one third of the people Francis cured were women or girls.[70] Thomas's evidence is slim, perhaps intentionally. The most one can say of Francis from his own writings and Thomas's *First Life* is that Francis welcomed women's conversions, was cautious in his relationships with them, and evinced no overt misogyny.

In contrast, Thomas's *Second Life* presents a misogynist Francis who assiduously avoided women. His new account of Francis's death omits the touching farewell scene at San Damiano (but perhaps because he also omits the procession with Francis's body to Assisi). Thomas gives due regard to Francis's affection for the "poor ladies," but what he gives with one hand, he immediately takes away with the other. In one passage, Thomas recounts that the "vicar" (Elias) had been "pestering" Francis to preach to his daughters at San Damiano, where Francis was staying toward the end of his life. Francis finally gave in, but rather than speak to the women, he showed them how they should consider themselves by sprinkling ashes around himself, then on his head, and quickly leaving. This is more than an eye-catching example of Francis's penitential preaching by deeds rather than words.[71] Thomas himself glosses the performance: "This was [Francis's] way of behaving with holy women; this was his way of visiting them, rare and constrained, but very useful! This was his will for all the brothers, whom he wanted to serve for the sake of Christ, whom they serve: that they might always, like winged creatures, beware of the nets before them."[72] Thomas's pen is a double-edged sword throughout the *Second Life*: Francis loved the women but wanted to have little to do with them. Thomas first praised the ladies as a "building much nobler" than the earthly San Damiano that Francis repaired; the order was a "polished collection of living stones" observing the "highest poverty and the beauty of every virtue." But he then underlined Francis's physical distance: "Though the father gradually withdrew his bodily presence from them, he still offered in the Holy Spirit, his affection to care for them."[73] Thomas's next pendulum swing is more dramatic: he first heaps more praise on the women, describing their signs of "highest perfection" and reminding readers that Francis "firmly promised them and others who professed poverty in a similar way of life, that he and his brothers would perpetually offer them help and advice. And he carried this out carefully as long as he lived, and when he was close to death he commanded it to be carried out without fail always, saying that one and the same Spirit had led the brothers and those little poor ladies [*illas pauperculas*] out of this world."[74] Although it would seem almost impossible for Thomas to significantly blunt this straightforward commitment, he then nimbly reverses course:

> The brothers were sometimes surprised that [Francis] did not often visit such holy handmaids of Christ in his bodily presence, but he would say: "Don't imagine, dear brothers, that I don't love them fully. For if it were a crime to cherish them in Christ, wouldn't it be even worse to have joined them to Christ? Not calling them would not have been harmful, but not to care for them after calling them would be the height of cruelty. But I am giving you an example, that as I do, so should you also do. I don't want one volunteering to visit them, but rather command that those who are unwilling and very reluctant should be assigned to their service, as long as they are spiritual men tested by a longstanding, worthy way of life.[75]

Francis's earthly distance from the women of San Damiano is mild compared to his unrestrained misogyny toward women in general:

> [Francis] ordered avoiding completely honeyed poison, that is, familiarities with women, by which even holy men are led astray. . . . He said that avoiding contagion when conversing with them, except for the most well-tested, was as easy as walking on live coals without burning his soles, as Scripture has it. But in order to speak by action, he showed himself an exemplar of virtue.
>
> Indeed the female even troubled him so much that you would believe this was neither caution nor good example, but fear or terror. When their inappropriate chattering made for competition in speaking, with face lowered with a humble and brief word, he called for silence.[76]

Thomas chatters on in this vein for several more passages; even holy women constitute dangerous temptations.[77] He follows this section, entitled "Against Familiarity with Women," with what must have seemed to him the next logical topic: "The Temptations He Endured." The *Second Life*, commissioned by the friars in part to set the record straight about Francis's true intentions, makes abundantly clear that associations with women, even holy women, were to be undertaken only with great reluctance. Thomas presented his *Second Life* to the general chapter of Lyon in July 1247, just days before Innocent was to issue his new *forma vitae*. If the Lesser Brothers sent a copy of the new *vita* to the pope, he was apparently unmoved. Indeed, he was about to move the friars much closer to women in the Order of San Damiano.

The Lesser Brothers in Innocent's Forma Vitae

The Lesser Brothers are woven into the very fabric of Innocent's 1247 *forma vitae*. Francis appears honorifically by way of his *Rule* (mentioned twice), his feast day, and the women's very formula of profession which they make to God, the Virgin Mary, the saints, and "to Saint Francis."[78] Clare of Assisi, by contrast, is not mentioned once. But it is the repeated mention of the Lesser Brothers (well over a dozen times) that crescendos into a sort of thematic dominance by the text's conclusion. The minister general could transfer sisters from one monastery to another.[79] He or one of the provincials would authorize who could enter the monastery (previously a papal prerogative),[80] decide when sisters could leave the enclosure for reasons such as founding or reforming another monastery,[81] and serve as visitator (unless they delegated another friar).[82] The sisters were to pray the Office after the manner of the Lesser Brothers. Indeed, the very prayers to be recited by illiterate sisters were lifted from the *Rule* of Francis.[83] While the women might have a chaplain who was not a friar, Innocent wanted only friars to hear the sisters' confessions, give them communion, and provide other sacraments. An exception might be made in cases of emergency, since, in keeping with previous privileges granted to the friars, Innocent did not require them to reside continually at the monasteries.[84] Innocent's *forma vitae* sheds fascinating light on a group of friars discussed apart from the priests, the *conversi*, brothers who resided at some, perhaps many of the monasteries. They were to fast just as the sisters did unless the abbess decided otherwise, and pray the same Office as the illiterate sisters, with the exception of the Office of the Blessed Virgin. Remarkably, both they and the monastery's chaplain, at the visitator's disposition, might have to promise obedience to the abbess, doubtless because she was the religious superior closest at hand.[85]

But the abbess's authority was effectively circumscribed by her new superiors, the Lesser Brothers, and she is mentioned only about as often as the friar visitator. Innocent's previous letters to both sisters and friars, for example, had described the abbess's election as belonging to the women without interference from the friars. Now his *forma vitae* required that the election be confirmed by the minister general or the pertinent provincial.[86] The authority Innocent invested in them was extreme and unequivocal. The Lesser Brothers would have complete control also over the Order of San Damiano's expansion: no new monastery could be founded unless their general chapter approved it.[87] Clearly, the sisters' new masters were the Lesser Brothers. In a letter to fourteen monasteries, Innocent wrote: "We fully entrust the care [*cura*] of you and all the monasteries of your Order with the authority of the present [document] to our beloved sons, the general and provincial ministers of the Order of Lesser Brothers. We decree that you remain under their—or others who might be ministers for a time—obedience, government [*regimine*], and teaching. You are firmly bound to obey them."[88]

Significantly, in this same passage, Innocent warned against the women falling under anyone else's supervision (*magisterio*) who might lead them to adopt other ways of life. His comment suggests a real and present threat. Indeed, women "feigning" to be followers of some sort of Francis of Assisi had been worrying the papacy for some time. In February 1241 Gregory IX had addressed a letter to archbishops and bishops demanding swift action against such women:

> It has come to our attention that some women [*nonnullae mulieres*] are running about your cities and dioceses falsely asserting that they are sisters of the Order of San Damiano. They go barefoot so that others accept their lying and cruel claim in good faith. They wear the habit and belt of the Nuns of that Order and also its chord [*chordula*]. Indeed, they are called the "barefoot ones," or "chord-wearers" and others even [call them] the "minoresses." The Nuns [of the Order of San Damiano], however, are enclosed perpetually so that they can give pleasing service to God. Since the aforementioned women's feigned religion [*religio*] results in confusion for the Order [of San Damiano], and disparagement of the Order of Lesser Brothers, and scandal for the Brothers and the Nuns, we instruct and command you all, through this Apostolic writing that, after a warning, when you will have made your request, you compel these women through ecclesiastical censure, without appeal, to put aside this sort of habit with its same belts and chords.[89]

Alberzoni believes the leadership of the Lesser Brothers lay behind the pope's directive,[90] although one could readily argue that Gregory, of his own accord, would have objected to non-cloistered women pretending to be religious. Such women posed an ongoing problem. In 1246 Innocent wrote to a Spanish monastery of the Order of San Damiano prohibiting *conversae*, that is, serving sisters, from leaving the monastery after making their profession. Some, he said, went to "other places" (*alia loca*), a term that could mean just anywhere but might also have indicated a religious settlement patterned after the Lesser Brothers' settlements, sometimes called *loca*, signifying "places" of abode. Innocent was particularly troubled by *conversae* who "wandered wretchedly throughout the world."[91] That same year he sent to the archbishops and bishops in Lombardy, the March of Treviso, and Romagna a vociferously worded condemnation of "little women" who wandered about, sometimes taking the name Lesser Sisters (*Sorores Minores*), a name neither the rule nor *formula* accorded even to the sisters of the Order of San Damiano. He warned the prelates not to be deluded by such women. They brought dishonor on the Lesser Brothers. The women had plans to build monasteries of the Order of San Damiano, founded by Francis, but Innocent asked the bishops to seek proper authorization from the Lesser Brothers or the Holy See. Popes continued to send such letters to prelates in northern Italy, France, and England well beyond Clare of Assisi's death in 1253.[92] Alberzoni points out Innocent's clever move in his 1246 letter: he calls Francis the founder not of the monastery of San Damiano, but of the very "Order of San Damiano." Noting the bond between Francis (and by extension, the Lesser Brothers) and the Order of San Damiano, Innocent thus managed to discredit and marginalize the *Sorores Minores*.[93] Innocent's *forma vitae* advanced his strategy further by delineating a juridic basis for that bond, symbolically linking the entire Order of San Damiano to Francis himself.

The Reception of Innocent's *Forma Vitae*

Scholars agree that Innocent's *forma vitae* was not warmly received but disagree about why it failed to take hold and who, specifically, was behind this failure. Many argue that the sisters of the Order of San Damiano (with Clare often figuring prominently) defeated the rule, and others point to the Lesser Brothers, but I propose that the most effective opponent of the pope's *forma vitae* was, instead, Cardinal Rainaldo.

Reception by the Order of San Damiano and Clare of Assisi

Livarius Oliger and Herbert Grundmann seem to have set the pattern for other historians. Both noted that Innocent's *forma vitae* was adopted by a few monasteries in Germany. Grundmann thought there was no evidence that it had been accepted by any monasteries in Italy, Spain, or France, whereas Oliger, on the basis of what now appears to be faulty evidence, thought it had been accepted in Italy.[94] Bert Roest comments that only a few Italian, German, and Spanish houses accepted it.[95] The near dearth of positive evidence showing that Innocent's *forma vitae* had been adopted constitutes a powerful argument from silence. Is it sufficient, however, to robustly prove the frequent claim that monasteries in the Order of San Damiano also strongly resisted Innocent's rule?[96]

In fact, there is only modest direct evidence indicating that women in the order overtly resisted Innocent's rule. The strongest explicit statement about how the women received the rule comes from Innocent himself when, in June 1250, he wrote to Rainaldo that no monastery should be forced to accept his 1247 *forma vitae*. He did not, he said, want any of the abbesses or nuns to be perturbed, clearly insinuating that some of the women in the Order of San Damiano were perturbed,[97] but how many? who were they? and what perturbed them? Scholars who try to identify this group have been forced to speculate. Most have pointed to the *forma vitae*'s provisions regarding possessions and concluded that monasteries emulating the poverty of San Damiano would have rejected Innocent's rule. One should bear in mind, however, the great diversity that reigned among the monasteries in this order, a diversity that Roberto Rusconi astutely called an "essential anarchy" and that, in part, propelled Innocent to devise a new rule.[98] Papal correspondence establishes that many monasteries had significant possessions. Few or none of these would have been perturbed by Innocent's permission allowing them to own goods, a permission they would have presumed prior to his legislation.

Clare's of Assisi's reaction to Innocent's rule and its brief provision regarding property has garnered even more comment,[99] although how scholars frame the issues varies. Grundmann argued that behind the widespread resistance to the rule "was the attitude of the house of St. Damian and of St. Clara herself. Accepting the new rule would have compelled this house to accept property and would have loosened its ties to the Franciscans."[100] On this point, however, the erudite scholar errs slightly. Innocent's rule compels no one to accept property: it simply allows (*liceat vobis*) them to receive and freely retain corporate possessions and to have a procurator to manage these possessions.[101] Moreover, San Damiano's Privilege of Poverty explicitly protected Clare's community from being compelled to accept possessions.[102] One might more reasonably speculate that Clare's commitment to poverty made her averse to even the mere mention of possible corporate possessions and a procurator. In 1245 Innocent had made a similar allowance for the friars, but it seemed contrary to the 1223 *Later Rule*—the very "*Rule* of Francis" Innocent admiringly cites in his *forma vitae*—and would be rejected outright in the 1253 rule Clare would help redact.[103] Although San Damiano's Privilege protected its poverty, Clare might very well have been concerned for those few other monasteries closely allied with San Damiano's practice of poverty. It is hard to imagine, however, that Clare's concern extended to all the monasteries in the Order of San Damiano since they lived such varied religious lives and, further, she exercised no administrative authority whatsoever over any of them. Furthermore, it seems Clare's star had dimmed since Gregory IX first accorded her and San Damiano symbolic leadership of the order in the 1220s. Innocent's 1247 *forma vitae* does not even mention her.

Some scholars do more than speculate about Clare's reaction. They describe it in graphic terms despite the fact that neither she nor any of her contemporaries left a single record of her thoughts regarding the new rule. Referring to the provision allowing property, for example, Grundmann writes that "this peril awoke once again the Franciscan rage of Clara Sciffi and cried out for a decision."[104] Others summon the picture of a wounded Clare, her heart aggrieved upon hearing of the rule.[105] Clare's character has so often come to life in such passages that it is almost a commonplace to imagine her bristling at the pope's new legislation. The usual culprit is the 1247 rule's allowance for corporate property.[106] Casagrande sensibly widens the net, concluding that the best way to show that Clare did not accept Innocent's rule is by comparing it point by point with the rule Clare herself redacted.[107] Although I will later suggest that Clare played a more circumscribed role in redacting the 1253 *forma vitae* than is commonly assumed, a witness for her canonization indeed testified that Clare was yearning to have that rule approved.[108] Yet even a comparison of differences between the 1247 and 1253 rules does not prove that Clare rejected Innocent's *forma vitae* out of hand. Absent any direct evidence of her views, Gilliat-Smith argued that Clare gracefully accepted the pope's rule. Pointing to the obedience she promised to Innocent IV in the later 1253 *forma vitae*, Gilliat-Smith finds it inconceivable that she "should have presumed to raise her hand against the Vicar of Christ, to reject a rule which he, in the legitimate exercise of his authority, had placed the whole order under strict obedience to accept, because, forsooth, it conceded a little more liberty in the matter of holding possessions in common than she deemed prudent."[109] Clearly, a dearth of evidence opens ample space for a spectrum of scholarly perspectives.

If the Clare-driven theme of religious poverty can inspire so much discussion on the basis of such modest evidence, why not consider other potentially off-putting issues as well? To offer but one pointed, small example, it seems plausible that numbers of women might have objected to the rule's requirement that there be a single monastic door, raised as high as possible, usually bolted shut, doubly so at night, and accessible by a ladder that was normally withdrawn.[110] One wonders how outsiders were supposed to enter the monastery in case of fire, another provision in Innocent's rule, or even more, how, in that event, the sisters were supposed to escape.[111]

A much more significant example to consider, however, regards the bond between the sisters and friars in the rule. Notably, the 1247 rule's treatment of possessions pales beside its extravagant attention to the Lesser Brothers' role in the women's life. Some scholars point to the possibility that Clare and her sisters could, in principle, have welcomed this new juridical relationship with the friars, had the rule not failed in other regards. Jean-François Godet notes that "Clare and her sisters became what they had always wanted to be, part of the Franciscan Order. . . . Clare's Franciscan ideal had finally achieved its juridical place within the Franciscan Order," although the rule was a betrayal in terms of its provisions regarding poverty.[112] Mueller too suggests that the sisters would, in principle at least, have welcomed the juridical relationship, but it was hollow in light of the rule's other provisions. For example, the relationship might also trouble the women because the rule gave the friars control over the women's foundation of new monasteries.[113] Casagrande emphasizes the negative character of the juridical ties. She notes that Gregory's *forma vitae* said nothing about poverty, possessions, or any defined relationship with the Lesser Brothers. She wonders if the very "openness" of Gregory's *forma vitae* might not explain its appeal over Innocent's *forma vitae*, which, by so defining the women's religious life, also eliminated some of its autonomy.[114] Alberzoni thinks that the enhanced ties Innocent posited between the women and Francis, the alleged founder of the *Order* of San Damiano, effectively undermined his special bond with Clare's particular monastery of San Damiano.[115] Gilliat-Smith approaches the question from a slightly different angle: monasteries bound to the Rule of Benedict from their very foundation—and this might include monasteries that subsequently transferred into the Order of San Damiano—might simply object to the "franciscanization" of their legislation, a key point to which I will return.[116]

Reception by the Order of Lesser Brothers

Many scholars contend that the Lesser Brothers were not pleased with Innocent's new *forma vitae*,[117] a view that aligns with my earlier discussion of the friars' resistance to papal expectations that they pastorally assist the Order of San Damiano. Other evidence suggests that some friars were resisting the new duties imposed upon them in Innocent's *forma vitae*. In May 1248 the pope wrote the provincial minister of the March of Ancona reminding him yet again of the Lesser Brothers' responsibilities toward the monastery of Ascoli Piceno; they were to care for, visit, and instruct the women (*curam gerens, eas visites, et informes*).[118] The letter suggests that the friars, for some reason, had not been acquitting themselves of these tasks, but we do not know why.

The friars, of course, were not a monolith. On the one hand, Thomas of Celano's heated treatment of the *cura monialium* and the dangers of women may have targeted friars too eager to enter women's monasteries. On the other hand, Innocent was close to many friars,[119] probably those more measured with respect to assisting monastic women, and some of these friars surely had a hand in redacting his *forma vitae*. Salimbene noted that he "always kept six Friars Minor with him as long as he lived, as I saw with my own eyes"[120] Innocent's chaplain, confessor, biographer, and one of his most intimate advisers was also a friar, Niccolò da Calvi. Indeed, Innocent appointed Niccolò bishop of Assisi after denying the post to Crescentius of Jesi.[121]

These friars, probably more receptive to the papacy's plan to engage the Lesser Brothers with the Order of San Damiano, did not represent the views of their leadership. Mueller, who attributes the failure of Innocent's *forma vitae* to the Lesser Brothers' resistance, singles out their minister general, John of Parma. He refused to implement the provisions in the new rule and this, writes Mueller, "left the sisters in a legal limbo. On 17 June 1248, Innocent wrote to Cardinal Rainaldo explaining the problem that the friars, whom he commissioned to care for and provide visitation for the sisters, and confirm the appointment of abbesses, were not doing their job. To make up for this lacuna, and knowing that he would not have his way with John of Parma, Innocent asked Cardinal Rainaldo to resume his role as the cardinal protector of the sisters."[122] But as my next discussion of Rainaldo's reaction to Innocent's new rule makes clear, this is not precisely what Innocent said.

Reception by Cardinal Rainaldo, Bishop of Ostia

Earlier, in March 1248, Innocent had written a cryptic letter that reveals Rainaldo's pivotal role regarding the women's various rules. He was writing to Rainaldo in Rainaldo's capacity as cardinal protector (the title retroactively assigned to this post) about a complaint Innocent had received, significantly, from the monastery of Monticelli near Florence. This was the very monastery that had requested and been granted permission in 1219 to adopt the regular observances (*observantias regulares*) of San Damiano and that many think later won a privilege of poverty under Clare's blood sister Agnes as abbess.[123] Innocent's brief missive notes that the women had professed the "rule of San Damiano," by which he meant Gregory's *forma vitae*. They were now seeking Innocent's assistance because the local provincial minister of the Lesser Brothers (possibly Thomas of Pavia) was demanding their obedience. The letter insinuates that the nuns objected to this, although no specific reasons are provided. Innocent concludes his letter by simply handing the matter over to Rainaldo for him to settle.[124]

Despite the letter's cryptic nature, four points can be gleaned. First, it shows that this particular provincial minister was apparently implementing Innocent's *forma vitae*, at least insofar as it gave him jurisdictional authority over the Monticelli monastery. Second, this concerned the women so much that they alerted the pope. Third, although we do not know the precise details of their objection, it seems obviously to revolve around the obedience Innocent's *forma vitae* required the women to give to the Lesser Brothers, not—or at least not stated—the *forma vitae*'s permission allowing the women to hold communal property. Finally, Innocent dealt with the matter not by informing the nuns that they owed obedience to the minister general as stipulated in the new *forma vitae*, but instead by writing Rainaldo, the cardinal protector, and telling him to do something (but what?) about it.

Rainaldo probably did nothing about it. He was in the process of forcing Innocent's hand, making him definitively backtrack on the very rule he had issued just eight months earlier in August 1247. This is transparent in Innocent's June 1248 letter, the letter Mueller cited as evidence that the friars were not implementing Innocent's *forma vitae*. The letter, which says nothing about the friars' failure to accept their new duties, instead shows that

Innocent was trying to reengage Rainaldo in his work as cardinal protector. It had come to his attention, Innocent wrote, that Rainaldo had given up his care (*cura*) and visitation of the monasteries of the Order of San Damiano because Innocent had entrusted it to the provincial ministers of the Lesser Brothers. The pope seems intent upon stroking and assuaging a prelate miffed at being displaced from a position that had been solely his. Rainaldo had apparently reacted to the involvement of the Lesser Brothers by withdrawing completely from his duties. It proved to be an excellent passive-aggressive gambit to regain the upper hand. Innocent's June 1248 letter came less than a year after he had issued his *forma vitae* and just months after he had charged Rainaldo with taking care of the Monticelli dustup. Deferential in tone, even slightly pleading, Innocent tells Rainaldo he does not want the women to be deprived of Rainaldo's helpful advocacy. Henceforth, writes Innocent, all the authority Rainaldo had previously held during the papacy of Gregory IX was to be fully restored. He mentions specifically the duty of correcting and reforming the monasteries (tasks Rainaldo could freely delegate to others) and of confirming the elections of abbesses[125]—all responsibilities Innocent's *forma vitae* had given away to the Lesser Brothers. These letters are clear evidence of how quickly Innocent's *forma vitae* was proving to be a mistake.

Importantly, Monticelli is not an isolated case: Rainaldo sent letters to various monasteries disquieted by the friars' new role in their lives. While the rather small number of monasteries emulating San Damiano's practice of poverty might have objected to Innocent's allowance of communal property, a greater number, it seemed, were perturbed about the new control exercised over them by the Lesser Brothers.[126] Far from resisting Innocent's *forma vitae*, some friars seem to have been embracing their new duties.

In October 1248 Innocent sent another letter to Rainaldo, one I have not seen discussed elsewhere and that I have included in Appendix A. It is almost identical to the letter the pope sent Rainaldo four months earlier reinstating all his previous authority. Annibali da Latera, the editor of this later letter, speculates that Innocent perhaps wrote Rainaldo a second time because the cardinal had refused to comply with the pope's first letter and had continued to ignore the women's monasteries.[127] Rainaldo's strategic pouting was paying a quick profit. The two letters differ in just one detail: whereas the first reinvested Rainaldo with the "visitation and care" the pope had handed over to the "provincial ministers," the second cited the "visitation and care" that he had handed over to the "minister general." Perhaps the pope was clarifying that neither the provincial ministers nor even the minister general of the

Lesser Brothers had authority that could trump Rainaldo's. In any case, the letter suggests that the cardinal was still on strike.

Several letters suggest, in fact, that the lines of authority were not altogether clear or, at least, that the Lesser Brothers continued to be involved in the *cura monialium*. In March 1250 Innocent wrote to the minister general, John of Parma, and the rest of the brothers noting that they would not, unless the pope made some express exception to this letter, have to accept any new responsibilities of visiting, correcting, or undertaking the *cura monialium*.[128] This implies, of course, that they were still performing these pastoral duties in other monasteries. Notably, Dominican men and women were experiencing the same push-pull; indeed, Innocent had earlier granted a similar privilege to Dominican men regarding the *cura monialium*.[129]

The letter Innocent eventually sent 6 June 1250, announcing that no monastery was to be forced to adopt his *forma vitae*, has naturally received prominent attention.[130] Some scholars see Clare as the prime mover prompting the pope to change his mind.[131] Such a speculative proposition fits the image of Clare as a strong woman, an image propagated so effectively in recent years. And although hard evidence about her life is relatively thin, it is plausible to think that if she wanted to oppose Innocent's *forma vitae*, she might have the wherewithal and will to do so. But there is no positive evidence that this is what happened. The evidence that exists points more securely to Rainaldo as the driving force behind the pope's change of heart. His letters to some monasteries in the Order of San Damiano suggest they too were involved. In Innocent's June 1250 letter reversing himself by no longer requiring monasteries to accept his *forma vitae*, he reiterated again that he wanted Rainaldo to undertake his "customary care" of the monasteries. Monasteries that had previously observed Gregory's *forma vitae*, wrote the pope, could continue to do so; the pope did not want the nuns to be perturbed. But the pope left the ultimate choice, importantly, up to Rainaldo, not the women. Rainaldo would judge which of the two *forma vitae* best served each monastery's interests. Of course, the women in these monasteries might very well have shared their opinion with Rainaldo and he might have had many reasons to comply with their wishes, but about this, little can be said for certain. That question awaits future archival investigations.

We do, however, have a record of what Rainaldo thought—in a remarkably detailed and powerfully worded letter he wrote to the abbess and sisters of Ascoli Piceno. The letter, overlooked almost entirely until now, casts important new light not only on the fortunes of the 1247 rule but also on

Rainaldo's role as cardinal protector for both the Order of San Damiano and the Order of Lesser Brothers. I have included the entire letter in Appendix B. Rainaldo sent it just three weeks after receiving the pope's June 1250 letter of reversal.[132] Ascoli Piceno was one of the monasteries that Innocent in 1246 had committed to the care of the Lesser Brothers *at the women's request*.[133] In May 1248 he reminded the provincial minister that the friars were to care for and visit the women.[134] By the time Rainaldo wrote to the monastery of Ascoli Piceno in late June 1250, however, it appears that the friars had usurped powers Rainaldo believed belonged to him alone, having been explicitly restored to him by the pope in his June and October 1248 letters and noted yet again in Innocent's early June 1250 letter giving Rainaldo the power to decide which *forma vitae* the women should follow.

Rainaldo's aggressive tone is unmistakable; no circumlocutions blunt the force of his opinion. He informs the sisters in no uncertain terms that he preferred Gregory's *forma vitae* to the new one. It was out of deference to "the Most Holy Father, the High Pontiff," he writes, that he had not resisted Innocent's *forma vitae* even though, in his modest opinion, he did not think it advanced the women's spiritual welfare. It is indeed possible that Rainaldo had not overtly opposed the pope's new legislation, but he hardly needed to since his abdication of his duties as cardinal protector had, without words, delivered his message. Rainaldo tells the sisters of Ascoli Piceno that he was unhappy not to have been consulted about Innocent's *forma vitae*. Although he knows they are aware that they have been placed once again under his care and jurisdiction, he clearly wants to drive the point home and, to that end, he sends them two written proofs of the pope's political change of heart. The first proof is a copy of the pope's June 1248 letter clarifying that he, Rainaldo, not the provincial ministers, holds jurisdiction over the women. Some of the provincial ministers, he is aware, have been ignoring the pope's mandate and arrogating to themselves jurisdiction that no longer belongs to them (more evidence that not all friars resisted the *cura monialium*). As if this were not enough, Rainaldo also sends the women a copy of Innocent's June 1250 letter announcing that the new *forma vitae* would no longer be binding; Rainaldo himself would have the authority to judge and determine which rule best served the sisters' spiritual interests. And it is his judgment, he writes, that they should observe not Innocent's *forma vitae*, but rather the one they had been observing, Gregory's *forma vitae*. Rainaldo bases his conclusion on his knowledge of the women's history and his careful consideration of both *formae vitae*.

This letter shows that it is not the case that the Lesser Brothers had simply refused to implement Innocent's *forma vitae*. Some friars were still interfering in monasteries that Rainaldo asserted were under his authority. In the letter Rainaldo also referred to a command he sent to the Lesser Brothers' general chapter (in Genoa, 1250) prohibiting them from exercising any jurisdiction over the women,[135] another indication that some friars were attempting to exercise such jurisdiction. The sisters, Rainaldo states, are to recur to him and the visitator he appoints for all matters related to their monastery and not recur at all to the Lesser Brothers. Some unnamed people (friars?), he notes, have been frightening the women, suggesting that if they held to certain rules of silence, fasting, bedding, and other matters (probably those mandated in Gregory's *forma vitae*) they would somehow be in danger of committing a mortal sin. Rainaldo concludes his letter ordering the sisters, his "daughters," under obedience to comply with his wishes. And lest their consciences be perturbed, he reminds them that he "understood, perceived, and knew the mind of your Founder." The founder, it is worth noting, was not Francis—as Innocent's *forma vitae* would have it—but Gregory IX.[136] Rainaldo's lengthy no-holds-barred letter, in contrast to the silence of Clare of Assisi and the—to date—more cryptic complaints of some sisters in the order, suggests that the most adamant and effective opponent of Innocent IV's *forma vitae* was the cardinal protector himself.

Chapter 8

The *1253 Forma Vitae*, ca. 1250 to 1253

Innocent IV showed a ready capacity to reverse course during controversies as seen, for example, during conflicts between the secular masters and mendicant orders[1] or in his own struggles with Frederick II.[2] Cumulatively, his about-turns suggest a pope who could be effectively lobbied by the competing voices around him. Rainaldo of Jenne proved to be just such a decisive force when he caused Innocent to backtrack on key provisions in his *forma vitae* less than a year after its promulgation in August 1247. Rainaldo proved just as influential in guiding the pope toward approving a new *forma vitae* for San Damiano just days before Clare's death in 1253. In fact, he probably played a significant role in redacting the *forma vitae*, albeit most scholarship ascribes the text principally to Clare. Innocent's waffling style was perhaps the optimal papal environment for Clare to push through a program of religious life that, until the late 1240s, the papacy had only reluctantly tolerated. Most scholars point to Innocent IV's 1247 rule as the catalyst for the *1253 forma vitae*, a sort of "last straw" galvanizing Clare to write her own rule.

But, remarkably, no source contemporary with Clare ever states that she wrote, dictated, or even thought of devising a religious rule. No later medieval source does either. The first suggestion that Clare had even a hand in writing the *1253 forma vitae* appeared around the turn of the twentieth century, when a few influential scholars argued that Clare was the text's principal author. Later in the twentieth century, fed probably by the burgeoning interest in women's history, claims that Clare composed a rule crescendoed to sometimes hyperbolic heights.

In this chapter I review what we know about how the *1253 forma vitae* came into being and consider its contents for what it reveals about monastic life in San Damiano. Revisiting the history of the rule's authorship, from the time of the rule's birth in the mid-thirteenth century until today, I will point to weaknesses in the evidence for Clare's sole or principal authorship and suggest other people who plausibly had a hand in the *forma vitae*'s composition.

Confirmation of the Privilege of Poverty

It was standard procedure for the papacy to reaffirm privileges from time to time, particularly when changed circumstances threatened the legitimacy of a privilege. A newly installed bishop might challenge a monastery's privilege, for example, or a change of popes might prompt a monastery to ask the new pontiff to reaffirm a privilege granted by a predecessor. San Damiano's Privilege of Poverty certainly figured among the most precarious of privileges, since Gregory IX, Innocent IV, and Rainaldo all consistently insisted that monasteries in the Order of San Damiano be encouraged to own property, receive rents, and otherwise be financially secured. It is, therefore, unsurprising that Clare sought to have her monastery's virtually unique Privilege of Poverty confirmed again toward the close of her life.

In April 1251, after some six years in Lyon, Innocent IV returned to Italy and took up residence in Perugia. Around then, Clare, who had been chronically ill for over twenty years,[3] took a turn for the worse. Clare's *Legend* reports that Rainaldo, hearing of her illness, set off from Perugia for Assisi, some twenty kilometers away. Described as a "father" to Clare, "a provider by his care [*cura*], [and] always a dedicated friend," he nourished Clare with the eucharist and her sisters with encouraging words. Clare "begged so great a father with her tears to take care of her soul and those of the other Ladies for the name of Christ. But, above all, she asked him to petition to have the Privilege of Poverty confirmed by the Lord Pope and the cardinals. Because he was a faithful helper of the Order, just as he promised by his word, so he fulfilled in deed."[4] Clare, no doubt aware that her days were numbered, wanted to ensure that her death would not also mean the demise of San Damiano's more radical form of poverty.

Rainaldo's Response: A Confirmation of a Privilege or a Forma Vitae*?*

For many years, most scholars have thought the evidence that Rainaldo remained true to his word was none other than the *1253 forma vitae*, confirmed by Rainaldo and Innocent IV. A parchment found in Assisi in the late nineteenth century, which I will call the Assisi parchment, contains this *forma vitae*. It combines five discrete items in this order:

1. Innocent's letter of confirmation, dated 9 August 1253
2. Rainaldo's letter of confirmation, dated 16 September 1252
3. The text proper of the new *forma vitae*
4. The date of Rainaldo's letter (item 2 above)
5. The date of Innocent's letter (item 1 above)

The Assisi parchment is often identified as *Solet annuere*, for the first words of the pope's letter, which, technically, contains all five items since, within it, the pope quotes Rainaldo's letter and the *forma vitae*. I shall reserve "pope's letter" for the portion of the text in the pope's voice, and "Rainaldo's letter"[5] for the portion of the text in Rainaldo's voice.

The Assisi parchment, written as a single paragraph, orders these five items such that Rainaldo's letter—beginning with its text (item 2) and concluding with its date (item 4)—encloses the *forma vitae* within it (item 3). Then Innocent's letter—beginning with its text (item 1) and concluding with its date (item 5)—encloses within it Rainaldo's text and the *forma vitae* (items 2–4). The image of the parchment in Figure 2 shows all five items written as a single continuous text.

Following is the list of items indented to illustrate the order and structure of texts within the Assisi parchment:

1. The text of Innocent IV's letter (9 August 1253) confirming Rainaldo's letter (item 2 below). Innocent's letter formally concludes with item 5 and includes items 2, 3, and 4 below.
   2. The text of Rainaldo's letter (16 September 1252), confirming the *1253 forma vitae* (item 3 below). Rainaldo's letter formally concludes with item 4 and includes item 3 below.
      3. The *1253 forma vitae* (finished before 16 September 1252 and confirmed by the above two letters).
   4. The date of Rainaldo's letter (item 2 above), 16 September 1252, written out.
5. The date of Innocent's letter (item 1 above), 9 August 1252, written out.

Figure 2. The *1253 Forma Vitae*: "The Assisi Parchment." Courtesy of the
Protomonastery of Santa Chiara, Assisi.

Because of its importance, I quote the text of item 2, Rainaldo's September
1252 letter, in full:

> Rainaldo, by divine mercy Bishop of Ostia and Velletri, to his most
> dear mother and daughter in Christ, the Lady Clare, Abbess of San
> Damiano in Assisi, and to her sisters, both present and to come,
> greeting and a fatherly blessing.
>   Beloved daughters in Christ, we approve your [plural] holy pro-
> posal in the Lord and we desire with fatherly affection to impart our
> kind favor upon your wishes and holy desires, because you have re-
> jected the splendors and pleasures of the world and, following the

footprints of Christ Himself and His most holy Mother, you have chosen to live bodily enclosed and to serve the Lord in the highest poverty that, in freedom of soul, you may be servants of the Lord. Acceding to your pious prayers, by the authority of the Lord Pope as well as our own, we, therefore, confirm forever for all of you and for all who will succeed you in your monastery, and we ratify by the protection of this document this form of life [*formam vitae*], the manner of holy unity and the highest poverty that your blessed Father Saint Francis gave you for your observance in word and in writing. It is as follows.[6]

Several features of this letter are noteworthy. First, he addresses it to "Lady Clare, Abbess of San Damiano" and her sisters but says nothing about the women's membership in the Order of San Damiano. This distinguishes his letter from others that he and the pope sent to individual monasteries. Those letters—for the twenty or so years prior to this letter—regularly identified monasteries as belonging to the Order of San Damiano. Scholars have long recognized that one peculiarity of Rainaldo's letter (and the pope's) was that it approved the *forma vitae* for the monastery of San Damiano alone, not any other monasteries in the order. Is this why both Rainaldo and Innocent failed to identify San Damiano as belonging to the Order of San Damiano?— perhaps, but I will return to this point below with a more startling possibility.

Second, according to the prose *Legend*, Clare had asked Rainaldo to have the "Privilege of Poverty confirmed by the pope and cardinals."[7] This was a very specific request and, if fulfilled, would have elicited a papal letter confirming the brief Privilege of Poverty that Innocent's predecessor, Gregory IX, had granted in 1228. But instead of that, Rainaldo's letter confirms the women's "holy proposal" (*sanctum propositum*) and a *forma vitae*, a legislative text much longer and more detailed than the 1228 Privilege of Poverty. And the pope's subsequent letter of August 1253 (item 1 of the Assisi parchment) confirms Rainaldo's September 1252 letter (item 2) with its confirmation. What is going on here? Why is Clare getting so much more than she asked for? It is true that the "holy proposal" and *forma vitae* that win Rainaldo's and the pope's confirmations are, at least, related to poverty. Clare employed the term *propositum* in her second letter to Agnes of Prague to refer to poverty, and, as my discussion of the *forma vitae* will show, poverty is central to that text's meaning. But why would Rainaldo not have responded to Clare's request in the most obvious and simple manner—by interceding on her behalf before the pope and obtaining a simple confirmation of the brief 1228 Privilege? Why would he have dramatically exceeded her expectations, confirming not only the Privilege's protection of poverty (contained and even strengthened within the *forma vitae*),[8] but also the new *forma vitae* itself?

The important codex of Messina might offer evidence that Rainaldo indeed did first obtain a simple confirmation of the Privilege. Dating this codex has been vexed, with estimates ranging widely, from about 1250 to 1450. Attilio Bartoli Langeli, whose study is the most exhaustive to date, places the manuscript in the late thirteenth century or even earlier. He believes its handwriting may even belong to Francis's and Clare's friend, Brother Leo (d. ca. 1270).[9] If Bartoli Langeli's dating is correct (a hypothesis still debated), the codex might have appeared around the time of Rainaldo's 1252 letter. The codex includes several related texts, including the pope's August 1253 letter of confirmation followed by Rainaldo's 1252 letter of confirmation. The first texts within the codex, for which I also indicate their folio placement, appear in this order:

1. The *1253 forma vitae* [1r–18v]
2. The date of Rainaldo's letter, 16 September 1252, written out [19r]
3. The date of Innocent's letter, 9 August 1253, written out [19r]
4. The Privilege of Poverty of Innocent (not indicated whether this is Innocent IV or Innocent III) [19r–21r]
5. The text of Innocent IV's letter of confirmation (9 August 1253), followed by a rubric in red that directs the reader to "see above" (seeming to point to item 4, the Privilege of Poverty) [21r–22r]
6. The text of Rainaldo's letter (16 September 1252) [22r–22v]

Notably, before the pope's letter (item 5) gives way to Rainaldo's letter (item 6), the scribe has interpolated an interesting rubric, which stands out because it is written in red rather than black ink like most of the codex. Here are the concluding words of the pope's letter: "Attentive, therefore, to your [Clare's and her sisters'] devout prayers, We [Innocent IV] approve and ratify what the Bishop [Rainaldo] has done in this matter and confirm it in virtue of Our Apostolic authority and support it in this document. To this end We include herein the text of Bishop [Rainaldo], word for word, which is the following." Then appears the scribe's remark in red ink: "Require retro," that is, "see back" or, in other words, "see above." And what comes before Innocent's letter?—a

Privilege of Poverty conceded by Pope Innocent (item 4). Moreover, the beginning of the pope's letter (item 5), which follows immediately after the Privilege (item 4), seems joined to the Privilege because no rubric separates the two texts; only a capital letter for the first word of the pope's letter marks the transition.[10] Bartoli Langeli believes that the Privilege in this manuscript is the counterfeit Privilege attributed to Innocent III, but there is no ordinal indicating which Pope Innocent is responsible for the Privilege.[11] I wonder, with Felice Accrocca, if the Messina codex might not preserve evidence that Rainaldo had indeed obtained exactly what Clare had requested, Pope Innocent IV's confirmation (item 5) of the Privilege of Poverty (item 4).[12] Evidence from the Messina codex is far too complex to conclude definitively that there had been, first, a simple confirmation of the Privilege of Poverty, but this hypothesis should be borne in mind.[13] Just two other manuscripts, besides the Messina codex, purportedly convey Innocent III's Privilege of Poverty; one of the manuscripts fails to name the pope, while the other, like the Messina codex, lacks an ordinal. Thus, these codices too perhaps contain Innocent IV's Privilege.[14]

A third striking feature of Rainaldo's letter in the Assisi parchment (and related to the preceding point) is that he states he is ratifying not a "privilege," but the "form of life [*formam vitae*], the manner of holy unity and the highest poverty that your blessed Father Saint Francis gave you for your observance in word and in writing. It is as follows." One expects a *forma vitae* to follow this remark and that is just the case in the Assisi parchment. Many scholars who have observed the disjuncture between Clare's request for confirmation of the Privilege of Poverty and Rainaldo's approval of the *forma vitae* have solved this dilemma by equating the Privilege with the *forma vitae* itself. That is, they assume that her request to have the Privilege approved was really a request to have the *forma vitae* (which contains the Privilege along with many other provisions) approved.[15] Eliding the two documents has certain advantages. It makes sense of the Assisi parchment with Rainaldo's (and Innocent's) approbations of a *forma vitae* rather than a privilege. It also ostensibly broadens the circle of textual references to the *forma vitae* because, while only one source (besides the *forma vitae* itself) mentions the *1253 forma vitae*, several sources refer to the Privilege. But it is critical to note that the two documents were clearly distinguished in the minds of Clare and her contemporaries.[16]

Sister Filippa's Testimony

Sister Filippa, whose testimony for Clare's canonization is by far the longest, provides the only extratextual reference to the *1253 forma vitae*. She explains how the text came about:

> At the end of her life, after calling together all her sisters, [Clare] entrusted the *Privilege of Poverty* to them. Her great desire was to have the rule of the order [*regula de l'ordine*] confirmed with a papal bull, to be able one day to place her lips upon the papal seal, and, then, on the following day, to die. It occurred just as she desired. She learned a brother had come with letters bearing the papal bull. She reverently took it even though she was very close to death and pressed that seal to her mouth in order to kiss it.[17]

Several points in Filippa's testimony merit attention. First, she clearly distinguished between the Privilege of Poverty, first approved in 1228, and the *forma vitae* or, in her words, the "rule of the order." This point is confirmed elsewhere in her testimony where she referred to the Privilege as a discrete document that Clare cherished and guarded carefully because she feared it could be lost.[18] So carefully did Clare (and her successors) guard this 1228 Privilege, in fact, that the document survives and is displayed today at the protomonastery of Santa Chiara in Assisi. The *forma vitae* contrasted with this Privilege insofar as the former was a much longer document including numerous provisions unrelated to possessions or poverty.

Second, however, by mentioning the "rule" just after the Privilege, Filippa implies that she sees a connection between them. This is simply because the *forma vitae* contained among its many provisions remarks that confirmed the radical poverty that Clare had sought to protect with the Privilege of Poverty. These remarks are inserted into the *forma vitae's* crucial chapter 6 and they probably explain, at least in part, Clare's "great desire," according to Filippa, to have the *forma vitae* of the order papally confirmed. If confirmed, Clare would thus succeed in embedding the sisters' right to live poorly within the very text of a papal bull, a far more solemn document than a mere privilege alone. Rainaldo had, it seemed, generously exceeded Clare's initial request, although we do not know how or why this happened. Perhaps after winning a privilege confirmed by Innocent IV, it occurred to Clare (or others) that the time was ripe for a more strategic request that would ensure more enduring protection for the women's commitment to poverty.

Third, Filippa is the only witness to mention the *forma vitae* (rule). Two other witnesses, including Clare's blood sister Beatrice, briefly referred to Clare's "love of the 'Privilege of poverty'" but said nothing at all about a rule or *forma vitae*.[19] If the canonization commissioners had thought it merited memorialization, they would have sought more testimony about it or, if such testimony was actually given, bothered to record it. It is worth noting that they were intensely interested in Clare's dying days, recording what six sisters had to say about them.[20] According to Filippa, it was a moment of high drama when the friar arrived with the rule. Clare's last earthly desire, indeed, probably the last dream holding her in this world, was to press the papal seal to her mouth and kiss it. That she died the next day seems hardly surprising.

But not only are the other witnesses silent (or silenced) regarding the rule, the prose *Legend* that Pope Alexander IV (Rainaldo) commissioned after Clare's death similarly says nothing. The hagiographer mentions the Privilege of Poverty, but not the rule, even though the canonization *Acts*, in which Filippa mentioned the rule, furnished much of his information.[21] In a passage where the *Legend* author was perhaps refashioning details of Filippa's testimony, he expands her brief mention of the Privilege to recount how Clare asked Rainaldo to have it confirmed and the prelate complied. But then instead of next relating how the friar arrived with the rule and Clare kissed its papal seal, the *Legend* author narrates an event not reported in the *Acts*: Pope Innocent IV came to visit Clare, and, extending his hand for her to kiss, she insisted instead on kissing his foot.[22] Is it possible that Clare's kiss has been transposed from the rule's papal seal to the papal foot? Notably, the *Versified Legend* also fails to mention the 1253 rule.[23]

Innocent IV's Confirmation of Rainaldo's Confirmation

Some scholars, especially those who do not elide the Privilege into the *forma vitae*, but rather recognize that the two documents are distinct, interpret the silence about the *forma vitae* as an intentional effort on the part of the papacy to suppress knowledge about a rule it did not want other monasteries clamoring to adopt. But if that were the case, why would Innocent IV ever have approved the rule in the first place?

The most common explanation is that Innocent wanted to grant Clare her last dying wish. Clare's final days, according to the *Legend*, created quite a stir, with prominent churchmen parading in to see her: the pope and cardinals visited; Rainaldo encouraged her during her "long martyrdom"; Brothers Juniper, Angelo, and Leo consoled her and her sisters; and the friars' provincial minister came to give Clare communion. Besides kissing Pope Innocent's foot, Clare asked him to forgive her sins, a request that took him aback because he believed his need for pardon greater than hers.[24]

Niccolò da Calvi, the pope's biographer, specified that Innocent visited Clare twice during her illness. Both visits might have taken place during the pope's residence in Assisi, from late April 1253 through that summer.[25] Some scholars think it was during one of these visits that Clare personally asked the pope to approve the *forma vitae*. Niccolò—a friar, papal adviser, and bishop of Assisi at the time—would quite possibly have accompanied Innocent. But like the Legend authors, he reports nothing about any rule Clare wanted the pope to approve.[26] So, with only Filippa's testimony and the *forma vitae* itself as evidence, it is anyone's guess how a privilege Clare wanted confirmed escalated into a full-blown rule approved in a papal bull.

Besides the silence of the official sources, there are a few, albeit inconclusive clues suggesting Innocent was less than enthusiastic about the *forma vitae*. First, Rainaldo's September 1252 letter delimited the rule's application by approving it for the "present and future sisters" of the monastery of San Damiano alone. Innocent's letter, signed just two days before Clare died, approved it for Clare and her sisters, with no mention of any "future sisters."[27] Is this a casual omission, "future sisters" being presumed within the reference to "sisters" and inferred also because Innocent's letter confirmed Rainaldo's? Second, and more suspicious, almost an entire year passed between Rainaldo's and the pope's approval, perhaps indicating Innocent's reluctance. Third, the *forma vitae* was never recorded in the papal register. Some scholars think the Assisi parchment is proof of a rushed job on the part of the papal chancery, trying to get the document into Clare's hands before she died.[28] The date of the pope's letter, 9 August 1253, is the date of his order that the *forma vitae* should be drawn up by the chancery, rather than the date of the *forma vitae*'s formal issue. Presumably, ordinary chancery procedures might have resumed after Clare's death; the *forma vitae* could then have been included in the papal register, but for some reason, it was not. It is true, however, that many, and maybe most of Innocent IV's documents never entered into the register.[29]

The *1253 Forma Vitae*: Contents

Filippa's claim—the sole clue about Clare's relationship to the *forma vitae*—is provocative as much for what it says as for what it omits: Clare's "great desire was to have the rule of the order confirmed with a papal bull, to be able one day to place her lips upon the papal seal, and, then, on the following day, to die."[30] Does this mean, as many have inferred, that Clare liked every feature of the *forma vitae*?—or, since Filippa tied this statement to Clare's love for the Privilege of Poverty, did she mean simply that Clare was delighted to have San Damiano's practice of poverty codified and confirmed with a papal bull? Recurring themes in the *forma vitae* provide some clues to the answer.

Poverty, the most pronounced theme in the *forma vitae*, is enshrined in the most unusual passages within the text and placed also in the text's very center, chapter 6, its heart, so to speak.[31] Although the Assisi parchment was written as one long paragraph, without any breaks, later versions divide the text into twelve chapters, perhaps to facilitate its reading in the monastic refectory,[32] to stress its likeness to Francis's 1223 rule for friars, or to otherwise play upon the symbolic number twelve. Chapter 6, later entitled "Not Having Possessions," includes the passages most securely tied to Clare of Assisi because she speaks in her own voice:

> After the Most High Heavenly Father saw fit by His grace to enlighten my heart to do penance according to the example and teaching of our most blessed father Saint Francis, shortly after his own conversion, I, together with my sisters, willingly promised him obedience. When the Blessed Father saw we had no fear of poverty, hard work, trial, shame, or contempt of the world, but, instead, we held them as great delights, moved by piety he wrote a form of life [*forma vivendi*] for us as follows: "Because by divine inspiration you have made yourselves daughters and handmaids of the most High, most Exalted King, the heavenly Father, and have taken the Holy Spirit as your spouse, choosing to live according to the perfection of the holy Gospel, I resolve and promise for myself and for my brothers always to have the same loving care and special solicitude for you as for them." As long as he lived he diligently fulfilled this and wished that it always be fulfilled by the brothers.[33]

As I noted in Chapter 2, Clare's inclusion of Francis's pithy and powerful *forma vivendi* anchors this longer *1253 forma vitae* in Francis's own words. Fernando Uribe thinks Clare probably knew that Gregory IX had, in his 1238 letter to Agnes of Prague, dismissed Francis's *forma vivendi* as mere "milk drink." That would make Clare's inclusion of it here in a rule to be solemnly approved by a later pontiff both poignant and pointed.[34] And after so simply summing up the sisters' beginning in penance, poverty, and adherence to Francis's example and teaching, Clare secured her sisters' future with Francis's own promise that the Lesser Brothers would perpetually care [have *cura*] for them. One might have thought this was enough to bind the women to poverty, but Clare drives her point home in the next passage with three more strategic insertions. She speaks again for herself and her sisters; she cites Francis's *Last Will* for the women; and she concludes by incorporating a few phrases from Gregory IX's Privilege of Poverty into her and her sisters' own solemn promise. Note Clare's extravagant use of absolute terms such as "never," "always," and "inviolably":

> In order that we as well as those who were to come after us would never turn aside from the holy poverty we had embraced, shortly before his death he repeated in writing his last wish for us. He said: "I, little brother Francis, wish to follow the life and poverty of our most high Lord Jesus Christ and of His most holy Mother and to persevere in this until the end; and I ask you, my ladies, and I give you my advice that you live always in this most holy life and poverty. And keep careful watch that you never depart from this by reason of the teaching or advice of anyone." As I, together with my sisters, have ever been solicitous to safeguard the holy poverty which we have promised the Lord God and blessed Francis, so, too, the abbesses who shall succeed me in office and all the sisters are bound inviolably to observe it to the end, that is, by not receiving or having possession or ownership either of themselves or through an intermediary, or even anything that might reasonably be called ownership, except as much land as necessity requires for the integrity and proper seclusion of the monastery, and this land may not be cultivated except as a garden for the needs of the sisters.[35]

The highly charged personal quality of this chapter is precisely what convinces most scholars that this is the work of Clare herself. The chapter has Clare's signature all over it, not just the dead-give-away pronouns, but also the very topics of poverty (including echoes of the Privilege), the descent from Francis, and the relationship with the Lesser Brothers, topics Clare touched on in her letters to Agnes of Prague and hagiographers and others who wrote about Clare also associated with her.

Only a few other very brief first-person statements appear elsewhere in the *forma vitae*. In two of three passages in which Clare speaks in her own singular voice, she notably speaks of poverty. First, Clare says "I admonish, beg, and encourage my sisters always to wear poor garments."[36] Second, in a chapter partly devoted to the subject of ownership and begging alms, she directly addresses her sisters: "This is that summit of the highest poverty which has established you, my dearest sisters, heiresses and queens of the kingdom of heaven; it has made you poor."[37] In both these passages, Clare takes her words almost verbatim from Francis's 1223 rule for the Lesser Brothers. Her only other "I" statement (about vices) is also, notably, right out of Francis's rule.[38] In other words, Clare consistently self-presents—whether within the crucial, central chapter six or in her three other brief "I" statements—as someone who is channeling Francis of Assisi.

Francis's voice is also present in other passages of the *forma vitae* that either closely paraphrase or quote directly from his 1223 rule. These include all the statements in chapter 8 on possessions and alms. Without analyzing further the remainder of the *1253 forma vitae* at this point, one can easily appreciate how on the mark Sister Filippa was: the Privilege of Poverty was certainly related to the *forma vitae* and, without a doubt, Clare would have longed to receive a papal document that so articulated some of her own desires for San Damiano. But should Clare be considered the sole or principal author of the *forma vitae*? In the course of answering this question, I will have reason to return to many other topics addressed in the text.

Who Authored the *1253 Forma Vitae*?

Francis and Hugo: Thirteenth to Late Nineteenth Centuries

To ask who authored the *1253 forma vitae* leads to another question: what does it mean to call anyone an author? The 1253 rule has many sources, a point everyone acknowledges. Even though Benedict of Nursia incorporated many and often lengthy verbatim passages from the *Rule of the Master* into his own rule, he is still considered the rule's true author because he consciously shaped the entire text. Clare's role in constructing the *1253 forma vitae* is often described in similar terms. Some of its commonly cited sources include the Rule of Benedict,[39] the *formae vitae* of Gregory IX and Innocent IV, Francis's 1221 rule (not approved by the papacy), and his 1223 papally approved rule. The editors of a volume that synoptically tracks, via parallel columns, the *forma vitae*'s dependence on these sources describe how Clare used her "creative freedom as author":

> Like the wise scribe of the gospel, who brings from the storeroom both the ancient and the new (cf. Mt 13,52), Clare takes from all others the expressive, juridic, [and] spiritual instruments she needs to codify her experience of following Christ [*sequela Christi*]. . . . And where these instruments prove less or show themselves to be inadequate for expressing the particular Franciscan identity of her Order of Poor Sisters and the newness of the charismatic experience she felt she conveyed, then, without any deferential fear, she adapts, transforms, omits, deliberately distances herself, and invents.[40]

Indeed, the most common statement made about Clare in the past few decades regards her authorship of the *1253 forma vitae*. Thirty years ago Thaddée Matura noted that it was "a great historical first" that Clare was "the first woman to compose a rule for women."[41] Matura had no idea, of course, that he was coining a phrase destined to be repeated many dozens of times over.[42]

Ann Matter is among the few scholars in the English-speaking world to raise a doubt about Clare as principal author of the rule. Matter observes that "there is no extant copy of the document [Clare] sent to Rome for approval, nor any surviving draft from Clare's own hand or community."[43] To this, I add that Clare is not cited as the rule's author or even minor contributor in any sources before the modern period—not in sources composed during her lifetime, not in the *Acts* for the process of her canonization, not in the early Legends, not in any medieval or even any early modern documents whatsoever. Indeed, Clare becomes the rule's author only in the late nineteenth century. How did this happen? What changed to make others think of her as the rule's principal architect and creator?

Until the late nineteenth century, discussions of the rule's composition completely sidelined Clare. The rule was first attributed to Francis—and this within the very Assisi parchment that contains the *forma vitae*. Innocent wrote in his 1253 letter introducing the *forma vitae* that he was confirming "the form of life that Blessed Francis gave you."[44] Rainaldo wrote in his 1252 letter introducing it that he was confirming "this form of life [*formam vitae*], the manner of holy unity and the highest poverty that your blessed Father Saint Francis gave you for your observance in word and in writing. *It is as follows*" (emphasis mine).[45] Rainaldo's "in word and in writing" does not specify how what "follows" had been written down. Did what Francis gave the women "in writing" (*scripto*) include more than his brief *forma vivendi* that Clare quoted in chapter 6? Nor does Rainaldo tell us who set down in writing what Francis passed on orally "in word" (*verbo*). He unambiguously, however, ascribes everything in the *1253 forma vitae* to Francis when he writes, "It is as follows." There is yet another suggestion in the Assisi parchment, somewhat more oblique, that the *forma vitae* was Francis's. Its first chapter opens: "The form of life of the Order of Poor Sisters that Blessed Francis established is this: to observe the Holy Gospel of our Lord Jesus Christ, by living in obedience, without anything of one's own, and in chastity."[46] These early, explicit attestations no doubt launched the long tradition of Francis as author of the *1253 forma vitae*, a tradition supported by Franciscan writers and texts including, for example, Ubertino da Casale (ca. 1305), the *Firmamentum trium Ordinum S. Francisci* (1512), and Francesco Gonzaga (1587).[47]

It was perhaps Brother Bernard of Besse, writing in 1279 or shortly thereafter, who launched a second long tradition that brought Gregory IX into the picture as Francis's coauthor. Bernard wrote: "In composing the rules or forms of living for their Orders [the Order of Lesser Brothers, the Order of San Damiano, and the Third Order], Lord Pope Gregory of holy memory, at that time in a lesser capacity [as Cardinal Hugo], united with blessed Francis through an intimate closeness, [and] devoutly supplied what the holy man lacked in knowledgeable judgment."[48] Bernard was probably thinking of Gregory's *forma vitae* composed around 1219 since this was the rule observed for so many years in most of the monasteries of the Order of San Damiano and it was still the rule most observed at the time Bernard was writing. It is true that Gregory took an avid interest and even had a hand in composing some rules. He claimed to have "stood by" Francis while he composed his 1223 rule for the friars. Gregory inventively put Francis forward as the model for lay penitents (whose origin predates Francis by generations); and Gregory was pope when the earliest rule for penitents appeared in a new version.[49] Gregory would certainly have made hay out of the fact that Francis had been his coauthor of a rule for nuns if that had been the case. But even Gregory would not go that far; he instead claimed merely that his *forma vitae* had been "accepted" by Francis, a claim made safely long after Francis had died.[50]

Brother Philip of Perugia, writing around 1306 about the first cardinal protectors of the Lesser Brothers, made this influential remark about the writing team of Francis and Hugo-Gregory: "Moreover, I heard this from elderly fathers, that [Hugo] arranged and wrote with our Father, blessed Francis, the rule of the sisters of the Order of San Damiano, now known as the 'Order of Saint Clare,' after the fashion of [*ad instar*] the rule of the Lesser Brothers. The Cardinal, owing to the rule's strictness, shed many tears while writing it, partly out of devotion and partly out of compassion."[51] Philip's confusion undermines his credibility. On the one hand, he shows his sensitivity to historical anachronism when he clarifies that the order had formerly been known as the Order of San Damiano. On the other hand, he conflates the *1253 forma vitae*, which was indeed loosely patterned after the 1223 rule of the Lesser Brothers, with Hugo's *forma vitae* composed around 1219. This confusion led Oliger to dismiss Philip's testimony out of hand.[52]

But Philip's hearsay, however muddled, proved tremendously influential among the Lesser Brothers' best-known chroniclers. Mariano of Florence (d. 1523), who wrote a lengthy chronicle of the Lesser Brothers[53] and also the first full-scale history of Clare's order,[54] adhered firmly to Philip's storyline of Francis and Hugo as coauthors. Writing in the wake of the order's Observant reform and incorporating both published and archival sources, Mariano echoed Philip almost verbatim: what Francis proposed, Hugo wrote out in his own hand, weeping from compassion and devotion and on account of the rule's strictness. Mariano adds that when the rule was finished, Francis went to San Damiano to explain it to Clare and her sisters. Hugo also succeeded, says Mariano, in persuading Francis to accept the pastoral care of all the monasteries in the order, not just San Damiano; thus all would observe the rule.[55]

The Portuguese chronicler Marcos of Lisbon (d. 1591) drew some of his information from Mariano of Florence but proved exceptional by giving Innocent IV a leading role in the rule's history. Marcos consulted archival sources in Spain, France, and Italy for his chronicle of the Order of Lesser Brothers, and he seems to have found a copy of the *1253 forma vitae* with its papal confirmation. He explained that after Innocent IV's 1247 rule failed—owing to the objections of Clare, San Damiano, and some other monasteries over the issue of the rule's relaxation of communal poverty—the pope allowed these women to return to the rule Francis had first given them and that Gregory IX had orally confirmed for Clare and the order. First approving Francis's rule *viva voce*, Innocent then confirmed it with a papal bull. After this account, Marcos published within his *Chronicle* a rule closely approximating the Assisi parchment and also, it is worth noting, a Privilege of Poverty granted, he wrote, by Innocent IV.[56] Marcos's account clearly mistakes the *1253 forma vitae* for a rule he thought Francis composed, Gregory confirmed, and Innocent reconfirmed.

The Irish friar Luke Wadding (d. 1657), by far the most influential chronicler in the Order of Lesser Brothers, published the first complete edition of Francis's writings in 1623, followed two years later by the first volume of his own prolific *Annales Minorum*, a chronicle of the order from its beginning until Wadding's own day.[57] Accepting Philip of Perugia's account, Wadding said Hugo assisted Francis by occasionally counseling moderation and by supplying words or phrases when these failed the less erudite Francis. Wadding conjectured that Francis composed the women's rule in 1224 since he modeled it on his 1223 rule for the friars. Francis, Wadding said, had just returned to Assisi when the women of San Damiano approached him and requested that he give them a written rule beyond what he had communicated to them orally, so that when he died they would have his rule to follow.[58] Wadding's scholarship was so consequential that most accounts of the rule until the late nineteenth century, and some thereafter, continued to present Francis as the rule's principal author, dictating to and assisted by Hugo.[59]

Wadding's edition of the *1253 forma vitae* was highly depersonalized compared to the Assisi parchment. While Clare's brief first-person statements in chapters two and eight remained, almost all the first-person plural statements (e.g., "our cardinal protector," "our life," "our form of poverty") appeared transposed to the third person. Most crucially, the highly personalized chapter six was radically truncated: it included the essence of the Privilege of Poverty, but had been entirely stripped of Clare's and Francis's first-person quotations. Oliger speculates that Wadding left these out because Francis's words were being recalled by Clare only after he had died (1226); if he had finished the rule in 1224, as Wadding believed, then Francis's "two letters"—as Wadding labeled the Francis quotations—must have been added after he had finished writing the women's rule.[60] Some scholars who were familiar with both Wadding's impersonal version and others that contained Clare's and Francis's first-person quotations considered Wadding's text superior. Lempp, for example, thought the personal passages were simply unsuitable within a rule.[61]

Clare Emerges as Author: The Twentieth-Century Turn

John of Capistrano, in his 1445 commentary on the *forma vitae*, did not address the question of authorship, but did provocatively allude in passing to what Francis and Clare "intended" regarding the sisters' work.[62] His fleeting remark suggests that some readers might have recognized Clare's contribution to the rule, but it would not be until the late nineteenth century that explicit recognition came. Editors and commentators had to notice, of course, the first-person pronouns within the rule, whether the few pronouns that appeared in Wadding's edition or the more plentiful pronouns in other editions.[63] In 1875, one anonymous editor tried to account for them. He noted that after Francis, assisted by Hugo, had finished compiling the rule, Clare made some "few trifling alterations," calling Francis "Saint" and "Blessed" whenever she mentioned him, "inserting two letters [the chapter 6 quotations] written by him to his beloved daughters at St. Damian's, and addressing the rule to her religious in her own name."[64] Twenty-five years later, Marianus Fiege cribbed this sentence (or was he himself the earlier anonymous editor?) almost verbatim, then added: "She thus made the Rule, as far as she could, her own, and directed it to her Religious in her own name and authority."[65] And in another way, even the anonymous writer of 1875, who called Clare's alterations "trifling," made the rule "hers" by linking it so inextricably to her deepest desires. After altering the rule, he writes, that

> she then presented it to the Holy See for confirmation, and for twenty-nine years this was the great object of all her prayers and tears. It was a struggle between the Saint's heroic love of poverty on the one hand, and on the other, the prudent hesitation of the Sovereign Pontiff to approve solemnly an Order founded on such absolute and hitherto unparalleled renunciation of all temporal property.
>
> But at length the prayers and patience of the Saint prevailed. The Rule, in all its primitive purity, was confirmed, first, by the Cardinal Protector, Raynald, Bishop of Ostia and Velletri (afterwards Pope Alexander IV) in the year 1252, and finally by Pope Innocent IV, who gave the solemn Bull of confirmation to St. Clare on the 9th August, 1253.[66]

Two scholars around the turn of the twentieth century helped turn the tide definitively in Clare's favor as the principal author of the *1253 forma vitae*.

Their studies proved so pivotal that they form part of scholarly discussions of the rule to this day. The first was the Italian savant and Vatican scholar, Giuseppe Cozza-Luzi (d. 1905), who undertook an analysis of the Assisi parchment. In 1893, Abbess Chiara Matilda Rossi of the protomonastery of Santa Chiara in Assisi had discovered it hidden in the folds of some garments guarded in a reliquary.[67] The abbess, who thought the relic garments had belonged to Clare, had begun to look for the rule because an abbess in France, troubled by the many variants among the rule's published editions, inquired about it so that a reliable version could be established. Cozza-Luzi's essay on the rule was wide ranging, covering not only the parchment but also the circumstances that led up to it and many individuals related to it, including Clare, Francis, and Innocent IV. But his study became renowned almost solely for his discussion of some marginal and other notes he found on the parchment. For over a century, it has been de rigueur to cite Cozza-Luzi's interpretations of the notes to corroborate the most widely held theory about the papacy's approval of the rule. Entirely overlooked, however, are Cozza-Luzi's preceding observations about Clare. Importantly, these provide the scaffolding on which he built his technical discussion of the Assisi parchment, his interpretations of its notes, and the principal role he accords to Clare as the rule's author.

I turn first, then, to this scaffolding. Cozza-Luzi sought at the outset of his essay to show unequivocally that Clare was on a par with or even better than Franciscan men. Her womanly heart, he wrote, could understand Francis not only as well as but perhaps better than the men who surrounded Francis. In contrast to earlier studies, Cozza-Luzi depicted Clare not as a mere assistant in founding the Order of San Damiano, but as the founder herself, who also knew herself to be the founder. She was worthy of more admiration than Francis, he wrote, because she accepted the task of leading souls at a younger age than Francis had.[68]

Cozza-Luzi subtly diminished Francis's centuries-old claim as the rule's principal author in two ways. First, although he obviously admired Francis as the creative genius behind "Franciscan poverty," he never referred to him as the 1253 rule's author or inspiration. In fact, within a single sentence he emphatically attributed the rule to Clare: "Clare alone dictated the rule" and she did so "after Francis's death."[69] Second, in a most revealing turn, Cozza-Luzi digressed to Dante Alighieri's treatment of Clare and the rule. In the *Paradiso*, Dante has the deceased Piccarda dei Donati, who in life had entered Clare's order, speaking to him:

> High merit and perfected love, she said,
> Ensky aloft a lady [Clare], by whose rule
> Maids in your world are veiled and habited.[70]

What most interested Cozza-Luzi in this passage is Dante's choice of words. Cozza-Luzi notes that the poet said the rule is "hers" (*sua*) when he put into Piccarda's mouth the phrase "by whose rule" (*a la cui norma*) the true followers are habited and veiled. That Dante's Italian term *norma* here signified "rule," Cozza-Luzi justified in a footnote. Without quite saying so, it is almost as if Cozza-Luzi was using Dante, who died some two generations after Clare, as a primary source to prove Clare was the 1253 rule's author.[71] Cozza-Luzi, who was then also busy publishing other material on Dante's *Paradiso*, seems to have had Dante very much on his mind.[72]

These and other arguments lay the groundwork for Cozza-Luzi's famous interpretations of the parchment's marginal and other notes. He interprets each note in the context of a visit by the pope to see Clare just before she died. Rainaldo had already confirmed San Damiano's commitment to highest poverty in 1252 "by the authority of the Lord pope," but Clare, thought Cozza-Luzi, was not satisfied. Rainaldo had given her hope for an altogether different sort of papal confirmation, so Clare, Cozza-Luzi said, was holding out for something in the pope's own name. Moved by her imminent death, Innocent decided to grant the *forma vitae* on 9 August 1253 and, extraordinarily, bring it to her himself the next day. Clare took the bull in her hands and kissed it (as Filippa had testified) "many times," Cozza-Luzi elaborated. The document had been sealed officially with the papal bull, but, Cozza-Luzi alleges, Clare was still not satisfied: she wanted Innocent to authorize it in his own handwriting. Although entirely out of keeping with papal practice, the pope decided to do so as a special favor to Clare, but then he, in turn, was not satisfied: of his own accord, he decided to write another comment on the parchment.[73]

Cozza-Luzi's imaginary scenario was a way for him to make sense of the notes he found on the parchment, notes he deciphered by "reviving" them with a chemical agent.[74] The first two notes, which he said were in the pope's own hand, appeared in the upper left margin of the parchment, on the same side containing Innocent's and Rainaldo's letters of confirmation and the text of the *forma vitae*. The first note—"Ad instar fiat. S."—was supposedly the pope's signature, which Cozza-Luzi rendered as "May it be done as it is here written," signed, following papal practice, with his baptismal name initial "S."

for Sinibaldus. The second note was what the pope allegedly added of his own volition, "Ex causis manifestis mihi et protectori fiat ad instar." Cozza-Luzi rendered this as "For the reasons made known to me and to the protector, may it be done as it is here said." There was yet this problem to resolve: the annotation "Ad instar fiat. S.," according to papal chancery procedures, indicated that the pope was giving his approval to a written document. The chancery would then use the annotated document to draw up a new formal version. When the papal seal was subsequently appended to that new version, it would become a solemn papal bull. Although Cozza-Luzi does not discuss this protocol, it is clear that he knew it was an unheard of breach of chancery protocol to have a pope's handwritten approval appear on the very bull itself. Moreover, he recognized that Rainaldo's confirmation of the *forma vitae* a year before Clare's death was made in the name of the pope and, Cozza-Luzi wrote, Clare knew this. Since no other confirmation was even required, Cozza-Luzi had to engage in some special pleading to explain the extraordinary circumstances. Clare, he writes, was not satisfied with Rainaldo's confirmation made in the pope's name and under his authority. She wanted the pope's own word, and the pope, knowing she was about to die and wishing to console her, decided to bring her the sealed papal bull himself. Still this was not enough for Clare. It was no use explaining to her that a sealed papal bull was already the most solemn confirmation possible. She asked the pope to write his approval on the bull in his own hand. So moved by her remarkable request, he complied, but then, unsatisfied himself, he decided gratuitously to write on the bull a second time. In Cozza-Luzi's account, the unheard of notes on the parchment, instead of undermining its authenticity, showed instead how special it was.[75]

Cozza-Luzi found two other notes on the back of the parchment in a hand he said was "almost contemporary" with the document itself. These notes, he thought, proved the authenticity of the parchment that "had filled Clare with consolation and which she had covered with her last kisses." His reading of the two notes was "Bull of confirmation of the rule of saint Clare given by Innocent IV" and "Clare touched and kissed this out of devotion many many times." Here was the proof, he wrote, that "the rule of the sisters was attributed to her [Clare] and not to others."[76] It should hardly be worth commenting that "rule of Saint Clare," a title early applied to the rule, does not qualify as proof that Clare composed the rule, but Cozza-Luzi here seems to interpret it just so. The genitive construction "rule of Clare" merely indicates *some* relation between the rule and Clare, without specifying what the relation was. For centuries, writers had used the phrase "rule of Saint Clare" to refer to the rule they thought Francis and Hugo had written and Clare and her sisters had observed.

Even if Cozza-Luzi's interpretations of all the parchment notes were correct, it is worth noting that they did not establish that Clare composed the rule. But Cozza-Luzi's enthusiastic study revolutionized scholars' view of the rule's approbation and composition. "It would be impossible to exaggerate the importance of this remarkable study," wrote Montgomery Carmichael in a 1904 essay on Francis's writings. Francis may have offered Clare a *formula vitae* when she began religious life and been the inspiration behind the rule, but Francis could no longer be considered its principal author. That honor, said Carmichael, belonged to Clare, who recast the rule in the days leading up to her death, incorporating into it and adapting various passages from the 1223 rule.[77] Two years later, Paschal Robinson echoed Carmichael's "recasting" language.[78] Then, in a series of four publications about Clare that appeared from 1910 to 1912, Robinson directly addressed the question of authorship. He said that except for the brief *forma vivendi* given at the beginning of Clare's and her sisters' religious life, Francis never wrote a rule for them, not in 1224 and certainly not later; he had no hand in the rule the pope approved in 1253.[79] Robinson's views on this last rule subtly shifted over time. Parting company with Cozza-Luzi, Carmichael, and others, in 1910 Robinson called Rainaldo the rule's "principal author." It was he who "closely copied the Rule of the Friars Minor." Clare "had a share in its compilation," particularly the personal passages, and Rainaldo's drafting and editing was "unquestionably prepared under the auspices of St. Clare."[80] Two years later, Robinson no longer called Rainaldo the "principal author": the cardinal "cast" the rule into legislative form, but "there can be no doubt that it was revised by St. Clare herself and that parts of it are her very own."[81] That same year, he wrote elsewhere that "St. Clare herself had a large share in [the rule's] compilation."[82] Robinson's slippage from thinking Clare had a share in the compilation of a work principally produced by Rainaldo to thinking she had a "large share" in a compilation Rainaldo cast before she revised it was remarkably restrained compared to other scholars' views.

The French Franciscan Livarius Oliger (d. 1951) produced the next major study upgrading Clare to author of her own rule. In 1912 he published a lengthy and deeply learned essay on the various rules associated with the Order of San Damiano, beginning with Francis's *forma vivendi* and concluding with the *1253 forma vitae*. He wrote in Latin, probably to make his work available to a wider reading public, an irony now that Latin is no longer the *lingua franca* of the scholarly world. One suspects his study is more often cited than actually read. Oliger positioned Clare as a sort of lynchpin in the story of the rule's genesis and approval. He was adamant that Clare absolutely refused to accept Innocent IV's 1247 rule. He also, importantly, accepted without reservation Cozza-Luzi's transcription of the marginal notes (corrected slightly by Robinson).[83] The first two notes were, he was absolutely convinced, handwritten by Innocent IV himself, although this opinion too seemed to rest on Cozza-Luzi's judgment. Oliger was perhaps more disturbed than Cozza-Luzi by the presence of Innocent's handwritten notes on a solemn bull and so added to the special pleading. A pope, he wrote, normally would have written only on a petition he was approving so it could subsequently be drawn up into a bull. But in this case, it appears that no such petition existed. The pope must have agreed orally to Clare's request. His decision to write directly on the bull both compensated for the unusual protocol and, given the extraordinary and hurried circumstances, underlined the document's legality.[84] Most momentously, Oliger concluded (but based on what?) that Clare should be considered the rule's author; she probably started writing it after she was displeased with Innocent IV's 1247 rule.[85]

Oliger's magisterial study essentially set the narrative for future discussions of the *1253 forma vitae*. But it is worth noting that his conclusions rested on diverse types of evidence, with some corroborated by multiple medieval sources and others dependent essentially on the work of scholars such as Cozza-Luzi. Where only circumstantial evidence existed, Oliger had to rely on his own plausible speculation; he posited, for example, that Clare wrote a rule between 1247 and 1252. Scholarly discussions since Oliger have varied on minor issues, such as quibbles about how many times the pope might have visited Clare; how, when, and where she made her request; or whether it was the pope himself or a friar who brought her the bull.[86] But, notably, many subsequent writers do not distinguish between conclusions Oliger documented with medieval sources and others based on his intuitive reasoning. So, for example, it is now common to read that Innocent IV's 1247 rule prompted Clare to start writing a rule and that the 1253 rule is wholly or virtually her own *oeuvre*.[87] Because this latter claim became so integral to the received wisdom about Clare, there has seemed to be no need for scholars to footnote it with corroborating evidence.

Clare's Oral Request and the Parchment's Notations Reconsidered

The absolute dearth of explicit medieval or even early modern testimony that Clare was sole or principal author of the *1253 forma vitae*, together with recent historical discoveries about the text, make this a propitious time to revisit Clare's role as author of the rule that came to bear her name. Recent analysis of the marginal notes severely undermines the oft-repeated account of Clare's moving oral request to Innocent IV and his rare decision to write his assent on a papal bull.

Except for Léopold Delisle, no one seems ever to have raised doubts about the marginal notes Cozza-Luzi made central to the pope's dramatic eleventh-hour approval of the *1253 forma vitae*.[88] Robinson offered a slightly revised reading of the notes, but no one else, it seems, ever rechecked them. The Assisi parchment was inaccessible to most scholars. Considered a relic itself after its rediscovery in the late nineteenth century, it was displayed in a reliquary that obscured its margins.[89] Most importantly, the chemical agent that Cozza-Luzi had applied to the first two notes to enhance their legibility soon rendered them illegible.[90] One wonders, in fact, how legible they were when Robinson reread them since, as will become clear below, he seems to have been unduly influenced by Cozza-Luzi's own reading.

In 2006, Stefano Brufani and Attilio Bartoli Langeli collaborated on a pair of studies on the parchment, made available to them by the community of sisters living in the protomonastery of Santa Chiara in Assisi. From the point of view of papal diplomatics, Bartoli Langeli found it "absurd" under any circumstances to think that a pope would write "Ad instar fiat" directly on a papal bull. It so contravened chancery practice of the period that only a "moment of collective madness" could conjure a scene in which the pope so acted.[91] But this, of course, is exactly what the scholarly community has been doing for the last century.

In papal diplomatics, "confirmation" of a preceding act is clearly distinguished from a *renovatio* or *innovatio*, a "renewal." Examples of confirmation include Rainaldo's 1252 letter confirming the *forma vitae* and Innocent IV's 1253 letter confirming Rainaldo's letter of confirmation. A confirmation of a text includes within it a word-for-word copy of the text that is being confirmed. And just so, Rainaldo's confirmation of the *1253 forma vitae* encloses that text word for word within his confirmation and, similarly, Innocent's confirmation of Rainaldo's confirmation includes the entirety of Rainaldo's confirmation (with the *1253 forma vitae*). A renewal, by contrast, is indicated by the phrase "Ad instar fiat," by which a pope, in his own handwriting, orders that a new document be drawn up "in imitation" of an earlier document formally issued by a previous pope. Innocent IV would not use the phrase "Ad instar fiat" to confirm either Rainaldo's letter or the *forma vitae*, neither of which were *papal* documents.[92] But who would?

The first of Brufani's and Bartoli Langeli's stunning claims is that the "Ad instar fiat" is not in Innocent IV's handwriting at all, as Cozza-Luzi thought. The note was instead a "renewal" issued in 1266 by Pope Clement IV (r. 1265–1268), who was newly approving his papal predecessor's (Innocent IV's) confirmation of Rainaldo's letter and the *forma vitae*. Bartoli Langeli based his conclusion not so much on paleographic grounds as on his own exposition of papal chancery procedures.[93] A multispectral analysis of the first note revealed, moreover, that it was not signed by "S," the first initial of Innocent IV's baptismal name; it might be an abbreviated "G," but is more likely another letter (and although Bartoli Langeli observes that Clement IV's baptismal name was "Guido," he is disinclined to conclude the note was signed by "G").[94]

Bartoli Langeli next concluded that Cozza-Luzi was entirely mistaken regarding the second note. It is not by the same hand as the first note, nor does it come even close to approximating Cozza-Luzi's Latin reading, rendered as "For the reasons made known to me and to the protector, may it be done as it is here said." Photos for each note buttress Bartoli Langeli's points. So few of the letters can be puzzled out for the second note (but enough to show Cozza-Luzi had erred) that, at the current state of technology, there is no decisive conclusion about the second note's meaning.[95]

The notes on the back of the parchment, which Cozza-Luzi thought were in a hand almost contemporary with the document and proved its authenticity, meet similar fates. The handwriting matches that of an archivist who made an inventory of documents in the protomonastery of Santa Chiara and annotated a number of them, including the 1228 Privilege of Poverty. He or she probably annotated the parchment sometime between 1323 and 1343, that is, about seventy to ninety years after Clare's death.[96] Cozza-Luzi's "Bull of confirmation of the rule of saint Clare given by Innocent IV" is correct except for the term "Bull," which cannot be fully deciphered and might approximate a term like *subietio*. Cozza-Luzi's "Clare touched and kissed this out of devotion many many times" is correct except for the currently indecipherable first term "Clare."[97] Brufani importantly asks whether this comment preserved a piece of oral history or simply repeated (and slightly elaborated) what Sister Filippa had reported in the process for Clare's canonization.[98]

How, if at all, might Brufani's and Bartoli Langeli's conclusions affect our understanding of the *forma vitae*? If they are correct, there is, on the one hand, far less justification for imagining the intense encounter (or encounters) between Innocent IV and Clare in the days prior to her death regarding, specifically, the *forma vitae*. With his handwriting now "removed" from the Assisi parchment, there was no breach of papal chancery protocol pointing to a unique papal favor. The papal notes on the parchment are now dated to 1266, which makes much more sense because Clement IV did indeed renew the texts contained in the Assisi parchment that year.[99] On the other hand, while the notes may have been written in 1266, the parchment appears to be an exemplar dated 9 August 1253, just two days before Clare's death.[100] The extraordinary feat of a new *forma vitae* being ordered by the pope for San Damiano in Clare's dying days thus stands. Sister Filippa, as the only contemporary of Clare to mention the *forma vitae*, had the last and only word about the matter: Clare entrusted the Privilege of Poverty to her sisters; she longed to have the "rule of the order" confirmed; a friar brought a letter to her on 10 August showing that the pope had so ordered it; she kissed the papal seal appended to the parchment and died the next day. According to the *Acts* for the canonization, Legends, and Niccolò da Calvi's life of Innocent, the pope had visited her. Whether they discussed the rule or not is now purely speculative, with no parchment notes to tip the matter one way or the other. But however that question is resolved, someone else besides Clare, either alone or with her, probably helped win the pope's approval.

The Multiple Voices in the 1253 Forma Vitae

The best witness about the truth of the *forma vitae*, however, is within its very text. I return to it now, still asking: who redacted this rule?

Clare's Contribution

Clare's contribution in chapter 6 is unambiguous. Altogether unusual for a religious rule, these highly personal passages are in Clare's voice and in Francis's voice, channeled by Clare. But many other voices speak throughout the rule. Elizabeth Petroff accounts for them by pointing to the rule's many sources, which include the Rule of Benedict, Francis's 1223 rule, and both Hugo-Gregory's and Innocent's *formae vitae*. She notes the dramatically more impersonal tone of most passages and says of the rule as a whole: "Less than half of the text is new, and even that seems boringly formulaic. . . . It is prescriptive legislation. Clare has chosen language that is both powerful and non-threatening; the words are not her own." Clare "makes no claim to originality" with this "patchwork of quotations." She presents chapter 6 as Francis's own writing and the text as a whole as a written version of the *forma vitae* he delivered orally. Petroff intriguingly sees this as a conscious strategy on Clare's part to use the words "of her masters" to achieve her own goals: "Clare is choosing a male voice, a male rhetoric, to safeguard the existence of her communities. For this is a revolutionary text intended to guide utopian communities of women in new roles for women in the Church."[101] Petroff is one of a number of commentators who helpfully highlight the novel features of this rule. Yet I wonder about that male voice or, in any case, the different voices in the text.

Others who attribute the 1253 rule to Clare and who similarly perceive multiple strands within the rule account for them in other ways. Chiara Augusta Lainati, who has long argued that Clare embraced Hugo's 1219 rule (including its strict provisions on enclosure), stresses how much Clare's *1253 forma vitae* adheres to the structure and order of topics Hugo laid out in the 1219 rule. While Clare may have begun work on her rule as early as 1238, states Lainati, it is most likely she wrote it after Innocent's rule appeared in 1247.[102] But regardless of when she began her redaction, Lainati considers it to be a highly conscious work of selection, adaptation, interpolation, and creative originality articulated in a more Franciscan idiom. Adhering to the order of Hugo's topics, Clare sometimes interrupted it to insert passages from Francis's 1223 rule or, as in chapter 6, from his *forma vivendi* and his *Last Will* for the sisters. Lainati is interested to see how Clare "seems not to care in the least that the original thread of Hugolino's text is broken" nor that the cumulative effect of her editing produces a "fragmented" document that sunders certain topics Lainati believes should logically be joined. Such fragmentation, rather than raising suspicions about Clare's sole redaction of the text, instead demonstrates for Lainati "Clare's true interest" in incorporating Franciscan themes such as poverty and spiritual unity.[103]

FRANCIS'S CONTRIBUTION

But perhaps a more elegant solution to the multiple voices within the document is to acknowledge that more than one person had a hand in its redaction. This is not to argue that the rule is simply a hodgepodge of texts lacking coherence. Poverty and the role of the Lesser Brothers at San Damiano are themes that carry throughout the rule. The voice of Francis is also heard throughout the text. A chapter that explains how the sisters were to be charitably corrected and that (in contrast to Hugo's 1219 rule) illiterate sisters should humbly remain so rather than seek literacy replicates, almost verbatim, a chapter in Francis's 1223 rule.[104] Other unmistakable echoes of Francis include the rule's teaching that fasting was not obligatory in times of manifest necessity,[105] that serving sisters should avoid certain types of encounters and relationships outside the monastery,[106] that the abbess should allow a sister to speak to her as if the sister was the lady and the abbess a handmaid,[107] and that the sisters should quickly replace via a new election any abbess they thought unqualified for their service and the general good.[108] The sisters were to recite the Office after the manner of the friars and, like the friars, could have breviaries if they were literate and, if not, were to recite a certain number of "Our Fathers."[109] Francis coined some of the *forma vitae*'s most unusual lines, such as the exhortation to community members to nourish each other spiritually like a mother nourishes her child.[110] The charitable relationships that typify community life in the *1253 forma vitae* parallel those that Francis fostered among his brothers.[111]

It is now commonly assumed that Francis was long dead when the 1253 rule was redacted, although no one knows when it was actually begun.[112] Francis's rule, other writings, and well-known teachings could have been incorporated into the *1253 forma vitae* by one or more other redactors, including Clare. Many scholars believe that the short quotation from Francis that Clare inserted into chapter 6—his *forma vivendi*, which is much more like a very general exhortation than a "form of life"—either belonged to a longer prescriptive document that is no longer extant or was one among several prescriptive writings the monastery of San Damiano had received from Francis over time.[113] Lainati correctly observes that the disappearance of such legislative texts makes it impossible for us to know just how many prescriptions in the *1253 forma vitae* were taken directly *from them* rather than from Francis's 1223 rule.[114] Lainati still holds to what are now minority positions: that Clare embraced Hugo's 1219 rule and that Francis accepted it for the Order of San Damiano (as Hugo-Gregory claimed in 1238). Her argument is thus thoroughly consistent when she both tracks the many ways in which Hugo's rule (along with Francis's) appears throughout the 1253 rule and argues, in tandem with claims first made in the late nineteenth century, that Clare was the mastermind behind the *1253 forma vitae*. Curiously, however, Lainati does not entertain the claims of the earliest sources, neither Philip of Perugia's 1306 assertion (allegedly received from earlier friars) that Francis and Hugo collaborated in writing the rule, nor Rainaldo's and Innocent IV's even earlier statements that Francis was the 1253 rule's author. Should not such explicit testimony in favor of Francis's contribution—corroborated up through the late nineteenth century—be weighted more heavily than the lack of any testimony whatsoever in favor of Clare as the principal or sole author of the rule?

Rainaldo of Jenne as Redactor

Another very likely contributor is the cardinal protector, Rainaldo of Jenne, redacting himself or having his curial underlings redact the rule. Many people have acknowledged that someone knowledgeable about canon law had to have assisted Clare.[115] Rainaldo has sometimes been mentioned in passing as a sort of collaborator, with Clare still as first author,[116] but perhaps only Robinson, writing a century ago, accorded the cardinal a leading role.[117] Rainaldo, experienced in canon law and an insider within the papal curia, had access to all the requisite canonical details. He was the churchman Clare turned to when she petitioned to have the Privilege confirmed. He showed himself to be more than obliging when, in September 1252, he confirmed the *forma vitae* that enshrined within it stronger statements about poverty than those contained in the Privilege. It was plausibly Rainaldo's politicking—his job, after all, as cardinal protector—that swayed the pope a year later on the eve of Clare's death to sign on to this momentous approval.

Rainaldo's successful overthrow of Innocent IV's 1247 rule showed how passionately invested he was in the details of any *forma vitae* regulating the monasteries in the Order of San Damiano. An admirer of the Lesser Brothers, for whom he was also cardinal protector, Rainaldo was nonetheless loathe to accept their jurisdictional oversight of the women's order. It is thus no surprise that the *1253 forma vitae* accorded key roles to the Lesser Brothers, but not a shred of the jurisdictional authority Innocent IV had extravagantly granted them. Their presence within the *forma vitae* and the roles it assigned them within San Damiano were prominent without being dominant. The *forma vitae*, for example, identified Clare as Francis's "little plant" and recalled that she promised him obedience and would now, with her sisters, promise it to his successors.[118] The sisters would celebrate the Office like the Lesser Brothers.[119] The friars' minister general and the provincial minister were to be present when the sisters elected their abbess.[120] The women's visitator (and probably their chaplain) was to be a Lesser Brother. Two lay brothers would assist the women materially, probably by begging on their behalf.[121] But real control remained solidly in Rainaldo's hands: the cardinal protector had the final word on which women could join the monastic community; he, with the pope, decided which outsiders could enter the monastery; and it was he who chose the Lesser Brother who would serve as the women's visitator.[122] The rule's final provision—that a single ecclesiastic be cardinal protector for both orders—cemented Rainaldo's oversight.[123] A very conscious strategic move, it allowed the women of San Damiano to have a special relationship with the Lesser Brothers but kept the chain of command eminently clear. Rainaldo, in fact, was so jealous of his position overseeing both orders that, in contrast to Gregory IX before him, he held onto his post as cardinal protector even after he became pope in late 1254.

OTHER SISTERS AS CONTRIBUTORS

Clare's sisters appear most often in the rule when they are spoken of in third-person, impersonal prescriptive passages—"let the sisters not appropriate"; "let no sister be permitted"; "when sick sisters are visited."[124] In chapter 6, Clare seems clearly to be speaking for herself and for her sisters when she articulates what "I, together with my sisters" promised.[125] But numbers of "we" statements elsewhere in the rule seem to capture the sisters speaking in a single voice as a community.[126] The pronoun "our" is employed when the community names outsiders who exercise some sort of authority vis-à-vis the sisters; for example, "our cardinal" (thrice), "our [cardinal] governor, protector, and corrector," "our Visitator";[127] and, somewhat similarly, "we ask . . . of the same Order a chaplain and a clerical companion . . . and two lay brothers."[128] These appointed individuals represent relationships that are meaningful to the entire community, indeed, are constitutive features of the monastery's life. Besides these, however, the most striking collective declarations intimate something about the unique character of the sisters' community life: "our poverty" (once) and "the form of our poverty" (twice);[129] "the form of our life" and "the tenor of our life" (a phrase found also in Francis's 1221 rule, which was not approved by the papacy);[130] and "our profession" and "the form of our profession" (five times).[131] Saying "*our form* of poverty" and "*our tenor* of life," instead of the simpler and unadorned "poverty" and "life," seems to convey that the sisters' poverty and life were distinct from the poverty and life at other monasteries. Recognizing that the *1253 forma vitae* probably grew out of practices that evolved over time indirectly acknowledges the sisters' contribution.[132] But their contribution would be even more direct if some or all of the many "we" statements were read as the sisters' own collective articulations consciously interjected into the text.

This brings me back to a point I raised earlier in this chapter, that neither Rainaldo's nor Innocent IV's letters confirming the *forma vitae* followed the usual practice of naming the order to which San Damiano belonged, the Order of San Damiano. More unusual yet is the rule's opening line, which follows the prelates' two letters in the Assisi parchment: "The form of life of the Order of the Poor Sisters that Blessed Francis established is this: to observe the Holy Gospel of our Lord Jesus Christ, by living in obedience, without anything of one's own, and in chastity."[133] Leading with the three vows is hardly novel, but mentioning the gospel evocatively ties the monastery to Francis of Assisi, and self-identifying as the Order of Poor Sisters is nothing short of revolutionary. It was tantamount to declaring the women's independence from (or within?) the Order of San Damiano. Francis founded not that order, as wishful-thinking popes would have it, but an Order of Poor Sisters. At a time when women calling themselves "lesser sisters" were being denounced by the church hierarchy, this new title was both clever and courageous.[134] Clare had identified her monastery as belonging to the "enclosed ladies" (or "Enclosed Ladies") in her first letter to Agnes of Prague (1234); in her second and third letters (respectively, 1235–1238 and 1238) she had said she was "Clare, of the poor ladies" (or "Poor Ladies"); in her last letter, written in 1253 just about the time this rule won approval, she wrote simply that she was "Clare . . . of his handmaids who live in the Monastery of San Damiano in Assisi."[135] In the 1253 rule she is referred to as "Sister" Clare.[136] Clare's and her sisters' self-awareness about following a particular path underlies the many "ours" peppering the *1253 forma vitae*: this is "our way of life," not that of others. Their *sui generis* self-identification explains why this rule is not even mentioned in the bull of Clare's canonization, Legends, and other early texts.[137]

Although anyone could have formulated such "we" statements, it seems intuitively sensible to consider that the community did so. Such statements might have transpired over time as the sisters learned from their experience and allowed it to shape their way (*forma*) of life. Their weekly chapter meetings, where the abbess was to consult them about everything regarding "the welfare and good of the monastery," would have constituted an ideal venue.[138] Clare conceivably could have been speaking for others, but attributing group statements to an individual when they could more transparently be attributed to the group seems unnecessarily circuitous. Such a move enhances Clare's role while, ironically, diminishing what many commentators consider one of the rule's most original features—described somewhat hyperbolically as the "democratization" of the community's form of governance, as "horizontal rather than vertical, collective rather than hierarchical."[139] There is, of course, hierarchy aplenty in this rule—hierarchy involving not only the various ecclesiastics but also the abbess. She was to admonish and correct the sisters; they were to obey her.[140] She was to make decisions regarding the sisters' clothing, fasting, confessions, work, correspondence, possessions, gifts of money, and punishments.[141]

But the rule invested the community of sisters with authority that is unusual for a medieval religious rule. Alongside the hierarchy, there reigns a surprising degree of reciprocity. Sister Pacifica had told the canonization commissioners that Francis had to compel Clare to take on the governance of the other sisters. Never in her letters does Clare refer to herself as abbess.[142] (The very frequency of the term's appearance throughout the *1253 forma vitae* is another clue that some individual/s besides Clare contributed significantly to the text). The relative equality of the sisters seems to extend to the serving sisters, whose tasks and license to leave the enclosure made them a group apart, but who seem to be included in the many collective designations of "sisters" within the monastery. No sense of superiority marks the comments about serving sisters made by the witnesses for Clare's canonization (some of whom may themselves have been serving sisters). Margaret Carney observes that the term "sister" appears in the 1253 rule sixty-eight times; the term "nun" once.[143] The sisters had significant say in the monastery's governance. They could remove the abbess if she were incompetent. They were to use their own judgment regarding the disposition of gifts sent to them by their families and others.[144] The sisters elected a council of eight (or more) "discerning" sisters, or "discreets" (*discretiores*), who would advise the abbess on a host of matters,[145] and in an apparent safeguard against this group becoming an ensconced power block, the rule authorized the community to elect new discreets when it seemed "useful and expedient."[146] All the sisters, including the youngest, were to be consulted about anything regarding the monastery's common good.[147] The *forma vitae* contained some community-minded provisions that were strikingly progressive: a majority of the community had to agree before a new member could join;[148] no significant debt could be incurred without the community's consent;[149] and the abbess shared the community's common life practices by, for example, wearing the same clothing, sleeping in the dormitory, and eating the same food in the common refectory.[150]

Above all, the tenor of relationships was to be marked by "mutual love and peace" and "perfect harmony."[151] The abbess was to strive to be loved rather than feared; she was to be a refuge for those in despair.[152] "Mercy," "charity," and being the servant (*ancilla*)—what Franciscans later termed *minoritas*—was to typify the abbess's governing style.[153] Because the *1253 forma vitae* is often praised in commentaries for its love, its rigor is sometimes passed over in silence (or perhaps embarrassment), but even its rigor is tinged with compassion. A sister who sinned mortally against the "form of our profession" was to be admonished two or three times. If she still did not amend her sin, she was to eat bread and water on the floor of the refectory in plain view of all or be punished even more if the abbess saw fit. But the rule added: "The abbess and her sisters, however, must beware not to become angry or disturbed on account of another's sin, for anger and disturbance prevent charity in oneself and in others."[154] As to other dissensions: "If it should happen, may it never be so, that an occasion of trouble or scandal should arise between sister and sister through a word or gesture, let her who was the cause of the trouble, before offering the gift of her prayer to the Lord, not only prostrate herself humbly at once at the feet of the other and ask pardon, but also beg her simply to intercede for her to the Lord that He forgive her. Let the other sister, mindful of that word of the Lord, 'If you do not forgive from the heart, neither will your heavenly Father forgive you,' generously pardon her sister every injury she has done to her."[155] The sisters were to care for others more "lovingly" than a mother cared for her child.[156]

The mutual charity that runs throughout the rule has sometimes fallen victim to a certain exceptionalism, as if this were the first rule to note such affective ties. As I have signaled in my notes, the Rule of Benedict and, even more, Francis's *Later Rule*, also give attention to brotherly love. But the *1253 forma vitae* goes farther, emphasizing still more the affective description of the sisters' life and elsewhere adding new passages, aspirational statements the rule makes concrete in its participatory governing structures.

In light of all of this, it simply strains credulity to think such a community did not, as a community, have a significant hand in forging the *forma vitae*, the "form of *our* life," as they called it (emphasis mine). Whatever leadership role Clare might have assumed in communicating the sisters' contributions, it is hard to imagine that she would not have included the ideas of not only the discreets but also the other sisters. If she was anything like the sisters who testified at the process for her canonization described her, she would not have imposed her own ideas on others but would rather have allowed her ideas to be shaped by the women around her.

Brother Leo (d. 1271?)

One final possible contributor is Brother Leo, the dear companion of Francis. Leo was Francis's scribe during his life; after it, he dedicated himself to memorializing Francis's words and deeds. Two of the three surviving examples of Francis's handwriting are a blessing and a letter the saint sent to his friend, documents Leo had the foresight to save.[157] When Minister General Crescentius put out his request in 1244 for the brothers to write down their recollections about Francis, Leo, together with Angelo and Rufino, responded generously. Their 1246 letter introducing what they wrote reveals that they were in touch with Brother Philip, San Damiano's visitator.[158] Numerous early Franciscan writers cite Leo and incorporate material they attribute to him into their own works, including Bonaventure, Salimbene, Conrad of Offida, Ubertino da Casale, and Angelo Clareno. Although no work survives that can be ascribed to Leo alone, "Leo material" abounds within fundamental works such as the *Assisi Compilation* and the *Mirror of Perfection*.[159]

Leo was among those Umbrian brothers who knew Francis well and, after his death, were displeased with the growing institutional physiognomy of the Order of Lesser Brothers. Leo lived in hermitages or very small communities not only out of fidelity to the friars' early practices, but probably also as a sort of protest against so many friars residing in larger town communities who relaxed their observance of the rule to undertake new pastoral and teaching duties.[160] He cultivated a close relationship with Clare and her community. Luigi Pellegrini believes Leo and two other friars constituted a small community living close by San Damiano; he points to a 1258 bequest that lists donations made to the "ladies of Saint Clare," a "Brother Leo," and two other friars, with just one other donee on the list intervening between the sisters and the friars.[161] Regardless of the identity of this Brother Leo, we are sure that Leo, Francis's companion, was close to Clare. He, together with Juniper and Angelo, was with Clare as she lay dying. The *Versified Legend* poignantly states that he kissed her bed while crying over her death.[162] After her death, it was Leo and Angelo who accompanied the bishop of Spoleto and the other commissioners when they went to San Damiano to interview Clare's sisters and collect data for her canonization.[163] The sisters no doubt welcomed the presence of their old and trusted friends. Bartoli Langeli speculates that Leo wanted to put his scribal (and perhaps authorial?) gifts to work on behalf of Clare as well as Francis. He argues that the Messina codex represents just such a text, containing as it does the *1253 forma vitae*, its letters of confirmation,

Pope Innocent's Privilege of Poverty, Clare's *Testament,* and *Blessing.* The handwriting, he thinks, belongs to Leo.[164]

Whether or not that is the case—indeed, some scholars date the Messina text to the fourteenth and the fifteenth centuries—there are still reasons to suppose that Leo might have served as a scribe or even redactor of the *forma vitae.* Both Bartoli Langeli and Accrocca believe Leo helped redact the *forma vitae.*[165] Besides his relationship with Clare and her sisters, and his well-known *métier* as scribe and author, Leo would have been thoroughly familiar with Francis's 1223 rule, which appears throughout the *forma vitae.* He too could have been the source for the few passages paralleling Francis's 1221 rule. There are also noteworthy parallels, quite possibly owing to Leo, between the *1253 forma vitae* and Thomas of Celano's *Second Life* of Francis (1246–1247). For example, Thomas quotes Francis's description of what the minister general of the Lesser Brothers should be like: "He must be without personal favorites, lest by loving some more than others, he create scandal for all. . . . Let him be someone who comforts the afflicted, and is the final refuge of the distressed, so that the sickness of despair does not overcome the sick because he did not offer healing remedies." These words appear almost verbatim in the *1253 forma vitae*'s description of the abbess.[166] Even more striking is Thomas's description of Francis's commitment to an "Order of holy virgins," which seems certainly to describe the women of San Damiano. Because Francis recognized that the women were marked with the signs of highest perfection and ready to suffer any loss or labor for Christ, "he firmly promised them, and others who professed poverty in a similar way of life, that he and his brothers would perpetually offer them help and advice. And he carried this out carefully as long as he lived."[167] What Thomas has put in the third person, speaking about Francis, Clare, in chapter 6 of the *forma vitae,* puts in Francis's first-person voice.[168]

Scholars who think Clare was the sole or principal author of the rule suggest that Clare was familiar with all these texts and used them to construct her rule. Perhaps, but the parallels might also be explained by Leo himself. It is well known that Thomas of Celano relied on Leo's writings in writing his *Second Life.* Perhaps Leo's material similarly informed the *1253 forma vitae,* either via written documents or what Leo remembered and collaboratively contributed to the rule as it was being redacted. Leo would have been a natural choice to help the sisters of San Damiano faithfully set down in a rule the promises Francis had made to the women and probably shared with Leo. Emblematic of the trust between Leo and the sisters is his gift to them between 1257 and 1260, shortly after Clare died, of a breviary that had belonged to Francis. He also gave them his precious *rotuli*—whether before or after Clare died, we do not know—described around 1305 by Ubertino da Casale as "scrolls written in [Leo's] own hand, which he entrusted to the monastery of Saint Clare to safeguard as a memory for posterity. . . . He had written many things in them, just as he had heard them from father [Francis's] mouth and had seen in his deeds."[169] Whether or not Clare or her sisters ever used the scrolls, the fact that Leo handed them over to her sisters rather than a community of friars attests to their close bonds. Bearing in mind also that Leo, as scribe or redactor, may have assisted Clare in writing her letters to Agnes of Prague, he should certainly be considered as a possible contributor to the *1253 forma vitae*, as should other Umbrian friars close to San Damiano.[170] We know, in fact, that Clare relied on a scribe when she wrote her fourth letter to Agnes, just when the *forma vitae* was being approved.[171] Perhaps there is symbolic significance in the fact that after Abbess Rossi found the rule in 1893, which she thought had been enfolded in Clare's garments, it came to light that the garments in the reliquary box had belonged both to Clare and to a friar. The friar was Brother Rufino, Clare's cousin and one of Leo's collaborators in collecting the stories that later found their way into Thomas of Celano's *Second Life* and the *Legend of the Three Companions*.[172]

In sum, Clare's insertion of her and Francis's heartfelt personal statements within the body of a legislative text makes it a singular document, to be sure. Equally notable is the plentiful internal and external evidence suggesting that Clare was part of a community of collaborators who collectively fashioned the unique *1253 forma vitae*.

Chapter 9

Clare's Last Words, ca. 1253

Three documents, besides the *1253 forma vitae*, are associated with Clare at the end of her life: her fourth letter to Agnes of Prague and two texts, the *Testament* and the *Blessing*, that she intended for her sisters. While Clare's authorship of her last letter to Agnes is universally accepted, scholars remain deeply divided about the last two texts. In this chapter, I review each of these documents and then conclude with some last words of my own about Clare of Assisi, the papacy, and the many women and men I have touched on in this book.

Clare's Last Letter to Agnes of Prague

Clare's fourth letter to Agnes of Prague was written shortly before Clare's death on 11 August 1253. Thematically coherent with her earlier letters to Agnes in the 1230s, we know that a significant hiatus in their correspondence preceded this letter. Clare notes at the outset: "Even if I have not written to you as frequently as both your soul and mine would have desired and longed for, do not for a moment wonder or believe in any way that the fire of my love for you burns any less sweetly in the deepest heart [*visceribus*] of your mother." Clare blamed her silence on the shortage of messengers and the dangerous roads.[1]

Alberzoni elaborates further about the possible reasons for this gap in Clare's correspondence. She suggests that Clare consciously quit writing to Agnes in 1238, the same year Gregory IX rejected Agnes's request for a new, more Franciscan *forma vitae* that included passages from the *forma vivendi* Francis had given to the women of San Damiano. Then, once Rainaldo had confirmed the *1253 forma vitae* (in September 1252), the rule that positioned Francis's *forma vivendi* in its very center, Clare resumed writing because she wanted, thinks Alberzoni, to encourage Agnes to now try to win the same legislation for her own monastery.[2] Alberzoni's theory is supremely cogent but remains speculative. Clare's fourth letter to Agnes says nothing at all about a *forma vitae*, not even obliquely. Perhaps one of the two friars charged with delivering Clare's letter could have communicated such a message orally, but why would Clare not be more straightforward within the letter itself? Could she have feared prying eyes? And why should we not take her at her (unambiguous) word that dangerous roads and a lack of messengers explained the hiatus? It is also worth pointing out that the hiatus, which most scholars put at about fifteen years—the length of time separating Clare's third and fourth surviving letters to Agnes—could have been less. Perhaps other letters sent during the intervening years, letters not considered important enough to preserve, simply did not survive.

What is most certain, however, is the intense bond of intimacy that now joined these two women. The very greetings in Clare's four letters chronicle the growing intensity of their bond. In her first letter to Agnes in 1234, when the two were just becoming acquainted, Clare's greeting employed the formal "you," the equivalent of "thou" in yesteryear's English, and focused on Agnes's royal lineage: "To the venerable and most holy virgin, the Lady Agnes, daughter of the most renowned illustrious king of Bohemia."[3] Clare's greeting in her second letter, probably written between May 1235 and early 1238, still invoked Agnes's royal lineage, but the "king" who is her "father" was now God instead of an earthly man. Moreover, Clare now spoke familiarly, employing the informal form of "you": "To the daughter of the King of kings, handmaid of the Lord of lords, most worthy spouse of Jesus Christ and therefore, very distinguished queen, the Lady Agnes."[4] Clare wrote her third letter in 1238, just the period in which Agnes was actively lobbying Pope Gregory for a more Franciscan *forma vitae* in lieu of his own and for permission to follow the fasting practices—at variance with Gregory's *forma vitae*—that Francis had given to Clare and her sisters. Clare's greeting in this letter shows that the two women had by then become sisters and comrades in arms. Both were at loggerheads with the pope. Clare was enlisting the aid of Minister General Elias (on the cusp of being removed from office by Gregory), and Agnes was drawing on her considerable political connections to win papal concessions. Clare's extravagant greeting notes Agnes's powerful royal connection: "To Agnes, sister in Christ, deserving of love before all other mortals, blood-sister of the illustrious king of Bohemia, but now sister and spouse of the most high king of heavens."[5] By the time Clare wrote her farewell letter in 1253, the two had become intimate soul mates. Clare addresses Agnes: "To the other half of her [Clare's] soul and repository of the special love of her deepest heart, [to the] illustrious queen, spouse of the Lamb of the eternal King, the Lady Agnes, her own dearest mother and, among all the others, her special daughter."[6] What besides years of shared travails might better explain why Clare now called Agnes—a woman Clare had never met in person—her "special daughter among all others" and "her own dearest mother"?

Medieval letter-writing also called for the writer to identify herself in her salutation. Two omissions from these salutations may also be telling. First, Clare never referred to herself as abbess, an unusual oversight if she had, in fact, ever thought of herself as abbess. It was, of course, the sort of title Francis eschewed. He wanted the leaders of his order to be known as "ministers," that is, "servants"; he barred them from using the title "prior," the religious term for superior; in fact, all the brothers were to be called "lesser brothers."[7] It is worth pointing out that although Agnes probably held the post of abbess at the time of Clare's second letter, and possibly the first and third as well, Clare never greeted her thus.[8] Second, whereas Clare's first letter had identified San Damiano as belonging to the "enclosed ladies," a term at the time synonymous with the Order of San Damiano, her last three letters acknowledged no such relationship. Of course, by the time Clare wrote her last letter to Agnes, the 1253 forma vitae had explosively identified her monastery with the Order of Poor Sisters, a name that seemed to signal an irreparable breach between Clare's monastery and the papally regulated Order of San Damiano.[9]

As already elaborated in Chapter 5, Clare's last letter highlights the same themes she had elaborated in her first three letters: living poorly and humbly, following Christ, contemplation, and divinization. This thematic unity has led some scholars to hypothesize a single scribe assisting Clare with all four letters.[10] A scribe certainly assisted Clare with her fourth letter because the terms *inquit* or *hoc inquit*, for "she says," appear in the text—the scribe's technique for assuring readers that what he or she wrote accurately represented what Clare dictated.[11] Whether slavishly verbatim or partly polished by the scribe, Clare's fourth letter, like the others, appears closely tied to her deeply felt affections and convictions. The consistency of Clare's themes across the years suggests that the letters powerfully delineate the contours of her spiritual teaching.

Clare's approaching death, coming after years of chronic illness, looms large in her last letter. Death, for Clare, would have represented not an end but a threshold to cross over into full life and union with God. The language of the letter, pronouncedly spiritual and lacking in apparent concrete details, lends it an ethereal cast. But for all Clare's attention in the letter to subjects such as Christ being the splendor of eternal glory and the power of contemplation being a path to union with the divine, it would be a mistake to read this letter as wholly otherworldly. Yes, Clare was leaving earth and its troubles far behind, and she also points Agnes forward to the heavenly banquet and radiant vision of God. But as Clare elaborates the notion of Christ the mirror whom Agnes should contemplate, she reminds her friend of the fundamental virtues of poverty, humility, and love. She anchors each of these in Christ's earthly life—its beginning, middle, and end. This life is the pattern for Agnes's as well, and Clare notes pointedly how Christ, the mirror, ended his days, out of love, on a cross, warning those who passed by that his suffering was beyond compare.[12]

Urging Agnes to consider this, she cryptically embeds a very this-worldly message within a lyrical biblical citation that could seem solely oriented toward the supernatural. Citing the Song of Songs and Isaiah, she tells Agnes to exclaim:

Draw me after you, Heavenly Spouse, we shall run in the fragrance of your perfumes! [Song 1:4]
I shall run and not grow weary [Isaiah 40:31]
until you bring me into the wine cellar [Song 2:4],
until your left hand is under my head and your right hand happily [*feliciter*] embraces me [Song 2:6; 8:3];
and you kiss me with the most blissful [*felicissimo*] kiss of your mouth [Song 1:1].[13]

Clare is very much aware, and hopeful, about this life and its struggles. She tells Agnes to study her own earthly face in the mirror and find herself adorned with those same virtues of poverty, humility, and love. When Clare urges Agnes to "run and not grow weary," her advice flows from a lifetime of personal experience and she knows Agnes still has farther to run.

Moreover, coded within one of Clare's allusions to the Song of Songs is a phrase pregnant with earthly significance. She knew she was echoing a phrase from the hard-fought 1228 Privilege of Poverty that she jealously guarded at San Damiano and wanted to enshrine within the papally approved *1253 forma vitae.*[14] Gregory's 1228 Privilege also concerned both the future life of divine love and an earthly life of material poverty:

> Nor does a lack of possessions frighten you from a proposal of this sort; for the left hand of the heavenly Spouse is under your head to support the weakness of your body. . . . He who feeds the birds of heavens and clothes the lilies of the field will not fail you in either food or clothing, until He ministers to you in heaven, when His right hand especially will more happily [*felicius*] embrace you in the fullness of his sight.[15]

Gregory associated the Song's "left hand of the heavenly Spouse" with the San Damiano women's brave embrace of a "lack of possessions." He tellingly inserted the term "happily" within the Song reference to God's "right hand," the hand that would "*happily* embrace" the women after their lifetime of trusting that he would care for their material needs just as he did for the birds of heavens and the lilies of the field. Clare's citations of the Song lack these explicit associations with material poverty, but she encodes them nonetheless by repeating Gregory's term "happily" and by citing the same verses. She counted, it seems, on Agnes recognizing that this final letter echoed the 1228 Privilege of Poverty, albeit the privilege of poverty that Agnes had won in 1238 had been articulated in different language.[16] The two women had by then been allies in the battle for Franciscan poverty for almost two decades.

Clare poignantly concludes her letter with an explicit farewell. Even as she acknowledges that her physical tongue will fall silent, she reminds Agnes of the inexpressible "love I have for you." Then, importantly, Clare seems to outline an alliance that will survive her own passing. She commends herself and her daughters to Agnes and her sisters. Into this circle she draws her own blood sister, Agnes of Assisi, then visiting from another monastery to be close to the dying Clare. Agnes of Assisi also belonged to a monastery that had struggled to protect its life of poverty. The blood sisters had plausibly discussed what the future might hold for their monasteries once Clare was gone. Clare significantly identified Agnes of Assisi as "our sister."[17] The pronoun "our" minimally included the three women, but it might also have embraced their communities. Clare might have been hoping that the *1253 forma vitae*, the rule that momentously defined her community as belonging to the Order of Poor Sisters, might be approved not only for her own community of San Damiano, but also for the communities of her other sister allies. Perhaps for

that reason, Clare's last sentence draws Agnes's attention to "our dearest bear-
ers of this letter," Brothers Amato and Bonagura, Lesser Brothers about whom
we know nothing but who were probably friar allies within her circle.[18] It
would have been entirely in character for the tenacious Clare, even at life's
end, to be thinking about an alliance of sisters and friends in this world who
would carry on after she was gone, perduring in the struggle to protect their
Franciscan form of life.

Clare's *Testament* and *Blessing*?

The two most disputed texts in the Clare corpus are certainly the *Testament*
and *Blessing* attributed to her.[19] In many respects, both capture features com-
pellingly consistent with Clare's life. On the other hand, the two texts are
surrounded by an array of open questions and suspicious circumstances that
cast doubt on their authenticity. I acknowledge at the outset that, after sifting
through all the evidence, I remain unsure about their authenticity. If they are
closely related to Clare, however, I think it probable that some significant
embellishments have been introduced into the texts.

Neither text can be dated with precision. If they are Clare's in some sense,
they would likely date to the end of her life and plausibly to her final days.
Since the exceedingly brief *Blessing* sounds a few of the same themes found in
the *Testament* and shares substantially the same manuscript history, I will
focus most of my remarks on the longer and more revelatory *Testament*.

The language of the *Testament* is powerfully compelling, far more so than
either her letters or the *1253 forma vitae*. Clare recounts in detail the foundation of the sisters' religious life, replete with a prophecy about the women ut-
tered by Francis, who is named repeatedly throughout the text. She sounds all
the central themes of her and Francis's vision of religious life, including penitence, poverty, humility, love, the mutual charity that joins the sisters, and
loving, service-oriented leadership, with no mention of the term "abbess." The
text also employs very specific terms found in Clare's or other early Franciscan
texts, including "mirror," "Lady Poverty," and "little plant," a metaphor for
Clare herself. The text is a tour de force of Franciscan themes.

The putative Clare in this text—whom, for ease of discussion, I will identify simply as Clare—says that she wrote the text so that what she recommended in it might "be better observed" by her present and future sisters.[20]
The *Testament* is so named because it passes on to Clare's sisters their

inheritance, so to speak. In some fifteen hundred words, Clare interpreted her sisters' origins, history, and essential identity and bound them, both living and to come, to remain faithful to the tradition she laid out before them. Clare showcases the sisters' intrinsic relationship to Francis, their commitment to poverty, the mutual charity that bonds them with one another, and their place vis-à-vis the Church, the pope, the cardinal protector, and the Lesser Brothers. Commonly characterized as the most personal and autobiographical of Clare's texts, Lainati calls it "a true reflection of Saint Clare's soul."[21] Such heartfelt sentiment can make debates about the text cut close to the bone for some Clare devotees.

Yet debates about the *Testament*'s authenticity have plagued it for centuries. I will here highlight some of the principal arguments scholars adduce against its authenticity and then track, in a point-counterpoint fashion, how those objections are answered by other scholars who either believe that the *Testament* is authentic or are open to the possibility.

Its weak manuscript history is almost always the first concern raised. Given the galvanizing tenor of Clare's words, one would expect it to have a solid manuscript tradition. Just five manuscripts contain it; Maleczek dates all of them to the fifteenth and sixteenth centuries.[22] A few proponents of its authenticity push back the dates of one or two of these manuscripts to the fourteenth century.[23] Bartoli Langeli, whose discussion of the Messina manuscript is the most exhaustive to date, has momentously proposed that it be dated to the thirteenth century. While a few scholars before him shared this view, it remains to be seen if his elaborate exposition will succeed in convincing other paleographers and scholars.[24] Marcos of Lisbon, in the late sixteenth century, and Luke Wadding, in the early seventeenth century, each published versions of the *Testament*. Both said they had found it in an "ancient record," a tantalizing phrase but one too vague to establish that they had seen a very early manuscript.[25] Godet suggests that no early manuscripts have survived because none were needed; when the sisters ceased to know Latin, they depended on vernacular translations. He adds that some "ancient" manuscripts survive in middle French, middle Italian, and middle Dutch.[26] Lainati places these in the fifteenth and sixteenth centuries, not particularly ancient for a text believed to have been originally redacted in the thirteenth century.[27]

Perhaps more troubling than the weak manuscript tradition is the fact that no early sources even mention that Clare left a testament. Many of the sisters testifying for Clare's canonization spoke about her dying days and recalled her various remarks. A few referred to the all-important Privilege of

Poverty that protected San Damiano's practice of poverty. Sister Filippa referred to the *forma vitae*, the text that similarly preserved the sisters' poverty and also attested to their relationship with Francis and his Lesser Brothers. It is remarkable that none of these sisters refers to the *Testament*—even if they had received it only orally from Clare—for in it, Clare personally, persuasively, and emphatically presents an account of her community's history and unique form of religious life.

The weak manuscript tradition and the silence of the early sources together amount to an argument *ex silentio* that has been repeatedly rejected as insufficient to prove anything about the text's authenticity; even Maleczek, one of the most powerful opponents of the *Testament*'s authenticity, has acknowledged that the negative argument is "not very persuasive."[28] Moreover, if Bartoli Langeli is correct in dating the Messina codex to the late thirteenth century, perhaps even to the hand of Brother Leo, then the manuscript tradition can no longer be considered weak.

This, however, is a large supposition and should be considered alongside an eye-catching syntony among the Latin manuscripts, vernacular translations, and first witnesses to the *Testament*: many have clear ties to the Franciscan Observant reform, which began among Umbrian friars in the mid-fourteenth century and spread to women in the early fifteenth century.[29] One of the Observant reform's main goals was to return to the original (and more rigorous) ideals of Francis and Clare. They were thus highly motivated to recover and propagate their founders' stricter rules and teachings.

Bracketing the still open question of the Messina codex's date, the *Testament* is first found and mentioned, importantly, in the Observant context. Sister Battista Alfani (d. 1523) included an Italian translation of the *Testament* in her late fifteenth-century *Legend of the Holy Virgin Saint Clare*. Alfani, a sister from the Observant monastery of S. Maria di Monteluce in Perugia, stated that Clare composed the *Testament* in order to "imitate her glorious father Saint Francis" (who also left a testament to his friars). Significantly, Alfani also claimed that it was a fellow sister who recorded Clare's dictation.[30] Alfani's monastery had become part of the reform movement in the mid-fifteenth century and then helped spread the reform to many other monasteries. Emore Paoli thinks, in fact, that Observant women were ultimately responsible for saving the *Testament* for posterity.[31] It is relevant to note that Alfani and her Monteluce sisters were known for their high level of culture and extremely productive *scriptorium*.[32] Remarkable too is the fact that all five manuscripts containing the *Testament* also include the *1253 forma vitae* and three include the Privilege of Poverty, all texts highly prized within the Observant milieu. And not long after Alfani finished her *Legend*, another Observant, the Franciscan Mariano of Florence, made repeated references to the *Testament* in his chronicle of Clare's order, completed in 1519.[33] Mariano's work constitutes one more example of the uncommon number of ties that join the *Testament* to the Observant movement.

Maleczek suggests that the Monteluce *scriptorium* was just the sort of environment that could give rise to the *Testament*. He elaborates at length how the Observants, male or female, had both motive and opportunity. Both Clare's *Testament*, he argues, and the disputed Privilege of Poverty purportedly issued in 1216 by Innocent III (an iconic figure in Franciscan accounts of their origins) were fabricated by Observants anxious to show that their rigorous ideals were rooted in Francis's and Clare's original intentions.[34] Forgery for such a noble cause was acceptable and relatively free of the negative valence it later assumed.[35] If, as Maleczek supposes, the earliest manuscripts and texts can be traced only as far back as the fifteenth century, or even if some can be traced back to the fourteenth century (as more scholars believe), then all the "earliest" evidence for the *Testament* could postdate the beginning of the friars' Observant reform movement.[36] This would powerfully corroborate Maleczek's suspicions that the Observant reform gave birth to the *Testament*. If, however, it could be shown that the Messina codex is, in fact, a thirteenth-century manuscript—a point that perhaps will never be resolved—then Maleczek's theory has to fall.

The style of the *Testament* has also troubled many scholars, but every suspicion spawns a counterargument. Scholarly evaluations run the gamut, and sometimes both suspicion and counterargument are articulated by the same scholar. For example, Zoppetti and Bartoli think the *Testament*'s fluent Latin contrasts with what we know about Clare's rather elemental literary formation. They resolve this inconsistency by pointing to Clare's letters, which prove her literary capacity (even as they also acknowledge possible scribal assistance).[37] Maleczek points to the disjuncture between the styles of Clare's letters and the *Testament* to argue that the latter is not Clare's creation.[38] Paoli, who thinks the *Testament* might be authentic, addresses the stylistic disjuncture by suggesting that a different scribe assisted Clare on each work.[39] Armstrong deals with what he finds to be a "constantly changing flow of styles" within the *Testament*—some passages smooth, others awkward—by suggesting that different sisters could have had a hand in composing it. Later, he alternatively suggests that Clare could have written the text in various stages.[40]

Marini, who accepts Clare as the principal author of the letters to Agnes, the *1253 forma vitae*, the *Testament*, and the *Blessing*, holds a minority perspective. The "basic unity" of style he finds across her writings establishes that she was their principal author.[41]

I cite the array of scholarly opinions about the *Testament*'s style not to argue for any single conclusion, but rather to show that *however* Clare's style is assessed, a solution may always be found to justify one's position regarding the text's authenticity. Furthermore, the relatively meager length of the Clare corpus, even if all texts are considered potentially authentic, undermines the importance of style as a criterion for judgment. The varied nature of the texts' genres, dates of composition, and possible degrees of collaborative assistance are sufficient to explain almost any stylistic diversity. In sum, assessments of Clare's style do little to advance arguments about the *Testament*'s authenticity.

Other knotty features of the *Testament* regard its contents. It refers, for example, to a privilege granted by Pope Innocent III. Clare says to her sisters: "Moreover, for greater security, I took care to have our profession of the most holy poverty that we promised our father [Francis] strengthened with privileges by the Lord Pope Innocent, in whose time we had our beginning, and by his other successors, that we would never in any way turn away from [that profession]."[42] Maleczek thinks this refers to Innocent III's alleged Privilege of Poverty, a text Maleczek has proved to most scholars' satisfaction to be a fifteenth-century forgery. The reference further convinced Maleczek that the *Testament* itself had been fabricated. While a few authors counter by simply asserting that Innocent III's Privilege in fact existed,[43] Paoli—who finds Maleczek's arguments against Innocent having issued a formal written privilege convincing—presents detailed explanations to explain Clare's troublesome statement. For example, "privilege" might have meant something besides a papal document. Although possible, I note that the sisters who testified for Clare's canonization used "privilege" precisely to denote a papal document. But Paoli suggests that Clare may have mentioned privileges granted by Innocent III and his successors merely to demonstrate that the women's commitment to poverty dated to San Damiano's very origins.[44]

Another passage that has long raised suspicions is a prophecy recounted early in the *Testament*. It emphatically ties the origins of Clare's order to the earliest days of Francis's conversion, *before* he even had any companions. Francis was rebuilding the church of San Damiano when he was suddenly enlightened by the Holy Spirit. Clare writes: "Climbing the wall of that church, he shouted in French to some poor people who were standing nearby: 'Come and help me in the work on the monastery of San Damiano, because there will as yet be ladies here who will glorify our heavenly Father throughout His holy, universal Church by their celebrated and holy manner of life.'"[45] The passage is practically a verbatim copy of a passage in the *Legend of the Three Companions*, a text containing significant material gathered in the late 1240s.[46] This earlier *Legend* passage proceeds to state that Gregory IX "approved" Clare's order, in contrast to the *Testament*, which pushes the approval back to Innocent III.[47] Lainati, the scholar who is probably most adept at harmonizing texts about and attributed to Clare, showing each to be "true," explains that the texts are perfectly compatible: the *Testament*'s passage regarded Innocent III's Privilege, while the *Legend*'s passage regarded Gregory IX's *forma vitae*.[48] Thaddée Matura (who accepts the *Testament*'s authenticity) seems more on the mark when he insightfully points out the text's polemical tone and "idealized hagiographic" portrayal of Francis. "Saint" Francis dominates the *Testament*, which was composed long after Francis's death.[49] The author of the *Testament* (Clare?) wants to underline how Francis's halo cast a sort of sanctifying light over all his projects, including the ladies who would reside in the very first church he repaired, a symbolic first step in his far grander project to repair the Church universal. What most troubles many scholars about this passage, however, is that it is a prophecy that came true. Such portents of the future strain credulity because they appear in texts composed only after the fact, once that predicted "future" lies safely in the past.

Clare issues a warning in her *Testament* that seems also to be another after-the-fact statement: "If it should happen at any time that these sisters leave this place [the monastery of San Damiano] and go elsewhere, let them be bound, wherever they may be after my death, to observe that form of poverty that we have promised God and our most blessed father Francis."[50] Clare's preemptive strike turned out to be prophetic. Just a few years after her death, the community of San Damiano abandoned the monastery and moved to the nearby town of Assisi, perhaps to be closer to Clare's body, perhaps because they had been urged there for greater protection within the town walls. City officials, interested in safeguarding Clare's relics, had taken her body to Assisi the very day following her death. The question is: why might Clare have suspected her community would leave San Damiano after she was gone? And is there some "bite" to be read in her admonition about preserving poverty?—for, in fact, the commune of Assisi spent lavishly to build the enormous new church in Assisi honoring Clare. It must have been substantially finished by 1265, when Alexander IV (Rainaldo) consecrated it. Maleczek thinks the imposing monastery alongside the church might also have been completed around then.[51] Is the author of the *Testament* looking backward (and from what year?) and imbuing Clare with a prescience she would not have had in 1253? Maleczek thinks so; someone, quite possibly in the Observant reform, wanted to point up the sisters' original poverty before such sumptuous build-ings existed.[52] Yet not all scholars accept Maleczek's logic. Lainati takes the *Testament*'s statements instead as proof that Clare knew (but how?) that the community was going to move.[53]

Besides the open question regarding a possible thirteenth-century manu-script version of the *Testament*, Maleczek's elegant and multifaceted argument against its authenticity has one significant weakness: he contends that the text emphasizes poverty all out of proportion to what it signified for Francis and Clare. Of Francis's four surviving texts written for the women—his (disputed) *Audite poverelle*, *Canticle of creatures*, *forma vivendi*, and *Last Will* (the last two being his brief quotations inserted into the *1253 forma vitae*)—only the *Last Will*, thinks Maleczek, stresses poverty. Therefore, he finds Francis's recom-mendation in the *Testament* that Clare and her sisters commit themselves to holy poverty to be out of sync with the thirteenth-century reality. He argues, furthermore, that in Clare's final years there would have been no reason for her to fight for her sisters' commitment to poverty. There was simply no dan-ger she could have foreseen at that time that her sisters were eventually going to abandon its practice. Moreover, the sisters testifying for Clare's canoniza-tion do not exalt poverty as a virtue particularly outstanding among Clare's many virtues, but—notes Maleczek—the Observant reformers do.[54]

Maleczek has, I think, overplayed his hand on this point. Aside from the obvious problem that the four Francis texts are too brief to be an accurate and balanced barometer of what Francis might have enjoined on Clare and her sisters, his *forma vivendi* most certainly did highlight poverty. While not using the word "poverty," Francis exhorted the women "to live according to the per-fection of the holy Gospel." In his writings, gospel living is always inextricably tied to a life of poverty and humility. "The perfection of the gospel," specifi-cally, recalls the story of the rich young man whom Jesus advised, "If you wish to be perfect, go, sell what you possess and give it to the poor," a line Francis and Clare enshrined in their rules and a practice their hagiographers recalled.[55] Moreover, we know directly from Clare's letters and her first-person state-ments within the *1253 forma vitae* that poverty was essential to her and Fran-cis's vision of religious life. Perhaps surprisingly, the term "poverty" appears with greater frequency in Clare's writings than in Francis's.[56] Indirect testimony further confirms poverty's importance for Clare. The *Bull of Canonization* and early Legends report her stand-off with Gregory IX over possessions. The very autograph of the Privilege of Poverty that she won from Gregory constitutes tangible evidence. In short, while it is the case that the treatment of poverty in the *Testament* is ramped up to a certain degree, it is also entirely in keeping with Francis's and Clare's thinking.

Maleczek is right that poverty was prominently featured within the Observant reform,[57] but that fails to distinguish the reform movement from Clare and Francis, who similarly valued poverty. If the goal of the Observant reform was to return the order to the pristine rigor of their founders' time, then one would expect Observant documents to sound the very themes of those founders. This in itself makes it difficult to ascertain whether the *Testament* belongs to the thirteenth-century founders or to their fifteenth-century imitators. As many proponents of the *Testament*'s authenticity have pointed out, there are no jarring themes within the text to lead to the conclusion that Clare—or someone close to her—could not have written it.[58] Its major themes all appeared, in fact, in the *1253 forma vitae*: Francis as inspiration and founder of the women's order; the centrality of poverty; mutual charity among the sisters; the place of the women's order vis-à-vis the pope, cardinal protector, and Lesser Brothers. An Observant friar or sister might have fabricated the *Testament* to provide further justification for a return to the *1253 forma vitae*, but the parallels between the two documents could be just as easily explained by positing a single author or authorial community for both.

The major stumbling blocks to accepting the *Testament* as authentically Clare's are, instead, its weak manuscript tradition; the silence of the early sources; its prominence within the Observant reform context; problematic passages within the text such as its reference to Innocent III's Privilege; uncanny predictions that come true; and some seemingly autohagiographical remarks by Clare herself, to which I will shortly return.

Brother Leo Again?

I have earlier suggested that Brother Leo might have had a significant hand in redacting the *1253 forma vitae* and, perhaps also, Clare's fourth letter to Agnes. Without disregarding Alfani's fifteenth-century claim that a sister took down Clare's dictated *Testament*, it is worth considering the possibility that Leo (together with a sister scribe?) helped redact the *Testament*, as some scholars have suggested.[59] His involvement would help explain some of the *Testament*'s notable, even perplexing, features.

Paoli points to two texts regarding Clare's last days that might suggest Leo's role in composing the *Testament*. First are Sister Filippa's comments to the canonization commissioners. She told them that "the whole night of that day during which [Clare] passed from this life, she admonished her sisters by preaching to them." Filippa also reported that at the end of Clare's life, she gathered her sisters together and "entrusted the *Privilege of Poverty* to them."[60] Filippa describes scenarios in which the dying Clare preaches to her sisters and impresses upon them the importance of their Privilege of Poverty. The second passage to note, from the prose *Legend*, reports that Clare "turned to her weeping daughters to whom she recalled in a praising way the divine blessings while entrusting them with the poverty of the Lord. She blessed her brothers and sisters and called down the fullest graces of blessings upon the Ladies of the poor monasteries, those in the present and those in the future. Those two blessed companions of the blessed Francis were standing there: Angelo was one of them who, while mourning himself, consoled those who were mourning; the other was Leo who kissed the bed of the dying woman."[61] Note here that Clare spoke about "blessings" and "poverty" to both "devoted brothers and sisters." In the *Testament*, too, Clare comments on God's blessings (which include what God has worked through their father Francis). She then moves to a vigorous recommendation about poverty, in which she reiterates her own and Francis's first-person statements included in the *1253 forma vitae*. The "blessed companions" whom Clare blessed included Angelo, Leo, and—we learn from another remark—Juniper.[62] Paoli suggests that Leo, who was present and heard what Clare said, might later have drafted her message into the text that became known as her *Testament*.[63] The man who did all he could to preserve Francis's words would perhaps have performed the same service for Clare.

This would explain not only certain affinities between Clare's *Testament* and Francis's *Testament*, but also the somewhat polemical and hagiographic character of Clare's *Testament*.[64] While either Clare or Leo might have been responsible for the idealized depiction of Francis, Leo, better than Clare, explains the hagiographic depiction of Clare herself within the *Testament*. In Clare's fourth letter to Agnes, she tells her to gaze upon the mirror *that is Christ*, a metaphor she then elaborates. But in the *Testament*, Clare and her sisters have curiously become that mirror: "For the Lord Himself has placed us as a model, as an example and mirror not only for others, but also for our sisters whom the Lord has called to our way of life as well, that they in turn might be a mirror and example to those living in the world."[65] Such a self-aggrandizing statement is more seemly coming from a writer other than Clare. Leo also had a motive: promoting Clare and her Poor Sisters could serve as an example or even rebuke to his fellow friars, many of whom he thought were abandoning Francis's way of poverty.

Leo's authorial contribution could also make sense of the *Testament* author's prescience regarding the future. Even if he was not one of the companions who compiled the *Legend of the Three Companions*, he would likely have been familiar with the story, repeated in the *Testament*, about Francis prophesying that ladies would one day live in San Damiano and bring glory to the Church. We know that Thomas of Celano's *Second Life* drew upon some of Leo's stories, and Thomas too recounts this episode, albeit in slightly different language.[66] Leo is thought to have died around 1271, well after Clare's community had transferred to the new monastery in Assisi. Leo as author could thus explain how "Clare" knew to warn her sisters about remaining poor even if they had to move. It is plausible, in short, that Clare's last words to her sisters, delivered orally, were redacted by or with the assistance of Leo, who might have also employed a bit of hagiographic license to strengthen Clare's words for posterity.

And, *mutatis mutandis*, some of the points I have raised regarding the *Testament* are pertinent for the briefer, approximately two-hundred-word *Blessing* as well. For example, scholars who believe the *Blessing* is authentically Clare's point to the same *Legend* passage quoted above that reports that Clare "called down the fullest graces of blessings" upon her present and future sisters. Although the passage says nothing about Clare's spoken words ever being written down, someone might have recorded them then or thereafter. Themes sounded in the brief *Blessing*, such as Clare's insistence that the sisters hold firm to what they promised—a clear allusion to poverty—that they care for each other, and that Francis was their father, accord well with what Clare wished for her sisters. But they also match the rhetoric of the late medieval Observant movement. Like the *Testament*, scholars point to Leo as the possible redactor of the *Blessing* because he was actually present when Clare "blessed" her brothers and sisters. And Leo could explain affinities between Clare's *Blessing* and another blessing that Francis bequeathed to Leo himself.[67] Finally, the *Blessing* contains a few phrases that sound more like the language a devotee might apply to Clare than language she would apply to herself. For example, in the *Blessing* (and the *Testament*), Clare describes herself in the first person as Francis's "little plant" (*plantula*), a moniker by which she is still known today.[68] Notably, the (likely earlier) *1253 forma vitae* referred to Clare in the third person, not in her own voice, as Francis's "little plant."[69] All three texts could have involved some sort of collaborative effort. Did the *Blessing* and *Testament*, perhaps both redacted by Leo only after Clare died, escalate the 1253 rule's third-person description of Clare as a "little plant" by having the sobriquet flow from her very own lips? Could the author once more be echoing Thomas of Celano? Composing his *First Life* at the behest of Gregory IX in 1228–1229 with Clare still alive, Thomas no doubt pleased the pope with his description of the women's order Gregory helped launch. Thomas called Francis the "planter" of the order (*religionem et ordinem*). He called Clare, within the order, its "first plant" (*prima planta*).[70] But the more pointed and endearing term *plantula*, "little plant," appears only much later. Besides the *1253 forma vitae*, composed while she was yet alive, the prose *Legend* composed shortly after her death also refers to Clare as Francis's *plantula*.[71] Even more striking, Clare herself—the putative Clare—in the *Testament* and *Blessing* refers to *herself* as Francis's *plantula*. Clare might have spoken about herself in this way, but something about the diminutive, overtly endearing, and almost immodest quality of "I, Clare . . . little plant of our most blessed father Saint Francis" strikes me more as the handiwork of an admiring hagiographer than Clare herself.[72]

Although the precise authorship of the *Testament* and *Blessing* might be debated, few would dispute that their principal themes regarding the sisters' material poverty, mutual charity, and relationship with Francis and his order are, in the main, valid reflections of Clare's vision of religious life for her sisters. It is their very agreement with themes prevalent in Clare's life and writings that makes discussion of their authenticity so vexed.

Conclusion

I have explored in this book the complex relationships between the thirteenth-century papacy, avid to regularize religious women, and Clare of Assisi and her network of allies. It is a micro-study that, in highlighting Clare and the papacy, illuminates a larger landscape including Francis of Assisi's Order of Lesser Brothers, Clare's community of San Damiano, and, importantly, penitent and religious women beyond San Damiano engaged in similar struggles to retain features of their religious life threatened by papal regularization. I wish to conclude by making some observations about the new image of Clare of Assisi that emerges from this book, but even more, about the communities surrounding Clare that bring this image into focus by newly placing her in perspective.

For centuries the historiography of Clare and the Order of San Damiano faithfully echoed themes shaped by the papacy and sounded in the early Legends. This Saint Clare was a conventional monastic saint in many respects—humble, ascetic, prayerful, enclosed—but a somewhat surprising rebel in a few others. Her early Legends report three crucial tussles she had with the papacy: she outright refused to accept property Pope Gregory IX pressed upon her community of San Damiano; she won an unusual papal privilege of poverty freeing San Damiano from having to accept such possessions; and she successfully rebuffed a papal decision that jeopardized the Lesser Brothers' relationship with her community. Clare could never quite qualify as a fully domesticated female saint. When around the turn of the twentieth century scholars began to incorporate Clare's own brief writings into their studies, her image remained essentially unchanged—a self-abnegating, ascetic saint bent on preserving her community's poverty and its ties to Francis of Assisi and his followers, in short, its intrinsic "Franciscan" identity. Scholars today still embrace this view.

But the traditional portrait of Clare has also proved significantly inaccurate in other respects. First and foremost, it has been a mistake to see her as a stand-alone figure, whether as a singular saint set before us to inspire or as an individual actor who so rises above her contemporaries that we hardly see them. This "great woman" approach has distorted Clare's significance. What I have tried to systematically lay out in this chronological study of her life is that Clare has a context and that understanding that context not only clarifies Clare's significance, but also helpfully brings to the fore the complex nexus of actors surrounding her. After turning first to Clare, I will circle out to comment on these other actors.

Clare's image remained relatively static for so long because the principal sources for her life were usually limited to hagiographic texts, her own brief corpus, and a few closely related documents such as the Privilege of Poverty. This narrow focus kept in place one of the great myths about Clare: that she founded—in deed and inspiration—the Order of San Damiano, the order known today as the Order of Saint Clare. Today, close study of numerous papal documents, *vitae*, letters, and other sources, most of which never mention Clare of Assisi or her community of San Damiano by name, upend the notion of Clare as founder.

First, in these documents we discover the papal response to the rapid proliferation of religious groups. Prelates like Jacques de Vitry in the early thirteenth century could still express enthusiastic approval for the ever-emerging new expressions of penitential life, including the early "lesser brothers and lesser sisters" linked to Francis. But increasing numbers of churchmen, including Pope Innocent III and pontiffs after him, concurred more readily with the Fourth Lateran Council's ambition to regiment a seemingly disordered situation. The overlapping trends typifying religious life in this ecclesial *zeitgeist* included shifts from diversity toward uniformity; autonomy toward dependence; episcopal to papal oversight; informal to formal regulation; and juridically separate religious groups (*religiones*) to juridically unified religious orders (*ordines*). Francis of Assisi's Order of Lesser Brothers is but one prominent, concrete example of these trends for penitent men. For Clare, her sisters, and other penitent women, however, the options were fewer because the papacy placed on them the added and related expectations that unenclosed or semi-enclosed communities accept strict claustration and that apostolically engaged communities adopt instead contemplation as their principal vocation. On the heels of these changes, curial authorities concluded that enclosed contemplative communities of women had to be secured by regular income. It was Cardinal Hugo, acting on the authority of Pope Honorius III, who initiated the first order of women's religious communities to be under the direct control of the papacy. He began organizing the "poor ladies of the valley of Spoleto or Tuscany," an oft-used title in the order's earliest years, only in late 1218. This, notably, was about seven years after Clare of Assisi and her sisters had begun their life as an independent house of penitents, inspired by Francis of Assisi and under the jurisdiction of the bishop of Assisi. Soon thereafter, the papacy imposed on Clare and her community Hugo's new *forma vitae* (c. 1219). Given along with the Rule of Benedict, which made the papal order canonical according to Lateran IV, Hugo's *forma vitae* prescribed how women in the new order were to conduct their religious life. These two texts transformed Clare's community from a house of female penitents under episcopal control into a monastery within a religious order founded, regulated, and overseen by the papacy.

The centuries-old narrative of Clare founding a religious order must now be replaced by a new narrative about how a religious order found Clare. Still, while Francis lived, she and her sisters could continue their Franciscan practice of poverty and close association with the friars. After all, Francis recognized the women as followers of his ideals, and Hugo recognized Francis as a charismatic leader not to be disrespected. But once Francis died in 1226 and Hugo became Pope Gregory IX in 1227, Gregory pressed Clare and her sisters to conform more fully with the papal order. Soon, in fact, the order was rebranded the Order of San Damiano, thus burnishing its credentials given "Saint" Francis's association with San Damiano, not to mention Clare's own rising star. Myth-making regarding the papal order escalated over the next years. By the mid-1230s, Julian of Speyer launched the thereafter popular notion that France had founded—not the individual religious house of San Damiano—but the Order of San Damiano itself. By the late 1230s, Gregory himself boldly claimed that Francis had fully accepted Hugo's *forma vitae* for the order. The die was cast for subsequent histories to present Francis, along with Clare, as the order's "true" founders.

Ostensibly, the revised portrait of Clare and her community that I have presented in this book takes them down a notch: no longer the founder and founding community of what would become one of the most renowned women's religious orders in western history, the San Damiano women become instead just one more house of penitents drawn into a papal program bent on regulating religious women. But this interpretation needlessly flattens an otherwise multidimensional story. Ironically, and as I have argued, although Clare and her sisters have now lost their role as the founding community in this women's order, new scrutiny of their minority position within the order trains important light on their strategies of resistance and self-preservation. Notably, Clare's three tussles with the papacy that I mentioned above were all with Gregory IX, the author of the *forma vitae* and the prime mover of the order's growth. Each clash occurred shortly after Francis had died and Gregory had become pope. Clare prevailed each time: she forcefully rejected the property he wanted to give San Damiano; she won (or wrung) from him the Privilege of Poverty; and she finessed him into reversing his decision impeding the entry of friars into San Damiano. The lesson here is not only about Clare—after all, these conflicts were always part of her narrative—but also about Gregory. While on the one hand he was resolute in propagating his papal order, on the other hand, he could repeatedly relent. As he had bowed before Francis's protection of San Damiano's *sui generis* status, so Gregory now bowed before Clare's insistent arguments. He knew when to respect the wishes of a charismatic and determined leader.

"Great woman" history still suits Clare in many respects, but an even greater story surrounds her. A network of women within the Order of San Damiano were part of a wider circle of resistance collectively attempting to forge a new style of religious life at loggerheads with papal ideals for the order. These women included Clare's community of San Damiano, Agnes of Prague, Clare's blood sister Agnes of Assisi, the monastery of Monteluce, other monasteries in Italy and Spain, and, as future research will no doubt show, other members and monasteries within the Order of San Damiano. Others outside the Order of San Damiano also contributed to the women's resistance. The numbers of Lesser Brothers sympathetic to Clare's and her allies' vision of religious life belie a too simple narrative pitting male churchmen against women religious. Women who can also be counted among those resisting papal regimentation include Cistercians, beguines, Dominicans, and the still rather opaque "lesser sisters." I now turn briefly to some of these allied individuals and groups.

Clare's community of San Damiano, it emerges, was in the papal order, but not of it. Resistance and self-preservation for San Damiano meant that even after they had been assigned Hugo's *forma vitae* and the Rule of Benedict, they continued to hew to the *forma vitae* that Francis himself had given them. Although the *forma vitae* Francis gave them is no longer extant beyond the few lines cited decades later within the *1253 forma vitae*, that such a text once existed is amply attested not only by Clare, but also by Gregory IX, Agnes of Prague (as Gregory reports), Bishop Rainaldo of Jenne (the future Pope Alexander IV), and Pope Innocent IV. No single voice from among the sisters of San Damiano, beyond Clare's, emerges with regard to Francis's *forma*, but as I have shown, it is highly probable that his text continued evolving over the years as he and quite likely the sisters themselves added to it, drawing lessons from their own communal life. Sparingly but consistently, documents—by Clare, about her, and about San Damiano—disclose the paramount place of Francis's legislation in their life. The voices of the San Damiano women are preserved in testimonies sifted and recorded by the commissioners gathering evidence for Clare's canonization. Some sisters tellingly noted the momentous Privilege of Poverty, and one even made much of Clare's great desire to have the *1253 forma vitae* solemnly approved with a papal bull. I return to their voices in that rule after considering the voices of other allies heard before that consequential text was written.

The better chronicled association between Clare and Agnes of Prague represents another key quarter of resistance to papal regularization. Clare's letters show how intent she was on leading Agnes's influential monastery into the circle of monasteries committed to Francis's and Clare's ideals; thus, her well-known partisan advice that Agnes follow the counsel of Elias of Assisi, minister general of the Lesser Brothers, rather than "someone" else in authority, probably Gregory IX. But new analysis of an array of papal letters, letters by or concerning members of Agnes's royal family, Agnes's *vita*, and other sources, while seldom mentioning Clare of Assisi or the community of San Damiano, reveals how persistent and multifaceted were Agnes's attempts to ally her monastery with Francis's and Clare's religious project. Agnes's bid to persuade Gregory to allow her monastery to follow a *forma vitae* she herself had compiled from Francis's *forma*, on the one hand, and Gregory's *forma*, on the other, failed miserably. Nevertheless, as I have shown through a close comparison of Gregory's and Clare's letters, Agnes also fought for and succeeded in winning the right to adapt Gregory's fasting rules to conform to those of Francis and Clare.

These sorts of incremental victories point to collaboration across a network of monasteries. Clare's blood sister Agnes of Assisi, a murkier figure, also won a significant concession from Gregory regarding her monastery's practice of poverty. Other monasteries within the Order of San Damiano similarly tried to assert control over the shape of their religious life. Sisters in the monastery of Monteluce daringly got rid of property even though the papacy had explicitly instructed them not to do so. Multiple monasteries from Italy, Bohemia, and Spain—and perhaps future research will turn up others—participated in a well-coordinated campaign to rid themselves of their unwanted legislation. In league with these monasteries, Agnes of Prague lobbied Gregory regarding the very validity of having two rules—Gregory's *forma vitae* and the Rule of Benedict—simultaneously reign over the women's lives. When Gregory resoundingly denied their petition, rather than give up, they strategically waited for a new pope. Indeed, their complaint about the legislation given them by the papacy was itself, as I have shown, a strategic move, a calculated pretext to free themselves to follow instead Francis of Assisi's prescriptions. The next pope, Innocent IV, recognized the gambit and was at first loathe to comply with the women's wishes. But their years-long campaign exposed the extent of their dissatisfaction and, eventually, he capitulated. Innocent wrote a new *forma vitae* that dropped the troublesome reference to the Rule of Benedict and bound the women instead to Francis of Assisi's 1223 rule. The women's victory was pyrrhic in the sense that Francis's rule bound them only with regard to the three vows. Nevertheless, their campaign highlighted the ability of enclosed women to organize across monasteries in an attempt to direct their own lives.

This women's narrative is itself incomplete, however, without acknowledging the essential role of their male allies. Here too the story of Clare of

Assisi and her sisters reflects wider trends beyond their own order, complicat-
ing claims that too starkly pit men's against women's orders. Historians have
long acknowledged that many male orders in this period wanted to stem the
tide or entirely free themselves of their pastoral obligations and administrative
ties to women's groups stylistically or even juridically associated with them.
Clare and the Order of Damiano illuminate key fissures in this narrative. It is
now more than ever transparent that Elias of Assisi, Francis's beloved early
companion and later minister general of the entire Order of Lesser Brothers,
was an intimate and integral ally of Clare, her blood sister Agnes of Assisi,
Agnes of Prague, their respective communities, and, no doubt, other women
in the order as well. Other friars important to Clare and her circle include
Philip Longo, Leo, Angelo, and Juniper, to name just a few. At the very time
that some Lesser Brothers, including their leadership, were indeed trying to
diminish their ties with the Order of San Damiano—including Clare and her
circle—other brothers helped them. These friars, often anonymous, continued to live alongside the women to assist them; they opened channels of com-
munication by carrying the women's letters from one monastery to the next;
and they quite probably conveyed oral messages that were too dangerous to
put into writing. Such a friar might just be the target of Gregory IX's warning
to Agnes of Prague, around the time she was lobbying for a more Franciscan
forma vitae, that she not to listen to "someone" giving her bad advice.

I have underlined Bishop Rainaldo of Jenne's key role in this drama. On
the one hand, as cardinal protector of the Order of San Damiano and the
Order of Lesser Brothers and as a future pope, he is easy to identify as a friend
to the papal program. Sources name him together with Gregory IX in trying
to press property on the community of San Damiano. Rainaldo continued as
cardinal protector under Innocent IV. On the other hand, as I have argued in
this book, Rainaldo's powerful role in undermining Innocent IV's new *forma
vitae* has been overlooked. His correspondence with the papacy and with
some monasteries in the Order of San Damiano points to the sisters' and especially to his concern that Innocent's *forma vitae* gave the Lesser Brothers too
much juridical authority over the women. Whereas the old narrative ties the
defeat of Innocent's rule to Clare, San Damiano, and allied monasteries committed to safeguarding communal poverty, this new narrative suggests that a
struggle about authority may be the more pertinent issue. If the women's role
in overthrowing Innocent's rule is to be preserved, moreover, this new narrative broadens the base of dissatisfaction to include not only the minority of
monasteries concerned about poverty, but also the many other monasteries

who would reasonably have cared very much about juridical changes affecting their life.

There are suggestive signs too of Rainaldo's pivotal, albeit measured, sympathy for Clare and her allies' religious commitments. First, Clare's famous (and victorious) clashes with Pope Gregory IX regarding poverty and the sisters' ties to the friars were memorialized for posterity in the two early Legends, both composed for Alexander IV, that is, Rainaldo himself, who became pope just after Clare's death. Second, it was Rainaldo who agreed to her dying request to have the Privilege of Poverty confirmed by Pope Innocent. While the Messina codex suggests that Rainaldo may have fulfilled that promise, we know for certain that he persuaded Innocent to confirm the far more significant *1253 forma vitae*. Third, and finally, Rainaldo likely had a hand in the very crafting of that *forma vitae*. In short, to a limited but significant degree, Rainaldo ranks among the men who lent support to Clare and her allies.

Turning finally to that momentous rule, I have argued forcefully in this book that it has been a mistake to attribute the *1253 forma vitae* to the sole or principal authorship of Clare of Assisi. A systematic analysis of that rule's attribution over the centuries shows that Clare was first declared the text's primary author only in the late nineteenth century based on faulty manuscript analysis and weak scholarly conjecture. Indeed, multiple voices appear in that text, not least among them the many "we" statements representing Clare's community of San Damiano. The women's collective voice stakes out new religious territory which they identify as "our form of life," including "our form of poverty." The *forma vitae* declares the sisters' intrinsic connection to Francis and relationship with the Lesser Brothers, whose participation in their life they delineate within the *forma*. Novel for any religious order, male or female, is the community of San Damiano's more participative model of religious governance. The sisters continue, not surprisingly, to be bound to the papacy, but with a startling twist: they no longer identify as the Order of San Damiano. They are instead the Order of Poor Sisters. I remarked above that the community of San Damiano had been in the papal order, but not of it. At the close of Clare's life, with the approval of the *1253 forma vitae*, one wonders to what extent they even thought they were in it.

While their trajectory has its own particularities, in broad outlines it recalls the experience of other women carving out their religious spaces within the thirteenth-century Church. Before the papacy started organizing religious women in earnest, it was hard even to distinguish them by name, much less by order. Beguines, *pinzochere*, lesser sisters, and penitents often shared similar features. They might manage hospices, come and go freely, and establish their own *forma vitae*. Beguines, Cistercian, and Dominican women, like women in the papal Order of San Damiano, were compelled over time to accept increasing church regulation and enclosure. Many of these women struggled, especially as they became more enclosed, with striking the right relationship with the religious men on whom they depended for the sacraments and other ministrations. Popes regularly inserted themselves into these matters, sometimes mandating closer ties, for example, between Dominican men and women, while at other times drawing stricter boundaries. Women who resisted papal regularization, like so many of the lesser sisters, it seems, were demonized by church authorities.

A final insight provided by Clare of Assisi and her sisters regards their persistent pursuit of their own vision of religious life. To be sure, their asymmetrical and subordinate position vis-à-vis the papacy and other churchmen allowed them limited room within which to maneuver. Yet, however disadvantaged by their status within the Church, they were able to exhibit stunning flashes of strategic politicking. They did so by building alliances across monasteries, in league with particular friars or prelates who supported their aims, and by playing what might truly be termed a long game. Clare's decades-long commitment to preserving San Damiano's Privilege of Poverty and relationship with the friars certainly fits this description as does Agnes of Prague's and other sisters' campaign to achieve a rule in closer harmony with Francis's and Clare's ideals. Clare's San Damiano sisters, after her death, continued the long game. The fact that they hung on to and preserved the very autograph exemplars of both the Privilege of Poverty and the *1253 forma vitae*—among the few documents to survive today from their community's beginnings—speaks volumes. Even after Pope Urban IV in 1263 devised another *forma vitae* for the order he newly named the Order of Saint Clare, the sisters from San Damiano, by then residing within the town walls of Assisi, managed to have the *1253 forma vitae* papally authorized again for their community. Clare and they had probably hoped more communities might adopt this rule.

Considering their thirteenth-century struggle and hope from today's vantage point, two striking facts stand out. First, communities of Clare's followers to this day still follow a diversity of rules. Quite evidently, the original papal project to establish a single uniform observance never managed to succeed. Second, in recent decades, a notable number of communities of Clare's followers around the world have decided to claim as their rule the very *forma vitae* forged by Clare and her allies. Remarkably then, the *1253 forma vitae*, granted as a concession to Clare's community alone and then threatened with extinction after her death, has managed to survive the centuries and expand its reach.

Appendix A.
Innocent IV, *Cum dilecto filio*, 28 October 1248

(From *Ad Bullarium Franciscanum . . . Supplementum*, ed.
Annibali da Latera, p. 19)

*Innocentius Episcopus, servus servorum Dei. Venerabili Fratri Ostien. Episcopo
salutem, et Apostolicam benedictionem.*

Cum dilecto filio Ministro Generali Ordinis Fratrum Minorum visitationem,
et custodiam Monasteriorum pauperum Monialium Inclusarum Ordinis
Sancti Damiani per nostras litteras commisisse dicamur, ac ob id, prout intel-
leximus, nec de ipsis curam geras, nec visitationis officium Monasteriis im-
pendi eisdem facias, ut solebas. Nos occasione hujusmodi nolentes illas tam
utili patrocinio destitui, Fraternitati tuae per Apostolica scripta mandamus,
quatenus de Monasteriis praedictis ad plenum consuetam, et solitam curam
gerens ut prius, Moniales jam dictas non desistas tuo patrocinio salutari, pro
aeternae mercedis cumulo, confovere. Circa correctiones autem, seu reforma-
tiones per te, vel per alios faciendas in eis, confirmationes quoque Abbatissa-
rum, ac Sororum receptiones, necnon et utilitates alias praedictarum illa utaris
auctoritate libere secundum dictum, praemissis litteris nequaquam obstantibus, quam olim a felicis recordationis Gregorio Papa praedecessore nostro tibi
concessam super iis dinosceris habuisse. Contradictores vero, si qui fuerint,
vel rebelles, eos per censuram Ecclesiasticam, appellatione remota,
compescas.

Datum Lugduni v. Kal. Novembris Pontificatus nostri Anno Sexto.

Appendix B.
Rainaldo of Jenne, *Etsi ea*, 27 June 1250

(From *Ad Bullarium Franciscanum . . . Supplementum*, ed.
Annibali da Latera, pp. 23–24 n. 4)

Raynaldus miseratione divina Ostien. et Velletren. Episcopus Carissimis in Domino filiabus Abbatissae, et Sororibus Monasterii S. Angeli Esculen. Ordinis Sancti Damiani, salutem et benedictionem paternam.

Etsi ea, quae pro concedenda vobis novae vitae formula Sanctissimo Patri nostro Summo Pontifici sunt suggesta, quantum ad suggestores et impetratores procedentes ad haec, nobis prorsus irrequisitis, prout ministrat nobis modicitas sensus nostri, in animarum vestrarum salutem non cedent, ac Ostien. Episcopo Patri vestro plurimum displicerent; reverentia tamen debita, ac devota prosequentes ordinationem Vicarii Jesu Christi, ei, quod factum erat, in nullo restitimus; et quia de grege sibi credito Dominus noster disponere poterat pro suae voluntatis beneplacito, et nos a magno eramus onere liberati, quod adhuc libenter vellemus, si vobis ad consolationem cederet, et propter depositionem hujus oneris Sponsarum, et talium Ancillarum Christi suffragia, Ostien. Protectori, et iis plurimum indignati non deficerent, ac vestrae orationes et lacrymae pro nobis apud piissimum Patrem, et justissimum Judicem non deessent, totum in humilitate, et subjectione omnimoda portabamus. Sed postea sicut Domino Papae placuit super cura, et jurisdictione Monasteriorum, et Dompnarum recepimus mandatum Apostolicum, quod vobis agnitum novimus, et tamen illud inspiciendum, et rememorandum in tenore suo devotioni vestrae insertum praesentibus destinamus. *Innocentius Episcopus etc. Venerabili Fratri Ostien. Episcopo etc. Cum dilectis filiis etc. Datum Lugduni etc. Innocentius Episcopus etc. Venerabili Fratri Ostien. Episcopo etc. Cum dilecto filio etc. Datum Lugduni etc.* Cujus mandati vim, et efficaciam quidam ex dilectis filiis nostris, et fratribus Ministri Provinciales pro sua voluntate glossantes, et

postillantes jurisdictione utebantur in praefatis Monasteriis, et in vobis, ac si
non essent in iis aliquae partes nostrae, aut nulla intercessisset auctoritas man-
datorum. Et ecce vos recepistis, et recipitis alias Papales Epistolas, et nos recip-
imus alias litteras Apostolicas, quas vobis mittimus praesentibus annotatas.
*Innocentius Episcopus etc. Venerabili Fratri Ostien. Episcopo etc. Inter personas
alias etc. Datum Lugduni etc.* Cum igitur vos ad susceptionem, et observan-
tiam praedictae novae formulae, seu antiquae taliter immutatae, cogendas
nullatenus videamus, sed potius observare debeatis antiquam formam vitae,
quam felicis recordationis vestri Patris, et Benefactoris Domini Papae Gregorii
ministerio, et sollicitis studiis in institutione vestri Ordinis suscepistis, quia
collatione, ac deliberatione habita diligenti, nos, qui de iis plene sumus in-
structi, longo tempore iterjecto, et quantum extendere possumus tenuem, et
exilem nostrae considerationis intuitum, Monasteriorum, et vestrum plene
initium novimus, et progressum videmus, quod per eam laudabiliter obser-
vandam melius vestrarum procuratur utilitas animarum, et quod vestrae saluti
non expedit praefatam novam regulam, vel immutatam taliter suscipere, et
servare, charitati veltrae tenore praesentium auctoritate, qua fungimur, et vir-
tute obedientiae districte praecipiendo mandamus, quatenus, sicut jussioni-
bus Apostolicis, atque nostris parere cupitis, saepedictam novam formulam
nullo modo Ministri alicujus, seu alterius Fratris Minoris mandato per se, vel
per alios Fratres directe, vel indirecte sic faciendo suscipientes, vel jam susceptam nullatenus observantes, supradictam vitae formam primam a vobis in vestri Ordinis susceptione susceptam, in quantum concesserit gratia Conditoris,
ad ipsius laudem, et gloriam, ad hororem Virginis gloriosae, et Beatorum
Apostolorum Petri et Pauli, ac Beatissimi Patris Domini Innocentii Summi
Pontificis, et Ecclesiae Romanae, perpetuis temporibus observetis. Et cum in
nova formula contineatur jurisdictio dilectissimis nostris Generali, et Provin-
cialibus Ministris Fratrum Minorum quondam in vobis et Monasteriis attrib-
uta, et nos eis prohibuerimus expresse per litteras nostras in Capitulo Generali,
quod se de usu jurisdictionis alicujus in vobis, et Monasteriis intromittere non
debeant, sed nos, et ea potius nostrae dispositionis arbitrio competentia, dante
Domino, beneplacito divino relinquant, nequaquam eis, quoad aliquam juris-
dictionem de caetero, sed nobis, et Visitatori nostro devote, et humiliter, ac
efficaciter intendatis. Verum, quia sic est in rescripto Apostolico, praedictum
mandatum nostrum a vobis impleri volumus, ut utamur verbis Summi Pontificis, *non obstantibus quibuslibet privilegiis vel indulgentiis, seu litteris Apostolicis impetratis hactenus, vel in posterum impetrandis.* Et ut omnis conscientiis
vestris auferatur turbationis materia, notum vobis, dilectae filiae, facimus per

praesentes, quod nos, qui mentem Instituentis agnovimus, sentimus, et scimus, quod Domini Gregorii supradicti non fuit intentio, nec est nostra, laqueum vobis inijcere, et in silentio, jejunio, lectis, et aliis pluribus, quae continentur in forma vitae ab ipso data, cum vester piissimus, et discretissimus fuerit, et tanta vos beneficiorum profusione prosequutus extiterit, ad transgressionem mortalis peccati, si vos contrarium contingeret facere, suis ordinationibus vos, sicut nobis ab aliquibus suggeritur, obligare, sed potius si quid rigiditatis est in serie antiquae formulae, quod vobis, vel vestrum aliquibus sit importabile, nos in hoc secundum Dominum salutem, et consolationem vestram libenter volumus pro loco, et tempore providere. Terrorem vobis, dilectissimae filiae, nullus incutiat, quia sic vobis adesse proponimus, sicut animae nostrae, et corporis proprii utilitati, et commodo proficere cogitamus. Caeterum per indeficientem orationum, et piorum vestrorum operum interventum continuato suffragio juvamen obsecramus, et petimus apud Deum.

Datum Perusii V. Kalendas Julii.

Abbreviations

1 Cel	Thomas of Celano. *Life of Saint Francis* [*First Life*]. Latin in *FF*, pp. 273–424. Trans. in *FAED*, vol. 1, pp. 180–308.
2 Cel	Thomas of Celano. *The Remembrance of the Desire of a Soul* [*Second Life*]. Latin in *FF*, pp. 441–639. Trans. in *FAED*, vol. 2, pp. 239–393.
1LAg	Clare's First Letter to Agnes of Prague. In *Letters*, ed. Mueller, pp. 28–37.
2LAg	Clare's Second Letter to Agnes of Prague. In *Letters*, ed. Mueller, pp. 54–61.
3LAg	Clare's Third Letter to Agnes of Prague. In *Letters*, ed. Mueller, pp. 74–83.
4LAg	Clare's Fourth Letter to Agnes of Prague. In *Letters*, ed. Mueller, pp. 90–99.
Acts	*The Acts of the Process of Canonization of Clare of Assisi.* Italian in *Santa Chiara d'Assisi sotto processo: Lettura storico-spirituale degli Atti di canonizzazione.* Ed. Giovanni Boccali. Assisi: Edizioni Porziuncola, 2003. Trans. in *CAED*, pp. 141–96.
Assisi Compilation	*The Assisi Compilation.* Latin in *FF*, pp. 1471–1690. Trans. in *FAED*, vol. 2, pp. 118–230.
BF	*Bullarium Franciscanum Romanorum Pontificum: Constitutiones, epistolas, ac diplomata* . . . . Ed. Giovanni Giacinto Sbaraglia. 4 vols. Rome: Typis Sacrae Congregationis de Propaganda Fide, 1759–1768.
CAED	*The Lady: Clare of Assisi: Early Documents.* Ed. and trans. Regis J. Armstrong. Rev. ed. New York: New City Press, 2006.

Earlier Rule	*The Earlier Rule*. Latin in *FF*, pp. 183–216. Trans. in *FAED*, vol. 1, pp. 63–86.
Escritos	*Escritos de Santa Clara y documentos complementarios*. Ed. and trans. Ignacio Omaechevarría. 2nd bilingual Latin-Spanish ed. Madrid: Biblioteca de Autores Cristianos, 1982.
FAED	*Francis of Assisi: Early Documents*. Ed. Regis J. Armstrong, J. A. Wayne Hellmann, and William J. Short. 3 vols. New York: New City Press, 1998–2001.
FF	*Fontes Franciscani*. Ed. Enrico Menestò and Stefano Brufani. Assisi: Edizioni Porziuncola, 1995.
FvI253	The *forma vitae* composed by Clare and collaborators and approved by Innocent IV in 1253. Latin: Federazione S. Chiara di Assisi. *Chiara di Assisi e le sue fonti legislative*. Trans. in *CAED*, pp. 108–26.
FvHugo	The *forma vitae* composed under Cardinal Hugo dei Conti di Segni [Gregory IX]. Latin: "La 'Cum omnis vera religio' del cardinale Ugolino. *Forma vite* primitiva per San Damiano ed altri monasteri." Ed. Giovanni Boccali. *Frate Francesco* 74 (2008): 435–77 (text: 456–76). This is the earliest (ca. 1220–1221) extant version. A close 1228 version is published in *Escritos*, pp. 214–29. Trans. in *CAED*, pp. 75–85.
FvInn	The *forma vitae* composed under Innocent IV. *Cum omnis vera religio* (6 August 1247). Latin in *Escritos*, pp. 237–59. Trans. in *CAED*, pp. 89–105.
Later Rule	*The Later Rule (1223)*. Latin in *FF*, pp. 169–81. Trans. in *FAED*, vol. 1, pp. 99–106.
LegCl	Thomas of Celano [?]. *Legend of Saint Clare*. Latin: *Legenda latina Sanctae Clarae Virginis Assisiensis*. Ed. Giovanni Boccali. Santa Maria degli Angeli: Edizioni Porziuncola, 2001. Trans. in *CAED*, pp. 277–329.
Letters	Clare of Assisi. *Clare's Letters to Agnes: Texts and Sources*. Ed. and trans. Joan Mueller. St. Bonaventure, N.Y.: Franciscan Institute, 2001. Latin and English.
Major Legend	*The Major Legend of Saint Francis (1260–1263)*. Latin in *FF*, pp. 775–961. Trans. in *FAED*, vol. 2, pp. 525–683.
Testament	Clare of Assisi [?]. "Testamento e benedizione di S.

Chiara: Nuovo codice latino." Ed. Giovanni Boccali. *AFH* 82 (1989): 283–92. This is the best Latin edition. A more accessible and close Latin edition is published in Clare of Assisi. *Écrits*. Ed. Marie-France Becker, Jean-François Godet, and Thaddée Matura, 166–84. Paris: Cerf, 1985; rev. ed., 2003. Trans. in *CAED*, pp. 60–65.

VLegCl   *The Versified Legend of the Virgin Clare*. Latin in *FF*, pp. 2347–2399. Trans. in *CAED*, pp. 199–261.

Notes

INTRODUCTION. RELIGIOUS WOMEN IN THE THIRTEENTH-CENTURY CHURCH

1. *Bull of Canonization*, vv. 28–29, in *FF*, p. 2333; trans. in *CAED*, vv. 43–44, p. 266.

2. On the *vita apostolica* movement, see Chenu, *Nature, Man, and Society*, pp. 202–69.

3. Thompson, *Cities of God*, esp. ch. 2, 7.

4. Casagrande, "An Order for Lay People."

5. All the medieval documents I draw on identify him as Hugo until he changes his name upon becoming Pope Gregory IX. On the nickname Hugolino, see Felten, *Papst Gregors IX*, p. 7.

6. See Bynum, "In Praise of Fragments," pp. 11–26.

7. *Acts*.

8. "Deeds of Blessed Francis," and "Little Flowers," in *FAED*, vol. 3, respectively, pp. 466–67; 590–91.

9. See, e.g., Peterson, *Clare of Assisi*.

10. Cozza-Luzi, *Chiara di Assisi secondo alcune nuove scoperte*.

11. Oliger, "De origine regularum"; Gilliat-Smith, *Saint Clare of Assisi*; Robinson, e.g., "Rule of St. Clare"; and Robinson, *Life of Saint Clare*.

12. Grau, *Leben und Schriften der heiligen Klara*; *Legend and Writings of Saint Clare*, ed. and trans. Franciscan Institute. See also A. Fortini, "Nuove notizie intorno a S. Chiara d'Assisi"; Grau, "Die päpstliche Bestätigung der Regel"; Grau, "Die Regel der hl. Klara"; and *Santa Chiara d'Assisi: Studi e Cronaca*.

13. Clare of Assisi, *Écrits*, ed. Becker, Godet, Matura.

14. For example, *Chiara: Francescanesimo al femminile*, ed. Covi and Dozzi; *Chiara di Assisi*; *Chiara d'Assisi e la memoria di Francesco*, ed. Marini and Mistretta; *Dialoghi con Chiara di Assisi*, ed. Giacometti; *Sainte Claire d'Assise et sa postérité*, ed. Brunel-Lobrichon et al.; *Chiara e il Secondo Ordine*, ed. G. Andenna and Vetere; *Chiara e la diffusione delle Clarisse*, ed. G. Andenna and Vetere; and *Convivium Assisiense 6* (known also as *Clara Claris Praeclara*) (2004).

15. Clare of Assisi et al., *Chiara di Assisi e le sue fonti legislative*, ed. Federazione S. Chiara (2003); see also the Federazione S. Chiara's *Chiara di Assisi: Una vita prende forma* (2005); and *Il Vangelo come forma di vita* (2007).

16. *FvHugo*; I will refer to this Latin version which dates to around 1221 or spring 1220. Unless there is a significant variant, I will use an accessible English translation (in *CAED*, pp. 75–85) based on a 1228 version (in *Escritos*, pp. 214–29) for quotations. To facilitate consultation, I will note differences in section numbers between the 1220–1221 version and the *CAED* translation even when I do not use the translation.

17. *Testament*: I will refer to this Latin edition. Unless there is a significant variant, I will use an accessible English translation (in *CAED*, pp. 60–65) based on the Latin edition Clare of Assisi, *Écrits*, pp. 60–65. For the *Blessing*, see Clare of Assisi [?], "Testamento e benedizione," pp. 293–94; trans. in *CAED*, pp. 66–67.

CHAPTER 1. CLARE'S CHILDHOOD AND CONVERSION TO RELIGIOUS LIFE, 1193 TO 1211

1. *Acts*.

2. For example, Grau, "Die Schriften der heiligen Klara," p. 231; Carney, *First Franciscan Woman*, pp. 22–23; La Grasta, "La canonizzazione di Chiara," pp. 301–2.

3. Guida, *Una leggenda in cerca d'autore*.

4. Boccali, "Tradizione manoscritta delle legende." The best Latin edition of the *Legend* to date is *LegCl*, ed. Boccali.

5. *LegCl*, Prologue 9–11.

6. *VLegCl*. Since the verse numbers differ in the Latin and English versions (both indicated in the Abbreviations list), I will provide verse numbers for each when I cite *VLegCl*.

7. For example, Cremascoli, "Introduzione," p. 2344; Boccali, "Tradizione manoscritta delle legende," p. 423, and esp. p. 451.

8. *VLegCl* III, 56 (*CAED*, III, 1).

9. See Lainati, "Processo di canonizzazione di Santa Chiara," vol. 2, p. 2308 n.16.

10. In *Acts*, the witnesses include seven religious sisters: I (Pacifica), 8, 41–42; II (Benvenuta da Perugia), 9–10; III (Filippa), 1–5; IV (Amata), 57; VI (Cecilia), 2–5, 16; XII (Beatrice, who was also Clare's blood sister), 14; XIII (Cristiana di Bernardo), 8; and two lay witnesses: XVII (Bona), 10–11; XVIII (Ranieri), 23. I indicate witnesses by Roman numerals and verses by Arabic numerals.

11. *Acts* XVII (Bona), 2, 15; see Boccali, *Santa Chiara d'Assisi sotto processo*, p. 78.

12. *Acts* II (Benvenuta da Perugia), 6; XIII (Cristiana di Bernardo), 9; XVII (Bona), 12; XX (Giovanni), 4. Clare's neighbor, Pietro, said Clare was about seventeen (XIX, 9, 12).

13. For example, Moorman, *History of the Franciscan Order*, e.g., pp. 32–39, 205–15, esp. 32.

14. For example, Kuster and Kreidler-Kos, "Neue Chronologie zu Clara," esp. pp. 6–10, although other dates and events in this chronology remain open to debate.

15. *Acts* XIX (Pietro), 3–5; trans. in *CAED*, "Nineteenth Witness," p. 194.

16. *Acts* XX (Giovanni), 8: "la corte de casa sua fusse de le maiure de la cità"; cf. *CAED*, "Twentieth Witness," p. 195.

17. *LegCl* I, 2 (*domus abundans et copiosae*). Its precise location is debated; see Abate, *La casa paterna*, pp. 1–20, and tables 1 and 2; A. Fortini, "Nuove notizie intorno a S. Chiara," pp. 23–29; Abate, "Nuovi studi sull'ubicazione della casa."

18. Della Porta et al., *Guide to Assisi*, pp. 125–26; A. Fortini, "Nuove notizie intorno a S. Chiara," 24–26.

19. A. Fortini, "Nuove notizie intorno a S. Chiara," pp. 15–19; Bartoli Langeli, in "Realtà sociale assisana," pp. 332–33 n. 33, questions Fortini's theory.

20. *Acts* II (Benvenuta da Perugia), 9. Cecilia is the sixth witness.

21. *Acts* XVII (Bona), 13.

22. For example, respectively, Omaechevarría, *Escritos*, p. 16; Santucci, "La Cattedrale," p. 91.

23. 1 Cel 52.

24. *Assisi Compilation* 80. For the *Assisi Compilation*, see *FAED*, vol. 2, pp. 118–230; see also *Mirror of Perfection*, ed. Sabatier, 61, in *FAED*, vol. 3, pp. 305–6.

25. *The Major Legend of Saint Francis* VI, 2; for the *Major Legend*, see *FAED*, vol. 2, pp. 525–683.

26. In retelling another Thomas of Celano story, Bonaventure places Francis in a hut in the cathedral canons' garden, thus situating Francis close to the center of ecclesiastical authority; 1 Cel 47; *Major Legend* IV, 4.

27. For example, *Mirror of Perfection*, ed. Sabatier, 105, in *FAED*, vol. 3, p. 353; Thomas, archdeacon of Spalato, *Historia Salonitarum*, in Habig, *St. Francis of Assisi: Writings and Early Biographies*, p. 1601.

28. On penitents, see Guarnieri, "Pinzochere"; Casagrande, "An Order for Lay People"; More, "According to Martha." Makowski, *A Pernicious Sort of Woman*, focuses on a slightly later period but includes helpful observations about the relationship between quasi-religious women and canonically recognized religious women.

29. For example, Francis, *The Testament* 1; *A Letter to the Entire Order* 44; *Earlier Exhortation*, ch. 1, 1–5; ch. 2, 1; in *FAED*, vol. 1, respectively, pp. 124, 120, 41, 43. Casagrande, "An Order for Lay People," pp. 39–43, and Cusato, "To Do Penance," discuss Francis's notion of *facere poenitentiam*.

30. *Acts* XII (Beatrice), 4; *LegCl* III, 1–3.

31. *Acts* XVII (Bona), 7.

32. *Acts* XII (Beatrice), 4–5; III (Filippa), 2; IV (Amata), 5; VI (Cecilia), 3; XVI (Ugolino), 9, 18; XVII (Bona), 7–9.

33. The "palm," *LegCl* IV, 5; *VLegCl* VII, 275 (*CAED*, VII, 12), in Italy was typically an olive branch. On the bishop's role, see Canonici, "Guido II d'Assisi," pp. 201–2; on Clare's relationship to the bishop, either Guido I or Guido II, see D'Acunto, *Assisi nel medioevo*, pp. 114–15, 119, 123–28.

34. *Acts* XII (Beatrice), 7; XVI (Ugolino), 19; XVIII (Ranieri), 16; XX (Giovanni), 14. Bona uses the verb "cut" rather than "tonsure"; XVII (Bona), 16.

35. Padovese, "Clare's Tonsure."

36. *LegCl* IV, 11. *VLegCl* VII, 280–82 (*CAED*, VII, 20–21), mentions only the brothers.

37. *Acts* XII (Beatrice), 8. On San Paolo, see Bigaroni, "I monasteri benedettini femminili," pp. 173–80.

38. *Acts* XII (Beatrice), 9–10; XVIII (Ranieri), 17–18; XX (Giovanni), 15.

39. *LegCl* V, 1–6 (trans. in *CAED*, p. 287; brackets in original); see also *VLegCl* VIII (*CAED*, VIII).

40. *LegCl* IV, 8; *VLegCl* VII, 281 (*CAED*, VII, 19).

41. Bigaroni, "I monasteri benedettini femminili," pp. 175–76.

42. This is the opinion of the editor, Boccali; *LegCl*, p. 31.

43. *VLegCl* VII, 297–99 (*CAED*, VII, 36–38).

44. Brufani, "Le 'legendae' agiografiche di Chiara," p. 345, suggests there was no plan at all; Dalarun, *Francis of Assisi and the Feminine*, p. 195, agrees.

45. Santucci, "La vicenda francescana-clariana," p. 193.

46. A. Fortini, "Nuove notizie intorno a S. Chiara," pp. 29–33.

47. *VLegCl* VIII, 311 (*CAED*, VIII, 13); and see *LegCl* V, 4–6.

48. *Acts* XII (Beatrice), 11.

49. A. Fortini, "Nuove notizie intorno a S. Chiara," p. 33.

50. Gregory IX, *Angelis gaudium* (11 May 1238), in *BF* I, p. 243.

51. Innocent IV, *In divini timore nominis* (13 November 1243), in *BF* I, pp. 316–17; Innocent IV, *Cum Universitati vestrae* (21 August 1244), in *BF* I, p. 350; and see Oliger, "De origine regularum," pp. 446–47.

52. *Acts* XII (Beatrice), 4–6; and see XIX (Pietro), 8–10.

53. Bartoli, *Clare of Assisi*, pp. 46–50, 53–54.

54. Santucci, "Sant'Angelo di Panzo," pp. 225–28; Casagrande and Merli, "Sulle tracce degli insediamenti clariani," pp. 21–24. By 1238, as Casagrande and Merli note, Gregory IX (Hugo) had regularized the community, which would then be governed by his *forma vitae* and the Rule of Benedict; see also A. Fortini, "Nuove notizie intorno a S. Chiara," p. 35.

55. For example, Santucci, "Sant'Angelo di Panzo," p. 225.

56. *LegCl* XVI. Agnes had perhaps been called Caterina prior to that moment; Boccali, *Santa Chiara d'Assisi sotto processo*, p. 156 n; Casolini, "Il nome di battesimo di s. Agnese," pp. 135–36. The fourteenth-century *Chronica XXIV Generalium*, p. 17, claims that Francis gave her the name "Agnes" after she joined Clare in religious life. The lateness of this source opens the claim to question.

57. *LegCl* XVI, 5–7.

58. *LegCl* XVI, 10; some Italian codices say fifteen days (Boccali, *Santa Chiara d'Assisi sotto processo*, p. 38 n. 79) as does the *vita* of Agnes of Assisi included within the *Chronica XXIV Generalium*, p. 174.

59. *LegCl* XVI, 13.

60. *LegCl* XVI, 14–30, quotations, respectively, vv. 14, 17–18, 21–22; trans. in *CAED*, pp. 303–4.

61. Agnes was in San Damiano by the summer of 1212 when a jar of oil was miraculously replenished; *Acts* I (Pacifica), 55, and see 43–58. Cecilia (VI, 49) and Benvenuta da Perugia (II, 23) also mention Agnes; the "carnal sister" who Benvenuta says witnessed Clare wearing a hair shirt must be Agnes rather than Beatrice, because Clare ceased wearing one after she fell ill in 1224 and Beatrice joined San Damiano in 1229.

62. *Acts* XII (Beatrice), 11–12.

63. *LegCl* V, 7; trans. mine (see also trans. in *CAED*, p. 287).

64. Righetti Tosti-Croce, "La chiesa di Santa Chiara ad Assisi," pp. 21–24.

65. Alberzoni, "Clare and San Damiano," pp. 3–7.

66. Alberzoni, "Intra in gaudium Domini," p. 20.

67. For example, *Acts* II (Pacifica), 62–63; III (Filippa), 39–40; IV (Amata), 36–40, 62–64; VI (Cecilia), 29–30.

68. Bigaroni, "San Damiano-Assisi," pp. 77–81, esp. 77, 77 n. 91.

69. Boccali, *Santa Chiara d'Assisi sotto processo*, p. 207 n, suggests Ortulana may have entered between 1226 and 1238. He conjectures, p. 225 n, that it may have been as early as 1226, when Cecilia says she heard Ortulana recount a story (VI, 34–36). Armstrong notes, *CAED*, p. 170 n. b, that Ortulana could have been simply visiting San Damiano then. I note further that Ortulana probably entered only in or after 1229, the year Clare's youngest sister, Beatrice, joined.

70. In *Escritos*, pp. 54–55.

71. *Acts* I (Pacifica), 11–16.

72. *Acts* IV (Amata), 36–40.

73. *Acts* VI (Cecilia), 34–36; trans. in *CAED*, p. 169; also reported by Filippa (III, 91–92) and Amata (IV, 51); see also XVII (Bona), 3. The *Bull of Canonization*, vv. 98–100, in *CAED*, p. 269, incorporates the story.

74. *VLegCl* V, 185–92 (*CAED*, V, 20–24); *LegCl* I, 9–11.

75. *Bull of Canonization*; trans. mine (cf. trans. in *CAED*, v. 43, p. 266). See also *VLegCl* V, 180–84 (*CAED*, V, 15–19); *LegCl* I, 3.

76. On his name, see *Acts* I (Pacifica), 10; XII (Beatrice), 1; XIX (Pietro), 3; and esp. XVI (Ugolino), 4; XX (Giovanni), 5.

77. On his noble status: I (Pacifica), 10; III (Filippa), 103; IV (Amata), 55; XVI (Ugolino), 3; XVIII (Ranieri), 19; XIX (Pietro), 4, and see 5; XX (Giovanni), 4.

78. *Acts* I (Pacifica), 6, 10.

79. *Acts* XIX (Pietro), 3, 8–9.

80. Vetere, "La condizione femminile nell'età di Chiara," pp. 18, 18 n. 24, believes Favarone and his older brother, Scipione, had to be in the search party though neither is named; see pp. 18, 18 n. 24, 20. None of the relatives who tried to seize Clare at San Paolo are named.

81. For example, A. Fortini, "Nuove notizie intorno a S. Chiara," pp. 9–10.

82. *Acts* XII (Beatrice), 17–20; trans. in *CAED*, p. 184.

83. Vetere, "La condizione femminile nell'età di Chiara," pp. 9–51.

84. *Acts* XIX (Pietro), 8–10; quotation, 9–10; trans. in *CAED*, pp. 194–95.

85. *LegCl* XIII, 2; trans. in *CAED*, p. 293; Vetere, "La condizione femminile nell'età di Chiara," pp. 32–33.

86. Hughes, "From Brideprice to Dowry," pp. 276–91, esp. 278, 288–89.

87. *Acts* XIII (Cristina di Bernardo), 31–32; trans. in *CAED*, p. 87, adapted.

88. *Acts* XIII (Cristiana di Bernardo), 1, seems to record one of the commissioner's or the notary's voice referring to Beatrice by name.

89. *Acts* XII (Beatrice), 6; trans. in *CAED*, p. 183. A. Fortini, "Nuove notizie intorno a S. Chiara," p. 11, takes this to mean that the inheritances were sold simultaneously, but this conflicts with those who suggest Clare sold her inheritance soon after entering San Damiano, e.g., *Acts* XIX (Pietro), 8–10; *LegCl* IX, 2.

90. Vetere, "La condizione femminile nell'età di Chiara," pp. 28, 35–51.

91. Coined in the sixteenth century, the term aptly describes the religious commitments, actions, and movements aligned with Francis of Assisi.

92. *Earlier Rule* I, 2.

93. *Later Rule* II, 7–8.

CHAPTER 2. THE EARLY SAN DAMIANO: A HOUSE OF PENITENTS, 1211 TO CA. 1216

1. *Fv1253*. I will cite *Fv1253* by chapter (Roman numeral), then verse (Arabic numeral). The quotation is *Fv1253*, VI, 1–5; trans. in *CAED*, pp. 117–18.

2. Uribe, "L'iter storico della Regola," pp. 237–38.

3. Suggesting 1212–1213: for example, Esser in Francis of Assisi, *Die Opuscula des hl. Franziskus*, p. 298; Da Campagnola, "Introduzione," p. 21. Suggesting 1215: Dalarun, "Francesco, Chiara e le altre," p. 30. Suggesting 1217–1221: Pozzi and Leonardi, *Scrittrici mistiche italiane*, p. 62.

4. For example, *FF*, pp. 117–19, and see 233–35.

5. *Earlier Rule* XII; trans. in *FAED*, vol. 1, pp. 63–64.

6. See Dozzi, *Il vangelo nella regola non bollata*. Around 1262, Jordan of Giano wrote that Francis had enlisted Caesar's help (Jordan of Giano, "Chronicle," p. 30).

7. Compare 2 Cel 209; *Major Legend* IV, 11.

8. 2 Cel 157; Vauchez, *Francis of Assisi*, pp. 94–100, 122–35.

9. *Assisi Compilation* 17; Ubertino da Casale, *Arbor vitae crucifixae Jesu*, bk. 5, ch. 5, trans. in *FAED*, vol. 3, p. 196 (Leo and Rufino); *Mirror of Perfection*, ed. Sabatier, Prologue, trans. in *FAED*, vol. 3, p. 253 (Leo and Bonizo); see also *Major Legend* IV, 11 (two companions assisted him).

10. Gregory IX, *Quo elongati* (28 September 1230), in *BF* I, p. 68; trans. in *FAED*, vol. 1, p. 571.

11. The phrase "perfection of the gospel" evokes Mt 19:21, where Jesus advises the rich young man that if he wishes to be perfect, he should sell all, give it to the poor, and then follow Jesus. Francis referred to this passage in *Earlier Rule* I, 2 and *Later Rule* II, 5.

12. Conwell, *Impelling Spirit*, pp. 294–98.

13. 1 Cel 32, 1.

14. 2 Cel 16, 1: *regula suae vitae*. Bonaventure calls it a "rule for living" (*vivendi regula*): *Major Legend* III, 9.

15. *Earlier Rule* I, 1; *Later Rule* I, 1.

16. Honorius III, in *Later Rule*, Bull 3.

17. See Francis's subsequent 1221 and 1223 rules legislating that new brothers be "received into obedience" (*Earlier Rule* II, 9; *Later Rule* II, 12) and the 1221 rule's prohibition against women being so received (*Earlier Rule* XII, 4); Alberzoni, "Un solo e medesimo spirito," pp. 386–87.

18. *Acts* I (Pacifica), 22–25; IV (Amata), 13–15; see also VI (Cecilia), 39–42. Although it is unclear whether Guido I or Guido II gave Clare a palm the night she left home, it was Guido II who commanded her to moderate her fasting; D'Acunto, *Assisi nel medioevo*, pp. 114–15, 127–28.

19. *Acts* I (Pacifica), 22–25; II (Benvenuta da Perugia), 26–29; IV (Amata), 12–15.

20. Canon 13, in "Lateran IV, 1215," in Tanner, *Decrees of the Ecumenical Councils*, vol. 1, p. 242; e.g., Gennaro, *Chiara d'Assisi*, pp. 40–43; Bartoli, *Clare of Assisi*, pp. 68, 70–71.

21. On *Ne nimia*, see Maccarone, *Studi su Innocenzo III*, pp. 307–27.

22. Canon 23, in "Council of Lyon II, 1274," in Tanner, *Decrees of the Ecumenical Councils*, vol. 1, p. 326.

23. Letter 1 in Jacques de Vitry, *Lettres de Jacques de Vitry*, pp. 71–78.

24. For example, Sabatier, "Note di viaggio di un prelato francese," pp. 106–7; Rusconi, "The Spread of Women's Franciscanism," pp. 41–43; Bartoli, *Clare of Assisi*, pp. 8, 67; Carney, *First Franciscan Woman*, pp. 44–45; Rotzetter, *Klara von Assisi*, p. 114; Pellegrini, "Female Religious Experience," pp. 111–12; Peterson, "Like a Beguine," pp. 66–67; Gennaro, *Chiara d'Assisi*, p. 21; Frugoni, *Una solitudine abitata*, pp. 21–22; Vauchez, *Clare of Assisi*, pp. 59–61.

25. For example, Sabatier, "Note di viaggio di un prelato francese," pp. 106–7.

26. Zarncke, *Der Anteil des Kardinals Ugolino*, pp. 28–30; McDonnell, *The Beguines and Beghards*, pp. 34–35 n. 121 (but cf. p. 97); Alberzoni, *Clare of Assisi*, pp. 113–53, esp. 115–16, 118–19; Dalarun, *Francis of Assisi and the Feminine*, pp. 30, 36; Knox, *Creating Clare of Assisi*, pp. 1–2.

27. On Jacques, see Hinnebusch's comments in Jacques de Vitry, *Historia Occidentalis*, pp. 3–15; Funk, *Jakob von Vitry*; Coen, "Jacques de Vitry."

28. Letter 1 in Jacques de Vitry, *Lettres de Jacques de Vitry*, p. 74, lines 70–72.

29. For the entire letter, see Letter 1, in Jacques de Vitry, *Lettres de Jacques de Vitry*, pp. 71–78; on the identity of the letter's recipients, see p. 6.

30. Sabatier, *Speculum perfectionis*, p. 295; Sabatier, *Life of St. Francis*, p. 429.

31. Letter 1, in Jacques de Vitry, *Lettres de Jacques de Vitry*, pp. 75–76, lines 107–29; trans. in *CAED*, p. 428.

32. Huygens, "Les passages des lettres de Jacques de Vitry," pp. 448–49.

33. Saint-Genois, "Sur des lettres inédites de Jacques de Vitry," pp. 29–33.

34. For a critique of Saint-Genois, see Huygens' comments in Jacques de Vitry, *Lettres de Jacques de Vitry*, pp. 11–13.

35. Sabatier, "Note di viaggio di un prelato francese," p. 108.

36. Röhricht, "Briefe des Jacobus de Vitriaco."

37. Huygens, "Les passages des lettres de Jacques de Vitry," p. 446, and see p. 448.

38. On the errors, see Huygens' comments in Jacques de Vitry, *Lettres de Jacques de Vitry*, pp. 11–13; Huygens, "Les passages des lettres de Jacques de Vitry," pp. 447–48.

39. Jacques de Vitry, *Vita Mariae Oigniacensis*; and see Thomas of Cantimpré, *Vita Mariae Oigniacensis*, esp. ch. 1, sec. 2, p. 573; ch. 3, sec. 15–17, pp. 577–78. On Jacques and women, see Muessig, *The Faces of Women in the Sermons of Jacques de Vitry*.

40. Jacques de Vitry, Letter 1, in *Lettres de Jacques de Vitry*, pp. 72–73, lines 49–61; p. 74, lines 76–81.

41. On the manuscript, see Huygens' comments in ibid., pp. 6–8.

42. 1 Cel 32; trans. in *FAED*, vol. 1, p. 210; see also Francis, *Testament* 14–15, in *FAED*, vol. 1, p. 125.

43. Jacques de Vitry, *Lettres de Jacques de Vitry*, p. 71, line 5; p. 72, lines 30–31.

44. Ibid., p. 38, and see the greetings on pp. 79, 101, 123, 134.

45. Varanini, "Per la storia dei Minori a Verona," pp. 92–105; Rigon, "Penitenti e laici devoti fra mondo monastico-canonicale e ordini mendicanti"; see also Alberzoni, *Clare of Assisi*, pp. 113–20, 141 n. 35.

46. *Homines*, which opens the fourth paragraph, here clearly means "men" rather than "people." Jacques employs both *vires* and *homines* to indicate men elsewhere in his writings; see, for example, his *Historia occidentalis*, where he employs both terms to distinguish the men from the women belonging to a single religious group: for *vir*, see p. 146, line 18; p. 147, line 5; for *homo*, see p. 147, line 14.

47. Röhricht's edition (followed by many scholars) also presents *hii autem* (in contrast to Huygens) and *Ipsi autem* as the beginning of new sentences; "Briefe des Jacobus de Vitriaco (1216–21)," pp. 103–4.

48. Mooney, "The 'Lesser Sisters'."

49. What appears in the manuscript to be a *punctus* here and in pericope 5 after *papa*, is part of the abbreviation for the term *papa*, "pope," rather than an indication of a textual pause.

50. The purpose of this *punctus* is unclear to me.

51. "Ipsi" is the only word capitalized in the passage. It may additionally be preceded by a *punctus*; the facsimile (or the manuscript itself?) appears marred at that place.

52. Letter 1, in Jacques de Vitry, *Lettres de Jacques de Vitry*, pp. 75–76, lines 107–29.

53. Van Asseldonk ("'Sorores minores': Una nuova impostazione," p. 611) is the only scholar to my knowledge who has discussed the ambiguities posed by *hii* and *Ipsi*. He argues that brothers and sisters were Jacques's subject from the passage's start through the comment about going into cities to undertake the apostolic activity. Several editions and translations accord generally with this interpretation by joining in a single paragraph the first three pericopes: e.g., *Escritos*, p. 35; Habig, *St. Francis of Assisi: Writings and Early Biographies*, p. 1608. Avoiding the problem of interpretation altogether are editions that keep all five pericopes together, without paragraphs, just as they appear in the manuscript: e.g., Leonardi, *La letteratura francescana*, pp. 234–35; Dalarun and Le Huërou, *Claire d'Assise: Écrits, Vies, documents*, pp. 831–32.

54. Mooney, "The 'Lesser Sisters'," pp. 24–25.

55. Pacifica di Guelfuccio, Benvenuta da Perugia, Balvina di Martino, Cecilia di Gualtieri, and Filippa di Leonardo; see Boccali's chronology in *Santa Chiara d'Assisi sotto processo*, pp. 37–38.

56. *Acts* I (Pacifica), 43–58.

57. *Servitiale*: e.g., *Acts* III (Filippa), 25; *sore servitrice*: XIV (Angeluccia), 37.

58. *FvHugo* 3 (*CAED*, sec. 4) and 4 (*CAED*, sec. 4).

59. *Acts* X (Angeluccia), 37–38.

60. Sensi, "Le Clarisse a Foligno nel secolo XIII"; text at p. 358.

61. On Jacques's evolving views of the Lesser Brothers, see Bird, "The Religious's Role," pp. 221–22.

62. Jacques de Vitry, *Historia occidentalis*, pp. 158–63; trans. in *FAED*, vol. 1, pp. 582–85.

63. Roger of Wendover, *Flowers of History*, vol. 2, pp. 462–65.

64. On papal hostility toward the lesser sisters and other women emulating the lifestyle of the Lesser Brothers, see Chapter 7, pp. 150–51.

65. Thompson, *Francis of Assisi*, p. 3 (2,000–3,000); Vauchez, *Francis of Assisi*, p. 5 (3,000–4,000).

66. *LegCl* XVI; see also *Acts* (Pacifica) 52–55.

67. *Acts* I (Pacifica), 6, 9.

68. *Acts* II (Benvenuta da Perugia), 5, 9.

69. *Acts* III (Filippa), 2, 21–22; but note, while Filippa claims she is Clare's "third" religious sister, Boccali's chronology (*Santa Chiara d'Assisi sotto processo*, pp. 38–39) presents her as the sixth after Clare.

70. *Acts* VII (Balvina di Martino), 2, 28.

71. *Acts* XIII (Cristiana di Bernardo), 2–7, 11.

72. *Acts* IV (Amata), 1, 4; XII (Beatrice), 22; and on Ortulana, see IV (Amata), 37.

73. On the questors, see III (Filippa), 35; and the *Bull of Canonization*, v. 59–60, in *FF*, p. 2335, in *CAED*, vv. 85–87, p. 268.

74. *Fv1253* XII, 5–7.

75. *Acts* V (Cristiana di Cristiano), 13; XIV (Angeluccia), 26.

76. See Boccali, *Santa Chiara d'Assisi sotto processo*, pp. 82–83, for a list of friars related to San Damiano.

77. I disagree with Boccali (*Santa Chiara d'Assisi sotto processo*, p. 82), however, that Thomas of Celano's report that Francis sent the friars out "two by two" helps determine that the number was probably "three to four"; 1 Cel 29, 3; 30, 1. Papal letters also suggest it was common for friars to reside at many monasteries: Gregory IX, *Licet velut ignis* (9 February 1237), in *BF* I, pp. 209–10; Innocent IV, *Paci, et tranquillitati* (17 July 1245), in *BF* I, p. 368; Innocent IV, *Cum, sicut ex parte vestra* (2 June 1246), in *BF* I, p. 413, and see p. 414; Innocent IV, *Licet olim quibusdam vestrum* (12 July 1246), in *BF* I, p. 420; see also Varanini, "Per la storia dei Minori a Verona," pp. 104–5.

78. Scholars differ slightly in calculating the year a given woman entered San Damiano; Boccali provides the best available chronology: *Santa Chiara d'Assisi sotto processo*, pp. 37–44.

79. *Acts* I (Pacifica), 17; see also VI (Cecilia), 5. *LegCl* VIII, 3 inventively retrojects into this event that Francis suggested Clare be called "abbess," a title she seems to have rejected and which was quite contrary to his own approach to organization among, minimally, the Lesser Brothers; see Rotzetter, *Klara von Assisi*, pp. 119–23.

80. 1 Cel 32; see 29, 31 for their numbers.

81. Casagrande, "Le compagne di Chiara," pp. 394–400; see p. 394 n. 28 for further literature on the social origins of the early sisters.

82. *FvHugo* 3 (*CAED*, sec. 4); 4 (*CAED*, sec. 4).

83. Alberzoni ("Clare and San Damiano," pp. 16–19) suggests around late summer 1221; Alberzoni, "Chiara d'Assisi e il Vangelo," pp. 228–29, more speculatively suggests around spring 1220.

84. *Acts* XIV (Angeluccia), 37–38.

85. *Fv1253* III, 10; enclosed sisters were not permitted to leave the monastery unless for some "useful, reasonable and justifiable matter" (II [Benvenuta da Perugia], 12).

86. Boccali, *Santa Chiara d'Assisi sotto processo*, pp. 69, 239 n; see *Acts* VIII (Lucia), 7.

87. *Acts* III (Filippa), 23–26; II (Benvenuta da Perugia), 11–13.

88. 1225: *Acts* XIV (Angeluccia), 4–6; see also 35; II (Benvenuta da Perugia), 31–32; III (Filippa), 99; VII (Balvina di Martino), 19–20; IX (Francesca), 17; X (Agnes), 7–9.

89. *Acts* I (Pacifica), 32–34; II (Benvenuta da Perugia), 39–40; VI (Cecilia), 39–43; IX (Francesca), 56–57; and see VIII (Lucia), 51–52.

90. *Earlier Rule* VII, 3–9; *Later Rule* V, 3.

91. *Acts* II (Benvenuta da Perugia), 26–29; I (Pacifica), 22–25; III (Filippa), 16–17; IV (Amata), 12–15; VI (Cecilia), 23; VII (Balvina di Martino), 10; X (Agnes), 10.

92. *Acts* VII (Balvina di Martino), 2, 10–12; and X (Agnes), 6, 22–25; see also III (Filippa), 15; IV (Amata), 16; VI (Cecilia), 23. On the illness, see I (Pacifica), 8, 67; XI (Benvenuta di Diambra Perugia), 9, 44.

93. *Acts* II (Benvenuta da Perugia), 28; IV (Amata), 15.

94. 3LAg 38–41; trans. in *Letters*, p. 81, and see p. 80 for the scriptural references.

95. *Acts* II (Benvenuta da Perugia), 21; trans. in *CAED*, p. 151; and see vv. 17–25; see also X (Agnes), 3.

96. *Acts* XX (Giovanni), 10; on the cloth (*stam[e]gna biancha*), see Boccali, *Santa Chiara d'Assisi sotto processo*, p. 308 n. for v. 10.

97. *Acts* II (Benvenuta da Perugia), 17–18, 23; see also X (Agnes), 2; and XIII (Cristiana di Bernardo), 20, who spoke of the roughness not only of Clare's garments but also of her "hairshirt" (*cilitii*).

98. *Acts* II (Benvenuta da Perugia), 25.

99. *Acts* VI (Cecilia), 44–47; trans. in *CAED*, p. 170. Cecilia also notes (vv. 48–50) that Clare's blood sister Agnes heard Clare's remarks, which allows us to place them during Clare's early years, but without the precision Boccali (*Santa Chiara d'Assisi sotto processo*, p. 39) suggests ("before 1219"), since exactly when Agnes left San Damiano is uncertain. Another incident Boccali (p. 39) thinks can be dated to sometime before 1217 is also uncertain: Balvina di Martino, who entered San Damiano before 1217 (VII, 2) reported that she "heard" that Clare had cured Benvenuta da Perugia by making the sign of the cross over her (VII, 16–17); Balvina's use of the past tense "heard" does not necessarily prove that the incident took place prior to her entrance, only that it took place prior to someone recounting it to her, which could have happened any time after she entered.

100. *Acts* III (Filippa), 1–4; IV (Amata), 2–3; VI (Cecilia), 4; on Clare's blood-sister Agnes, see *LegCl* XI, 1–11.

101. Alfani, *Vita et leggenda*, p. 170; Knox, *Creating Clare of Assisi*, pp. 174–75.

CHAPTER 3. THE HOUSE OF PENITENTS BECOMES A MONASTERY, CA. 1211 TO 1228

1. For example, Lester, *Creating Cistercian Nuns*; Smith, "Prouille, Madrid, Rome."

2. See, for example, Oliger, "De origine regularum," pp. 181–84.

3. On *Ne nimia* and San Damiano, see Chapter 2 above, p. 35.

4. For example, Omaechevarría, "La 'regla' y las reglas," pp. 95, 110, and *Escritos*, pp. 206–7, thinks Clare adopted the Rule of Benedict, at least in broad outline, in 1216, as a direct result of Lateran IV's legislation.

5. On Hugo, see Maleczek, *Papst und Kardinalskolleg*, pp. 126–33.

6. Maccarone, *Studi su Innocenzo III*, pp. 316–18. For example, the Dominicans, bound by the broad Rule of Augustine, were governed in practice by their own constitutions; Oliger, "De origine regularum," p. 204.

7. On *"forma vitae"* as constitutions, see Leclercq, "Qu'est-ce que vivre selon une règle?"; Gregory IX, *Angelis gaudium* (11 May 1238), in *BF* I, p. 243.

8. For example, Oliger, "De origine regularum," pp. 427–28; Omaechevarría, "La 'regla' y las reglas."

9. Zarncke, *Der Anteil des Kardinals Hugolino*, pp. 26–77.

10. Grundmann, *Religious Movements*, pp. 112–13.

11. Rusconi, "The Spread of Women's Franciscanism," pp. 40–56; Maleczek, "Authenticity of the Privilege," pp. 25–31; Pellegrini, "Female Religious Experience," pp. 97–112; Alberzoni, e.g., "Clare and San Damiano."

12. Benvenuti Papi, "La fortuna del movimento damianita in Italia," pp. 72–74; see also Maleczek, "Authenticity of the Privilege," pp. 26–27. It is possible that San Salvatore di Colpersito should be added to this list; see Alberzoni, *Clare of Assisi*, p. 35, and esp. pp. 68–69 n. 41.

13. Pásztor, "Esperienze di povertà al femminile"; Bartoli, "La povertà e il movimento francescano femminile," esp. 226–29.

14. Honorius III, *Litterae tuae* (27 August 1218), in *Escritos*, pp. 39–41. To maintain their episcopal exemption (e.g., from dues and tithes), the communities had to remain without possessions, receive no tithes themselves, and not allow burials on their land, acts that might cause friction with bishops who jealousy guarded such rights.

15. Maccarone, *Studi su Innocenzo III*, pp. 272–78; Bolton, "Daughters of Rome," pp. 107–15.

16. Sensi, "Women's Recluse Movement," p. 324; Roest, *Order and Disorder*, pp. 17–18, 21–22.

17. *BF* I, pp. 10–15; each letter is enclosed within a letter sent later by Pope Honorius III. The dates of Hugo's and Honorius's letters to each house are, respectively: Lucca (30 July; 19 September); Siena (29 July; 19 September); Perugia (29 July; 24 September).

18. Levi, *Registri dei cardinali Ugolino d'Ostia e Ottaviano*, pp. 153–54; Latin reprint in Alberzoni, *Clare of Assisi*, pp. 212–13.

19. See the 1228 version of his *forma vitae* in *Escritos*, p. 214. The earliest known version dates to ca. spring 1220 to late summer 1221 (see Chapter 2 above, n. 83); for it and an early Italian translation, see *FvHugo*, pp. 456–76. I will refer to the 1220–1221 Latin version but, unless there is a significant variant, use an accessible English translation (in *CAED*) based on the 1228 version. For ease of consultation, I will also note differences in section numbers between the 1220–1221 version and the *CAED* translation even when I do not use the translation.

20. *BF* I, p. 14.

21. Muratori, "Vita Gregorii IX papae," p. 575.

22. 1 Cel 19.

23. See Appendix B, p. 226 above.

24. Hugo, *Prudentibus virginibus* (27 July 1219) (contained within Honorius III, *Sacrosancta Romana ecclesia* [9 December 1219]), in *BF* I, p. 4.

25. For example, Omaechevarría, "La 'regla' y las reglas," p. 95.

26. References to Francis's contributions are found in 3LAg 36; Gregory IX, *Angelis gaudium* (11 May 1238), in *BF* I, p. 243; Rainaldo's letter of 16 September 1252 (*FvI253*, Prologue 2); Innocent IV's letter of 9 August 1253 (*FvI253*, Prologue 1); and Clare's own remarks (*FvI253* VI, 2–4); see also *Assisi Compilation* 85.

27. Pellegrini, "Female Religious Experience," p. 110; Lainati, "La regola francescana e il II Ordine," pp. 230–33.

28. Sevesi, "Il monastero delle Clarisse in S. Apollinare," pp. 343–45; Alberzoni, *Francescanesimo a Milano*, pp. 46–52, 178, 208.

29. *FvHugo* 1; trans. in *CAED*, sec. 2, p. 75.

30. *FvHugo* 1; trans. in *CAED*, sec. 2–3, pp. 75–76.

31. Hugo, *Prudentibus virginibus* (27 July 1219), in *BF* I, p. 4; Hugo, *Prudentibus virginibus* (29 July 1219), in *BF* I, p. 14.

32. *FvHugo* 2–3; trans. in *CAED*, sec. 4, p. 76.

33. Benedict of Nursia, *Rule of St. Benedict*, ch. 67, does not list reasons for leaving the enclosure, but suggests that it was common.

34. *FvHugo* 3; trans. in *CAED*, sec. 4, pp. 76–77.

35. Gregory IX, *Inter Venerabilem* (4 August 1227), in *BF* I, p. 32.

36. *FvHugo* 12 (*CAED*, sec. 10).

37. *FvHugo* 6, 12 (*CAED*, sec. 6, 10).

38. *FvHugo* 15; trans. in *CAED*, sec. 13, p. 85.

39. *FvHugo* 13 (*CAED*, sec. 11).

40. *FvHugo* 15; trans. in *CAED*, sec. 13, p. 84.

41. Lainati, "The Enclosure of St Clare," p. 58.

42. *FvHugo* 14; trans. in *CAED*, sec. 16, p. 85.

43. *FvHugo* 7; Freeman, "Klarissenfasten im 13. Jahrhundert," pp. 220–21.

44. Scholars differ on the definition of *pulmentum*: Gilliat-Smith, *Saint Clare of Assisi*, pp. 200–201, adduces medieval evidence that suggests it refers to a soup or similar cooked dish, perhaps with fish, that could be eaten with bread; Freeman, "Klarissenfasten im 13. Jahrhundert," pp. 225, 236–43, examining the term in other rules, states it refers to all cooked foods.

45. *FvHugo* 7; Benedict of Nursia, *Rule of St. Benedict*, ch. 39–40; *Earlier Rule* III; *Later Rule* III. Freeman, "Klarissenfasten im 13. Jahrhundert," pp. 217–42, discusses fasting in the Middle Ages, in Hugo's *forma vitae*, and in other religious rules; see esp. pp. 232–35.

46. *FvHugo* 14; trans. in *CAED*, sec. 12, p. 83.

47. Alberzoni, *La nascita di un'istituzione*, pp. 19–20; Maleczek, "Authenticity of the Privilege," p. 29.

48. *FvHugo* 16; trans. in *CAED*, sec. 14, p. 85.

49. Rusconi, "Spread of Women's Franciscanism," p. 47.

50. On penitent women at this time, see Guarnieri, "Pinzochere"; Sensi, "Women's Recluse Movement," pp. 319–23.

51. *Acts* III (Filippa), 1–4.

52. Mooney, "Nuns, Tertiaries, and Quasi-Religious," pp. 85–86; and for a later illuminating case, McLaughlin, "Creating and Recreating Communities of Women."

53. *LegCl* XVII, 4–8. On the date: Guida, *Una leggenda in cerca d'autore*, 37–38.

54. *Chronica XXIV Generalium*, p. 183.

55. Esser, "Die Briefe Gregors IX," pp. 278, 281–83; and see Omaechevarría, in *Escritos*, pp. 351–52. A supposed lynch pin for the 1220 date is a trip Hugo may have made to Assisi with

Francis after Francis returned from the East, but there is no medieval evidence for Hugo's trip. Esser's speculation depends on Jordan of Giano's questionable report in 1262 about Francis's request to Honorius III that Hugo become the friars' protector.

56. For example, Alberzoni, *Clare of Assisi*, p. 39.

57. On the images, see Debby, *The Cult of St Clare*, index entry "St. Francis of Assisi: Images with St. Clare," p. 167.

58. *Earlier Rule* XII; trans. in *FAED*, vol. 1, p. 73.

59. *Fv1253* VI, 1; trans. in *CAED*, p. 117.

60. *Earlier Rule* II, 9; *Later Rule* II, 12.

61. *Later Rule* XI.

CHAPTER 4. TURNING POINT: NEGOTIATING SAN DAMIANO'S SINGULARITY, CA. 1226 TO 1230

1. Dalarun, *Francis of Assisi and the Feminine*, p. 52.

2. *Earlier Rule* XII; *Later Rule* XI.

3. Gregory IX, *Quoties cordis* (14 December 1227), *BF* I, pp. 36–37 (misdated 14 November 1227); see Rusconi, "The Spread of Women's Franciscanism," p. 52; Alberzoni, *Clare of Assisi*, pp. 43–44.

4. *Fv1253* VI, 4–5; and on the friars' presence at San Damiano, see Chapter 2 above, nn. 73–77.

5. 3LAg 36; *Fv1253*, Prologue 1–2; VI.

6. *Assisi Compilation* 83, in *FF*, pp. 1594–99.

7. 1 Cel 62.

8. *Fv1253* VI, 4; trans. in *CAED*, p. 118.

9. Alberzoni, *Clare of Assisi*, pp. 44–45, 49.

10. Gregory IX, *Deus Pater* (1228), in *BF* I, p. 37. On the date and attribution, see Esser, "Die Briefe Gregors IX. an die hl. Klara," pp. 284–90.

11. Marino di Eboli's formulary, bk. 1: Vat. lat. 2976 (cited in *Escritos*, p. 354); Wadding, *Annales Minorum*, 3rd ed., vol. 3, an. 1251, no. XVI–XVII, pp. 272–73; the letter, with the rubric, is also in *BF* I, p. 37.

12. Esser, "Die Briefe Gregors IX. an die hl. Klara," pp. 284–90; Alberzoni, "Da *pauperes domine* a *sorores pauperes*," p. 48; see also Dalarun and Le Huërou, *Claire d'Assise: Écrits, Vies, documents*, p. 891.

13. For example, Zoppetti and Bartoli, *S. Chiara d'Assisi: Scritti e documenti*, p. 396; Mueller, *Companion to Clare*, pp. 76–77.

14. Latin text: Esser, "Die Briefe Gregors IX. an die hl. Klara," pp. 283–84; quotation, p. 283; trans. in *CAED*, p. 131.

15. Trans. in *CAED*, pp. 131–32.

16. He refers to his troubles also in *Magna sicut dicitur*, a letter circulated to several monasteries: for example, to the communities of San Apollinare in Milan (28 July 1227), in Alberzoni, *Francescanesimo a Milano*, p. 209; and Santa Maria in Siena (12 August 1227), in *BF* I, pp. 33–34.

17. Latin text: Esser, "Die Briefe Gregors IX. an die hl. Klara," pp. 283–84; trans. mine (cf. trans. in *CAED*, p. 132).

18. On Rainaldo's pertinence to the family of the counts of Jenne rather than the

sometimes-cited counts of Segni, see Paravicini Bagliani, *Cardinali di curia*, pp. 41–53. "Father and Lord": "Carta . . . del cardenal Rainaldo," in *Escritos*, p. 358; see also 1 Cel 100.

19. The original is in the Archivio di Stato, Siena; for the letter, see "Carta . . . del cardenal Rainaldo," in *Escritos*, pp. 358–61; and Oliger, "De origine regularum," pp. 445–46.

20. "Carta . . . del cardenal Rainaldo," in *Escritos*, p. 358.

21. Alberzoni, "Clare and San Damiano," p. 18.

22. "Carta . . . del cardenal Rainaldo," in *Escritos*, p. 358; Alberzoni, *Clare of Assisi*, p. 111 n. 50.

23. Trans. in *CAED*, pp. 133–34.

24. Boccali, *Santa Chiara d'Assisi sotto processo*, p. 176 n. for v. 74; Oliger, "De origine regularum," pp. 207–8.

25. Gregory IX, *Solet annuere* (30 October 1228), *BF* I, pp. 46–47.

26. On the appearance of this title in 1229 and the 1230s, see Alberzoni, *Clare of Assisi*, pp. 45, 76 n. 101. Earlier examples may yet be found.

27. Gregory IX, *Sincerum animi tui* (30 August 1234), in *BF* I, pp. 134–35.

28. *FvHugo* 14 (*CAED*, sec. 12).

29. Jordan of Giano, "Chronicle," pp. 28–30.

30. Rusconi, "The Spread of Women's Franciscanism," pp. 47–49. On the rift: Knox, "Audacious Nuns."

31. Alberzoni, "Chiara d'Assisi e il Vangelo," pp. 227–30.

32. "Instrumentum quo Villanus episcopus," in Oliger, "Documenta originis Clarissarum," p. 98; see also Gregory IX, *Magna, sicut dicitur* (12 August 1227), in *BF* I, pp. 33–34.

33. *Acts* XVII (Bona), 8; VI (Cecilia), 4.

34. *Acts* XII (Beatrice), 11.

35. *Acts* VI (Cecilia), 3–5.

36. Gregory IX, *Sicut manifestum est* (17 September 1228), *BF* I, p. 771; trans. in *CAED*, p. 87.

37. Millane, "Privilege of Poverty of 1228."

38. *VLegCl* XII, 424–26; trans. in *CAED* XII, 20–22, p. 215.

39. *FvI253* VI, 6–9; trans. in *CAED*, p. 118. In a brief exhortation that Francis allegedly addressed to the San Damiano community in 1225, he calls them "little poor ones" and recommends careful use of alms; Francis of Assisi [?], "Canto di esortazione"; for bibliography regarding the text's disputed authenticity, see Dalarun, *Francis of Assisi and the Feminine*, p. 74 n. 11.

40. *Acts* II (Benvenuta da Perugia), 74–77; trans. in *CAED*, p. 155.

41. *Acts* III (Filippa), 37–38; trans. in *CAED*, pp. 157–58; "[Rainaldo]" my addition.

42. *Acts* I (Pacifica), 39–40.

43. For example, Boccali, *Santa Chiara d'Assisi sotto processo*, p. 176 n. for v. 74, and see p. 63; Mueller, *Privilege of Poverty*, pp. 38–39.

44. *Acts* III (Filippa), 38; trans. in *CAED*, p. 158.

45. *VLegCl* XII, 424–34; trans. in *CAED*, XII, 20–30, p. 215.

46. Alberzoni, *Clare of Assisi*, pp. 41–45, and see 76 n. 99; Oliger, "De origine regularum," pp. 414–17.

47. Muratori, "Vita Gregorii IX papae," p. 575. Similarly, the *vita* of Innocent IV (r. 1243–1254), written by Innocent's contemporary, confessor, and close adviser, says that Gregory "built and founded at his own expense many monasteries and religious houses": Niccolò da Calvi, "Niccolò da Calvi e la sua vita d'Innocenzo IV," p. 78.

48. *LegCl* IX, 9–15.

49. Elsewhere, the author mentions the Privilege, but without identifying the pope; *LegCl* XXVI, 16. "First draft" (*primam notulam*): *LegCl* IX, 11.

50. *BF* I, p. 50 n. e.

51. Maleczek, "Authenticity of the Privilege," pp. 1–52; also arguing against the authenticity of a 1216 privilege, see C. Andenna, "Chiara d'Assisi: La questione dell'autenticità del 'Privilegium paupertatis' e del Testamento"; C. Andenna, "Chiara di Assisi: Alcune reflessioni," pp. 558–63. For alternative hypotheses and critiques of Maleczek, see Kuster, "Clare's *Testament* and Innocent III's *Privilege of Poverty*" (an essay that has failed to persuade most scholars); Paoli, "Introduzione," pp. 2237–51; Cusato, "Hypothesis on the Origin of the *Privilegium Paupertatis*." In Chapter 9, I discuss challenges to Maleczek's dating of the manuscripts.

52. Gregory IX, *Sicut manifestum est* (17 September 1228), in *BF* I, p. 771; trans. in *CAED*, p. 87, adapted.

53. Mueller, *Privilege of Poverty*, p. 40; Millane, "Privilege of Poverty of 1228," p. 42.

54. *LegCl* IX, 12–15; trans. in *CAED*, p. 294.

55. *Acts* III (Filippa), 37–38.

56. In the Protomonastery of Santa Chiara in Assisi.

57. Gregory granted a privilege of poverty to the monastery of Monteluce in *Sicut manifestum est* (16 June 1229), in *BF* I, p. 50 (still extant in the State Archives of Perugia, S. Pietro, cass. III, n. 3); and to the monastery of Agnes of Prague in *Pia credulitate tenentes* (15 April 1238), in *BF* I, pp. 236–37. Both privileges were perhaps short-lived or differently invoked since plentiful evidence points to each monastery's possessions; see for example, Oliger, "De origine regularum," pp. 415–17.

Whether or not the privilege was also granted to the monastery of Monticelli is more difficult to determine. A late fourteenth-century source places Clare's blood sister Agnes of Assisi there and includes her letter to Clare, with no internal indications regarding its provenance. Agnes reports that the pope (Gregory IX) had satisfied her regarding Clare's and Agnes's position vis-à-vis owning property, but she does not explicitly mention a papal privilege; see *Chronica XXIV Generalium*, p. 176. Alberzoni, *Clare of Assisi*, p. 78 n. 120, notes that the superior of the monastery of Monteluce was also named "Agnes" and that she was not called "abbess," a term Clare of Assisi (and quite possibly Agnes of Assisi) eschewed. Perhaps a scribal or some other error mistakenly placed Clare's blood sister at Monticelli instead of Monteluce: while no evidence (besides Agnes's oblique reference) exists for a privilege at Monticelli, an autograph of the Monteluce privilege is still extant.

58. 1 Cel 18–20.

59. 1 Cel 19; trans. in *FAED*, vol. 1, p. 197.

60. 1 Cel 20; trans. in *FAED*, vol. 1, p. 199.

61. 1 Cel 37; trans. in *FAED*, vol. 1, p. 216.

62. For example, Habig, *St. Francis of Assisi: Writings and Early Biographies*, pp. 260, 569 n. 133.

63. 1 Cel 36; trans. in *FAED*, vol. 1, p. 215.

64. Folliet, "Les trois catégories de chrétiens"; Folliet, "Les trois catégories de chrétiens a partir de Luc"; Oexle, "Tria genera hominum."

65. *In Hexaemeron*, xxii, 18–23, in Bonaventure, *Doctoris seraphici S. Bonaventurae*, vol. 5, pp. 440–41.

66. Julian of Speyer, *Life of Saint Francis*, IV, 14, 23 (in *FF*; and *FAED*, vol. 1). On the inspirational but not institutional association between Francis and lay penitents, see Meersseman, *Dossier de l'ordre de la pénitence*, pp. 5–7; Stewart, "*De illis qui faciunt penitentiam*"; and Casagrande, "An Order for Lay People," pp. 43–54.

67. Francis of Assisi, *Testament*, 34–39; trans. in *FAED*, vol. 1, p. 127.

68. *Later Rule* XI; trans. in *FAED*, vol. 1, p. 106.

69. For example, 1LAg 2; 2LAg 2, 25; 3LAg 2, 4, 42; *FvI253* I, 1, 4–5.

70. Gregory IX, *Quo elongati* (28 September 1230), in *BF* I, p. 70.

71. Alberzoni, *La nascita di un'istituzione*, p. 29.

72. Thomas of Eccleston, "The Coming of the Friars Minor," p. 153.

73. Salimbene de Adam, *Chronicle*, p. 52.

74. Rigon, "Antonio di Padova e il minoritismo," p. 189, and see pp. 187–90.

75. Gregory IX, *Mira circa nos* (19 July 1228), in *BF* I, p. 44, sec. 7.

76. Gregory IX, *Quo elongati* (28 September 1230), in *BF* I, p. 68 (trans. in *FAED*, vol. 1, p. 571); on the *Testament*, p. 68.

77. Ibid., in *BF* I, p. 70; trans. in *FAED*, vol. 1, p. 575; "[brothers]" my addition.

78. *VLegCl* XXIX, 1140–42; trans. in *CAED*, XXIX, 69–70, p. 240.

79. *LegCl* XXIV, 7–10; quotation, 8; trans. in *CAED*, p. 312.

80. Bartoli, "Gregorio IX, Chiara d'Assisi e le prime dispute," p. 107.

81. *LegCl* XXIV, 7–10; *VLegCl* XXIX, 1143–44 (*CAED*, XXIX, 71–72).

82. *FvI253* VI, 4; trans. in *CAED*, p. 118.

83. *Acts* VI (Cecilia), 34–36; quotation, 35; trans. in *CAED*, p. 169.

84. 1 Cel 18.

85. A. Fortini, *Nova vita di San Francesco*, vol. 3, pp. 428–31, esp. 429.

86. In *Escritos*, pp. 54–55.

87. *Acts* I (Pacifica), 56; and see Boccali, *Santa Chiara d'Assisi sotto processo*, p. 80; Casagrande, "Le compagne di Chiara," p. 388. On the date, see Sensi, "Il patrimonio monastico di S. Maria di Vallegloria," pp. 77–83.

88. *Acts* I (Pacifica), 42.

89. For example, see Agnes of Assisi's letter to Clare, in the late fourteenth-century *Chronica XXIV Generalium*, pp. 175–77; trans. in *CAED*, pp. 404–5. Alberzoni suggests the monastery may instead have been Monteluce; see above, this chapter, n. 57.

90. *Acts* VII (Balvina di Martino), 27; trans. in *CAED*, p. 172.

CHAPTER 5. CLARE'S LETTERS TO AGNES OF PRAGUE, CA. 1234 TO 1238

1. Wadding, *Annales Minorum*, 3rd ed., vol. 4, an. 1257, no. VIII–XXVII, pp. 90–91.

2. Melissano de Macro, *Annalium Ordinis Minorum supplementa*, no. XX, p. 72.

3. For example, Grau, "Schriften der heiligen Klara," pp. 202–5.

4. For example, Grau and Schlosser, *Leben und Schriften der heiligen Klara*, pp. 222–24; Dalarun and Le Huërou, *Claire d'Assise: Écrits, Vies, documents*, pp. 139–41.

5. Vyskočil, *Legend of Blessed Agnes*, p. 150.

6. A German version of the letters was the earliest known until Achille Ratti (later Pius XI) found an early (ca. 1280–1330) Latin manuscript version; Ratti, "Un codice pragense a Milano"; Seton "Letters from Saint Clare to Blessed Agnes," pp. 509–11. On other mss. and editions of the letters, see Paoli, "Introduzione," pp. 2224–25; Mueller, in *Letters*, pp. 1–4.

7. *Acts* X (Agnes), 27.

8. *VLegCl* XXIX, 1131–32 (*CAED*, XXIX, 59–60); see also *LegCl* XXIV, 5.

9. Van den Goorbergh and Zweerman, *Light Shining Through a Veil*, p. 11.

10. For example, Bartoli, *Clare of Assisi*, pp. 6–7; Armstrong, Introduction to "The Letters of Agnes of Prague," *CAED*, pp. 39–42; Maleczek, "Authenticity of the Privilege," pp. 64–65.

11. Mueller, *Companion to Clare*, pp. 130–31.

12. Matura, "Claire, 'Écrivain,'" in *Écrits*, pp. 33–34.

13. Aizpurúa, *Il cammino di Chiara*, p. 62.

14. Balestracci, *Cilastro che sapeva leggere*; Black, *Education and Society in Florentine Tuscany*, esp. ch. 3–4.

15. Mooney, "Wondrous Words," pp. 277–83.

16. *Acts* X (Agnes), 46; Ps 115:16.

17. *Acts* XIV (Angeluccia), 34–35 (the translation in *CAED*, p. 188, has only "I saw water"); see also X (Agnes), 32.

18. Boccali, *Santa Chiara d'Assisi sotto processo*, p. 255 n. for v. 27.

19. Bonaventure, "Sermo 1, de sancto Marco Evangelista," in *Doctoris seraphici s. Bonaventurae*, vol. 9, p. 519; cited in Muessig, "The Vernacularization of Late Medieval Sermons," pp. 272–73, and see also 267–74.

20. Seton, "Letters from Saint Clare," pp. 509–11.

21. Raurell, "La lettura del 'Cantico dei cantici,'" pp. 232–39; Mueller, in *Letters*, pp. 107–48; and "The Legend of Saint Agnes of Rome," in ibid., pp. 253–65.

22. Johnson, "Clare, Leo, and the Authorship of the Fourth Letter," pp. 91–97, charts the three verses and indicates translations that misunderstand their meaning; Marini, "'Ancilla Christi, plantula sancti Francisci,'" p. 128, notes two of the verses.

23. Muessig, "The Vernacularization of Late Medieval Sermons," pp. 267–71, 274.

24. Paoli, "Introduzione," p. 2223 n. 3.

25. Johnson, "Clare, Leo, and the Authorship of the Fourth Letter," pp. 98–100; Bartoli Langeli, *Gli autografi*, pp. 93–103, esp. 95; and see Marini, "'Ancilla Christi, plantula sancti Francisci,'" p. 128 n. 58. On the gift of the breviary, much of which is in Leo's own hand, see Brooke, *The Image of St Francis*, pp. 4–6.

26. On these and other questions regarding medieval authorship, see Minnis, *Medieval Theory of Authorship*; and Tylus, *Reclaiming Catherine of Siena*.

27. On Agnes and for further bibliography, see *Letters*, pp. 5–11; Klaniczay, *Holy Rulers and Blessed Princesses*, pp. 204–5; Newman, "Agnes of Prague and Guglielma of Milan"; I thank Professor Newman for sharing an advance copy of her essay.

28. Vyskočil, *Legend of Blessed Agnes*, p. 145. On Agnes's suitors, see Marini, *Agnese di Boemia*, pp. 43–54; and, with some caveats, Vyskočil, *Legend of Blessed Agnes*, pp. 140–46, 234–35 n. 21.

29. Mueller, "Agnes of Prague and the Juridical Implications of the Privilege," p. 262, esp. n. 3.

30. Vyskočil, *Legend of Blessed Agnes*, pp. 146–47.

31. Ibid., p. 147. Gregory IX notes in a letter written shortly after Agnes began her religious life that her brother King Wenceslas provided the land, and that he, together with the local bishop and chapter, agreed to hand both institutions over to the Holy See; Gregory IX, *Sincerum animi tui fervorem* (30 August 1234), in *BF* I, p. 134. Later, Gregory noted that Agnes "built" the institutions: *Cum relicta seculi* (18 May 1235), in *BF* I, p. 156.

32. Vyskočil, *Legend of Blessed Agnes*, pp. 146–48; Marini, *Agnese di Boemia*, p. 61.

33. See Alberzoni, "Clare and San Damiano," pp. 30–31.

34. Mueller, *Companion to Clare*, pp. 78–79.

35. Friedrich, *Codex diplomaticus et epistolarius regni Bohemiae*, pp. 65–66.

36. Gregory IX, *Sincerum animi tui fervorem* (30 August 1234), in *BF* I, p. 134.

37. Přemysl's letter and King Wenceslas's confirmation of it (2 Oct. 1234) are quoted within

Gregory IX's letter to the brothers of the hospital, *Filius Summi Regis* (18 May 1235), in *BF* I, pp. 156–58; Přemysl's letter, pp. 156–58.

38. Queen Constance's letter is within Gregory IX's letter to the brothers of the hospital, *Filius Summi Regis* (18 May 1235), in *BF* I, p. 159.

39. 2LAg 10; trans. in *Letters*, p. 56.

40. 3LAg 14 and 41; trans. in *Letters*, respectively, pp. 77 and 81.

41. See also Pozzi's remarks in Clare of Assisi, *Lettere ad Agnese*, pp. 46–56.

42. See above, this chapter, n. 21.

43. 3LAg 4; trans. in *Letters*, p. 74.

44. 3LAg 24–26.

45. 2LAg 22.

46. 4LAg 20; trans. in *Letters*, pp. 94–95. At times, Clare associates a third virtue with poverty and humility, e.g., faith (2LAg 7), and charity (4LAg 18).

47. Mueller, *Companion to Clare*, pp. 78–79.

48. Gregory IX, *Cum relicta seculi* (18 May 1235), in *BF* I, p. 156.

49. Gregory IX, *Sincerum animi tui fervorem* (30 August 1234), in *BF* I, pp. 134–35. The translation in *CAED*, pp. 351–52, omits the letter's closing and inadvertently replaces it with the conclusion of the letter Gregory sent the next day to the friars' custodian in Bohemia, directing him to make Agnes abbess; see *BF* I, pp. 135–36.

50. Newman, "Agnes of Prague and Guglielma of Milan" p. 565.

51. Vyskočil, *Legend of Blessed Agnes*, p. 147; for Přemysl's donation letter, see *BF* I, pp. 157–58; for Queen Constance's donation letter, see *BF* I, p. 159.

52. For example, Mueller, *Companion to Clare*, pp. 78–79, 127–28, 141–42. The English trans. in *CAED*, pp. 353–54, remains ambiguous. For a translation closer to the Latin, see Dalarun and Le Huërou, *Claire d'Assise: Écrits, Vies, documents*, pp. 917–18.

53. Hamburger, "Art, Enclosure and the *Cura Monialium*," p. 115, and see the diagram of the monastic complex, ca. 1234, on p. 116.

54. Gregory IX, *Prudentibus Virginibus* (25 July 1235), in *BF* I, pp. 171–72.

55. 2LAg 8–9; trans. in *Letters*, pp. 56–57.

56. 2LAg 2; trans. in *Letters*, pp. 54–55.

57. 2LAg 3–7; trans. in *Letters*, pp. 54–55, adapted.

58. 2LAg 11; trans. in *Letters*, pp. 56–57.

59. Conwell, *Impelling Spirit*, pp. 341–52.

60. For example, Salimbene de Adam, *Chronicle*, pp. 325–36.

61. Gen 29:16; Marini, "'Ancilla Christi, plantula sancti Francisci,'" in *Chiara di Assisi* (1993), pp. 136–37 n. 76.

62. Armstrong, "Starting Points," pp. 79–80.

63. 2LAg 11; trans. in *Letters*, pp. 56–57.

64. 2LAg 18–20; trans. in *Letters*, pp. 58–59.

65. Gregory IX, *Mira circa nos* (19 July 1228), in *BF* I, p. 43.

66. 2LAg 13–14, trans. mine (cf. trans. in *Letters*, pp. 56–57).

67. Angelo Clareno, "Angelus Clarenus Ad Alvarum Pelagium," p. 143.

68. 2LAg 15–18; trans. in *Letters*, pp. 58–59.

69. Robinson, "Writings of St. Clare," pp. 438–39, where he also implies a certain separation when he refers to the brothers' and sisters' "close relations." He was perhaps influenced by a Latin translation of Clare's letter in which she called Elias not merely "minister general," but "minister general of the whole order," an order Robinson thus thought included the women.

70. Salimbene de Adam, *Chronicle*: "Order of St. Clare" (e.g., pp. 12, 30–32); "St. Clare of the Order of St. Francis" (p. 462); "Order of St. Francis" also denoted the Order of Lesser Brothers (e.g. p. 20).

71. *FV1253* VI, 4; trans. in *CAED*, p. 118.

72. On Clare's trust in Elias, see Alberzoni, *Clare of Assisi*, pp. 48–55.

73. *Chronica XXIV Generalium*, pp. 176–77.

74. Barone, *Da frate Elia*, p. 74; Sedda, "La 'malavventura' di frate Elia," p. 221.

75. In September 1220 Francis handed over governance of the brothers to Pietro Catani. Pietro died March 1221, at which point Elias took over. On Elias as minister general, see Accrocca, "Frate Elia ministro generale," pp. 61–90.

76. *Letter to the Entire Order*, 2, 38, 47, in *FAED*, vol. 1.

77. 1 Cel 98; Sedda, "La 'malavventura' di frate Elia," pp. 219–20, 247–49; Barone, *Da frate Elia*, pp. 29–30.

78. 1 Cel 98.

79. This changed after Elias's deposition as minister in 1239; Barone, *Da frate Elia*, pp. 29–30, 45, and see 31–72.

80. For example, Salimbene de Adam, *Chronicle*, pp. 13, 74, 149, and see 152, 157.

81. Alberzoni, "Frate Elia," pp. 91–121 discusses the complex relations among Elias, Clare, Gregory IX, and Frederick II; on Gregory and Elias, see also Barone, *Da frate Elia*, pp. 44–72, 141–60; and Cusato, "*Non propheta, sed prophanus apostata*," pp. 255–83. Sedda, "La 'malavventura' di frate Elia," pp. 215–300, systematically analyzes the nuanced images of Elias presented in sources through Bonaventure; see also Sedda, "La deriva storiografica," pp. 123–44.

82. Gregory IX, *Quoniam, ut ait Apostolus* (7 March 1234), in *BF* I, p. 148.

83. Gregory IX, respectively, *Attendentes sicut convenit* (30 March 1237), in *BF* I, p. 211; and *Monasterium vestrum* (24 May 1237), in *BF* I, p. 224.

84. Mueller, "Agnes of Prague and the Rule," pp. 164–65; Mueller, *Privilege*, pp. 71–72.

85. The letter is published in *Regesta diplomatica nec non epistolaria Bohemiae et Moraviae*, ed. K.J. Erben, pt. 1 (Prague: Haase, 1855), p. 429, and reprinted in Seton, *Some New Sources*, p. 175; Latin and English are in Vyskočil, *Legend of Blessed Agnes*, p. 286.

86. Gregory IX, *Prudentibus Virginibus* (14 April 1237), in *BF* I, pp. 215–16.

87. Gregory IX, *Omnipotens Deus* (14 April 1237), in *BF* I, pp. 216–17.

88. Gregory IX, *Pia credulitate tenentes* (15 April 1238), in *BF* I, pp. 236–37; quotation, p. 237; trans. in *CAED*, p. 356. It is curious that Gregory entrusted the hospital to the canons on 14 April 1237 and granted Agnes's community its privilege one year and one day later on 15 April 1238, events one might expect to have transpired on sequential days. Friedrich, *Codex diplomaticus et epistolaris regni Bohemiae*, pp. 195–98, dates *Prudentibus Virginibus* similarly to the *BF* (14 April 1237) when it cites the year of Gregory's papal reign, but (in a typo?) also gives the date 14 April 1238.

89. Van den Goorbergh and Zweerman, *Light Shining Through a Veil*, pp. 299–300; Fassbinder, *Die selige Agnes von Prag*, pp. 98–99.

90. 1LAg 10, trans. in *Letters*, pp. 30–31.

91. 4LAg 28–32, trans. in *Letters*, pp. 96–97; and see Leclercq, "St. Clare and Nuptial Spirituality," pp. 171–78.

92. Van den Goorbergh and Zweerman, *Light Shining Through a Veil*, p. 238.

93. 1LAg 12, 24; 4LAg 1, 4; see Schlosser, "Mother, Sister, Bride," pp. 233–49.

94. *Earlier Exhortation*, 7–10, and see *Later Admonition and Exhortation*, in *FAED*, vol. 1, respectively, pp. 41–42 and 49; Alberzoni, "Da *pauperes domine* a sorores pauperes," pp. 51–52,

suggests a parallel with Rainaldo of Jenne's August 1218 letter, which addressed Clare and her sisters as mothers, sisters, daughters, and spouses.

95. La Grasta, "La canonizzazione di Chiara," pp. 311–12.

96. 2LAg 21; trans. in *Letters*, pp. 58–59, adapted.

97. *Angelis gaudium* (11 May 1238), in *BF* I.

98. 3LAg 3–4; trans. in *Letters*, pp. 73–74.

99. 3LAg 6; trans. in *Letters*, pp. 74–75; see also 2LAg 20.

100. 3LAg 15; trans. in *Letters*, pp. 76–77.

101. For example, 3LAg 6, 28 (pride); 20 (false glories).

102. 3LAg 27–28; and see 4, 7, 25 on poverty and humility.

103. 3LAg 4; trans. in *Letters*, pp. 74–75.

104. In Van den Goorbergh and Zweerman, *Light Shining Through a Veil*, trans. Sister Frances Teresa, p. 141 (cf. trans. of 3LAg 8 in *Letters*, pp. 74–75).

105. 3LAg 4; trans. in *Letters*, pp. 74–75.

106. Marini, " 'Ancilla Christi, plantula sancti Francisci,' " p. 141; Marini suggests that this anticipates Thomas of Celano's account in the *Second Life* (1246–1247) of Innocent III dreaming of Francis upholding a collapsing Church; see also Pozzi's remarks in Clare of Assisi, *Lettere ad Agnese*, p. 52.

107. 3LAg 12–14; trans. in *Letters*, pp. 76–77.

108. 3LAg 18–19; trans. in *Letters*, pp. 78–79.

109. 3LAg 21–22; trans. in *Letters*, pp. 78–79.

110. 3LAg 24–26; trans. in *Letters*, pp. 78–79. I have adapted the translation of "her footsteps" to "his footsteps." Both translations are grammatically correct, but "his footsteps" is consistent with every other statement that Clare makes about following Christ in poverty and humility; "her footsteps" finds no support in any statements Clare makes about Mary; on this, see Mooney, "*Imitatio Christi* or *Imitatio Mariae?*" pp. 60–67. Other translations that sensibly render this as "his" footsteps: Francis of Assisi and Clare of Assisi, *Francis and Clare*, p. 201; Clare of Assisi, *Écrits*, p. 107; *Escritos*, p. 391; Pozzi and Leonardi, *Scrittrici mistiche italiane*, pp. 65–66; Zoppetti and Bartoli, *S. Chiara d'Assisi: Scritti e documenti*, p. 99; Dalarun and Le Huërou, *Claire d'Assise: Écrits, Vies, documents*, p. 130.

111. See Menestò, "Vite dei santi e processi di canonizzazione," pp. 182–85, esp. 185.

112. Freeman, "Klarissenfasten im 13. Jahrhundert," pp. 220–27, 232–35.

113. Gregory IX, *Cum, sicut propositum* (9 April 1237), in *BF* I, p. 215

114. The text of this *forma vitae* is found in an unpublished letter (4 March 1238), Archivio di Stato di Trento; see *Escritos*, p. 213 n.

115. Gregory IX, *Pia meditatione pensantes* (5 May 1238), in *BF* I, pp. 240–41.

116. The medieval meaning of "refectio" is "repast" or "meal," rather than "refreshment," as some English translations render it.

117. Compare Mueller's table in *Letters*, pp. 230–31, for a somewhat different interpretation of three of these documents; and see pp. 221–29.

118. *Earlier Rule* III, 12; *Later Rule* III, 8; 3LAg 36.

119. Frugoni, *Una solitudine abitata*, p. 43, similarly dates Clare's letter.

120. 3LAg 36; trans. in *Letters*, p. 80. Clare cannot here mean either Francis's 1221 rule or the papally approved 1223 rule because their fasting guidelines differ from what Clare set down in her letter to Agnes; cf. *Early Rule* III; *Later Rule* III.

121. Marini, "La 'forma vitae' di san Francesco," pp. 184–91.

122. *FVr253*, Prologue.

123. 3LAg 38, 40; trans. in *Letters*, pp. 80–81.

124. 4LAg 9, 13, 31, 32; trans. in *Letters*, pp. 92–93, 96–97.

125. 3LAg 11; trans. in *Letters*, pp. 76–77.

126. 4LAg 15–17; trans. in *Letters*, pp. 94–95; see 1LAg 10–11.

127. 4LAg 18; trans. in *Letters*, pp. 94–95; I render *caritas* as "love" instead of "charity" to accord with v. 23, where *caritas* is rendered as "love."

128. Gen 1:26–27; 1 Cor 4:4.

129. Mueller, *Letters*, p. 101, nn. 24 and 29, p. 102 n. 3, correctly notes that these three terms, *principium*, *medio*, and *fine*, denote periods in time rather than the mirror's "border," "surface," and "depth"; cf. Armstrong, "Clare of Assisi: The Mirror Mystic," p. 200; and *CAED*, p. 56 n. a.

130. 4LAg 19; trans. in *Letters*, pp. 94–95.

131. 2LAg 11; trans. in *Letters*, pp. 56–57.

132. 4LAg 20–21; trans. in *Letters*, pp. 94–95.

133. 4LAg 22–23; trans. in *Letters*, pp. 94–95.

134. 1 Jn 3:2. In the thirteenth century, the author of this letter was thought to be the evangelist John.

135. 1 Cor 13:12.

CHAPTER 6. CONTESTED RULES, LATE 1230S TO CA. 1246

1. 1239: *Acts* XI (Benvenuta di Diambra), 1–8; see also II (Benvenuta da Perugia), 5–55; III (Filippa), 28–29; IV (Amata), 24–27; V (Cristiana di Cristiano), 10; IX (Francesca), 41; XIII (Cristiana di Bernardo), 22; XIV (Angeluccia), 21. 1241: *Acts* VII (Balvina di Martino), 31–36.

2. *Acts* V (Cristiana di Cristiano), 12–15; XIV (Angeluccia), 23–30; XV (Balvina da Porziano), 3–6; see also VI (Cecilia), 57–58.

3. See *Escritos*, pp. 212–13, for six known versions of this redaction of the *forma vitae*. Archival research will likely yield more.

4. Regarding Prague: Gregory IX, *Cum, sicut propositum est* (9 April 1237), in *BF* I, p. 215; *Pia meditatione pensantes* (5 May 1238), in *BF* I, pp. 240–41; for other monasteries, *BF* I, passim.

5. Gregory IX, *Cum saeculi vanitate* (4 April 1237), in *BF* I, p. 213.

6. Vyskočil, *Legend of Blessed Agnes*, pp. 147–48, and see also 152.

7. In Meersseman, *Dossier de l'ordre de la pénitence*, pp. 92–112, and see 8–16; see also Bartoli, "Gregorio IX e il movimento penitenziale," pp. 47–60.

8. Alberzoni, "Curia Romana e regolamentazione."

9. 3LAg 36; trans. in *Letters*, p. 80.

10. *Angelis gaudium* (11 May 1238), in *BF* I, p. 243.

11. Gregory IX, *Angelis gaudium* (11 May 1238), in *BF* I, p. 243; trans. in *CAED*, p. 361.

12. Gilliat-Smith, *Saint Clare of Assisi*, pp. 196–97.

13. See, for example, his letters to the houses of Lucca, Siena, and Perugia in 1219, in *BF* I, respectively, pp. 11, 12, 14.

14. Innocent IV, *In divini timore nominis* (13 November 1243), in *BF* I, p. 316.

15. Gregory IX, *De Conditoris omnium* (9 May 1238), in *BF* I, p. 242.

16. See Francis's first and second versions of his *Letter to the Faithful*, in *FAED*, vol. 1, pp. 41–51.

17. See Chapter 4 above, pp. 80–81.

18. Gregory IX, *Angelis gaudium* (11 May 1238), in *BF* I, p. 243; trans. in *CAED*, p. 361.

19. Robinson, "Writings of St. Clare," p. 439.

20. Gregory IX, *Angelis gaudium* (11 May 1238), in *BF* I, p. 243; trans. in *CAED*, respectively, pp. 361, 362; the triple ellipse in the third quotation indicates a phrase from earlier in the translation erroneously repeated.

21. Gregory IX, *Angelis gaudium* (11 May 1238), in *BF* I, p. 243; trans. mine (cf. trans. in *CAED*, p. 361).

22. Alberzoni, *Clare of Assisi*, pp. 53–54.

23. Gregory IX, *Etsi omnium illa* (22 November 1236), in *BF* I, pp. 206–7.

24. Thomas of Eccleston, "The Coming of the Friars Minor," p. 156; Alberzoni, *Clare of Assisi*, p. 56. Salimbene de Adam writes at length about Elias's faults but fails to note any relationship between Elias and religious women; e.g., *Chronicle*, pp. 75–87, 149–56.

25. Roggen, *Spirit of St. Clare*, pp. 74–75; Robinson, "St. Clare," p. 41; Oliger, "De origine regularum," p. 427, maintains that Clare did not "fully accept" Gregory's rule.

26. Gregory IX, *Angelis gaudium* (11 May 1238), in *BF* I, p. 243; Lainati, "The Enclosure of St Clare," pp. 5–6 n. 3, 47–49, 51; Omaechevarría, "La 'regla' y las reglas," p. 110; Innocent IV, *In divini timore nominis* (13 November 1243), in *BF* I, p. 316.

27. Lester, *Creating Cistercian Women*, pp. 23, 36, 39–42.

28. *Acts* VI (Cecilia), 18–19; VII (Balvina di Martino), 5–6; and see XII (Beatrice), 20.

29. For example, Alberzoni, "Chiara d'Assisi e Agnese di Boemia," p. 447; Vauchez, *Francis of Assisi*, p. 89.

30. Lainati, "The Enclosure of St Clare," p. 4.

31. Benedict of Nursia, *Rule of St. Benedict*, ch. 58; and see ch. 33, 40, 48.

32. *Fvi253* II, 7; trans. in *CAED*, p. 110; cf. *Earlier Rule* II, 4; *Later Rule* II, 5.

33. *Fvi253* VI, 2; trans. in *CAED*, pp. 117–18.

34. 2LAg 15; trans. in *Letters*, pp. 58–59.

35. Robinson, "Writings of St. Clare," p. 439.

36. For example, Smith, "Prouille, Madrid, Rome," p. 348.

37. Possibly too, San Salvatore de Colpersito; Alberzoni, *Clare of Assisi*, pp. 35, 68–69 n. 41.

38. Sensi, "Le Clarisse a Foligno," esp. p. 358.

39. See Chapter 4 above, n. 57.

40. Honorius III, *Litterae tuae nobis* (27 August 1218), in *BF* I, pp. 1–2.

41. Gregory IX, *Indigentiam Monasterii* (3 January 1228), in *BF* I, pp. 38–39.

42. Gregory IX, *Sicut manifestum est* (16 June 1229), in *BF* I, p. 50; the autograph is still preserved at the monastery.

43. Gregory IX, *Ad faciendam vobis* (18 July 1231), in *BF* I, p. 73.

44. Gregory IX, respectively, *Quoniam, ut ait Apostolus* (7 March 1235), in *BF* I, p. 148; and *Si quibuslibet piis locis* (1 September 1235), in *BF* I, p. 177. Höhler, "Il monastero delle Clarisse di Monteluce," pp. 165–68, notes other donations besides those I cite; the donations lead him reasonably to think that the monastery had become rich.

45. Gregory IX, *Attendentes, sicut convenit* (30 March 1237), in *BF* I, p. 211 (the donation); Gregory IX, *Monasterium vestrum* (24 May 1237), in *BF* I, p. 224 (the tithe).

46. Gregory IX, *Statum Monasterii vestri* (13 March 1239), in *BF* I, p. 260 (Monteluce); see p. 259 for the same letter to Spoleto (17 February 1239) and Spello (16 March 1239); only the letter to Spoleto has the full text.

47. Oliger, "De origine regularum," p. 416; Gilliat-Smith, *Saint Clare of Assisi*, pp. 240–43.

48. Innocent IV, *Cum, sicut accepimus* (20 May 1244), in *BF* I, p. 341.

49. Oliger, "De origine regularum," p. 202, and see pp. 414–17.

50. Compare *Sicut manifestum est* (16 June 1229), in *BF* I, p. 50; and *Sicut manifestum est* (17 September 1228), in *BF* I, p. 771 (*CAED*, p. 87).

51. In *Escritos*, pp. 54–55.

52. Omaechevarría, "L'Ordine di S. Chiara sotto diverse Regole," p. 145.

53. Innocent IV, *In divini timore nominis* (13 November 1243), in *BF* I, pp. 315–17.

54. *FvHugo* 1; trans. in *CAED*, sec. 3, p. 76.

55. Innocent IV, *In divini timore nominis* (13 November 1243), in *BF* I, p. 316; trans. in *CAED*, p. 372.

56. Ibid.; I here provide my own translation because it more accurately reflects how closely Innocent's Latin copies Gregory's earlier letter, *Angelis gaudium* (11 May 1238), in *BF* I, p. 243, quoted earlier in this chapter; cf. trans. in *CAED*, pp. 372, 361.

57. Gilliat-Smith, *Saint Clare of Assisi*, p. 192.

58. Vyskočil, *Legend of Blessed Agnes*, p. 151.

59. Ibid.; Latin text in Nemec, *Agnese di Boemia*, p. 81.

60. *LegCl* IX, 13; trans. in *CAED*, p. 294; see also *VLegCl* XII, 430: *ob sevas corrupti temporis iras* (because of the cruel violence of a corrupt time; trans. in *CAED*, XII, 25, p. 215).

61. Vyskočil, *Legend of Blessed Agnes*, pp. 108–11, 127; Klaniczay, *Holy Rulers and Blessed Princesses*, p. 240, points out also Agnes's imitation of her cousin, Elizabeth of Hungary.

62. Agnes's monastery did accept possessions; e.g., see Vyskočil, *Legend of Blessed Agnes*, p. 152.

63. On Agnes's political influence, see ibid., pp. 278–79.

64. Oliger, "De origine regularum," pp. 446–47, presents Rainaldo's introductory remarks to the papal letter, but not the letter; both Rainaldo's and Innocent's letters are dated 15 April 1244. For the text of the letter, see *BF* I, p. 350, which publishes an identical letter sent 21 August 1244.

65. Innocent IV, *Cum Universitati vestrae* (21 August 1244), in *BF* I, p. 350; and see p. 349.

66. On the letter being addressed, specifically, to Clare and her sisters: Robinson, "Inventarium omnium documentorum," p. 417. Alberzoni, *Francescanesimo a Milano*, p. 191, notes an autograph of the same letter sent to and preserved by the monastery of San Apollinare in Milan.

67. Innocent IV, *Cum vobis, sicut ceteris sororibus*, to the monastery of Barcelona (5 July 1245) and the monastery of Salamanca (23 August 1245), respectively, in Fita, "Fundación y primer período," pp. 293–94; and Vásquez, "La 'forma vitae' hugoliniana," pp. 110–11. The letter to the monastery in Barcelona was dated the same day that Innocent participated in the second session of the First Council of Lyon. The editor speculates that the letter's provisions were treated at the council, but this is unlikely since similar letters had previously been sent.

68. Innocent IV, *Cum universitati vestrae* (21 August 1244), in *BF* I, p. 350; trans. mine (cf. trans. in *CAED*, p. 374); and see Innocent IV, *In divini timore nominis* (13 November 1243), in *BF* I, pp. 316–17.

69. Innocent IV, *In divini timore nominis* (13 November 1243), in *BF* I, p. 316.

70. *FvHugo* 1; trans. in *CAED*, sec. 3, p. 76.

71. Innocent IV, *Solet annuere* (13 November 1245): for the quotation, see Vásquez, "La 'forma vitae' hugoliniana," p. 101. Vásquez, "La 'forma vitae' hugoliniana," p. 97 no. 5, notes the text's location in the Vatican Register of Innocent IV. The text is published in *BF* I, pp. 394–99, but with many errors, including, apparently, Innocent's more assertive ownership of the *forma vitae*; on the errors, see Vásquez, "La 'forma vitae' hugoliniana," pp. 96, 101, 104–6.

72. Vásquez, "La 'forma vitae' hugoliniana," pp. 102–3.

73. Innocent IV, *Piis votis omnium* (13 November 1243), in *BF* I, pp. 314–15.

CHAPTER 7. INNOCENT IV'S FORMA VITAE AND ITS AFTERMATH, 1247 TO 1250

1. *FvInn*. This edition in *Escritos* is based on an original manuscript in the archives of Santa Clara de Burgos, published by Manuel de Castro in *Boletín de la Real Academia de la Historia* 171, cuad. 1 (1974): 158–72; it indicates variants signaled by Eubel, *Bullarii Franciscani Epitome*, pp. 241–46; see *Escritos*, p. 236. For another edition, based on the Vatican Register, see *BF* I, pp. 476–83. Innocent's *forma vitae* is henceforth *FvInn*, which I will cite by section number.

2. Innocent IV, *Quoties a Nobis petitur* (23 August 1247), in *BF* I, p. 488.

3. Innocent IV, *In divini timore nominis* (13 November 1243), in *BF* I, p. 317; and Innocent IV, *Cum Universitate vestrae* (21 August 1244), in *BF* I, p. 350: "vestrarum mentium fluctibus."

4. For example, *BF* I, p. 488 n. b.

5. Innocent IV, *Quoties a Nobis petitur* (23 August 1247), in *BF* I, p. 488.

6. For example, Omaechevarría, "La 'regla' y las reglas," passim; Rotzetter, *Klara von Assisi*, pp. 278–86; and Casagrande, "La regola di Innocenzo IV."

7. For example, Bartoli, *Clare of Assisi*, pp. 177–78.

8. Innocent IV, *Inter personas* (6 June 1250), in Eubel, *Bullarii Franciscani Epitome*, p. 249; also in Annibali da Latera, *Ad Bullarium Franciscanum . . . Supplementum*, pp. 22–23.

9. Bynum, *Holy Feast, Holy Fast*, pp. 101–2.

10. *FvInn* 4; on *pulmentis* as "potages" or cooked foods, see Chapter 3 above, n. 44.

11. *FvInn* 6.

12. Gregory IX, *Vestris piis supplicationibus inclinati* (31 May 1241), in *BF* I, p. 295; Innocent IV, *Vestris piis supplicationibus* (21 October 1245), in *BF* I, p. 388. See Mueller's comments in *Letters*, pp. 233–35, on Agnes of Prague's influence.

13. *FvInn* 10–11; trans. mine.

14. Innocent IV, *Cum, sicut ex parte vestra* (2 June 1246), in *BF* I, pp. 413–14.

15. Innocent continued to grant privileges regarding possessions to monasteries in the order, e.g., Innocent IV, *Devotionis vestre precibus* (15 April 1248), to the enclosed nuns of San Apollinare in Milan (in Alberzoni, *Francescanesimo a Milano*, pp. 220–21), and similarly entitled letters to the monasteries of Ascoli Piceno (21 April 1248), in *BF* I, p. 512, and Todi (11 May 1250), in *BF* I, p. 542.

16. *FvInn* 11.

17. Innocent IV, *Quanto studiosus* (19 August 1247), in *BF* I, pp. 487–88.

18. *FvHugo* 3 (*CAED*, sec. 4); *FvInn* 1.

19. *FvInn* 5; trans. in *CAED*, pp. 94, 95; cf. *FvHugo* 9–10 (*CAED*, sec. 9).

20. *FvInn*, respectively, 5, 7, 10.

21. *FvInn*, respectively, 2, 3, 7, 10. On the chalice being withdrawn: Jungmann, *Mass of the Roman Rite*, pp. 510–13.

22. *FvHugo* 15 (*CAED*, sec. 13); and cf. *FvHugo* 9.

23. *FvInn* 5, in *Escritos*, p. 244; trans. mine.

24. *FvInn* 5.

25. *FvHugo* 15 (*CAED*, sec. 13).

26. *FvInn* 9; trans. mine.

27. *FvHugo* 15 (*CAED* sec. 13); *FvInn* 9.

28. Grau, "Introduction," p. 5.

29. *FvInn*, Prologue; trans. in *CAED*, p. 90.

30. Innocent IV, *In divini timore nominis* (13 November 1243), in *BF* I, pp. 315–17; and see above, Chapter 6, pp. 119–23.

31. Lemmens, "Miszellen," p. 322.

32. For example, see Chapter 4 above, pp. 81–87; Grundmann, *Religious Movements*, pp. 109–24, 130–34.

33. Innocent IV, *Paci, et tranquillitati* (17 July 1245), in *BF* I, pp. 367–68.

34. Innocent IV, *Paci, et saluti* (16 October 1245), in *BF* I, pp. 387–88; cf. *FvHugo* 14 (*CAED*, sec. 12).

35. Innocent IV, *Vestris piis supplicationibus* (21 October 1245), in *BF* I, p. 388; Grundmann, *Religious Movements*, pp. 108–9.

36. *Later Rule* XI; trans. in *FAED*, vol. 1, p. 106

37. Innocent IV, *Ordinem vestrum* (14 November 1245), in *BF* I, p. 402. *FAED*, vol. 2, p. 779, has noteworthy errors in its interpretation of *Ordinem vestrum*: line 4 should read "only the cloistered nuns of the Order of San Damiano" rather than "especially the cloistered nuns . . ."; lines 7 and 8 incorrectly state that the brothers can enter "other areas of the monastery" (i.e., the outer cloister) with permission of their superiors; the Latin instead states that this permission allows the brothers to enter the inner cloister of "other communities of nuns," that is, communities not belonging to the Order of San Damiano.

38. Pisanu, *Innocenzo IV e i francescani*, pp. 201–4.

39. Innocent IV, *Paci, et saluti dilectarum* (8 November 1245), in *BF* I, p. 393, and see n. g.

40. Innocent IV, *Paci, et saluti dilectarum* (18 September 1246), in *BF* I, p. 424, and see n. i.

41. Innocent IV, *Cum, sicut ex parte vestra* (2 June 1246), in *BF* I, p. 413, and see n. g; Innocent IV, *Cum, sicut ex parte vestra* (27 May 1248), in *BF* I, p. 517; Innocent IV, *Cum personae quorumdam* (5 February 1252), in *BF* I, p. 593.

42. Innocent IV, *Cum, sicut ex parte vestra* (2 June 1246), in *BF* I, pp. 413–14.

43. See Wadding, *Annales Minorum*, 3rd ed., vol. 3, an. 1247, no. 43, p. 189.

44. Innocent IV, *Licet olim quibusdam vestrum* (12 July 1246), in *BF* I, p. 420.

45. For example, Innocent IV, *Paci, et saluti* (18 September 1246), in *BF* I, p. 425; Innocent IV, *Paci, et saluti* (5 July 1247), in *BF* I, p. 467.

46. See Grundmann, *Religious Movements*, pp. 92–137, esp. 108–22.

47. Both letters are similarly entitled and dated: Innocent IV, *Illius dilectionis affectus* (10 May 1247), in *BF* I, respectively, pp. 453–54, 454.

48. Salimbene de Adam, *Chronicle*, p. 166.

49. See Innocent IV's letters in *BF* I, pp. 502–5; Niccolò da Calvi, "Niccolò da Calvi e la sua vita d'Innocenzo IV," pp. 36–37, 52–54; Brooke, *Early Franciscan Government*, pp. 247–55. Thomas of Eccleston, "The Coming of the Friars Minor," in *XIIIth Century Chronicles*, p. 160, says Crescentius "asked" to be released from the post.

50. *Chronica XXIV Generalium*, p. 262; see also *Legend of the Three Companions*, in *FAED*, vol. 2, pp. 66–68; 2 Cel, Prologue 1; Salimbene de Adam, *Chronicle*, p. 166.

51. 1 Cel, respectively, 95, 98.

52. 1 Cel 69.

53. 1 Cel 18–19; trans. in *FAED*, vol. 1, p. 197; adapted.

54. 1 Cel 116–17.

55. Burr, *The Spiritual Franciscans*, p. 16.

56. Thomas of Eccleston, "The Coming of the Friars Minor," pp. 156–57.

57. 2 Cel 28, 34, 144, 207, 216; and see Sedda, "La 'malavventura' di frate Elia," pp. 240–49.

58. Elias's support of Frederick II had alienated Gregory; Cusato, "*Non propheta, sed prophanus apostata*," pp. 255–83. Jordan of Giano reported that friars complained of Elias's

irregularly sending visitators to provinces of the order to advance his own plans; Jordan of Giano, "Chronicle," p. 65.

59. 2 Cel 112; trans. in *FAED*, vol. 2, p. 322.

60. Jacopa di Settesoli was a wealthy noblewoman devoted to Francis and his brothers; see, for example, *Assisi Compilation* 8, 12; Thomas of Celano, *Treatise on the Miracles* 37–39; see also Dalarun, *Francis of Assisi and the Feminine*, passim.

61. 2 Cel 204; trans. in *FAED*, vol. 2, p. 378; see also *VLegCl* V, 168–69 (*CAED*, V, 4).

62. Dalarun (*Francis of Assisi and the Feminine*, pp. 194–95) suggests that Thomas's silence is owing also to the fact that brothers who provided Thomas with information for the *Second Life*, in response to Crescentius's call for information about Francis, were simply silent about Clare.

63. *Earlier Rule* XII, 1–4; trans. in *FAED*, vol. 1, pp. 72–73, adapted; see also "Fragments," 31–32, in *FAED*, vol. 1, p. 89.

64. See, for example, Weinstein and Bell, *Saints and Society*, pp. 81–97.

65. *Earlier Rule* XII, 5; XIII, 1; trans. in *FAED*, vol. 1, p. 73.

66. *Later Rule* XI, 2–4; trans. in *FAED*, vol. 1, p. 106.

67. Oliger, "Descriptio codicis S. Antonii," p. 383; trans. in Dalarun, *Francis of Assisi and the Feminine*, pp. 61–62.

68. Dalarun, *Francis of Assisi and the Feminine*, pp. 61–62; Knox, "Audacious Nuns."

69. 1 Cel, respectively, 37, 36, 90 (and see 23, 62, 85, 124 for his preaching to both women and men).

70. Francis cured thirty-two boys and men (1 Cel 64–66, 68, 128–31, 133–50); sixteen women and girls (1 Cel 63–64, 67, 69–70, 127, 132, 134, 136, 138, 141–42, 150); and two people whose sex is not specified (1 Cel 64, 138).

71. *Earlier Rule* X.

72. 2 Cel 207; trans. in *FAED*, vol. 2, p. 380.

73. 2 Cel 204; trans. in *FAED*, vol. 2, p. 378.

74. 2 Cel 204, pp. 378–79.

75. 2 Cel 205; trans. in *FAED*, vol. 2, p. 379.

76. 2 Cel 112; trans. in *FAED*, vol. 2, pp. 321–22.

77. 2 Cel 113–114.

78. *FvInn*, Prologue (rule), 1 (profession, rule), 4 (feast day).

79. *FvInn* 1.

80. *FvInn* 6.

81. *FvInn* 1.

82. *FvInn* 12.

83. *FvInn* 2; *Later Rule* III; and cf. *Earlier Rule*, III.

84. *FvInn* 7, 12.

85. *FvInn* 12, which also describes the habit *conversi* wore.

86. Innocent IV, *Cum, sicut ex parte vestra* (2 June 1246), in *BF* I, pp. 413–14; Innocent IV, *Licet olim quibusdam vestrum* (12 July 1246), in *BF* I, p. 420; *FvInn* 12.

87. *FvInn* 12.

88. *FvInn* 12; trans. in *CAED*, p. 103. Elsewhere, Innocent called the superior of a community of friars serving a monastery in Pamplona the "guardian" of the monastery, a name typically reserved for the friars' own governmental hierarchy; *Escritos*, p. 235 n. 5.

89. Gregory IX, *Ad audientiam nostram* (21 February 1241), in *BF* I, p. 290.

90. Alberzoni, *Clare of Assisi*, p. 126.

91. Innocent IV, *Ex parte vestra* (5 October 1246), in *BF* I, p. 427.

92. For the text of this letter, see Innocent IV, *Cum harum rector* (20 April 1250), in *BF* I, p. 541. Alberzoni, *Clare of Assisi*, pp. 127, 146 nn. 77–82, provides information regarding the dates and locations of some other letters: 2 October 1246 to prelates in Lombardy, the March of Treviso, and Romagna, in Alberzoni, *Francescanesimo a Milano*, pp. 219–20; 10 October 1246 to prelates in southern France, in Archives de l'Hérault, H: *Visitation*, 14 A; 17 August 1251 to prelates of France, in Archives du monastère de Périgueux, Bibl. Nat., Fond français, *Perigord*, 35, f. 2 (the location of these last two archival sources is found in Agathange de Paris, "L'origine et la fondation des monastères de Clarisses en Aquitaine au XIIIe siècle," *CF* 25 [1955]: 7 n. 7); 17 August 1251 to prelates of England, in *Register of Walter Giffard, Lord Archbishop of York*, ed. William Brown (Durham: Andrews & Co., 1904), pp. 93–94.

93. Alberzoni, *Clare of Assisi*, pp. 127–28; and see Casagrande, "La regola di Innocenzo IV," pp. 75–76.

94. Oliger, "De origine regularum," p. 427; Grundmann, *Religious Movements*, p. 123; echoed by Rotzetter, *Klara von Assisi*, p. 286. Oliger's argument depended on a letter dated 1250, thus after Innocent's 1247 *forma vitae*; a similar letter from 1246 has since been located, rendering Oliger's argument moot.

95. Roest, *Order and Disorder*, p. 51 n. 38.

96. For example, Grundmann, *Religious Movements*, p. 123; Omaechevarría, in *Escritos*, p. 259; Rotzetter, *Klara von Assisi*, pp. 279, 286; Uribe, "L'iter storico della Regola," p. 235.

97. Innocent IV, *Inter personas alias* (6 June 1950), in Eubel, *Bullarii Franciscani Epitome*, p. 249.

98. Rusconi, "The Spread of Women's Franciscanism," p. 56.

99. For example, Oliger, "De origine regularum," p. 427; Omaechevarría, "La 'regla' y las reglas," p. 116; Omaechevarría, "L'Ordine di S. Chiara sotto diverse Regole," p. 144; Frugoni, *Una solitudine abitata*, p. 46; Alberzoni, *Clare of Assisi*, p. 61.

100. Grundmann, *Religious Movements*, p. 123; see also Mueller, *Privilege of Poverty*, p. 108.

101. *FvInn* 11.

102. Gilliat-Smith, *Saint Clare of Assisi*, p. 259; Alberzoni, *Clare of Assisi*, p. 59.

103. Innocent IV, *Ordinem vestrum* (14 November 1245), in *BF* I, pp. 400–401; *Later Rule* IV, 1; *Fv1253* VI, 12. In a belabored passage, Innocent argues that *Ordinem vestrum*'s gloss actually accords with the *Later Rule*.

104. Grundmann, *Religious Movements*, p. 123; "Sciffi" is now rejected as Clare's surname.

105. Cozza-Luzi, *Chiara di Assisi secondo alcune nuove scoperte*, p. 35, and see pp. 34–37.

106. For example, Costa, "Le regole Clariane," pp. 816, 828–32; Federazione S. Chiara, *Chiara di Assisi: Una vita prende forma*, p. 100.

107. Casagrande, "La regola di Innocenzo IV," p. 78.

108. *Acts* III (Filippa), 107.

109. Gilliat-Smith, *Saint Clare of Assisi*, pp. 258–59; and see Cozza-Luzi, *Chiara di Assisi secondo alcune nuove scoperte*, p. 35, 35 n. 2.

110. *FvInn* 9.

111. *FvInn* 6.

112. Godet, "New Look at Clare's Gospel Plan of Life," p. 25; and see Godet, "Francis and Clare and the Second Order," p. 123.

113. Mueller, *Privilege of Poverty*, pp. 107–8; see also Zoppetti and Bartoli, *S. Chiara d'Assisi: Scritti e documenti*, pp. 328–29.

114. Casagrande, "La regola di Innocenzo IV," p. 79; also noted briefly by Carney, *First*

Franciscan Woman, p. 76; Rotzetter, *Klara von Assisi*, p. 286; Frugoni, *Una solitudine abitata*, p. 46.

115. Alberzoni, "Clare and San Damiano," pp. 35–36.

116. Gilliat-Smith, *Saint Clare of Assisi*, p. 255.

117. For example, Gilliat-Smith, *Saint Clare of Assisi*, p. 255; Frugoni, *Una solitudine abitata*, p. 46.

118. Innocent IV, *Cum, sicut ex parte dilectarum* (27 May 1248), in *BF* I, p. 517.

119. Pisanu, *Innocenzo IV e i francescani*, pp. 227–33.

120. Salimbene de Adam, *Chronicle*, p. 201, and see p. 455.

121. Brooke, *Early Franciscan Government*, p. 255; and see Thomas of Eccleston, "The Coming of the Friars Minor," p. 175; Pisanu, *Innocenzo IV e i francescani*, pp. 169–71, 179–80 (on Crescentius, p. 170). Innocent's *vita*: Niccolò da Calvi, "Niccolò da Calvi e la sua vita d'Innocenzo IV," pp. 76–120; on Niccolò's appointment as bishop, pp. 36–37, 52–54.

122. Mueller, *Privilege of Poverty*, p. 113; and see Mueller, *Companion to Clare*, pp. 86–87.

123. On the possible confusion between the monasteries of Monticelli and Monteluce, see Chapter 4 above, n. 57.

124. Innocent IV, *Dilectae in Christo filiae* (28 March 1248), in *BF* I, pp. 511–12; on the minister provincial's identity, see p. 512 n. a.

125. Innocent IV, *Cum dilectis filiis* (17 June 1248), in Eubel, *Bullarii Franciscani Epitome*, p. 247.

126. Polli, *Le clarisse di San Michele a Trento*, for example, provides evidence from sisters in Trent; Federazione S. Chiara, *Chiara di Assisi: Una vita prende forma*, p. 99 n. 34, refers to other examples.

127. Innocent IV, *Cum dilecto filio* (28 October 1248), in Annibali da Latera, *Ad Bullarium Franciscanum . . . Supplementum*, p. 19, and see n. 1.

128. Innocent IV, *Inspirationis divinae* (6 March 1250), in *BF* I, p. 538.

129. Grundmann, *Religious Movements*, p. 131.

130. Innocent IV, *Inter personas* (6 June 1250), in Eubel, *Bullarii Franciscani Epitome*, p. 249.

131. For example, Grundmann, *Religious Movements*, p. 123.

132. Rainaldo, *Etsi ea* (27 June 1250), in Annibali da Latera, *Ad Bullarium Franciscanum . . . Supplementum*, pp. 23–24 n. 4. The letter is briefly mentioned in Federazione S. Chiara, *Chiara di Assisi: Una vita prende forma*, pp. 99–100.

133. Innocent IV, *Cum, sicut ex parte vestra* (2 June 1246), in *BF* I, pp. 413–14.

134. Innocent IV, *Cum, sicut ex parte dilectarum* (27 May 1248), in *BF* I, p. 517.

135. There is some debate about the year of this chapter; Brooke, *Early Franciscan Government*, p. 257, suggests 1251, but Rainaldo refers to the chapter within his letter of July 1250. See also Omaechevarría, "La 'regla' y las reglas," p. 114.

136. Rainaldo knew Gregory well: he worked in Gregory's curia, followed in his footsteps as bishop of Ostia and cardinal protector of the orders of Lesser Brothers and San Damiano (and later as pope), and was related to Gregory; Boespflug, "Alexander IV," pp. 22–23.

CHAPTER 8. THE 1253 FORMA VITAE, CA. 1250 TO 1253

1. Pisanu, *Innocenzo IV e i francescani*, pp. 212–27.

2. Paravicini Bagliani, "Innocent IV," pp. 790–91.

3. *Acts* I (Pacifica), 67.

4. *LegCl* XXVI, 12–16; quotation 15–16; trans. in *CAED*, p. 314; see also *VLegCl* XXX, 1226–37; trans. in *CAED*, XXX, 57–68, p. 243.

5. Sometimes identified as *Quia vos dilectae* for its first words.

6. *Fv1253*, Prologue; trans. in *CAED*, pp. 108–9.

7. *LegCl* XXVI, 16.

8. *Fv1253* VI, 10–15.

9. Bartoli Langeli, *Gli autografi*, pp. 106–8, 125–30; Bartoli Langeli, "I libri dei frati," pp. 303–4.

10. Bartoli Langeli, *Gli autografi*, p. 113, and table 22, folios 21v–22r.

11. Ibid., p. 113; but see also p. 128, where he seems to entertain Innocent IV as a possibility.

12. See Accrocca, "The 'Unlettered One' and His Witness," pp. 281–82; Accrocca's description of the various texts in the Messina codex is dense; it is helpful to consult Bartoli Langeli, *Gli autografi*, pp. 112–13, and his photographic reproduction of the codex in tables 12–38, esp. 21–22.

13. Among the textual oddities in the Privilege that require explanation is that it resembles the text of the Privilege attributed to Innocent III and thought to be a forgery; see Maleczek, "Authenticity of the Privilege," pp. 1–42, 46–48.

14. Capitani, "Chiara per Francesco," pp. 103–12.

15. For example, Grau, "Die päpstliche Bestätigung der Regel," p. 318; Alberzoni, *Clare of Assisi*, p. 59; and Boccali's comments in *LegCl*, p. 44.

16. Also distinguishing the two documents: Maleczek, "Authenticity of the Privilege," pp. 38–40; Brufani, "Note di storia," pp. 77–78; and see Accrocca, "The 'Unlettered One' and His Witness," pp. 281–82.

17. *Acts* III (Filippa), 106–7; trans. in *CAED*, p. 162; adapted to read "rule of the order" (instead of "*Form of Life* of the Order") to more literally reflect the Italian.

18. *Acts* III (Filippa), 37–38; and see VII (Balvina di Martino), 18; XII (Beatrice), 20; see also Brufani, "Note di storia," p. 78.

19. *Acts* VII (Balvina di Martino), 18; XII (Beatrice), 20.

20. *Acts* III (Filippa), 71, 75, 84–85, 87, 107–9; IV (Amata), 6–61; IX (Francesca), 48–49; X (Agnes), 45–46; XI (Benvenuta di Diambra), 33–34; XIV (Angeluccia), 32.

21. *LegCl*, Preface 9; "*recensitis actibus*" refers to the *Acts*, rather than to Clare's "recent deeds" (cf. trans. in *CAED*, p. 278).

22. *LegCl* XXVI, 8–XXVII, 7.

23. See *VLegCl* XXX, 1235–40 (*CAED*, XXX, 65–71).

24. *LegCl* XXVII, 4–10.

25. Niccolò da Calvi, "Niccolò da Calvi e la sua vita d'Innocenzo IV," pp. 113–14.

26. Ibid., sec. 33, p. 111.

27. For example, Brufani, "Note di storia," pp. 76–78.

28. For example, Omaechevarría, *Las Clarisas a través de los siglos*, pp. 220–21; Bartoli Langeli, "Note di diplomatica," pp. 101–2.

29. Bartoli Langeli, "Note di diplomatica," p. 101 n. 13.

30. *Acts* III (Filippa), 107; trans. in *CAED*, p. 162; adapted to read "rule of the order" (instead of "*Form of Life* of the Order") to more literally reflect the Italian.

31. Godet, "Lettura della forma di vita," p. 285; Godet, "New Look at Clare's Gospel Plan of Life," pp. 70–80; Marini, "'Ancilla Christi, plantula sancti Francisci,'" pp. 121–22. On

poverty, see Acquadro and Mondonico, "La Regola di Chiara," pp. 153–54, 166–68, 194–202; and Acquadro, *Sulle orme di Gesù povero*.

32. Lainati, *Novus ordo, novus vita*, pp. 71–72. Some versions divided the rule into fourteen chapters; Oliger, "De origine regularum," p. 431. Accrocca, "The 'Unlettered One' and His Witness," pp. 279–80, suggests the chapter divisions might have appeared in a version that preceded the Assisi parchment.

33. Trans. in *CAED*, pp. 117–18.

34. Uribe, "L'iter storico della Regola," p. 215.

35. *Fv1253* VI, 6–15; trans. in *CAED*, pp. 118–19. On the women's poverty, see also a brief exhortation Francis allegedly wrote for them: Francis of Assisi [?], "Canto di esortazione," p. 18; see Chapter 4 above, n. 39.

36. *Fv1253* II, 24; trans. in *CAED*, p. 112; and see *Later Rule* II, 16–17.

37. *Fv1253* VIII, 4; trans. in *CAED*, pp. 119–20; and see *Later Rule* VI, 4.

38. *Fv1253* X, 6; and see *Later Rule* X, 7.

39. Sainte-Marie, "Presence of the Benedictine Rule."

40. Clare of Assisi et al., *Chiara di Assisi e le sue fonti legislative*, p. 11; this work presents a new critical edition of the *1253 forma vitae*.

41. Clare of Assisi, *Écrits*, p. 30.

42. For example, Bartoli, *Clare of Assisi*, p. 6; Petroff, "Medieval Woman's Utopian Vision," pp. 66–67; *CAED*, p. 106; *Letters*, pp. 9–10; and see Kreidler-Kos, Röttger, and Kuster, *Klara von Assisi*, p. 114.

43. Matter, "Canon of Religious Life," p. 81; see also Lynn, "The Body and the Text," p. 85.

44. *Fv1253*, Prologue; trans. in *CAED*, p. 108.

45. *Fv1253*, Prologue; trans. in *CAED*, p. 109.

46. *Fv1253* I, 1–2; trans. in *CAED*, p. 109.

47. Oliger, "De origine regularum," p. 432, cites Francesco Gonzaga, *De origine seraphicae Religionis* (Rome: Dominici Basa, 1587), p. 3; and Nicholaus Glassberger, *AF* 2 (1887), p. 72. For the relevant Latin passages for Ubertino da Casale, *Arbor vitae crucifixae Jesu*, bk. 5, ch. 6, and *Firmamentum trium Ordinum* (Paris 1512), see Oliger, "De origine regularum," pp. 442 and 433, respectively.

48. Bernard of Besse, *Book of the Praises of Saint Francis*, in *FAED*, vol. 3, p. 65.

49. Gregory IX, *Quo elongati* (28 September 1230), in *BF* I, p. 68; Meersseman, *Dossier de l'ordre de la pénitence*, pp. 1–11, 92–112.

50. Gregory IX, *Angelis gaudium* (11 May 1238), in *BF* I, p. 243.

51. Philip of Perugia, *Catalogus Cardinalium, qui fuerunt Ordinis Protectores*, p. 709.

52. Oliger, "De origine regularum," pp. 198–99; and see 190, 199, 202–3 for convincing evidence that Francis did not help Gregory compose his *forma vitae*.

53. Only his book-length summary survives: *Compendium chronicarum Ordinis FF. Minorum*.

54. Mariano of Florence, *Libro delle degnità et excellentie del Ordine*.

55. Ibid., sec. 44–46, pp. 58–59. Knox, *Creating Clare of Assisi*, pp. 144–56, on Mariano's treatment of the *forma vitae* and the Clarisses at the time of the Observant reform.

56. Marcos of Lisbon, *Crónicas da Ordem dos Frades Menores*, bk. 8, ch. 19, pp. 212–13, 213–16 (the rule). In the nineteenth century, scholars similarly attributed a Privilege of Poverty to Innocent IV: Demore, *Vie de sainte Claire d'Assise*, pp. 236–38; and José de Madrid, cited by Locatelli, *Vita di S.ᵃ Chiara*, pp. 87–88 n. 1, but whose work (probably his *Primera [segunda, etc.] parte de las chronicas de los frailes menores capuchinos*, 5 vol. [Madrid: Carlos Sanchez, 1644–1691]) I have been unable to consult.

57. Francis of Assisi, *B. P. Francisci Assisiatis Opuscula*, 3 vols.; Wadding, *Annales Minorum*, 1st ed.

58. Wadding, *Annales Minorum*, 3rd ed, vol. 2, an. 1224, no. I, p. 88; text of the rule, pp. 89–96.

59. For example, *First Rule of the Glorious Virgin S. Clare* (1665), pp. 3–8; Locatelli, *Vita di S.ᵃ Chiara* (1854), pp. 82–95, esp. 85, and see 333–52; Francis of Assisi, *Opuscoli del Serafico Patriarca S. Francesco* (1880), pp. 184–85 n. a; Francis of Assisi, *Works of the Seraphic Father St. Francis* (1890), p. 69; Fiege, *Princess of Poverty* (1900), pp. 139–44; *St. Clare and Her Order* (1912), p. 53; Lazzeri, "La 'Forma Vitae' di S. Chiara" (1954), pp. 79–84; see also De Chérancé, *Saint Francis of Assisi* (1900), p. 104.

60. Francis of Assisi, *B. P. Francisci Assisiatis Opuscula*, Epistles IV–V, pp. 16–19.

61. Oliger, "De origine regularum," p. 430; Oliger notes that Wadding seems to have drawn his text from the *Firmamentum Trium Ordinum* (Paris, 1512) which included the quotations; Lempp, "Die Anfänge des Clarissenordens," p. 235 n. 2.

62. John of Capistrano, "Explicatio primae regulae," p. 512; on John and his commentary, see Knox, *Creating Clare of Assisi*, pp. 132–43.

63. A translation essentially following Wadding: Francis of Assisi, *Works of the Seraphic Father St. Francis* (1890). Translations preserving most or all of the first-person statements: *First Rule of the Glorious Virgin S. Clare* (1665); *Regla de la gloriosa santa Clara* (1700), pp. 1–45; *Regla de la gloriosa santa Clara* (1850), pp. 4–18; Locatelli, *Vita di S.ᵃ Chiara* (1854), pp. 333–52.

64. *First Rule of Saint Clare* (1875), pp. 1–3; quotation, p. 3.

65. Fiege, *Princess of Poverty*, p. 143.

66. *First Rule of Saint Clare* (1875), pp. 3–4.

67. Soon thereafter an erroneous belief that the parchment had been buried with Clare and lost for centuries grew up and is still repeated today. Clare's body was exhumed after six centuries in 1850. The parchment had long before been known and seems to have been lost track of only during the last few decades, at most, of the nineteenth century; see Van Leeuwen, "Clare's Rule," pp. 75–76 n. 19; and, esp. Brufani, "Note di storia," pp. 68–71, 71 n. 20, 74–75.

68. Cozza-Luzi, *Chiara di Assisi secondo alcune nuove scoperte*, pp. 9–10.

69. Ibid., pp. 10–11; quotation, p. 11.

70. Dante Alighieri, *Paradiso*, canto 3, vv. 97–99.

71. Cozza-Luzi, *Chiara di Assisi secondo alcune nuove scoperte*, pp. 11–14, 12 n.1; quotation, p. 12.

72. Clovio and Cozza-Luzi, *Il Paradiso Dantesco*.

73. Cozza-Luzi, *Chiara di Assisi secondo alcune nuove scoperte*, pp. 36–41.

74. Ibid., pp. 41, 45; Robinson, "Inventarium omnium documentorum," p. 417.

75. Cozza-Luzi, *Chiara di Assisi secondo alcune nuove scoperte*, pp. 37–41, and see 25–26.

76. Ibid., pp. 41, 45.

77. Carmichael, "Writings of St. Francis," pp. 158–60; quotation, p. 160 n. 3.

78. Robinson, *Writings of Saint Francis*, p. 76.

79. Robinson: *Life of Saint Clare*, pp. xv–xvi, 95, 97; "Writings of St. Clare," p. 441; "Rule of St. Clare," pp. 402–4, 408; "St. Clare," pp. 47–48.

80. Robinson, "Writings of St. Clare," pp. 441–42; and see Robinson, *Life of Saint Clare*, pp. 96–97.

81. Robinson, "Rule of St. Clare," p. 413.

82. Robinson, "St. Clare," p. 47.

83. Robinson's slight emendations to two notes did not affect their interpretation: "Ex

causis manifestis mihi et protectori mon(asterii?)"; "Hanc (?) beata Clara tetigit et obsculata est pro devotione pluribu(s et?) pluribus vicibus"; Robinson, "Inventarium omnium documentorum," p. 417.

84. Oliger, "De origine regularum," pp. 427, 429, 429 n. 5.

85. Ibid., pp. 427–35.

86. For example, Grau,"Die päpstliche Bestätigung der Regel," pp. 317–23, discusses these.

87. Dalarun (in Dalarun and Le Huërou, *Claire d'Assise: Écrits, Vies, documents*, pp. 148–49) notes that Clare drew on earlier rules for some of the text, but that about two-thirds of it are her own, except for some slight interventions by Rainaldo and Innocent IV (e.g., references to Clare as abbess).

88. Léopold Delisle, curator of manuscripts at the Bibliothèque Nationale, suggested in a letter to Cozza-Luzi that the first two notes were papal chancery notations rather than Innocent IV's own writing. Cozza-Luzi cryptically responded that the marginal notes were not of the type Delisle discussed in "Forme des abbréviations et des liaisons," pp. 121–24; Cozza-Luzi's response appeared in a note added to a reprint of *Chiara di Assisi secondo alcune nuove scoperte*; see his "Chiara di Assisi ed Innocenzo IV," part 4, p. 904 n. 2. Delisle's essay is, indeed, not particularly illuminating vis-à-vis the parchment's notes, but his letter to Cozza-Luzi on 5 January 1895, which I have been unable to locate, might reveal more; it is cited in *Seraphicae legislationis textus originales*, p. 15.

89. Brufani, "Note di storia," pp. 85–86.

90. Ibid., pp. 72–73, 73 n. 26; and Bartoli Langeli, "Note di diplomatica," p. 94.

91. Bartoli Langeli, "Note di diplomatica," pp. 95–96.

92. Ibid., pp. 96–98.

93. Ibid., pp. 96–101, 104; and see Brufani, "Note di storia," p. 73 n. 26.

94. Bartoli Langeli, "Note di diplomatica," p. 104.

95. Ibid., pp. 103–5, and plates 7–10.

96. Brufani, "Note di storia, p. 74, and see n. 32.

97. Bartoli Langeli, "Note di diplomatica," pp. 105–6, and plates 11–12.

98. Brufani, "Note di storia," p. 79.

99. Clement IV, *Solet annuere* (31 December 1266), in *BF* III, p. 107.

100. Bartoli Langeli, "Note di diplomatica," pp. 100–101.

101. Petroff, "Medieval Woman's Utopian Vision," pp. 71–72.

102. 1238: Lainati, "La regola francescana e il II ordine," p. 228. After 6 August 1247: Lainati, "Il Testamento," pp. 211–12.

103. Lainati, "La regola francescana e il II ordine," pp. 237–41; quotation, p. 240.

104. *Fv1253* X; *Later Rule* X; cf. *FvHugo* 5 (*CAED*, sec. 5). Francis's 1223 rule and the 1253 rule are compared in Clare of Assisi et al., *Chiara di Assisi e le sue fonti legislative*.

105. *Fv1253* III, 11; *Later Rule* III, 9.

106. *Fv1253* IX, 13–15; *Later Rule* XI, 1, 3.

107. *Fv1253* X, 1, 4–5; *Later Rule* X, 5–6.

108. *Fv1253* IV, 7; *Later Rule* VIII, 4.

109. *Fv1253* III, 1–4; *Later Rule* III, 1–3; cf. *FvInn* 2.

110. *Fv1253* VIII, 16; *Later Rule* VI, 8.

111. Carney, *First Franciscan Woman*, pp. 139–71.

112. Acquadro and Mondonico, "La regola di Chiara," p. 151, give a *terminus post quem* of 1247, not only because they think Innocent IV's rule prompted Clare to begin writing, but also because the *1253 forma vitae* has passages apparently borrowed from Thomas of Celano's *Second*

Life; below I point out that Thomas and the *forma vitae* might both have borrowed from an earlier source.

113. Kuster, "Schriften des Franziskus an Klara," p. 170 n. 24, has assembled a lengthy list of such scholars.

114. Lainati, "La regola francescana e il II Ordine," pp. 230–33.

115. For example, Armstrong, in *CAED*, p. 29; see also Marini, "'Ancilla Christi, plantula sancti Francisci,'" pp. 112, 128.

116. For example, Alberzoni, "Da *pauperes domine* a *sorores pauperes*," p. 54; Mueller, "Agnes of Prague and the Rule," p. 166.

117. Robinson, "Rule of St. Clare," p. 413; Robinson, "St. Clare," p. 47.

118. *Fv1253* I, 3–5.

119. *Fv1253* III, 1–2, and see v. 5.

120. *Fv1253* IV, 2.

121. *Fv1253* XII, 5–7.

122. *Fv1253* II, 2; XI, 7; XII, 1.

123. *Fv1253* XII, 12–13.

124. *Fv1253* VIII, respectively, 1, 7, 19; trans. in *CAED*, pp. 119, 120, 121.

125. Carney, *First Franciscan Woman*, p. 78, supposes Clare's community added points; Mueller, *Companion to Clare*, p. 14, is certain.

126. Lynn, "The Body and the Text," pp. 84–85, 93.

127. *Fv1253* II, 2; XI, 7; XII, 1 (our cardinal); XII, 12 (governor, protector, and corrector); XII, 1 (our Visitator).

128. *Fv1253* XII, 5; trans. in *CAED*, p. 125.

129. *Fv1253* XII, 6; II, 13; IV, 5.

130. *Fv1253* IV, 23; II, 6; *Early Rule* II, 3.

131. *Fv1253*, respectively, X, 3; and II, 20, 23; IX, 1; X, 1; XII, 3.

132. For example, Carney, *First Franciscan Woman*, p. 78.

133. *Fv1253* I, 1–2; trans. in *CAED*, p. 109.

134. Accrocca, "The 'Unlettered One' and His Witness," p. 281; and see Acquadro and Mondonico, "La regola di Chiara," p. 166; Alberzoni, "Da *pauperes domine* a *sorores pauperes*," pp. 55–56.

135. Trans. in *Letters*, pp. 28–29, 54–55, 74–75, 90–91.

136. *Fv1253* I, 5.

137. Accrocca, "The 'Unlettered One' and His Witness," p. 281.

138. *Fv1253* IV, 15–18; trans. in *CAED*, p. 115.

139. Respectively, Matura in Clare of Assisi, *Écrits*, pp. 46–47; and Petroff, "Medieval Woman's Utopian Vision," pp. 72–73; quotation, p. 73.

140. *Fv1253* X, 1, 3.

141. *Fv1253*, respectively, II, 17; III, 9–10; III, 12; VII, 3 (the vicaress could also make decisions about work); VIII, 7, 8, 11; IX, 3.

142. *Acts* I (Pacifica), 1, 17.

143. Carney, *First Franciscan Woman*, pp. 170, 170 n. 78

144. *Fv1253*: incompetence (IV, 7; see *Later Rule* VIII, 4); gifts (VIII, 9–10).

145. *Fv1253* IV, 23; this provision is original to the *1253 forma vitae*, but perhaps inspired by the "elders" (*seniores*) in Benedict of Nursia, *Rule of St. Benedict*, ch. 3, 12

146. *Fv1253* IV, 24; cf. Benedict of Nursia, *Rule of St. Benedict*, ch. 21, 5–6.

147. *Fv1253* IV, 17–18; see Benedict of Nursia, *Rule of St. Benedict*, ch. 3, 2.

148. *Fv1253* II, 1–2. *Later Rule* II, 1, states that provincial ministers admit members.

149. *Fv1253* IV, 19.

150. *Fv1253* IV, 13.

151. *Fv1253*: "mutual love and peace" (IV, 22; and see Benedict of Nursia, *Rule of St. Benedict*, ch. 66, 11; *FvHugo* 14 [*CAED*, sec. 12]); "perfect harmony" (IV, 3; and see Benedict of Nursia, *Rule of St. Benedict*, ch. 64, 1). See also Carney, *First Franciscan Woman*, pp. 159–71, 196–215.

152. *Fv1253* IV, 9–12; and see Benedict of Nursia, *Rule of St. Benedict*, ch. 64, 15.

153. *Fv1253*: "mercy" (IX, 17; and see *Later Rule* VII, 2); "charity" (IX, 5; X, 1; and see *Later Rule* VII, 3; X, 1); "servant" (*ancilla*) (X, 4–5; see also X, 1; and see *Later Rule* X, 1, 5–6); and on the abbess, see Acquadro and Mondonico, "La regola di Chiara," pp. 181–91.

154. *Fv1253* IX, 1–5; quotation, 5; trans. in *CAED*, p. 121; see *Later Rule* VII, 3.

155. *Fv1253* IX, 6–10; trans. in *CAED*, pp. 121–22; this passage is largely original to the *1253 forma vitae*, but see, for example, Benedict of Nursia, *Rule of St. Benedict*, ch. 69, 3; ch. 71, 6–8.

156. *Fv1253* VIII, 16; and see *Later Rule* VI, 8; Mooney, "Francis of Assisi as Mother," pp. 301–32.

157. Bartoli Langeli, *Gli autografi*, pp. 13–56.

158. "Letter," in *Legend of the Three Companions*, in *FAED*, vol. 2, pp. 66–67; specifically, "visitator of the poor ladies."

159. Bartoli Langeli, *Gli autografi*, pp. 94–101.

160. Da Campagnola, "Gli spirituali umbri," pp. 82, 88–89 n. 50; Bartoli Langeli, *Gli autografi*, p. 95.

161. Pellegrini, "I Frati Minori ad Assisi," pp. 127–28; Accrocca, "The 'Unlettered One' and His Witness," p. 280 n. 42, corrected Pellegrini, who thought the friars were mentioned "immediately" after the ladies. The bequest: Bartoli Langeli, *Le carte duecentesche*, pp. 83–84.

162. *VLegCl* XXXII, 1319–26, 1336–39 (*CAED*, XXXII 37–43; 53–56); and see *LegCl* XXIX, 7–8, 12.

163. *Acts*, Prologue 43.

164. Bartoli Langeli, *Gli autografi*, pp. 125–30, and see 106–8; Bartoli Langeli, "I libri dei frati," pp. 303–4.

165. Bartoli Langeli, *Gli autografi*, p. 125; Accrocca, "The 'Unlettered One' and His Witness," p. 280.

166. 2 Cel 185; trans. in *FAED*, vol. 2, p. 365; *Fv1253* IV, 10–12.

167. 2 Cel 204; trans. in *FAED*, vol. 2, p. 378.

168. *Fv1253* VI, 4–5.

169. Ubertino da Casale, *Arbor vitae crucifixae Jesu*, bk. 5, ch. 5; trans. in *FAED*, vol. 3, pp. 198–99.

170. See Chapter 5 above, pp. 93–94, and n. 25. Paoli ("Introduzione," p. 2223 n. 3), noting the stylistic differences between Clare's letters to Agnes of Prague and the *1253 forma vitae*, suggests that a scribe other than the one she employed for her correspondence assisted with the redaction of the rule. The stylistic differences could, I note, be owing simply to the varying genres of letters and legislation.

171. Johnson, "Clare, Leo, and the Authorship of the Fourth Letter," pp. 91–97; and see Chapter 5 above, p. 93.

172. Ottavio Ringhieri, *Tesoro sacro delle Reliquie, che si conservano nel santuario di S. Chiara d'Assisi* (Bologna: Longhi, 1741), pp. 21–22; quoted in Brufani, "Note di storia," p. 87 n. 80.

1. 4LAg 4–6; quotation, 4–5; trans. in *Letters*, pp. 90–91.

2. Alberzoni, *Clare of Assisi*, p. 55.

3. 1LAg 1; trans. in *Letters*, pp. 28–29.

4. 2LAg 1; trans. in *Letters*, pp. 54–55.

5. 3LAg 1; trans. in *Letters*, pp. 74–75.

6. 4LAg 1; trans. in *Letters*, pp. 90–91.

7. *Earlier Rule* IV; VI, 3; *Later Rule* X, 1, 6.

8. The first letter was possibly written before Gregory IX's letter *Sincerum animi carissimae* (31 August 1234), in *BF* I, pp. 135–36, which said Agnes should be abbess of the monastery. The third letter was probably written after Gregory IX's *De Conditoris omnium* (9 May 1238), in *BF* I, pp. 241–42, which was addressed to "daughter Agnes, handmaid of Christ" rather than to "Agnes, abbess," indicating that Agnes was perhaps no longer abbess, but see Marini, *Agnese di Boemia*, pp. 97–98 n. 25.

9. Alberzoni, "De *pauperes domine* a *sorores pauperes*," p. 54.

10. For example, Paoli, "Introduzione," p. 2223 n. 3.

11. Johnson, "Clare, Leo, and the Authorship of the Fourth Letter," pp. 91–97; see also Marini, "'Ancilla Christi, plantula sancti Francisci,'" p. 128.

12. 4LAg 18–25.

13. 4LAg 30–33; trans. in *Letters*, pp. 96–97, and see 101 n. 36; translation adapted from "right arm blissfully" to "right hand happily," consonant with the Latin [*dextera feliciter*], to underline the similarities between Clare's and Gregory's texts.

14. Mueller in *Letters*, p. 102 nn. 34–35.

15. Gregory IX, *Sicut manifestum est* (17 September 1228), in *BF* I, p. 771; trans. in *CAED*, p. 87.

16. Gregory IX, *Pia credulitate tenentes* (15 April 1238), in *BF* I, pp. 236–37.

17. 4LAg 35–39.

18. 4LAg 40; trans. in *Letters*, pp. 98–99.

19. The best critical edition of Clare's *Testament* is based on all five Latin manuscripts and takes into account Wadding's 1628 published version, drawn from what he identified simply as an "ancient record"; *Testament*, pp. 283–92. The best English translation is based on the Latin edition in Clare of Assisi, *Écrits*, pp. 166–84, using four manuscripts; trans. in *CAED*, pp. 60–65.

20. *Testament*, v. 79; trans. in *CAED*, p. 65.

21. Lainati, "Il Testamento," p. 215.

22. Maleczek, "Authenticity of the Privilege," pp. 42–52. Boccali describes the five manuscripts in *Testament*, pp. 276–81. Ciccarelli, "Contributi alla recensione degli scritti di S. Chiara," pp. 349–55, and Godet, Clare of Assisi, *Écrits*, pp. 23–27, each discuss four manuscripts. For the Messina manuscript, see Bartoli Langeli, *Gli autografi*, pp. 104–30, tables 12–28.

23. Godet in Clare of Assisi, *Écrits*, pp. 21–27; Lainati, "Il Testamento," pp. 207–11; Boccali in *Testament*, pp. 278–79.

24. Bartoli Langeli, *Gli autografi*, pp. 115–24; see pp. 106–7 for the opinions of eight other scholars, including three who earlier dated the manuscript to the thirteenth century: Giacomo Macrì (1903), Zeffirino Lazzeri (1954), and Mario Sensi (1994).

25. Marcos of Lisbon published a Portuguese version (*Crónicas*, ch. 35); Wadding published a Latin version (*Annales Minorum*, 3rd ed., vol. 3, an. 1253, no. V, pp. 340–43); some scholars

believe Wadding may have taken his text from Mariano of Florence and his reference to an "ancient record" from Marcos; see Oliger, "De origine regularum," pp. 187–88 n. 4.

26. Godet in Clare of Assisi, *Écrits*, pp. 23–24.

27. Lainati, "Il Testamento," p. 208.

28. For example, Robinson, "Writings of St. Clare," p. 444; Lainati, "Il Testamento," p. 207; Kuster, "Clare's *Testament* and Innocent III's *Privilege of Poverty*," pp. 183–86; Maleczek, "Authenticity of the Privilege," p. 52.

29. Knox, *Creating Clare of Assisi*, pp. 123–56.

30. Alfani, *Vita et leggenda*, p. 241, and see pp. 241–52.

31. Paoli, "Introduzione," p. 2237.

32. Boccali in Alfani, *Vita et leggenda*, pp. 9–15; Maleczek, "Authenticity of the Privilege," pp. 46–51, 65–80.

33. Mariano of Florence, *Libro delle degnità et excellentie del Ordine*, sec. 18, 36, 142, 144, 146, 161, 184; on the date of completion, see sec. 730.

34. Maleczek, "Authenticity of the Privilege."

35. C. Andenna, "Chiara d'Assisi: La questione dell'autenticità del 'Privilegium paupertatis' e del Testamento," p. 597.

36. Maleczek, "Authenticity of the Privilege," pp. 42–52.

37. Zoppetti and Bartoli, *S. Chiara d'Assisi: Scritti e documenti*, p. 116.

38. Maleczek, "Authenticity of the Privilege," p. 63.

39. Paoli, "Introduzione," p. 2223 n. 3.

40. Armstrong in *CAED*, pp. 29, 59.

41. Marini, " 'Ancilla Christi, plantula sancti Francisci,' " p. 154.

42. *Testament*, vv. 42–43; trans. in *CAED*, p. 62.

43. For example, Lainati, "Il Testamento," pp. 206, 213.

44. Paoli, "Introduzione," pp. 2238–42.

45. *Testament*, vv. 12–14; trans. in *CAED*, pp. 60–61.

46. *Legend of the Three Companions* 24, in *FAED*, vol. 2, p. 83; see also 1 Cel 18. A letter introducing the *Legend* suggests that it was compiled by Leo, Angelo, and Rufino, but on difficulties surrounding the letter's claim, see Pellegrini, "Introduzione," pp. 1355–71.

47. *Legend of the Three Companions* 24, in *FAED*, vol. 2, p. 83.

48. Lainati, "Il Testamento," pp. 213–14.

49. Matura in Clare of Assisi, *Écrits*, pp. 62–63.

50. *Testament*, v. 52; trans. in *CAED*, p. 63.

51. Scholars disagree about the date of the move; negotiations had begun by 1255; construction on the new church began in 1257 and seems to have been substantially finished in 1260; see Bigaroni, "Origine e sviluppo storico della chiesa," p. 19; and Meier, "Protomonastero e chiesa di pellegrinaggio," pp. 100–101, both in Bigaroni, Meier, and Lunghi, *La Basilica di S. Chiara*. Bartoli Langeli, *Gli autografi*, p. 115 n. 23, places the move between 1257 and 1265. By October 1257, when Alexander IV addressed a letter to the "Abbess and Sisters of the monastery of Saint Clare in Assisi," it is clear that some of the sisters had moved; see Robinson, "Inventarium omnium documentorum," p. 419.

52. Maleczek, "Authenticity of the Privilege," p. 55.

53. Lainati, "Il Testamento," p. 200.

54. Maleczek, "Authenticity of the Privilege," pp. 61–63, 69, 78–80.

55. *Earlier Rule* I, 2; *Later Rule* II, 5; *Fvr253* II, 7. Hagiographers: e.g.: Cel I, 24; Cel II, 80, 190; Bonaventure, *Major Legend* III, 3; *LegCl* IX, 13.

56. Bartoli, "La povertà e il movimento francescano femminile," p. 231.

57. Maleczek, "Authenticity of the Privilege," p. 78.

58. For example, Robinson, "Writings of St. Clare," p. 443; Lainati, "Il Testamento," p. 207.

59. For example, Bartoli Langeli, *Gli autografi*, pp. 95, 106 n. 7, and see p. 128; Knox, *Creating Clare of Assisi*, pp. 13–14.

60. *Acts* III (Filippa), 81, 106; trans. in *CAED*, respectively, pp. 160, 162.

61. *LegCl* XXIX, 9–12; trans. in *CAED*, p. 316.

62. *LegCl* XXIX, 7.

63. Paoli, "Introduzione," pp. 2250–51.

64. Ibid., pp. 2248–51.

65. *Testament*, vv. 19–20; trans. in *CAED*, p. 61.

66. 2 Cel 13. There is no scholarly consensus regarding the chronological order or precise relationships between Thomas of Celano's *Second Life* and related texts containing material probably first gathered in response to Crescentius's 1244 request; see Accrocca, "Nodi problematici delle Fonti Francescane," pp. 580–92.

67. Paoli, "Introduzione," pp. 2251–54, summarizes arguments.

68. *Blessing*, v. 6; *Testament*, v. 37; see also *Testament*, vv. 48–49, where the putative Clare herself calls together with her sisters Francis's "little plant."

69. *Fvr253* I, 3.

70. 1 Cel 116; see also *Assisi Compilation* 13, 85; and for word plays on Clare as the "plant" or "little plant" of her mother "Ortulana," which means "gardener," see, respectively, *Bull of Canonization*, vv. 28–29, in *FF*, p. 2333; trans. in *CAED*, vv. 43–44, p. 266; and *LegCl* I, 3; XXII, 13.

71. *LegCl* I, 3; XXII, 13; trans. in *CAED*, p. 67.

72. *Blessing*, v. 6.

Bibliography

PRIMARY SOURCES

Alfani, Battista. *Vita et leggenda della seraphica vergine Sancta Chiara.* Ed. Giovanni Boccali. Assisi: Porziuncola, 2004.

Analecta Franciscana. 12 vols. Ad Claras Aquas (Quaracchi): Ex Typographia Collegii S. Bonaventurae, 1885–1983.

Angelo Clareno. "Angelus Clarenus Ad Alvarum Pelagium. Apologia pro vita sua." Ed. Victorin Doucet. *Archivum Franciscanum Historicum* 39 (1946): 63–200.

Annibali da Latera, Flaminio Maria, ed. *Ad Bullarium Franciscanum . . . Supplementum.* Rome, 1780.

Armstrong, Regis J., ed. and trans. *The Lady: Clare of Assisi: Early Documents.* Rev. ed. New York: New City Press, 2006. (*CAED*)

Armstrong, Regis J., J. A. Wayne Hellmann, and William J. Short, eds., *Francis of Assisi: Early Documents.* 3 vols. New York: New City Press, 1998–2001. (*FAED*)

Bartoli Langeli, Attilio, ed. *Le carte duecentesche del sacro convento di Assisi: (Istrumenti, 1168–1300).* Padua: Centro Studi Antoniani, 1997.

Benedict of Nursia. *RB 1980: The Rule of St. Benedict in Latin and English.* Ed. Timothy Fry. Collegeville, Minn.: Liturgical Press, 1981.

Boccali, Giovanni, ed. *Santa Chiara d'Assisi sotto processo: Lettura storico-spirituale degli Atti di canonizzazione.* Assisi: Edizioni Porziuncola, 2003. (*Acts*)

Boehmer, Heinrich, ed. *Analekten zur Geschichte des Franciscus von Assisi.* Tübingen: J. C. B. Mohr (Paul Siebeck), 1904.

Bollandus, Johannes, and Godefridus Henschenius, eds. *Acta sanctorum . . . editio novissima.* Paris: Palmé, 1863–.

Bonaventure of Bagnoregio. *Doctoris seraphici S. Bonaventurae . . . Opera omnia.* Ad Claras Aquas (Quaracchi): Ex Typographia Collegii S. Bonaventurae, 1882–1902.

Chronica XXIV Generalium. In *Analecta Franciscana* 3 (1897).

Clare of Assisi. *Clare's Letters to Agnes: Texts and Sources.* Ed. and trans. Joan Mueller. St. Bonaventure, N.Y.: Franciscan Institute, 2001. (*Letters*)

———. *Écrits.* Ed. Marie-France Becker, Jean-François Godet, and Thaddée Matura. Paris: Cerf, 1985; rev. ed., 2003.

———. *Lettere ad Agnese; La visione dello specchio.* Ed. Giovanni Pozzi and Beatrice Rima. Milan: Adelphi, 1999.

Clare of Assisi? "Testamento e benedizione di S. Chiara: Nuovo codice latino." Ed. Giovanni Boccali. *Archivum Franciscanum Historicum* 82 (1989): 273–305. (*Testament*)

Clare of Assisi et al. *Chiara di Assisi e le sue fonti legislative: Sinossi cromatica*. Ed. Federazione S. Chiara di Assisi delle Clarisse di Umbria-Sardegna. Padua: Messaggero, 2003. (*FvI253*)

Dalarun, Jacques, ed. *François d'Assise: Écrits, Vies, témoignages*. 2 vols. Paris: Cerf, 2010.

Dalarun, Jacques, and Armelle Le Huërou, eds. *Claire d'Assise: Écrits, Vies, documents*. Paris: Cerf, 2013.

Dante Alighieri. *Paradiso*. Trans. Dorothy L. Sayers and Barbara Reynolds. Baltimore: Penguin, 1962.

Eubel, Conrad, ed. *Bullarii Franciscani Epitome sive Summa Bullarum in eiusdem Bullarii quattuor prioribus tomis relatarum, addito supplemento* . . . . Apud Claras Aquas: Typis Collegii S. Bonaventurae, 1908.

Fita, Fidel, ed. "Fundación y primer período del monasterio de Santa Clara en Barcelona: Bulas inéditas de Gregorio IX, Inocencio IV y Alejandro IV." *Boletín de la Real Academia de la Historia* 27 (1895): 273–314.

The First Rule of the Glorious Virgin S. Clare. Audomari (St. Omer): Typis Thomæ Geubels, 1665.

The First Rule of Saint Clare, and the Constitutions of St. Coletta. London: Thomas Richardson and Sons, 1875.

Fonti francescane: scritti e biografie di san Francesco d'Assisi, cronache e altre testimonianze del primo secolo francescano, scritti e biografie di santa Chiara d'Assisi. 2 vols. Assisi: Movimento Francescano, 1977.

Francis of Assisi. *B. P. Francisci Assisiatis Opuscula*. Ed. Luke Wadding. 3 vols. Antwerp, 1623.

————. *Die Opuscula des hl. Franziskus von Assisi: Neue textkritische Edition*. Ed. Kajetan Esser. Grottaferrata [Rome]: Editiones Collegii S. Bonaventurae ad Claras Aquas, 1976.

————. *Opuscoli del Serafico Patriarca S. Francesco d'Assisi volgarizzati col testo a fronte da un religioso cappuccino di Toscana*. Florence, 1880.

————. *Works of the Seraphic Father St. Francis of Assisi*. 2nd ed. London: R. Washbourne, 1890.

Francis of Assisi? "Canto di esortazione di San Francesco per le 'Poverelle' di San Damiano." Ed. Giovanni Boccali. *Collectanea Franciscana* 48 (1978): 5–29.

Francis of Assisi and Clare of Assisi. *Francis and Clare: The Complete Works*. Trans. Regis J. Armstrong and Ignatius C. Brady. New York: Paulist, 1982.

Friedrich, Gustav, ed. *Codex diplomaticus et epistolaris regni Bohemiae*. With Zdeněk Kristen. Vol. 3. Prague: Sumptibus Comitiorum Regni Bohemiae, 1907.

Grau, Engelbert, ed. *Leben und Schriften der heiligen Klara von Assisi*. Werl, Westf.: Dietrich Coelde-Verlag, 1952.

Grau, Engelbert, and Marianne Schlosser, eds. *Leben und Schriften der heiligen Klara von Assisi*. 8th ed. Kevelaer: Coelde; Butzon & Bercker, 2001.

Habig, Marion A., ed. *St. Francis of Assisi: Writings and Early Biographies: English Omnibus of the Sources*. 4th rev. ed. Chicago: Franciscan Herald Press, 1983.

Hugo [Hugolino] dei Conti di Segni. "La 'Cum omnis vera religio' del cardinale Ugolino. *Forma vite* primitiva per San Damiano ed altri monasteri." Ed. Giovanni Boccali. *Frate Francesco* 74 (2008): 435–77. (*FvHugo*)

Jacques de Vitry. *The Historia Occidentalis of Jacques de Vitry: A Critical Edition*. Ed. John Frederick Hinnebusch. Fribourg: University Press, 1972.

————. "Jacobi vitriacensis (1180–1240): Sermones ad Fratres Minores." Ed. H. a L. [Hilarin Felder]. *Analecta Ordinis Minorum Capuccinorum* 19 (1903): 22–24, 114–22, 149–58.

————. *Lettres de Jacques de Vitry, 1160/1170–1240, évêque de Saint-Jean d'Acre*. Ed. R. B. C. Huygens. Leiden: Brill, 1960.

————. *Vita Mariae Oigniacensis*. In *Acta sanctorum . . . editio novissima*. June. Vol. 5, 542–72. Paris: Palmé, 1867.

John of Capistrano. "Explicatio primae regulae S. Clarae auctore S. Ioanne Capistranensi (1445)." Ed. Donatus van Adrichen. *Archivum Franciscanum Historicum* 22 (1929): 336–57, 512–28.

Jordan of Giano. "Chronicle of Brother Jordan of Giano." In *XIIIth Century Chronicles*, trans. Placid Hermann, pp. 1–77. Chicago: Franciscan Herald Press, 1961.

The Legend and Writings of Saint Clare of Assisi. Ed. and trans. Franciscan Institute. St. Bonaventure, N.Y.: Franciscan Institute, 1953.

Leonardi, Claudio, ed. *La letteratura francescana*. Vol. 1. [Rome]: Fondazione Lorenzo Valla, 2004.

Levi, Guido, ed. *Registri dei cardinali Ugolino d'Ostia e Ottaviano degli Ubaldini*. Rome: Forzani, 1890.

Marcos of Lisbon. *Crónicas da Ordem dos Frades Menores*. Porto: Faculdade de Letras da Universidade do Porto, 2001.

Mariano of Florence. *Compendium chronicarum Ordinis FF. Minorum*. Ad Claras Aquas: Typ. Collegii S. Bonaventurae, 1911.

———. *Libro delle degnità et excellentie del Ordine, della seraphica madre delle povere donne Sancta Chiara da Asisi*. Ed. Giovanni Boccali. Florence: Edizioni Studi Francescani, 1986.

Mellissano de Macro, Antonio. *Annalium Ordinis Minorum supplementa: ab anno 1213 ad annum 1500*. Ed. Antonio-Maria di Torre. Turin, 1710.

Menestò, Enrico, and Stefano Brufani, eds. *Fontes Franciscani*. Assisi: Edizioni Porziuncola, 1995. Latin and Italian texts of Francis's and Clare's writings and numerous thirteenth- and early fourteenth-century texts about them. (*FF*)

Muratori, Ludovico Antonio, ed. "Vita Gregorii IX papae." In *Rerum Italicarum Scriptores*, vol. 3, pt. 1, pp. 575–87. Milan, 1723.

Nemec, Jaroslav, ed. *Agnese di Boemia: la vita, il culto, la "Legenda."* Padua: EMP, 1987.

Niccolò da Calvi. "Niccolò da Calvi e la sua vita d'Innocenzo IV, con una breve introduzione sulla istoriografia pontificia nei secoli XIII e XIV." Ed. Francesco Pagnotti. *Archivio della Società Romana di Storia Patria* 21 (1898): 5–120; Vita: pp. 76–120.

Omaechevarría, Ignacio, ed. and trans. *Escritos de Santa Clara y documentos complementarios*. 2nd bilingual Latin-Spanish ed. Madrid: Biblioteca de Autores Cristianos, 1982. (*Escritos*)

Philip of Perugia. *Catalogus Cardinalium, qui fuerunt Ordinis Protectores*. In *Analecta Franciscana* 3 (1897): 708–12.

Pozzi, Giovanni, and Claudio Leonardi, eds. *Scrittrici mistiche italiane*. Genoa: Marietti, 1988.

Regla de la gloriosa santa Clara, con las Constituciones de las Monjas Capuchinas. Santiago de Chile, 1850.

Regla de la gloriosa santa Clara, constituciones de las monjas capuchinas, y sus ceremonias. . . . Cordoba, Spain: En la Oficina de D. Juan Rodríguez de la Torre, 1700.

Roger of Wendover. *Flowers of History*. Trans. J. A. Giles. 2 vols. 1849. Reprint New York: AMS, 1968.

Sabatier, Paul, ed. *Speculum perfectionis seu, S. Francisci Assisiensis legenda antiquissima*. Paris: Fischbacher, 1898.

Salimbene de Adam. *The Chronicle of Salimbene de Adam*. Trans. Joseph L. Baird, Giuseppe Baglivi, and John Robert Kane. Binghamton, N.Y.: MRTS, 1986.

Sbaraglia, Giovanni Giacinto, ed. *Bullarium Franciscanum Romanorum Pontificum: Constitutiones, epistolas, ac diplomata* . . . . 4 vols. Rome: Typis Sacrae Congregationis de Propaganda Fide, 1759–1768. (*BF*)

Seraphicae legislationis textus originales. Ad Claras Aquas (Quaracchi): Ex Typographia Collegii S. Bonaventurae, 1897.

Tanner, Norman P., ed. *Decrees of the Ecumenical Councils.* Vol. 1. London: Sheed & Ward; Washington, D.C.: Georgetown University Press, 1990.

Thomas of Cantimpré. *Vita Mariae Oigniacensis, Supplementum.* In *Acta sanctorum . . . editio novissima*, June. Vol. 5, 572–81. Paris: Palmé, 1867.

Thomas of Celano. *Treatise on the Miracles of Saint Francis.* In *Francis of Assisi: Early Documents*, ed. Armstrong, Hellmann, and Short, vol. 2, 399–468.

Thomas of Celano? *Legenda latina Sanctae Clarae Virginis Assisiensis.* Ed. Giovanni Boccali; Ital. trans. Marino Bigaroni. Santa Maria degli Angeli: Edizioni Porziuncola, 2001. (*LegCl*)

Thomas of Eccleston. "The Coming of the Friars Minor to England." In *XIIIth Century Chronicles*, trans. Placid Hermann, pp. 79–191. Chicago: Franciscan Herald Press, 1961.

Ubertino da Casale. *Arbor vitae crucifixae Jesu.* Turin: Bottega d'Erasmo, 1961. Partial trans. of Book 5 in *Tree of the Crucified Life of Jesus.* In *Francis of Assisi: Early Documents*, ed. Armstrong, Hellmann, and Short, vol. 3, 146–203.

Vyskočil, Jan Kapistrán, ed. *The Legend of Blessed Agnes of Bohemia and the Four Letters of St. Clare.* Trans. Vita Buresh. N.p., 1963. Originally published as *Legenda blahoslavené Anežky a čtyři listy Sv. Kláry.* [Prague: Universum, 1932.]

Wadding, Luke, ed. *Annales Minorum, in quibus res omnes trium Ordinum a S. Francisco institutorum ex fide ponderosius asseruntur, calumniae refelluntur, praeclara quaeque monumenta ab oblivione vendicantur.* 1st ed. Vols. 1–7. Lyon, 1625–1648. Vol. 8. Rome, 1654.

———. *Annales Minorum: seu Trium ordinum a S. Francisco institutorum Annales.* 3rd ed. Ed. Josephi Mariae Fonseca ab Ebora. 32 vols. Florence: Ad Claras Aquas (Quaracchi): Tipografia Barbera, Alfani e Venturi proprietari, 1931–.

Zoppetti, Ginepro G., and Marco Bartoli, eds. and trans. *S. Chiara d'Assisi: Scritti e documenti.* Assisi: Editrici Francescane, 1994.

SECONDARY SOURCES

Abate, Giuseppe. *La casa paterna di s. Chiara e falsificazioni storiche dei secoli XVI e XVII intorno alla medesima santa e a s. Francesco d'Assisi.* Assisi: Casa Editrice Francescana, 1946. Extract, *Bollettino della Deputazione di storia patria per l'Umbria* 41 (1944): 34–160.

———. "Nuovi studi sull'ubicazione della casa paterna di s. Chiara d'Assisi." Extract, *Bollettino della Deputazione di storia patria per l'Umbria* 50 (1953): 111–44.

Accrocca, Felice. "Frate Elia ministro generale." In *Elia di Cortona tra realtà e mito*, 61–90.

———. "Nodi problematici delle Fonti Francescane: A proposito di due recenti edizioni." *Collectanea Franciscana* 66 (1996): 563–98.

———. "The 'Unlettered One' and His Witness: Footnotes to a Recent Volume on the Autographs of Brother Francis and Brother Leo." Trans. Edward Hagman. *Greyfriars Review* 16 (2002): 265–82.

Acquadro, Chiara Agnese. *Sulle orme di Gesù povero: Chiara d'Assisi e il suo itinerario di vita.* S. Maria degli Angeli, Assisi: Edizioni Porziuncola, 2014.

Acquadro, Chiara Agnese, and Chiara Cristiana Mondonico. "La Regola di Chiara di Assisi: Il Vangelo come forma di vita." *Convivium Assisiense* 6 (2004): 147–232.

Aizpurúa, Fidel. *Il cammino di Chiara d'Assisi: Corso base di francescanesimo: vita, scritti e spiritualità.* Trans. Ginepro Zoppetti. 2nd ed. Padua: Messaggero di Sant'Antonio, 2005.

Alberzoni, Maria Pia. "Chiara d'Assisi e Agnese di Boemia: Edizioni e studi recenti." *Rivista di Storia della Chiesa in Italia* 57 (2003): 439–49.

———. "Chiara d'Assisi e il Vangelo come forma di vita." *Franciscana* 10 (2008): 223–54.

———. "Clare and San Damiano Between the Order of the Friars Minor and the Papal Curia." Trans. Edward Hagman. *Greyfriars Review* 20 (2011): 1–45.

———. *Clare of Assisi and the Poor Sisters in the Thirteenth Century.* Ed. Jean François Godet-Calogeras. St. Bonaventure, N.Y.: Franciscan Institute, 2004.

———. "Clare of Assisi and Women's Franciscanism." Trans. Edward Hagman. *Greyfriars Review* 17 (2003): 5–29.

———. "Curia Romana e regolamentazione delle Damianite e delle Domenicane." In *Regulae-Consuetudines-Statuta: studi sulle fonti normative degli ordini religiosi nei secoli centrali del Medioevo. Atti del I e del II Seminario internazionale di studio del Centro italo-tedesco di storia comparata degli ordini religiosi,* ed. Cristina Andenna and Gert Melville, 501–37. Münster: LIT, 2005.

———. *Francescanesimo a Milano nel Duecento.* Milan: Edizioni Biblioteca Francescana, 1991.

———. "Frate Elia tra Chiara d'Assisi, Gregorio IX e Federico II." In *Elia di Cortona tra realtà e mito,* 91–121.

———. "'Intra in gaudium Domini, Domini tui videlicet, Praedicatorum Ordinis': Diana d'Andalò e Chiara d'Assisi: Da *sorores* a *moniales.*" *Franciscanum* 12 (2010): 1–42.

———. *La nascita di un'istituzione: L'Ordine di S. Damiano nel XIII secolo.* N.p.: CUSL, [1996].

———. "Da *pauperes domine* a *sorores pauperes*: La negazione di un modello di santità itinerante femminile." In *Pellegrinaggi e culto dei santi: Santità minoritica del primo e secondo ordine,* ed. Benedetto Vetere, 37–59. [Galatina?]: M. Congedo, 2001.

———. "'Un solo e medesimo spirito ha fatto uscire i frati e quelle donne poverelle da questo mondo [malvagio]' (2*Cel* 204.)" In *Maschile e femminile, vita consecrata francescanesimo: Scritti per l'VIII centenario dell'Ordine di Santa Chiara (1212–2012),* ed. Paolo Martinelli, 385–402. Bologna: EDB, 2012.

Andenna, Cristina. "Chiara d'Assisi: La questione dell'autenticità del 'Privilegium paupertatis' e del Testamento. Tavola rotonda: Rome, 19 Febbraio 1997." *Rivista di Storia della Chiesa in Italia* 51 (1997): 595–99.

———. "Chiara di Assisi: Alcune reflessioni su un problema ancora aperto." *Rivista di Storia e Letteratura Religiosa* 34 (1998): 547–79.

Andenna, Giancarlo. "Les Clarisse nel novarese (1252–1300)." *Archivum Franciscanum Historicum* 67 (1974): 185–267.

Andenna, Giancarlo, and Benedetto Vetere, eds. *Chiara e il Secondo Ordine: Il fenomeno francescano femminile nel Salento. Atti del Convegno di studi in occasione dell'VIII centenario della nascita di Santa Chiara, Nardo, 12–13 novembre 1993.* Galatina (Lecce): Congedo, 1997.

———, eds. *Chiara e la diffusione delle Clarisse nel secolo XIII. Atti del Convegno di studi in occasione dell'VIII centenario della nascita di Santa Chiara, Manduria, 14–15 dicembre 1994.* Galatina (Lecce): Congedo, 1998.

Armstrong, Regis J. "Clare of Assisi: The Mirror Mystic." *The Cord* (1985): 195–202.

———. "Starting Points: Images of Women in the Letters of Clare." *Collectanea Franciscana* 62 (1992): 63–100.

Balestracci, Duccio. *Cilastro che sapeva leggere: Alfabetazzazione e istruzione nelle campagne toscane alla fine del Medioevo (XIV–XVI secoli).* Ospedaletto (Pisa): Pacini, 2004.

Barone, Giulia. *Da frate Elia agli Spirituali.* Milan: Edizioni Biblioteca Francescana, 1999.

Bartoli, Marco. *Clare of Assisi.* Trans. Sister Frances Teresa. Quincy, Ill.: Franciscan Press, 1993.

———. "Gregorio IX, Chiara d'Assisi e le prime dispute all'interno del movimento francescano." *Rendiconti* 25 (1980): 97–108.

———. "Gregorio IX e il movimento penitenziale." In *La "supra montem" di Niccolò IV (1289): Genesi e diffusione di una regola*, ed. Raffaele Pazzelli and Lino Temperini, 47–60. Rome: Ed. Analecta TOR, 1988.

———. "La povertà e il movimento francescano femminile." In *Dalla 'sequela Christi' di Francesco d'Assisi all'apologia della povertà*, 223–48. Spoleto: Centro italiano di studi sull'alto Medievo, 1992.

Bartoli Langeli, Attilio. *Gli autografi di frate Francesco e di frate Leone.* Turnhout: Brepols, 2000.

———. "I libri dei frati: La cultura scritta dell'Ordine dei Minori." In *Francesco d'Assisi e il primo secolo di storia francescana*, ed. Maria Pia Alberzoni et al., 283–305. Turin: Einaudi, 1997.

———. "Note di diplomatica." Part 2, 93–106. In Attilio Bartoli Langeli and Stefano Brufani, "La lettera Solet annuere di Innocenzo IV per Chiara d'Assisi (9 agosto 1253)." *Franciscana* 8 (2006): 63–106, and tables 1–12.

———. "La realtà sociale assisiana e il patto del 1210." In *Assisi al tempo di San Francesco. Atti del V convegno internazionale, Assisi, 13–16 ottobre 1977*, 273–336. Assisi: La Società, 1978.

Benvenuti Papi, Anna. "La fortuna del movimento damianita in Italia (sec. XIII): Propositi per un censimento da fare." In *Chiara di Assisi* (1993), 57–106.

Bigaroni, Marino. "I monasteri benedettini femminili di S. Paolo delle abbadesse, di S. Apollinare in Assisi e S. Maria di Paradiso prima del Concilio di Trento." In *Aspetti di vita benedettina nella storia di Assisi*, 171–231. Assisi: Accademia Properziana del Subasio, 1981.

———. "San Damiano-Assisi: The First Church of Saint Francis." Trans. Agnes Van Baer. *Franciscan Studies* 47 (1987): 45–97.

Bigaroni, Marino, Hans-Rudolf Meier, and Elvio Lunghi. *La Basilica di S. Chiara in Assisi.* Perugia: Quattroemme, 1994.

Bird, Jessalyn. "The Religious's Role in a Post-Fourth-Lateran World: Jacques de Vitry's *Sermones ad status* and *Historia occidentalis*." In *Medieval Monastic Preaching*, ed. Carolyn Muessig, 209–29. Leiden: Brill, 1998.

Black, Robert. *Education and Society in Florentine Tuscany: Teachers, Pupils and Schools, c. 1250–1500.* Leiden: Brill, 2007.

Boccali, Giovanni. "Tradizione manoscritta delle legende di Santa Chiara d'Assisi." *Convivium Assisiense* 6 (2004): 419–500.

Boespflug, Thérèse. "Alexander IV." In *The Papacy: An Encyclopedia*, 3 vols., ed. Philippe Levillain and John W. O'Malley, vol. 1, 22–24. New York: Routledge, 2002.

Bolton, Brenda M. "Daughters of Rome: All One in Christ Jesus!" In *Women in the Church*, ed. W. J. Sheils and Diana Wood, 101–15. Cambridge, Mass.: Blackwell, 1990.

Brooke, R. B. and C. N. L. Brooke. "St Clare." In *Medieval Women*, ed. Derek Baker, 275–87. Oxford: Blackwell, 1978.

Brooke, Rosalind B. *Early Franciscan Government: Elias to Bonaventure.* Cambridge: University Press, 1959.

———. *The Image of St Francis: Responses to Sainthood in the Thirteenth Century.* Cambridge: Cambridge University Press, 2006.

Brufani, Stefano. "Le 'legendae' agiografiche di Chiara del secolo XIII." In *Chiara di Assisi* (1993), 325–55.

———. "Note di storia, agiografia e iconografia clariana." Pt. 1, 65–92. In Attilio Bartoli Langeli and Stefano Brufani, "La lettera Solet annuere di Innocenzo IV per Chiara d'Assisi (9 agosto 1253)." *Franciscana* 8 (2006): 63–106 and tables 1–12.

Brunel-Lobrichon, Geneviève et al., eds. *Sainte Claire d'Assise et sa postérité: Actes du Colloque* *international organisé à l'occasion du VIIIe centenaire de la naissance de sainte Claire: UNE-SCO, 29 septembre–1 octobre 1994.* Nantes: Association Claire Aujourd'hui, 1995.

Burr, David. *The Spiritual Franciscans: From Protest to Persecution in the Century After Saint Francis.* University Park: Pennsylvania State University Press, 2001.

Bynum, Caroline Walker. *Holy Feast and Holy Fast: The Religious Significance of Food to Medieval Women.* Berkeley: University of California Press, 1987.

———. "In Praise of Fragments: History in the Comic Mode." In *Fragmentation and Redemption: Essays on Gender and the Human Body in Medieval Religion,* 11–26. New York: Zone, 1991.

Canonici, Luciano. "Guido II d'Assisi: Il vescovo di San Francesco." *Studi Francescani* 77 (1980): 187–206.

Capitani, Ovidio. "Chiara per Francesco." In *La presenza francescana tra medioevo e modernità,* ed. Mario Chessa and Marco Poli, 103–12. Florence: Vallecchi, 1996.

Carmichael, Montgomery. "The Writings of St. Francis." *The Month* (January 1904): 156–64.

Carney, Margaret. *The First Franciscan Woman: Clare of Assisi and Her Form of Life.* Quincy, Ill.: Franciscan Press, 1993.

Casagrande, Giovanna. "Chiara e le compagne attraverso il testo del Processo." In *Dialoghi con Chiara,* ed. Giacometti, 1–20.

———. "Le compagne di Chiara." In *Chiara di Assisi* (1993), 383–425.

———. "An Order for Lay People: Penance and Penitents in the Thirteenth Century." Trans. Edward Hagman. *Greyfriars Review* 17 (2003): 39–54.

Casagrande, Giovanna, and Sonia Merli. "Sulle tracce degli insediamenti clariani scomparsi (secc. XIII–XIV)." In *Presenza Clariana nella storia di Assisi,* ed. Francesco Santucci, 17–79. Assisi: Accademia Properziana del Subasio, 1994.

Casolini, Fausta. "Il nome di battesimo di s. Agnese." *Chiara d'Assisi: Rassegna del Protomonastero* 2 (1954): 135–36.

———. "La regola di Innocenzo IV." *Convivium Assisiense* 6 (2004): 71–82.

Chenu, M.-D. *Nature, Man, and Society in the Twelfth Century: Essays on New Theological Perspectives in the Latin West.* Ed. and trans. Jerome Taylor and Lester K. Little. Chicago: University of Chicago Press, 1968.

Chiara di Assisi. Atti del XX convegno internazionale, Assisi, 15–17 ottobre 1992. Spoleto: Centro italiano di studi sull'alto Medioevo, 1993.

Ciccarelli, Diego. "Contributi alla recensione degli scritti di S. Chiara." *Miscellanea Francescana* 79 (1979): 347–74.

Clovio, Giuli, and Giuseppe Cozza-Luzi. *Il Paradiso dantesco nei quadri miniati e nei bozzetti, di Giulio Clovio.* Rome, 1893.

Coen, Maurice. "Jacques de Vitry." In *Biographie nationale, Supplement.* Académie Royale des sciences, des lettres et des beaux-arts de Belgique, vol. 31, suppl. 3, cols. 465–74. Brussels: Bruylant, 1962.

Convivium Assisiense 6 (2004). Alternate title: *Clara Claris Praeclara: L'esperienza cristiana e la memoria di Chiara d'Assisi in occasione del 750° anniversario della morte. Atti del Convegno Internazionale, Assisi, 20–22 novembre 2003.* S. Maria degli Angeli: Edizioni Porziuncola, 2004.

Conwell, Joseph F. *Impelling Spirit: Revisiting a Founding Experience: 1539, Ignatius of Loyola and His Companions.* Chicago: Loyola Press, 1997.

Costa, Francesco. "Le regole Clariane: Genesi e confronto." *Miscellanea Francescana* 98 (1998): 812–35.

Covi, Davide, and Dino Dozzi, eds. *Chiara: Francescanesimo al femminile. Atti del XX convegno internazionale, Assisi, 15–17 ottobre 1992.* Rome: Dehoniane-Edizioni Collegio San Lorenzo, 1992.

Cozza-Luzi, Giuseppe. *Chiara di Assisi secondo alcune nuove scoperte e documenti.* Rome, 1895. Reprint "Chiara di Assisi ed Innocenzo IV," parts 1–4, *L'Arcadia, Periodico di Scienze, Lettere ed Arti* 7–8.9 (Settembre 1895–1896): 694–714; 7–8.10 (Ottobre 1895–1896): 777–92; 7–8.11 (Novembre 1895–1896): 867–79; 7–8.12 (Dicembre 1895–1896): 903–7, with updated note, p. 904 n. 2. Reprint *Un autografo di Innocenzo IV e memorie di Santa Chiara di Assisi,* Rome, 1896. Reprint *Chiara di Assisi ed Innocenzo IV,* Rome, 1897.

Cremascoli, Giuseppe. "Introduzione" a *Legenda Versificata Sanctae.* In *Fontes Franciscani,* ed. Menestò and Brufani, 2341–45.

Cusato, Michael F. "From the *Perfectio Sancti Evangelii* to the *Sanctissima Vita et Paupertas*: An Hypothesis on the Origin of the *Privilegium Paupertatis* to Clare and Her Sisters at San Damiano." *Franciscan Studies* 64 (2006): 123–44.

———. "*Non propheta, sed prophanus apostata*: The Eschatology of Elias of Cortona and His Deposition as Minister General in 1239." In *That Others May Know and Love: Essays in Honor of Zachary Hayes, OFM,* ed. Michael F. Cusato and F. Edward Coughlin, 255–83. St. Bonaventure, N.Y.: Franciscan Institute, 1997.

———. "To Do Penance/*Facere poenitentiam.*" *The Cord* 57 (2007): 3–24.

Da Campagnola, Stanislao. "Introduzione" a *Francisci Assisiensis: Opuscula.* In *Fontes Franciscani,* ed. Menestò and Brufani, 3–22.

———. "Gli spirituali umbri." In *Chi erano gli spirituali. Atti del III Convegno internazionale: Assisi, 16–18 ottobre 1975,* 71–105. Assisi: La Società, 1976.

D'Acunto, Nicolangelo. *Assisi nel medioevo: Studi di storia ecclesiastica e civile.* Assisi: Accademia Properziana del Subasio, 2002.

Dalarun, Jacques. "Francesco, Chiara e le altre." In *Chiara d'Assisi e la memoria di Francesco. Atti del Convegno per l'VIII centenario della nascita di S. Chiara, Fara Sabina, 19–20 maggio 1994,* ed. Alfonso Marini and M. Beatrice Mistretta, 35–39. Città di Castello: Petruzzi, 1995.

———. *Francis of Assisi and the Feminine.* Trans. Paula Pierce and Mary Sutphin. St. Bonaventure, N.Y.: Franciscan Institute, 2006.

De Chérancé, Léopold. *Saint Francis of Assisi.* Trans. R. F. O'Connor. 3rd ed. London: Burns and Oates, 1900.

Debby, Nirit Ben-Aryeh. *The Cult of St Clare in Early Modern Italy.* Burlington, Vt.: Ashgate, 2014.

Delisle, Léopold. "Forme des abbréviations et des liaisons dans les lettres des papes au XIIIe siècle." *Bibliothèque de l'École des Chartes* 48 (1887): 121–24.

Della Porta, Pier Maurizio, Ezio Genovesi, and Elvio Lunghi. *Guide to Assisi: History and Art.* Trans. Mary O'Bringer and Julia Perry. Assisi: Editrice Minerva, 2005.

Demore, François. *Vie de sainte Claire d'Assise.* Paris: A. Bray, 1856.

Dozzi, Dino. *Il vangelo nella regola non bollata di San Francesco d'Assisi.* Rome: Istituto Storico dei Cappuccini, 1989.

Elia di Cortona tra realtà e mito. Atti dell'Incontro di studio (Cortona, 12–13 luglio 2013). Spoleto: Fondazione Centro italiano di studi sull'alto Medioevo, 2014.

Esser, Kajetan. "Die Briefe Gregors IX. an die hl. Klara von Assisi." *Franciscan Studies* 35 (1953): 274–95.

Fassbinder, Maria. *Die selige Agnes von Prag: Eine königliche Klarissin.* Werl, Westf.: Dietrich-Coelde, 1957.

———. "Untersuchungen über die Quellen zum Leben der hl. Klara von Assisi." *Franciscan Studies* 23 (1936): 296–335.

Federazione S. Chiara di Assisi delle Clarisse di Umbria-Sardegna. *Chiara di Assisi: Una vita prende forma: Iter storico.* Padua: Messaggero, 2005.

———. *Il Vangelo come forma di vita: In ascolto di Chiara e della sua Regola.* Padua: Messaggero, 2007.

Felten, Joseph. *Papst Gregors IX.* Freiburg: Herder, 1886.

Fiege, Marianus. *The Princess of Poverty: Saint Clare of Assisi and the Order of Poor Ladies.* Evansville, Ind.: Poor Clares of the Monastery of S. Clare, 1900.

Folliet, Georges. "Les trois catégories de chrétiens a partir de Luc (17, 34–36), Matthieu (24, 40–41) et Ézéchiel (14, 14)." In *Augustinus Magister: Congrès international augustinien, Paris, 21–24 septembre 1954,* vol. 2, 631–44. Paris: Études Augustiniennes, 1954.

———. "Les trois catégories de chrétiens: Survie d'un thème augustinien." *L'Année Théologique Augustinienne* 14 (1954): 81–96.

Fortini, Arnaldo. *Nova vita di San Francesco.* 4 vols. in 5. Assisi: Porziuncola, 1959.

———. "Nuove notizie intorno a S. Chiara d'Assisi." *Archivum Franciscanum Historicum* 46 (1953): 3–43. Trans. "New Information About Saint Clare of Assisi," trans. M. Jane Frances. *Greyfriars Review* 7 (1993): 27–69 (with some errors and omissions).

Fortini, Gemma. "The Noble Family of St. Clare of Assisi." Trans. Finbarr Conroy. *Franciscan Studies* 42 (1982): 48–67.

Freeman, Gerard Pieter. "Klarissenfasten im 13. Jahrhundert." *Archivum Franciscanum Historicum* 87 (1994): 217–86.

Frugoni, Chiara. *Una solitudine abitata: Chiara d'Assisi.* Rome: Laterza, 2006.

Funk, Philipp. *Jakob von Vitry, Leben und Werke.* Leipzig: Teubner, 1909. Reprint Hildesheim: Gerstenberg, 1973.

Gemelli, Pia. "Giacomo da Vitry e le origini del movimento francescano." *Aevum* 39 (1965): 474–95.

Gennaro, Clara. *Chiara d'Assisi.* Magnano, Italy: Qiqajon, 1995.

———. "Il francescanesimo femminile nel XIII secolo." *Rivista di Storia e Letteratura Religiosa* 25 (1989): 259–84.

Giacometti, Luigi, ed. *Dialoghi con Chiara di Assisi. Atti delle Giornate di studio e riflessione per l'VIII centenario di Santa Chiara, celebrate a S. Damiano di Assisi: ottobre 1993–luglio 1994.* Assisi: Edizioni Porziuncola, 1995.

Gilliat-Smith, Ernest. *Saint Clare of Assisi: Her Life and Legislation.* London: J.M. Dent, 1914.

Godet, Jean François. "Lettura della forma di vita." *Vita minorum* 3 (1985): 239–301. See also Godet-Calogeras, Jean François.

———. "A New Look at Clare's Gospel Plan of Life." *Greyfriars Review* 5, Supplement (1991): 1–84. See also Godet-Calogeras, Jean François.

Godet-Calogeras, Jean François. "Francis and Clare and the Emergence of the Second Order." In *The Cambridge Companion to Francis of Assisi,* ed. Michael J. P. Robson, 115–25. Cambridge: Cambridge University Press, 2012. See also Godet, Jean François.

Golubovich, Girolamo. *Biblioteca bio-bibliografica della Terra Santa e dell'Oriente Francescano.* Quaracchi-Florence, 1906.

Grau, Engelbert. "Introduction." In *The Legend and Writings of Saint Clare of Assisi,* ed. and trans. Franciscan Institute, 1–14.

———. "Die päpstliche Bestätigung der Regel der hl. Klara (1253)." *Franziskanische Studien* 35 (1953): 317–23.

———. "Die Regel der hl. Klara (1253) in ihrer Abhängigkeit von der Regel der Minderbrüder (1223)." *Franziskanische Studien* 35 (1953): 211–73.

———. "Die Schriften der heiligen Klara und die Werke ihrer Biographen." In *Movimento religioso femminile e francescanesimo nel secolo XIII*, 195–238. Assisi: Società Internazionale di Studi Francescani, 1980.

Grundmann, Herbert. *Religious Movements in the Middle Ages: The Historical Links Between Heresy, the Mendicant Orders, and the Women's Religious Movement in the Twelfth and Thirteenth Century, with the Historical Foundations of German Mysticism*. Trans. Steven Rowan. Notre Dame, Ind.: University of Notre Dame Press, 1995.

Guarnieri, Romana. "Pinzochere." In *Dizionario degli istituti di perfezione*, coll. 1721–49. Rome: Edizioni Paoline, 1980.

Guida, Marco. *Una leggenda in cerca d'autore: La "Vita" di santa Chiara d'Assisi: Studio delle fonti e sinossi intertestuale*. Brussels: Société des Bollandistes, 2010.

Hamburger, Jeffrey F. "Art, Enclosure and the *Cura Monialium*: Prolegomena in the Guise of a Postscript." *Gesta* 31 (1992): 108–34.

Höhler, Peter. "Il monastero delle Clarisse di Monteluce in Perugia (1218–1400)." In *Il movimento religioso femminile in Umbria nei secoli XIII–XIV*, ed. Roberto Rusconi, 159–82. Perugia: Regione dell'Umbria; Scandicci (Florence): Nuova Italia, 1984.

Hughes, Diane Owen. "From Brideprice to Dowry in Mediterranean Europe." *Journal of Family History* 3 (1978): 262–96.

Huygens, R. B. C. "Les passages des lettres de Jacques de Vitry relatifs à saint François d'Assise et à ses premiers disciples." In *Hommages à Léon Herrmann*, 446–53. Brussels: Latomus, 1960.

Johnson, Timothy. "Clare, Leo, and the Authorship of the Fourth Letter to Agnes of Prague." *Franciscan Studies* 62 (2004): 91–100.

Jungmann, Joseph A. *The Mass of the Roman Rite: Its Origins and Development ("Missarum Sollemnia")*. Trans. Francis A. Brunner. Rev. ed. Charles K. Riepe. New York: Benziger, 1961.

Klaniczay, Gábor. *Holy Rulers and Blessed Princesses: Dynastic Cults in Medieval Central Europe*. Trans. Éva Pálmai. Cambridge: Cambridge University Press, 2000.

Knox, Lezlie S. "Audacious Nuns: Institutionalizing the Franciscan Order of Saint Clare." *Church History* 69 (2000): 41–62.

———. *Creating Clare of Assisi: Female Franciscan Identities in Later Medieval Italy*. Leiden: Brill, 2008.

Kreidler-Kos, Martin, Ancilla Röttger, and Niklaus Kuster. *Klara von Assisi: Freundin der Stille: Schwester der Stadt*. Kevelaer: Topos, 2005.

Kuster, Niklaus. "Clare's *Testament* and Innocent III's *Privilege of Poverty*: Genuine or Clever Forgeries?" Trans. Nancy Celaschi. *Greyfriars Review* 15 (2001): 171–252.

———. "Schriften des Franziskus an Klara von Assisi: Eine Spurensuche zwischen *plura scripta* und dem Schweigen der Quellen." *Wissenschaft und Weisheit* 65 (2002): 163–79.

Kuster, Niklaus, and Kreidler-Kos, Martina. "Neue Chronologie zu Clara von Assisi." *Wissenschaft und Weisheit* 69 (2006): 3–46.

La Grasta, Giovanna. "La canonizzazione di Chiara." In *Chiara di Assisi* (1993), 301–24.

Lainati, Chiara Augusta. "The Enclosure of St Clare and of the First Poor Clares in Canonical Legislation and in Practice." *The Cord* 28 (1978): 3–15, 47–60.

———. "Introduzione" to sources on Clare. In *Fonti francescane* (1977). Vol. 2, 2211–40.

———. *Novus ordo, novus vita: Un nuovo ordine, una nuova vita: Regola di santa Chiara di Assisi del 9 agosto 1253*. Matelica: Monastero Clarisse S. Maria Maddalena, 2001.

————, ed. "Processo di canonizzazione di Santa Chiara." In *Fonti francescane* (1977). Vol. 2, 2299–2383.

————. "La regola francescana e il II Ordine." *Vita Minorum* 44 (1973): 227–49.

————. "Il Testamento di Santa Chiara." *Forma Sororum* 23 (1986): 196–220.

Lazzeri, Zeffirino. "La 'Forma Vitae' di S. Chiara e le Regole sue e del suo Ordine." In *Santa Chiara d'Assisi: Studi e cronaca*, 79–121.

Leclercq, Jean. "Qu'est-ce que vivre selon une règle?" *Collectanea Cisterciensia* 32 (1970): 155–63.

————. "St. Clare and Nuptial Spirituality." Trans. Edward Hagman. *Greyfriars Review* 10 (1996): 171–78.

Lemmens, Leonhard. "Miszellen." *Zeitschrift für Kirchengeschichte* 24 (1903): 321–23.

Lempp, Edouard. "Die Anfänge des Clarissenordens." *Zeitschrift für Kirchengeschichte* 13 (1892): 181–245.

Lester, Anne E. *Creating Cistercian Nuns: The Women's Religious Movement and Its Reform in Thirteenth-Century Champagne.* Ithaca, N.Y.: Cornell University Press, 2011.

Locatelli, Vicenzo. *Vita di S.ᵃ Chiara di Assisi.* Naples: Gabriele Sarracino, 1854.

Lynn, Beth. "The Body and the Text: The Community at San Damiano that Produced the Text Known as the *Form of Life of the Poor Sisters.*" *Spirit and Life* 17 (2012): 83–94.

Maccarone, Michele. *Studi su Innocenzo III.* Padua: Antenore, 1972.

Makowski, Elizabeth M. *A Pernicious Sort of Woman: Quasi-Religious Women and Canon Lawyers in the Later Middle Ages.* Washington, D.C.: Catholic University of America Press, 2005.

Maleczek, Werner. *Papst und Kardinalskolleg von 1191 bis 1216: Die Kardinäle unter Coelestin III. und Innocenz III.* Vienna: Österreichischen Akademie der Wissenschaften, 1984.

————. "Questions About the Authenticity of the Privilege of Poverty of Innocent III and of the Testament of Clare of Assisi." Trans. Cyprian Rosen and Dawn Nothwehr. *Greyfriars Review* 12, Supplement (1998): 1–80.

Marini, Alfonso. *Agnese di Boemia.* Rome: Istituto Storico dei Cappuccini, 1991.

————. "'Ancilla Christi, plantula sancti Francisci': Gli scritti di santa Chiara e la Regola." In *Chiara di Assisi* (1993), 107–56.

————. "La 'forma vitae' di san Francesco per San Damiano tra Chiara d'Assisi, Agnese di Boemia ed interventi papali." *Hagiographica* 4 (1997): 179–95.

Marini, Alfonso, and M. Beatrice Mistretta, eds. and trans. *Chiara d'Assisi e la memoria di Francesco. Atti del Convegno per l'VIII centenario della nascita di S. Chiara, Fara Sabina, 19–20 maggio 1994.* Città di Castello: Petruzzi, 1995.

Matter, E. Ann. "The Canon of Religious Life: Maria Domitilla Galluzzi and the *Rule* of St. Clare of Assisi." In *Strong Voices, Weak History: Early Women Writers and Canons in England, France, and Italy*, ed. Pamela Joseph Benson and Victoria Kirkham, 78–98. Ann Arbor: University of Michigan Press, 2005.

McDonnell, Ernest W. *The Beguines and Beghards in Medieval Culture: With Special Emphasis on the Belgian Scene.* New Brunswick, N.J.: Rutgers University Press, 1954.

McLaughlin, Mary Martin. "Creating and Recreating Communities of Women: The Case of Corpus Domini, Ferrara, 1406–1452." *Signs* 14 (1989): 293–320.

Meersseman, G. G. *Dossier de l'ordre de la pénitence au XIIIe siècle.* Fribourg: Editions Universitaires, 1961.

Menestò, Enrico. "Vite dei santi e processi di canonizzazione come proposta di un modello di santità." In *Dalla "sequela Christi" di Francesco d'Assisi all'apologia della povertà*, 173–201. Spoleto: Centro italiano di studi sull'alto Medioevo, 1992.

Millane, Pacelli. "Privilege of Poverty of 1228: Rooted in the Canticle of Canticles." *Spirit and Life* 11 (2004): 39–49.

Minnis, Alastair J. *Medieval Theory of Authorship: Scholastic Literary Attitudes in the Later Middle Ages.* 2nd. ed. Philadelphia: University of Pennsylvania Press, 2010.

Mooney, Catherine M. "Francis of Assisi as Mother, Father and Androgynous Figure in Some Early Sources." In *The Boswell Thesis: Essays on Christianity, Social Tolerance, and Homosexuality*, ed. Mathew Kuefler, 301–32. Chicago: University of Chicago Press, 2006.

———. "*Imitatio Christi* or *Imitatio Mariae*? Clare of Assisi and Her Interpreters." In *Gendered Voices: Medieval Saints and Their Interpreters*, ed. Catherine M. Mooney, 52–77, 207–20. Philadelphia: University of Pennsylvania Press, 1999.

———. "The 'Lesser Sisters" in Jacques de Vitry's 1216 Letter." *Franciscan Studies* 69 (2011): 1–29.

———. "Nuns, Tertiaries, and Quasi-Religious: The Religious Identities of Late Medieval Italian Holy Women." *Medieval Feminist Forum* 42 (2006): 68–92.

———. "Wondrous Words: Catherine of Siena's Miraculous Reading and Writing According to the Early Sources." In *Catherine of Siena: The Creation of a Cult*, ed. Jeffrey Hamburger and Gabriela Signori, 263–90. Medieval Women: Texts and Contexts 13. Turnhout: Brepols, 2013.

Moorman, John. *A History of the Franciscan Order: From Its Origins to the Year 1517.* Oxford: Clarendon, 1968.

More, Alison. "According to Martha: Extra-Regular Religious Women and the Gospel Life." *Franciscana* 10 (2008): 255–80.

Mueller, Joan. "Agnes of Prague and the Juridical Implications of the Privilege of Poverty." *Franciscan Studies* 58 (2000): 261–87.

———. "Agnes of Prague and the Rule of St. Clare." *Studies in Spirituality* 13 (2003): 154–67.

———. *A Companion to Clare of Assisi: Life, Writings, and Spirituality.* Leiden: Brill, 2010.

———. *The Privilege of Poverty: Clare of Assisi, Agnes of Prague, and the Struggle for a Franciscan Rule for Women.* University Park: Pennsylvania State University Press, 2006.

Muessig, Carolyn. *The Faces of Women in the Sermons of Jacques de Vitry.* Toronto: Peregrina, 1999.

———. "The Vernacularization of Late Medieval Sermons: Some French and Italian Examples." In *Medieval Multilingualism: The Francophone World and Its Neighbours*, ed. Christopher Kleinhenz and Keith Busby, 267–84. Turnhout: Brepols, 2010.

Newman, Barbara. "Agnes of Prague and Guglielma of Milan." In *Medieval Holy Women in the Christian Tradition c. 1100–c. 1500*, ed. Alastair Minnis and Rosalynn Voaden, 557–79. Turnhout: Brepols, 2010.

Oexle, Otto Gerhard. "Tria genera hominum: Zur Geschichte eines Deutungsschemas der sozialen Wirklichkeit in Antike und Mittelalter." In *Institutionen, Kultur und Gesellschaft im Mittelalter: Festschrift für Josef Fleckenstein zu seinem 65. Geburtstag*, ed. Lutz Fenske, Werner Rösener, and Thomas Zotz, 483–500. Sigmaringen: Thorbecke, 1984.

Olgiati, Felice and Chiara Augusta Lainati. "Scritti di Chiara d'Assisi." In *Fonti francescane* (1977), vol. 2, 2241–98.

Oliger, Livarius. "Descriptio codicis S. Antonii de Urbe unacum appendice textuum de S. Francisco." *Archivum Franciscanum Historicum* 12 (1919): 321–401.

———. "Documenta originis Clarissarum, Civitatis Castelli, Eugubii (a. 1223–1263)." *Archivum Franciscanum Historicum* 15 (1922): 71–102.

———. "De origine regularum ordinis s. Clarae." *Archivum Franciscanum Historicum* 5 (1912): 181–209, 413–47.

Omaechevarría, Ignacio. *Las Clarisas a través de los siglos*. Madrid: Cisneros, 1972.

———. "L'Ordine di S. Chiara sotto diverse Regole." *Forma Sororum* 15 (1978): 141–53.

———. "La 'regla' y las reglas de la orden de Santa Clara." *Collectanea Franciscana* 46 (1976): 93–119.

Padovese, Luigi. "Clare's Tonsure: Act of Consecration or Sign of Penance?" Trans. Madonna Balestrieri. *Greyfriars Review* 6 (1992): 67–80.

Paoli, Emore. "Introduzione" a *Clarae Assisiensis: Opuscula*. In *Fontes Franciscani*, ed. Menestò and Brufani, 2223–60.

Paravicini Bagliani, Agostino. *Cardinali di curia e 'familiae' cardinalizie: Dal 1227 al 1254*. Vol.1. Padua: Antenore, 1972.

———. "Innocent IV." In *The Papacy: An Encyclopedia*. 3 vols., ed. Philippe Levillain and John W. O'Malley, vol. 2, 790–93. New York: Routledge, 2002.

Pásztor, Edith. "Esperienze di povertà al femminile." In *La conversione alla povertà nell'Italia dei secoli XII–XIV. Atti del XXVII Convegno storico internazionale, Todi, 14–17 ottobre 1990*, 369–89. Spoleto: Centro italiano di studi sull'alto Medioevo, 1991.

Pellegrini, Luigi. "Female Religious Experience and Society in Thirteenth-Century Italy." In *Monks and Nuns, Saints and Outcasts: Religion in Medieval Society*, ed. Lester K. Little, Sharon A. Farmer, and Barbara H. Rosenwein, 97–122. Ithaca, N.Y.: Cornell University Press, 2000.

———. "Introduzione" a *Legenda Trium Sociorum*. In *Fontes Franciscani*, ed. Menestò and Brufani, 1355–71.

———. "I Frati Minori ad Assisi tra due e trecento." In *Assisi anno 1300*, ed. Stefano Brufani and Enrico Menestò, 113–37. Assisi: Porziuncola, 2002.

Peterson, Ingrid J. *Clare of Assisi: A Biographical Study*. Quincy, Ill.: Franciscan Press, 1993.

———. "Like a Beguine: Clare Before 1212." In *Clare of Assisi: Investigations*, 47–67. Clare Centenary Series 7. St. Bonaventure, N.Y.: Franciscan Institute, 1993.

Petroff, Elizabeth Alvida. "A Medieval Woman's Utopian Vision: The Rule of St. Clare of Assisi." In Petroff, *Body and Soul: Essays on Medieval Women and Mysticism*, 66–79. New York: Oxford University Press, 1994.

Pisanu, Leonardo. *Innocenzo IV e i francescani (1243–1254)*. Rome: Edizioni Francescane, 1968.

Polli, Giuliana. *Le clarisse di San Michele a Trento: Ricostruzione dell'archivio ed edizione dei documenti (1193–1500)*. Trent: Società di Studi Trentini di Scienze Storiche, 2014.

Ratti, Achille. "Un codice pragense a Milano con testo inedito della vita di S. Agnese di Praga." *Rendiconti dell'Istituto Lombardo di Scienze e Lettere*, ser. 2, 29 (1896): 392–96.

Raurell, Frederic. "La lettura del 'Cantico dei cantici' al tempo di Chiara." In *Chiara: Francescanesimo al femminile*, ed. Covi and Dozzi, 188–289.

Righetti Tosti-Croce, Marina. "La chiesa di Santa Chiara ad Assisi: architettura." In *Santa Chiara in Assisi. Architettura e decorazione*, ed. Alessandro Tomei, 21–41. Cinisello Balsamo (Milan): Silvana, 2002.

Rigon, Anton. "Antonio di Padova e il minoritismo padano." In *I compagni e la prima generazione minoritica. Atti del XIX convegno internazionale, Assisi, 17–19 ottobre 1991*, 167–99. Spoleto: Centro italiano di studi sull'alto Medioevo, 1992.

———. "Penitenti e laici devoti fra mondo monastico-canonicale e ordini mendicanti: Qualche esempio in area veneta e montovana." *Ricerche di storia sociale e religiosa* 17–18 (1980): 51–73.

Robinson, Paschal. "Inventarium omnium documentorum, quae in Archivio Protomonasterii S. Clarae Assisiensis nunc asservantur." *Archivum Franciscanum Historicum* 1 (1908): 413–32.

————, ed. and trans. *The Life of Saint Clare, ascribed to Fr. Thomas of Celano*. Philadelphia: Dolphin, 1910.

————. "The Rule of St. Clare and Its Observance in the Light of Early Documents." *Ecclesiastical Review* 46 (1912): 398–414. Reprinted as a monograph, Philadelphia: Dolphin Press, 1912.

————. "St. Clare." In *Franciscan Essays*. Ed. Paul Sabatier et al., vol. 1, 31–49. Aberdeen: University Press, 1912.

————. *The Writings of Saint Francis of Assisi*. Philadelphia: Dolphin Press, 1906.

————. "The Writings of St. Clare of Assisi." *Archivum Franciscanum Historicum* 3 (1910): 433–47.

Robson, Michael. *The Franciscans in the Middle Ages*. Woodbridge: Boydell, 2006.

Roest, Bert. *Order and Disorder: The Poor Clares Between Foundation and Reform*. Leiden: Brill, 2013.

Roggen, Heribert. *The Spirit of St. Clare*. Trans. Paul Joseph Oligny. Chicago: Franciscan Herald Press, 1971.

Röhricht, Reinhold. "Briefe des Jacobus de Vitriaco (1216–21)." *Zeitschrift für Kirchengeschichte* 14 (1894): 97–118.

Rotzetter, Anton. *Klara von Assisi: Die erste franziskanische Frau*. 3rd ed. Freiburg im Breisgau: Herder, 1993.

Rusconi, Roberto. "The Spread of Women's Franciscanism in the Thirteenth Century." Trans. Edward Hagman. *Greyfriars Review* 12 (1998): 35–75.

Sabatier, Paul. *Life of St. Francis of Assisi*. New York: Scribner's, 1905.

————. "Note di viaggio di un prelato francese in Italia (Jacques de Vitry 1216)." *Bollettino della Società Umbra di Storia Patria* 1 (1895): 106–13.

Sainte-Marie, Henri de. "Presence of the Benedictine Rule in the Rule of St. Clare." Trans. Sergius Wroblewski. *Greyfriars Review* 6 (1992): 49–65.

Saint-Genois, Jules. "Sur des lettres inédites de Jacques de Vitry, évêque de Saint-Jean d'Acre, cardinal et légat du pape, écrites en 1216." *Mémoires de l'Académie Royale des Sciences, des Lettres et des Beaux-Arts de Belgique* 23 (1849): 1–43.

Santa Chiara d'Assisi: Studi e cronaca del VII Centenario, 1253–1953. Assisi: Comitato Centrale per il VII Centenario Morte S. Chiara, 1954.

Santucci, Francesco. "La Cattedrale e il Francescanesimo." In *La cattedrale di San Rufino in Assisi*, ed. Francesco Santucci, 88–91. Cinisello Balsamo (Milan): Silvana, 1999.

————. "Sant'Angelo di Panzo Near Assisi." Trans. Lori Pieper. *Greyfriars Review* 8 (1994): 219–38.

————. "La vicenda francescana-clariana e il culto mariano ad Assisi." In *Itinerari del sacro in Umbria*, ed. Mario Sensi, 183–207. Florence: Octavo, 1998.

Schlosser, Marianne. "Mother, Sister, Bride: The Spirituality of St. Clare." Trans. Ignatius McCormick. *Greyfriars Review* 5 (1991): 233–49.

Sedda, Filippo. "La deriva storiografica di frate Elia nelle fonti francescane trecentesche." In *Elia di Cortona tra realtà e mito*, 123–44.

————. "La 'malavventura' di frate Elia. Un percorso attraverso le fonti biografiche." *Il Santo* 41 (2001): 215–300.

Sensi, Mario. "Le Clarisse a Foligno nel secolo XIII." *Collectanea Franciscana* 47 (1977): 349–63.

————. "Il patrimonio monastico di S. Maria di Vallegloria a Spello." *Bollettino della Deputazione di Storia Patria per l'Umbria* 81 (1984): 77–149.

————. "The Women's Recluse Movement in Umbria During the 13th and 14th Centuries." Trans. Edward Hagman. *Greyfriars Review* 8 (1994): 319–45.

Seton, Walter. "The Letters from Saint Clare to Blessed Agnes of Bohemia." *Archivum Francisca-num Historicum* 17 (1924): 509–19.

———. *Some New Sources for the Life of Blessed Agnes of Bohemia*. Aberdeen: University Press, 1915.

Sevesi, P. M. "Il monastero delle Clarisse in S. Apollinare di Milano." *Archivum Franciscanum Historicum* 17 (1924): 338–64, 520–44; 18 (1925): 226–47, 525–58; 19 (1926): 76–99.

Smith, Julie Ann. "Prouille, Madrid, Rome: The Evolution of the Earliest Dominican *Instituta* for Nuns." *Journal of Medieval History* 35 (2009): 340–52.

St. Clare and Her Order: A Story of Seven Centuries. Ed. author of *The Enclosed Nun*. London: Mills and Boon, 1912.

Stewart, Robert M. *"De illis qui faciunt penitentiam": The Rule of the Secular Franciscan Order: Origins, Development, Interpretation*. Rome: Istituto Storico dei Cappuccini, 1991.

Thompson, Augustine. *Cities of God: The Religion of the Italian Communes, 1125–1325*. University Park: Pennsylvania State University Press, 2005.

———. *Francis of Assisi: A New Biography*. Ithaca, N.Y.: Cornell University Press, 2012.

Tylus, Jane. *Reclaiming Catherine of Siena: Literacy, Literature, and the Signs of Others*. Chicago: University of Chicago Press, 2009.

Uribe, Fernando. "L'iter storico della Regola di S. Chiara: Una prova di fedeltà al Vangelo." In *Dialoghi con Chiara*, ed. Giacometti, 211–40.

Van Asseldonk, Optatus. " 'Sorores minores': Una nuova impostazione del problema." *Collectanea Franciscana* 62 (1992): 595–634.

Van den Goorbergh, Edith A. and Theodore H. Zweerman. *Light Shining Through a Veil: On Saint Clare's Letters to Saint Agnes of Prague*. Trans. Aline Looman-Graaskamp and Sister Frances Teresa. Leuven: Peeters, 2000.

Van Leeuwen, Peter. "Clare's Rule." Trans. Joseph Oudeman. *Greyfriars Review* 1 (1987): 65–76.

Varanini, Gian Maria. "Per la storia dei Minori a Verona nel Duecento." In *Minoritismo e centri veneti nel Duecento*, ed. Giorgio Cracco, 92–125. Trent: Argentarium, 1983.

Vásquez, Isaac. "La 'forma vitae' hugoliniana para las Clarisas en una bula desconocida de 1245." *Antonianum* 52 (1977): 94–125.

Vauchez, André. *Francis of Assisi: The Life and Afterlife of a Medieval Saint*. Trans. Michael F. Cusato. New Haven, Conn.: Yale University Press, 2012.

Vetere, Benedetto. "La condizione femminile nell'età di Chiara e la sua esperienza di vita." In *Chiara e la diffusione delle Clarisse nel secolo XIII*, ed. Andenna and Vetere, 9–51.

Weinstein, Donald, and Rudolph M. Bell. *Saints and Society: The Two Worlds of Western Christendom, 1000–1700*. Chicago: University of Chicago Press, 1982.

Wood, Jeryldene M. *Women, Art, and Spirituality: The Poor Clares of Early Modern Italy*. Cambridge: Cambridge University Press, 1996.

Zarncke, Lilly. *Der Anteil des Kardinals Ugolino an der Ausbildung der drei Orden des heiligen Franz*. Leipzig: Teubner, 1930. Reprint Hildesheim: Gerstenberg, 1972.

Index

Acknowledgments

In Fall 2009, The Franciscan Institute at St. Bonaventure University invited me to be the Joseph A. Doino Visiting Professor of Franciscan Studies, Franciscan Institute, New York. That fellowship launched this book and shaped its contours in ways that would not have been possible without access to the Institute's remarkable library of Franciscan sources. I am grateful to the colleagues who hosted me: Michael Blastic OFM, Margaret Carney OSF, Michael Cusato OFM, Jean François Godet-Calogeras, and Alison More.

Beverly Mayne Kienzle and E. Ann Matter offered me their sage advice on particular topics. Lezlie S. Knox and Carolyn Muessig generously read the entire manuscript and improved it with their astute observations. I thank too those who kindly assisted me with obtaining photos and the permissions to publish them: Elvio Lunghi for the cover photo; the University Library, Ghent, for Jacques de Vitry's letter; and Stefano Brufani, Sr. Chiara Agnese Acquadro, and the Protomonastery of Saint Clare in Assisi for the 1253 *forma vitae*. I want especially to acknowledge Anne Kenny, Manager of the Interlibrary Loan Office at Boston College, who readily tracked down every single request for a publication, no matter how difficult.

I am grateful to many former teachers who have influenced my scholarship and opened new ways of thinking about medieval religion, Latin, law, and religious orders: Giles Constable, Ralph Hexter, and the late John Boswell.

A few people I can never sufficiently thank. Caroline Walker Bynum introduced me to medieval religious history and spirituality and has, over the years, been the most generous mentor and colleague one could hope for. Francine Cardman was tireless in reading drafts of the entire manuscript, always improving it with her incisive observations. Brinton Lykes patiently listened to me think through so many puzzles regarding Clare of Assisi, thirteenth-century religious women, and popes that she should be made an honorary medievalist. Most of all, I thank each of these women for being unfailing friends through thick and thin.

CPSIA information can be obtained
at www.ICGtesting.com
Printed in the USA
LVHW111548091021
699917LV00007B/5

9 780812 225075